Multinational Corporations and Global Justice

Multinational Corporations and Global Justice

Human Rights Obligations of a
Quasi-Governmental Institution

Florian Wettstein

Stanford Business Books
An Imprint of Stanford University Press
Stanford, California

Stanford University Press

Stanford, California

© 2009 by the Board of Trustees of the Leland Stanford Junior University.

Printed in the United States of America on acid-free, archival-quality paper

Library of Congress Cataloging-in-Publication Data

Wettstein, Florian.

Multinational corporations and global justice : human rights obligations of a quasi-governmental institution / Florian Wettstein.

p.   cm.

Includes bibliographical references and index.

ISBN 978-0-8047-6240-3 (cloth : alk. paper)

1. International business enterprises—Moral and ethical aspects.   2. Social responsibility of business.   3. Human rights.   I. Title.

HD2755.5.W473   2009

174'.4—dc22   2009011621

Typeset by Westchester Book Composition in Minion, 10/14

Contents

Preface

THIS BOOK IS ABOUT HUMAN BEINGS and their just coexistence in a global society—and it is about corporations. We cannot discuss global justice without taking these powerful institutions into account. The practical realization of global justice will be virtually impossible without paying adequate attention to the role of large corporations. Thus the perspective on multinational corporations in this book is derived from the primary emphasis on global justice. The connection also holds the other way around; if we are to truly understand the role and responsibility of multinational corporations in the global political economy, we cannot discuss them without paying adequate attention to the concept of global justice. Corporations are built by and for human beings, and they have been built with a purpose—a public purpose. It is important to remind ourselves of this purpose behind economic ideas today. More than ever, during the last three decades we have disconnected the concept of the corporation from its humanistic foundations and studied it in a social vacuum. We tend to discuss the theories of modern corporations and the conclusions we draw from them without ever taking a closer look at the normative assumptions on which they inevitably are built.

Any book about corporations is at the same time a book about human beings and society; however, we have come to forget that the corporation is designed to serve the people, rather than the other way around. This in itself speaks volumes about how we see and interpret the world today. There are no books that do not contain and promote specific worldviews. We cannot escape the normativity of our own being and writing, no matter how hard we try. We can either state those worldviews explicitly and make them the subject of the book itself, or we can try to obscure them behind the veil of theory and sell them as quasi-objective truths. The former is the more honest approach; the latter, however, is the more common one.

Developing a picture of the corporation that is not disconnected from but is based on and embedded in a holistic conception of just human coexistence takes time. It takes time not only for the writer but also for the reader to work through the moral and political-philosophical foundations on which a normative account of corporate responsibility can and must be built. The structure of this book is a reflection of these insights. Rather than forcing the perspective on the corporation onto a conception of global justice, I will let it emerge from and through it. The result will be a better and more integrated understanding of the corporation's role and place within society—an understanding of the corporation as an instrument for human beings rather than as an end in itself. The place of the corporation in society conditions the place of the corporation in the structure of this book; it does not come first but derives naturally from the vision of justice in 21st-century global society.

An analysis located at the intersection of economy, society, and politics is naturally multiperspectival. If it also has an explicitly normative focus, it is likely to be controversial. Thus not everyone will agree with the suggestions and conclusions put forth in this work. However, initial disagreement sparks debate and discussion and therefore builds the breeding ground for inclusive and holistic solutions to complex problems. I hope that the readers of this book will be as diverse and different in their perspectives and opinions as society can be. Its interdisciplinary approach should provide entry points for various fields to take part in the discussion. However, for truly fruitful solutions to emerge, I hope that any disagreement sparked by the theses put forth in this book is motivated by one shared goal, the sincere practical concern for achieving justice and humanity in the global era.

As is the case for all such works, this book would not have been possible without many people to whom I would like to express my special gratitude. Peter Ulrich has been the face, heart, and soul of business ethics in the German-speaking area for the last two decades. His part in this book can hardly be overstated. He has been a mentor and a seemingly inexhaustible source of inspiration, mental challenge, and support. He has provided direction and advice far beyond this specific project. I can only hope that some of his ingenuity is reflected in this work. My thanks to Peter Ulrich can be extended to everyone with whom I shared time and space at the Institute for Business Ethics at the University of St. Gallen in Switzerland, of which he was the founding director between 1987 and 2009. In particular, I would like to mention Dorothea Baur, Markus Breuer, Johannes Hirata, York Lunau, Thomas Maak, and Ulrich Thielemann. Many of our conversations have, in one way or another, found their way into this book.

I was lucky enough to be able to share and discuss the theses of this book with Otfried Höffe, who directs the Research Center for Political Philosophy (Philosophisches Seminar) at Eberhard Karls University in Tübingen, and to benefit from his guidance, knowledge, and insight. Sandra Waddock was a guarantor of good discussions during my time at Boston College and after. I would also like to thank everyone associated with the Program on Human Rights and Justice at MIT, especially its director, Balakrishnan Rajagopal, for providing a wonderful platform for its fellows for researching and writing a book like this one. The same goes for the faculty of the innovative and remarkable Business and Society Program at York University in Toronto, of which I was a part in 2006–2007, as well as my current "home," the Department of Ethics and Business Law around Ken Goodpaster at the University of St. Thomas in Minneapolis–St. Paul.

I could not have wished for a better editor for this work than Margo Beth Crouppen. Her trust in and enthusiasm for this project were tremendously motivating, and her wonderful support from the very beginning to the very end of the process was invaluable. I also thank Terry Macdonald and Guido Palazzo for their insightful advice. Finally, I would like to thank my parents and, most important, my wife, Rose, for her patience and support throughout the long process of writing this book.

Multinational Corporations and Global Justice

Chapter 1

Introduction

A Plea for Global Justice

W E ARE LIVING IN AN AGE OF PARADOX. The current stage of globalization is said to be shrinking time and space, but the emotional distance between different parts of the world, between different classes within countries, and between us and our less privileged neighbors next door seems to widen. Thus, although globalization is supposed to bring people closer together, its individualistic and competitive stance instead has driven them apart. People of all races and nationalities are said to be "linked more deeply, more intensely, more immediately than ever before" (UNDP 1999, 30). They are becoming profoundly interconnected within one worldwide community of fate (D. Held 1995b, 228; 2000, 424; Höffe 2002c, 14ff.), but their individual fates could not be more different from one another. For some people, globalization brings unprecedented freedom from physical and spatial constraints, but for others it undercuts the possibility of domesticating the locality on which they inevitably and inherently depend (Bauman 1998, 18). The advantage of the one is the disadvantage of the other; luck on one side is matched with harm and misfortune on the other; lavish and excessive wealth is nourished by the extreme poverty, starvation, and humiliation it helps maintain.

Modernity, Inequality, and the Neoliberal Project of the Global Market

"Being a spectator of calamities taking place in another country," according to Susan Sontag, "is a quintessential modern experience" (Sontag 2003, 18). This is the flip side of the globalization coin. The display in the media of humanitarian horrors and social grievances in distant parts of the world unhinges us from the sheltered, and in itself distinctly modern, context of our nationally organized, bounded societies. It robs us of the option of pretending that we did not know and forces us to replace inward-looking ignorance with an open global perspective.

If witnessing distant social grievances is an inherently modern experience, however, so must be the challenge that inevitably derives from it. We cannot escape the normative consequences of living alongside poverty and starvation in the developing world. Within an increasingly integrated world society, the quest for global justice is turning into the single most complex and at the same time most pressing and important challenge of the 21st century. Thus globalization does not render all our modern achievements simply irrelevant, as some postmodern skeptics proclaimed somewhat prematurely during the 1990s. Rather, we will have to rethink, reformulate, and justify them anew in the global context. It is modernity itself that formulates the challenge for the new era; and the sheer dimensions of poverty, starvation, and inequality on a worldwide scale make the challenge of this "second modernity" (Beck 2000, 58) without precedent.

But as we speak about and refer to global justice, we stand in front of the pile of shards and broken promises left behind by the misguided neoliberal project of a global market society.[1] The dream of the neoliberal architects of the global market was one of liberty and global prosperity—provided and secured by the magic of an unleashed, self-regulating market on a global scale. The euphoria was disarming when in the early 1980s Margaret Thatcher and Ronald Reagan steered their economies on a bold new course of deregulation, liberalization, and privatization. Their belief was that their neoliberal policies provided both the simple but effective answer to the exploding cost of the Western welfare state and the much-needed remedies for the economic "underdevelopment" in the Third World. When in the waning days of the 1980s the East collapsed under the heavy weight of its similarly failed ideology, the world was left, it seemed, with no alternative path to progress and development than the one built by global neoliberal capitalism. The final chapter of human history had been written (Fukuyama 1992); no questions seemed to remain open.

Today, however, more questions are open again than are answered. The enthusiastically proclaimed end of the business cycle in the realm of the emerging "New Economy" in the mid-1990s turned out to be a chimera. The seemingly unstoppable economic upheaval that provided the fuel for the neoliberals' defense of their project was only a gigantic bubble, and when it finally burst at the turn of the new millennium, it propelled the world economy into the first tailspin of truly global dimensions—for many hardworking employees a fatal scenario in a society that had replaced the commitment to social security and justice with the blind belief in everlasting economic growth. Today the level of inequality in the industrialized world is back to where it was in the 1920s; and symptomatically, it is most evident in those countries that embraced the neo-liberal course most profoundly.

During the heydays of neoliberal economic globalization in the 1990s, the gap between the richest and the poorest parts of this world widened. At the beginning of this new millennium, 15.6 percent of the world's people shared a total of 81 percent of global income, while the remaining 19 percent of the income must suffice for the other 84.4 percent of human beings. The income gap between the richest fifth of people living in the richest countries and the poorest fifth living in the poorest countries increased from 30 to 1 in 1960 to 60 to 1 in 1990, and to 74 to 1 in 1997 (Pogge 2004, 264f.). This trend is ongoing (World Bank 2008, 7f.). In 46 countries people were poorer in the early 2000s than they were in 1990, and twenty-five countries saw more of their people go hungry than in the early 1990s. Consequently, in the early years of the new millennium more than 1.2 billion people worldwide lived below the international poverty line, and more than 800 million were undernourished (Pogge 2003, 118). Thirty thousand children died every day of preventable causes (Robinson 2005, 25), and a third of all human deaths were related to poverty (Pogge 2003, 118). More than 1 billion human beings had no access to clean water, and 2.6 billion did not have access to basic sanitation (Robinson 2005, 25f.). Furthermore, more than 880 million people lacked access to basic health services, 854 million adults were illiterate, approximately 1 billion had no adequate shelter, and 2 billion had no electricity (Pogge 2003, 118). For an unprecedented number of countries, as Mary Robinson (2005, 25) concluded, the human development indicators did not improve but got worse during the 1990s. Only the targeted efforts based on and toward the UN Millennium Development Goals in the past few years have started to show some improvement in these numbers. The improvements, much needed as they are, tend to be highly concentrated on specific geographical areas, while first of all sub-Saharan Africa but also South Asia are falling farther behind in almost all of the projected goals. And overall, still, 1 billion people continue to live in extreme poverty today, 75 million children of primary school age remain without access to education, 190,000 children under the age of five die of preventable diseases every week, every 30 seconds one child loses the battle against malaria, and still half of the developing world lacks basic sanitation (World Bank 2008, 2). In sub-Saharan Africa and South Asia, 35 percent of children under the age of five are affected by moderate to severe stunting caused by malnutrition. Globally, malnutrition accounts for 3.5 million deaths each year (World Bank 2008, 9). The list goes on and on.

Yet a remarkable number of economists still insist on the adequacy and continuation of the neoliberal project. They blame the remaining obstructions to the free global market for the persistence of deprivation and human misery and opt for an even more vigorous course of global deregulation, liberalization, and privatization. Some do admit that their policies might cause some initial suffering, but they see this suffering as the inevitable price we must pay in order to move on to a more prosperous and just future; all we need, they assert, is more patience for the effects of their remedies to kick in and the benefits of the global competitive markets to "trickle down" to even the poorest of the poor—as if a quarter century was not enough. They still believe, or pretend to believe, that the rising tide of the global economy will eventually lift all boats, but they fail to see that the boats not strong enough for the fast-rising tide have started to sink. The higher the tide rises, the deeper these boats get pulled underwater. The question they have not answered yet is when—if at all—this "trickle-down" effect will start to set in (Wettstein 2008, 248).

Nobel laureate Joseph Stiglitz (2001, vii) sees no empirical evidence and "little historical support" for the existence of a trickle-down effect. For millions of the global poor, economic growth did not equal economic development (Tavis 1982a, 5). In many parts of the developing world neoliberal policies did not even create the economic growth necessary for anything to trickle down in the first place (Stiglitz 2002a, 20). Rather than providing a path for developing countries to catch up, the growth-induced development strategies proposed and enforced in the realm of the so-called Washington Consensus led to a further marginalization of poor countries in the global economy. At a certain level, as Ivan Illich (1978) showed, economic growth modernizes and thus perpetuates poverty rather than alleviating it. It increases our dependency on the market and forces low-income classes to spend an ever-increasing share of their budget in order to satisfy their basic needs. Furthermore, it is well known that beyond the struggle for the realization of the most basic material needs, personal well-being is not only a function of absolute income but also crucially depends on relative measures and one's actual position within the purchasing-power hierarchy (Ulrich 1986, 119). It is exactly this inability of market-based growth strategies to address relative problems that makes the reintegration of the justice focus into economic rationality an urgent necessity. Lacking this focus, however, we are moving in the direction of universalizing rather than eliminating the social conditions of the Third World today (Ulrich 2004a, 9).

Both the intellectual and the empirical foundations of the trickle-down argument are weak, if not nonexistent. "Trickle-down economics," Joseph Stiglitz (2002a, 78) asserts, "was never much more than just a belief, an article of faith." It is the belief of the last ideologues of a fading orthodoxy that has defeated itself. By systematically eliminating the human factor from its core, it has distanced itself from its inherently practical basis. After a quarter century of rapid integration of global markets, this has become only too obvious today. But still in 2000 economist Rudiger Dornbusch kept asserting, "Now the economy is on a bold new course that turns back to where we came from, economic liberalism and individualism, competition and opportunity" (Dornbusch 2000, 25).

Surprisingly, this was after the New Economy of the "roaring nineties" (Stiglitz 2003) collapsed like a house of cards. The "blissful world" Dornbusch (2000, 25) still envisioned had already been unmasked as a world of empty promises. Global market competition has predominantly improved the existing opportunities of those who have much already and eroded the ones of those who have little. Economic liberalism and individualism, praised by Dornbusch, have deepened the divide between rich and poor within, as well as between, countries. Today the world is a more unjust place than ever before in history; the sheer dimensions of human suffering are beyond comprehension. From any reasonably reflective standpoint, Dornbusch's "blissful world" denotes a world without justice. In light of the harsh realities that hundreds of millions of human beings are facing today, his ideological assertions appear nothing but cynical.

The Inadequacy of the Utilitarian Worldview and Rawls's Failed Attempt to Correct It

For Dornbusch and his mainstream economist colleagues, justice does not matter, at least as long as it does not have any instrumental value for furthering their economistic goals. Economists think and speak in utilitarian terms that reduce justice to a mere function of collective welfare. In other words, in the mind of the utilitarian, justice attains value and relevance only insofar as it enhances the common good; it does not have any normative significance on its own (Höffe 2002b, 15).

The problem with utilitarianism is its implicit justification of individual misery with reference to overall societal progress or welfare. It is based on a simplistic formula that measures the condition of society simply by adding up individual utilities (Sen 1973, 15). What matters is a net increase in their overall sum, that is, a positive balance of utility losses and gains; the questions of who wins and who loses and by how much are considered irrelevant. On the contrary, where the misery of one person leads to a greater increase in the welfare of others, suffering even turns into a moral imperative. For utilitarians, aggregate utility gains outweigh even the most fundamental inequalities in their distribution (Sen 1980, 202).

What is problematic about the utilitarian perspective is not its consequentialist or teleological stance per se. Any plausible ethical theory must have some specific idea about the good in society (C. Jones 2001, 30). Rather, the problem is its exclusive focus on the good and thus the exclusion or, more precisely, the subordination of the perspective on the ethically right. Thus utilitarians regard those societies as properly arranged whose institutions maximize the net aggregate satisfaction of the individuals who belong to it. Not the interpersonal distribution of the economic pie but its maximum growth is of relevance to utilitarians. In other words, the (ethically) correct distribution is considered the one that yields the maximum aggregate fulfillment of personal desires (Rawls 1971, 24ff.). Only in the few exceptional cases in which a just distribution is at the same time the most efficient one does "justice" actually matter to utilitarians.

It is not necessary to provide a full critique of philosophical utilitarianism at this point. Its fundamental shortcomings and flaws have been widely discussed, and I will touch on many of them in the course of this book. Utilitarianism largely lost its justificatory credibility with the publication of John Rawls's tremendously influential critique *A Theory of Justice* (1971). It is evident that no reasonable account or perspective of justice can possibly permit the sacrifice of one person's most fundamental freedoms for the benefit of others. "The rights secured by justice," as Rawls (1971, 28) argued correctly, "are not subject to political bargaining or to the calculus of social interests."

Nevertheless, Rawls was not entirely successful in his crusade against utilitarianism. Although he succeeded in dismantling the flawed foundation of philosophical utilitarianism, at the same time his theory provided fuel for the less ambitious, implicitly confirmatory rather than ultimately justificatory utilitarian doctrines of neoliberalism.[2] It is this subtler utilitarian stance that still shines through in today's mainstream economic thinking. For example, in his second principle of justice, the "difference principle," Rawls argued that social and economic inequalities must be arranged so that they are reasonably expected to be to everyone's advantage (Rawls 1971, 60). This rather ambiguous formulation reinforces rather than mitigates the economic utilitarian argument that resources are to be allocated according to the principle of highest productivity. It is precisely the economists' argument that an efficient allocation will enable society to achieve the highest economic output, which in turn will leave all its members better off. Hence they see the market as one of the cases in which an unequal distribution actually does work to the advantage of all. Even Rawls's own critique is thus not free of concessions to utilitarianism, and these concessions—combined with his theory's contractarian basis—build the grounds on which many mainstream economists express their explicit affinity to Rawls's egalitarian thinking. Rawls's explicit rejection of utilitarianism was sufficient to end its appeal as a justificatory moral philosophy, but it cannot serve as a consistent critique of the modern market economy. After all, both Rawls's theory of justice and neoliberal economic theories are based on the same problematic assumption of human beings as fully rational, entirely self-interested, and mutually indifferent individuals. Thus Rawls's account of justice is systematically unsuitable as a normative basis for this book.

The rejection of utilitarianism as an adequate ethical theory contains an implicit normative claim for the rightness of the justice perspective. In an age in which globality has become an irreversible reality (Beck 2000, 15), however, justice must increasingly be thought of in global terms. The most plausible interpretation of global justice, as I attempt to show in this book, is one based on the concept of human rights. The focus on human rights is able to overcome the shortcomings of both the utilitarian and the contractarian perspectives that weigh so heavily on Rawls's theory. It avoids the radical individualism underlying the latter without falling into the trap of a potentially disenfranchising communitarianism of the former. As such, it provides a walkable path of well-understood universalism that understands individual rights and dignity as a precondition rather than a contradiction of a functioning community. In our increasingly global society, the ethical minimum of human rights might be all we can hope for, but if we value pluralism of cultures, religions, and worldviews, it might indeed be all we need. The aim and the purpose of human rights are not to impose a preconditioned set of values on cultures and peoples but to protect their differences by appeal to our shared humanity. This is an ideal worth striving for, even in a time when it seems to become more distant.

We might not be able to undo globalization and perhaps should not, but we can shape and direct it in a fundamentally different direction than it is heading now. If the last three decades of globalization have made one thing clear, it is that global justice will not simply emerge as a by-product of a globalized economy. The moral duty to transform our global economy and to make justice happen is ours. We can no longer put off this fundamental task—there is too much at stake for humankind. For any society that prioritizes justice for all over the privileged interests of a few, the inescapable normative implications deriving from extreme poverty and incomprehensible human misery must render any talk about the end of history unacceptable. The question we face at the doorstep to a global society, however, is: who is effectively able to turn history around?

It Is Time to Act—But for Whom?

"Normative reflection on transnational commitments," Pablo De Greiff and Ciaran Cronin (2002, 28) rightly note, "has lagged behind the reality of transnational social and economic integration" for too long. Global justice was indeed not a major concern of moral and political philosophy until the last quarter of the 20th century. With the exception of classical Stoic philosophy and a few later contributions during the Enlightenment period, among them most famously Kant's brilliant essay "To Eternal Peace" (2001b), the concept of justice was rarely explored from a truly global angle.

The rapid global integration of an ever-growing number of social and societal domains by the end of the 20th century, however, rendered global justice an immediate practical concern and put it back on the political and philosophical agenda. Although this has led to a vivid debate on the nature and relevance of global justice, scholars in the field have remained surprisingly silent about the question of obligations. One laudable exception in this regard is Onora O'Neill. O'Neill (1991, 279) justifiably criticized the debate on global justice for focusing solely on the implications that different approaches to global justice would have for international distribution if there were actors and recipients for whom these implications were pertinent. Those involved in the debate did not, however, specify who those actors and recipients are and what duties they must bear. Therefore, they have successfully managed to get around the discussion of the most controversial part of the global justice debate. The "deep and consequential disagreements," as Thomas Pogge (2001b, 1) concurs, are not about technical matters and implementation questions but about who must bear what responsibility. Unless we start defining and allocating moral obligations, the practical impact of our reflections and discussions about principles of global justice will necessarily remain small. From this perspective, this book is a deliberate attempt to extend the discussion of global justice to questions of obligations and obligation bearers.

The sheer dimensions of the inequality and injustice that characterize and determine our global human coexistence render the question of who is obliged to make what contribution not only of existential importance but also of great controversy. In this book I will argue that the largest obligations of justice must be assigned to those agents and agencies with the most extensive capabilities to make positive contributions to the transformation of unjust situations into just ones. It is from this perspective that I will focus on a specific actor that has acquired superior capabilities but has nevertheless largely escaped the screen in regard to questions of justice so far: the large multinational corporation.

There is increasing agreement to the claim that corporations' responsibilities must not be confined to the abdication of doing harm but must include positive contributions to the solution of pressing societal problems (Marsden 2000, 9f.). For Henry Shue (1988, 697), the failure to harness the "gargantuan force" of these transnational actors for the solution of some of our most persistent problems is a lost opportunity of spectacular dimensions. Although this claim may make sense intuitively, we still lack the normative foundation on which to consistently formulate such responsibilities. On what basis can we legitimately attach extensive moral obligations to multinational corporations' or any other agent's capabilities? This book will provide an answer to this pressing and important question and therefore will lead the way to approaching human misery and global inequality from an entirely new perspective. The missing normative foundation, I will argue, is provided by the concept of global justice. Hence multinational corporations must be theorized as agents of justice at the global level. Those who argue that this is not what we designed corporations for miss one crucial point: the way we did design them in the realm of neoclassical economic theory has evidently failed to meet the requirements of a just society. This alone is sufficient to create a demand for an alternative perspective on these important social institutions.

Multinational corporations are generally defined as corporations that own and control activities (Buckley and Casson 1976, 1), that is, operations or income-generating assets (G. Jones 1996, 4), in more than one country. The characteristic feature of contemporary multinational corporations is their cross-border organizational structure (Berghoff 2004, 127), which commonly distinguishes them from companies that merely export their goods and services from their home bases (G. Jones 1996, 5), as well as from so-called free-standing companies (Wilkins 1998a; 1998b, 107). Free-standing companies, a phenomenon first analyzed and described by Mira Wilkins in the mid-1980s, do not grow out of existing domestic corporations, as is typical of multinationals (G. Jones 2003, 357), but are "set up in one country for the purpose of doing business outside that country" (Wilkins 1998a, 3). Hence they conduct business exclusively abroad.

International business is anything but a new phenomenon. Its roots reach back to Italian and German multinational banking networks in the Middle Ages, to the large international trading companies of the 16th century—the so-called chartered companies—and more recently to the first modern multinationals of the late 19th century. Chartered companies were in many regards the direct ancestors of the modern multinational corporation. Such companies, located in the Netherlands, England, and France, maintained and facilitated lucrative trade routes to geographically distant overseas destinations for which they were granted monopolies through royal charters. They were organized as stock companies, some of which already had sophisticated administrations and functionally differentiated management structures (Berghoff 2004, 84). Characteristically, they were named after geographic locations, such as the English East India Company or, in the case of one corporation with a particularly exotic destination, the Company of Distant Parts. These companies were forerunners, but not real prototypes, of the modern multinational corporation. They were trading rather than manufacturing companies and operated predominantly within colonial territory, that is, in the spheres of influence of their own nations and not under the jurisdiction of foreign sovereign states (Jacoby 1973, 96).

The era of the modern corporation was heralded by the English Joint Stock Companies Act of 1856 (Micklethwait and Wooldridge 2003, 49f.), which established the two key legal features that still characterize the corporation as an institution today: limited liability and the transferability of ownership (Williamson 1986, 133). The railroads were not only the first truly modern corporations but at the same time the first modern multinationals in history (A. D. Chandler 2002, 81ff.; Micklethwait and Wooldridge 2003, 60f., 162). The profound changes that led to the characteristic transnational structure of today's multinational corporations, however, occurred only after 1970. Before 1970 a multinational's foreign subsidiaries were mostly seen as tools for expanding the comparative advantages—mostly technological and managerial expertise (Williamson 1986, 158)—of their headquarters across borders. Consequently, foreign subsidiaries were structured as copies of their headquarters, but on a smaller scale. This typical structure of the so-called multidomestic corporation changed dramatically when corporations started to organize their value chains globally (Gilpin 2000, 165; M. T. Jones 2000, 946; Berghoff 2004, 143f.). Competitive advantage was now sought through the global combination of industrial locations with different comparative advantages. Accordingly, corporations started to split up their activities and carry them out at the location with the lowest factor costs. The overarching goal of multinational business was no longer to provide a superior alternative to exporting goods and to avoid customs but to reach an optimal resource allocation within the global economy (Berghoff 2004, 143f.). International and multidomestic strategies were supplanted by truly global strategies (M. T. Jones 2000, 949). Multinational corporations started to perceive competition as global competition involving all units, irrespective of their location. Thus the fight for market shares shifted to the global level; strategies were crafted on the basis of a corporation's global position (Vernon 1998, 14).

When during the 1980s, as a consequence of globalizing value chains, more and more managing functions and responsibilities were transferred to different locations, multinationals' formerly centralized, hierarchical structures turned into polycentric organizations. In other words, multinational corporations turned into transnational networks (Bartlett and Ghoshal 1991, 75ff.; M. T. Jones 2000, 946; Scherer 2003, 97; Berghoff 2004, 144) or "global webs" (R. B. Reich 1995, 165) and eventually into truly global organizations. Today's multinationals, as the German business historian Hartmut Berghoff (2004, 144) confirms, define themselves as "world businesses" whose home is the entire globe.

The notion of the "global corporation" is not uncontested. Opponents claim that even such allegedly "global" companies are still decisively influenced by the state, its history, and its culture. Therefore, the notion of the global corporation is claimed to create a false image of some kind of rootless, footloose, or even stateless firm (e.g., Ruigrok and van Tulder 1995; Doremus et al. 1998) when in fact multinationals are hardly more than "national firms with international operations" (Hu 1992). The sharp distinction between the "national" and the "global" on which these objections are based, however, seems unsuitable for adequately capturing the true nature of today's multinational corporations. It conceals that corporations can become increasingly global in their character even without completely abandoning their roots or cutting all ties to their home countries (Hout, Porter, and Rudden 1998, 289ff.). As long as the global order consists of nation-states and as long as there is no transnational law under which multinational corporations can be formed, that is, as long as they can be incorporated only under national law, even "global" corporations will inevitably consider one particular state their "home country." They will naturally be influenced by the policies and legal laws of different states and therefore actively seek close relationships with the respective governments wherever possible. The crucial point that most opponents seem to overlook, however, is that the strategic use of their multinational structure increasingly allows them to choose the rules by which they do or do not want to abide. Thus the pressure to seek and maintain good business-government relationships tends to shift from businesses to governments (Stopford and Strange 1991).

Hence we must not confuse a corporation's close relationship to a government with its heightened commitment or loyalty to that particular country. On the contrary, it is precisely the trend to decreasing loyalty that ties governments even more strongly to corporations: "Corporate uncoupling is from the nation itself, and it involves abandonment of loyalty to any particular nation's interests or those of its citizens, even as ties to the nation's government may intensify" (Derber 2002, 72).

In order to prove that there is no such thing as a global corporation, opponents have suggested a variety of different measures and criteria, for example, the share of sales generated abroad, a corporation's assets abroad, the number of workers abroad, or the number of foreigners on company boards (e.g., Hu 1992, 109; Ruigrok and van Tulder 1995). What is striking about these statistics is that they are all based on the corporation's owned assets. The new network strategies of multinational corporations, however, are increasingly based on the aspect of control. In other words, today's companies can exercise multinational influence even without owning any activities in other countries (Weissbrodt 2005, 287). Hence in order to capture their true internationality, we must define the very borders of the firm anew; we must broaden our attention to those corporations that command and control global networks of contractors and strategic partners, rather than focusing exclusively on direct ownership of subsidiaries.

Thus characterizing multinational corporations as global institutions is linked to the influence or, more precisely, the potential influence of their global strategies. From a broad stakeholder perspective, which includes all groups and individuals potentially affected by a corporation's business operations, multinational corporations' business decisions, as well as the political implications deriving from them, have the potential to attain a truly "global reach" (Barnet and Müller 1974). Therefore, it is important that we look not only at direct influence but also at patterns of indirect influence. A strategic decision of a corporation to invest in China instead of Vietnam, for example, quite evidently affects both countries. "They are," Susan Strange once noted in connection with the jobs of Brazilian and German car workers, "competing for the same share of the cake" (Strange 1988, 81). Hence under conditions of systemic interconnectedness the scope of a multinational corporation's influence far exceeds the mere number of countries in which it actually maintains operations. The very fact that no corporation covers the full globe—and therefore can indeed be a "global" corporation in the truest sense of the word—is itself a result of their global strategies and thus of their capacity to choose between different locations. As much as exclusion is an inherent part of the current stage of globalization, it is also a defining moment of global corporate strategies. There is no contradiction in multinationals being of inherently global character and at the same time concentrating on preferred locations. These concepts are neither opposed to each other nor mutually exclusive but are, in fact, inherently interwoven within multinationals' global strategies.

It is precisely in this context of diminishing state control, combined with the spread of underregulated global markets, that the multinational corporation has advanced to one of the major institutions, if not *the* major institution, in the global political economy. It has at least partly escaped from the regulatory grip of national governments and has assumed a position of authority not only over people and markets but to an increasing extent even over governments. Today these transnational network organizations are effectively operating in what I will call "quasi-governmental" (see also Derber 1998; Rondinelli 2002, 2003) positions at the global level. It is this position of authority that gives rise to novel obligations of justice for multinational corporations, that is, obligations that have traditionally been associated exclusively with govern-ments. Hence it is not so much the phenomenon of multinational business per se that is at the core of this book, but its novel political role in the emerging transnational economy.

The Ethical Perspective on Business

For many people who earn their livelihood in the corporate world, business ethics sounds like an oxymoron. Clearly, the public image of the economy and its leading representatives is not at its best. The scandals that shook the busi-ness world in the early 2000s and led to the collapse of large multinational corporations—symbols of the 21st-century global economy—such as World-com, Global Crossing, and most notably Enron and the downfall of some of the largest banking institutions on the planet (Bear Stearns, Lehman Broth-ers) in the current subprime debacle have caused lasting damage to the public trust not only in the social responsibility but also in the very effectiveness of our economy and its economic leaders.

However, the visible misconduct of individual managers and directors only scratches the surface of the public's image of business as a morals-free domain. Much more profoundly, the widespread idea of business as a some-how amoral affair is based on the deep-seated belief that the economy works most effectively if its participants strictly pursue their own self-interest. This belief has been shaped and promoted successfully by neoclassical economists for more than a century. However, the very image of the economy as an amoral domain turns out to be based on particular interests and derived from specific normative ideals. It is based on a particular idea and understanding of what the economy's role should be in society. In other words, the very belief in the amoral economy is itself based on a normative-ethical position.

It is questionable whether people would perceive business ethics as an oxymoron if they were aware that those same neoclassical economists who pretend that there is no room for ethical reflection in economic affairs—Friedrich von Hayek or Milton Friedman, for example—can, in a broad sense, be considered business ethicists themselves. Their claims are no less based on specific normative-ethical ideas about the role of business in society than those of any other outspoken business ethicist. Therefore, their theories and statements are anything but free of normativity. The only difference is that business ethicists make their normative assumptions explicit and open them to critical reflection and justification, while economic liberals tend to hide theirs behind the veil of pseudo-objectivity of an allegedly value-free economic science.

Thus mainstream economists promote an image of the market as a purely functional and thus impersonal mechanism for the efficient creation of value. The questions they leave unaddressed, however, are the ones about what values shall be created and for whom (Ulrich 2008, 185ff.). These inherently and explicitly normative-ethical questions are systematically prior to the questions of instrumental efficiency that dominate neoclassical economic thought; they address the very meaning and goals of economic activity to which all instrumental questions regarding the strategies of how to achieve them most efficiently must ultimately refer. Such normative-ethical questions are far from being answered in today's economy. On the contrary, they reappear with all their ambiguity and controversy at the global level today. To consider them as settled denotes a deep disrespect for the dignity of all those people whose daily lives are dominated by deprivation and unfulfilled economic needs.

Hence doing business has never been and will never be an amoral or value-neutral affair. Any interpretation of the "right" way to do business, whether in terms of maximizing profits or, as in this book, in terms of social justice, is ultimately based on a specific normative-ethical idea about the function and legitimacy of business in society. From this point of view, business or economic ethical analysis neither merely provides a missing value basis for economic theory and practical business conduct nor denotes the simple application of ethics to the (otherwise value-free) economic realm. It is not a mere complement to but an actual critique of existing foundations of economic theory and practice. The normative standpoint is integral to economic theory; it has always been and will always be there and cannot be removed. Robert Cox (1985, 207) rightly claimed, "Theory is always *for* someone and *for* some purpose"; it always has a perspective and cannot be divorced from "a standpoint in time and space." Hence, above all, ethical reflection in the economic realm aims at rendering the normative assumptions underlying mainstream economic thought visible and at renewing them on the basis of an ethically more sound foundation. This is the critical task and mission of an "integrative" understanding of business ethics as developed and promoted by the Swiss business ethicist Peter Ulrich (1998, 2001a, 2002a, 2008). It will build the normative-methodological foundation of this analysis.

Analyzing the role of the large multinational corporation from the standpoint of global justice is thus only half as exotic an idea as it might appear at first. Any statement about the proper role and function of the corporation must ultimately be based on a normative-ethical idea about the constitution of society at large. Within such a normative conception of society the concept of justice is arguably of most fundamental importance. From this point of view, it is rather surprising that a systematic and holistic analysis of the private corporation's role in social justice has not yet been conducted. Although at the global level this gap of normative research can at least partly be explained by the persistent controversy surrounding the underlying concept of global justice, one would think that at least at the domestic level there would be plenty of reasons to engage in such an assessment. This book will confirm that the increasing power of (multinational) corporations renders the holistic assessment of their societal role from a genuine justice perspective ever more urgent.

Recent years have seen a flood of books and articles about corporate social responsibility or corporate citizenship, but the conventional interpretations of these concepts that have dominated this literature so far only scratch the surface of a true justice perspective. They often focus only on the concrete impacts of business conduct without extensive prior reflection on the general institutional role and purpose of corporations in society. Therefore, the concept of justice seldom plays a major role in statements derived from such approaches. On the contrary, precisely because they lack a consistent normative foundation, many contemporary approaches to corporate social responsibility, as we will see, are not able to pose a serious critique of the neoclassical business model, let alone to challenge its underlying normative assumptions. Some of them even turn out to be based on the same normative foundations as neoclassical economics itself.

From a justice perspective, the newly emerging debate on business and human rights is more productive than are the conventional approaches to corporate social responsibility. It is one of the central beliefs of this book that human rights are the most promising starting point for elaborating on corporations' moral obligations and that the young and dynamic debate on business and human rights is leading the way to new approaches to theorizing and thinking about business. Thus it seems even more surprising than in the case of conventional concepts of corporate social responsibility that so far, the business and human rights debate has not been systematically assessed or informed by the concept of justice. Jeremy Waldron even claimed that modern theorists in general "have not written nearly enough about the relation between liberal theories of rights and liberal theories of justice" (Waldron 1993, 27). Nevertheless, in recent years there has been a significant increase in the popularity of rights-based interpretations of justice that is connected directly to the growing interest in global justice. Thus it is first of all the scholars in the global justice debate who are engaged in conceptualizing the connection between (human) rights and justice today. This is not a coincidence, because the quest for global justice has given a new sense of urgency to the claim of universality, both normatively and empirically. Because I take Waldron's concern seriously, a declared goal of this book is not only to bring the promising debate on business and human rights forward but to take it to a new normative level by restating its claims through the lens of a consistent account of rights-based global justice. Additionally, by systematically connecting human rights to the concept of justice, it will contribute to the analytical-ethical foundation of both theories of rights and theories of justice.

Readers should not expect this theory to lead to a comprehensive list of concrete obligations of justice for multinational corporations. Normative-ethical statements, as I pointed out earlier, are inherently critical. As such, they do not contain direct advice about how one must act in a specific situation. After all, no theory of justice can determine in advance what options and courses of action will be open for a particular actor in a specific situation (O'Neill 1986, 153). Therefore, statements about how one ought to act must necessarily remain rather general. Normative-ethical analysis provides general orientational principles, that is, reasons and justifications to guide human action, but without predetermining the actions themselves (Pieper 2003, 12). Hence the determination of the final obligations of particular corporations will always be dependent on the actual context and circumstances in which they conduct their business. What the reader can and should expect, however, is a clear statement of the conceptual nature of corporate obligations of justice, as well as a general systematization and categorization of such obligations that can provide guidance for their practical specification in concrete cases. An analysis like this one can provide a foundation or "a starting point" (O'Neill 1986, 153) for deliberation, that is, a basis to which the practical public discourse regarding the distribution of such obligations can refer in concrete cases; however, it can never replace the need for public deliberation.

The theorization of the multinational corporation as a quasi-governmental institution put forth in this book will not only earn agreement but also likely lead to controversial discussions and even opposition. Such controversy, however, is not a defeat but the very essence of critical reasoning. To spark a debate by challenging established perceptions and categories is thus the aim of introducing a controversial notion like the quasi-governmental institution.

The notion of the quasi-governmental institution inevitably puts the issue of power and authority in the global political economy on the agenda. It helps render those power relations more visible that have traditionally been covered up and denied by the dominant economic liberal ideology. Power always implies corresponding responsibilities. Thus it is often easier for powerful agents or those who defend and act in their interests to deny its existence than to deal with the moral obligations deriving from it. Among the harshest opponents of the theory of the quasi-governmental institution put forth in part II of this book will thus arguably be those persons who represent the current corporate establishment views. It is neither an easy nor a particularly grateful task to stand up against such established ideological beliefs and deeply rooted ways of thinking. As Onora O'Neill (1986, 43) writes, this is especially true for "reasoning which is addressed to institutions and their officers." However, rising to this challenge and formulating new ideas and solutions are inevitable for intellectual thought not to stagnate and fall into indifference or even backwardness. Provoking opposition and offending sensibilities are thus part of the business of critical thinking. They require a thick skin and some healthy trust in one's own intellectual capacity. "Sapere Aude!—Have the courage to use your own intelligence!" (Kant 2001a, 135) was the Kantian creed for the Enlightenment period. It has lost none of its relevance.

Outlook and Further Arguments

This book is divided into three parts. An inquiry into the foundations of rights-based global justice in part I provides its analytical-ethical foundation. Part II contains an analysis of multinational corporations' quasi-governmental roles and thus the precondition for their theorization as what I will call primary agents of justice in part III. Part III, then, draws the normative-ethical conclusions from the combination of parts I and II by putting forth a systematic assessment of the multinational corporation's obligations of (global) justice.

The elaborations in part I start with a general inquiry into the principles of global justice (chapter 2). Before developing a substantive theory, however, I clarify the formal constitution and justification of the concept of justice in general. Filling the resulting formal notion of justice with content will lead us toward an egalitarian conception of rights-based justice that, taken to the global level, must be thought of as inherently cosmopolitan. From this perspective, I argue that global justice must essentially be interpreted as human development.

After clarification of the principles of global justice, the logical next step is to assess what obligations derive from them and for whom they are prescriptive. Accordingly, the next two chapters unfold a general perspective on obligations of global justice (chapter 3) and on the respective obligation bearers (chapter 4). More specifically, they clarify the status of obligations of justice within the full spectrum of moral requirements, the basic shape and nature as well as the (necessary and sufficient) conditions for obligations of justice, and the criteria for determining the agents that are to be held responsible. Regarding obligations of justice in general, I argue that we must change our perspective from focusing on the causal involvement of specific actors in committing human rights violations to their superior capabilities to alleviate existing deprivations. Regarding the bearers of obligations of justice, I introduce a basic heuristic for the determination of primary and secondary agents of justice that is based on the concepts of power and authority. Although the role of the primary agent of justice was traditionally monopolized by the state, recent transformations in the global political economy have brought about a shift to grant a larger role to nonstate actors in this regard. Arguably one of the most prominent nonstate actors is the multinational corporation.

Part II of this book provides in-depth evidence of this shifting role of multinational corporations. The (descriptive) notion of the quasi-governmental institution is closely connected to multinationals' new (normative) status as primary agents of justice. Conceptually, the theory of the quasi-governmental institution is based on what I call "the neoliberal paradox" (chapter 5). The neoliberal paradox essentially is the (unintended) implicit politicization of multinational corporations within the reverse process of a combined depoliticization of the economy and economization of politics. In other words, the political and regulatory vacuum in the global economy has led to a tremendous increase of multinational corporations' political power, and with it, to the implicit politicization of virtually all its actions, its decisions, and, ultimately, its very nature.

The sources of multinational corporations' political power are to be identified within the structures of the global political economy. This is the conclusion of an in-depth assessment of the nature and the historical foundations, as well as the ingredients and sources, of multinational corporations' new political power.

However, multinational corporations are acting in quasi-governmental roles only when power is effectively transformed into authority. Hence in order to complete the conceptual foundations of the theory of the quasi-governmental institution, I examine the systematic relationship between the concepts of power and authority (chapter 6). This provides an adequate perspective from which the various ways in which multinational corporations factually act like governments can systematically be assessed (chapter 7). I show that as de facto governments, multinational corporations increasingly govern people, markets, governments, and, by taking over the role of rule makers in the global political economy, even themselves.

Finally, part III provides a systematization and categorization of multinational corporations' obligations of justice. From a rights-based perspective, these obligations must essentially be understood as human rights obligations. This systematization derives its basic shape from the conceptual elaborations on obligations of justice in chapter 3 and its content from the substantive principles of justice developed in chapter 2. This last part of the book begins with some important preliminary conceptual reflections on the nature of corporate obligations of justice. I show the novelty of this approach by contrasting these basic conceptual insights with the main normative assumptions behind three distinct current approaches to interpreting corporate responsibilities: the neoclassical business model, conventional concepts of corporate social responsibility and corporate citizenship, and the current debate on business and human rights (chapter 8). After these preliminary elaborations, I present a holistic framework or taxonomy of obligations of justice for the quasi-governmental institution (chapter 9), followed by a short outlook on the implications of such an approach for the quest for global democracy (chapter 10). The brevity of the concluding chapter must not lead readers to wrong conclusions regarding its tremendous importance. I am not trying to promote a society in which corporations permanently replace governments; I do not strive for a world governed by private institutions. The goal is to restore democracy and the rule of law in the global age. Thus a state in which corporations take the role of primary agents of justice can always be only a state in transition. To spell out their respective moral responsibilities in this time of disorder, however, is of no less importance, both because they must ultimately contribute to the achievement of the ideal and because this transitional state is without a doubt the reality in which humanity will have to coexist, at least within the foreseeable future.

This book takes a combined actor- and structure-oriented perspective on human rights obligations. Such a combined approach avoids, on the one hand, the shortcomings of a purely actor-oriented perspective, which inevitably neglects the fact that today's most pervasive and persistent human rights problems are largely structurally induced. On the other hand, it corrects the blindness of purely structural approaches to powerful actors that factually control such seemingly "impersonal" structures. Hence a combined approach will put primary emphasis on those actors with the potential to transform unjust structures into just ones. The unification of the two perspectives will effectively take place within the concept of "structural power" introduced in part II of this book. Accordingly, the main categories of obligations identified in part III will be the ones directly aimed at the transformation of the current global system. Such a combined actor-oriented and structural perspective is endemic to the focus on multinational corporations. Multinational corporations not only are actors that control global economic structures but have in fact, as we will see, largely internalized those structures. Hence it is precisely in the form of multinational corporations that structures effectively become actors and actors become structures (Galtung 1994, 36).

PART I

Toward Rights-Based Cosmopolitan Justice

Principles, Obligations, and Agents

Chapter 2

Principles of Global Justice

T HE TASK OF JUDGING WHAT IS JUST," Onora O'Neill (1996, 182) claimed, "begins with fixing principles of justice." Consequently, a theory about obligations of justice must also begin with the formulation of sound principles, because we cannot charge different agents with such obligations without a profound understanding of what is to be considered just or unjust. Hence, taking initial critical thoughts about the global market as a starting point, the following section aims at the development of a consistent conception of global justice that is able to provide normative orientation and practical guidance for the transformation of our global economy.

In chapter 1 I rejected utilitarianism on the basis of its incompatibility with the justice perspective. However, I have not yet provided a sound argument why the justice perspective is to be considered superior to utilitarianism. I simply assumed the rightness of justice as the primary guiding ideal for society. Consequently, I will start the following elaborations with a defense and a basic formal definition of the justice perspective in general. From there, I will move step by step toward a rich substantive conception of rights-based justice. Extending this rights-based notion of justice into the global realm will lead to a cosmopolitan understanding of justice, which I will, as a conclusion, interpret as a conception of justice as human development.

Establishing Justice: The Indispensability of the Justice Perspective

In its colloquial use, the term *justice* rarely leads to real confusion. It seems that we all understand one another when we refer to justice, at least conceptually.

Imagine one of our fellow human beings complaining about a particular injustice done to her. We might well disagree with the way she defends her claim and try to prove otherwise, but in most cases we will not contest the correct use of the term *justice*. Thus we seem to be on common ground at least regarding the basic context to which the term refers. When we are casually discussing the justice or injustice of institutions, practices, or actions that affect our everyday life, we do not need to provide preliminary conceptual elaborations on what exactly we mean by justice; we simply presuppose a basic common understanding in this regard. Even utilitarian thinker John Stuart Mill (2001, 42) seemed fascinated by "the powerful sentiment and apparently clear perception which that word recalls with a rapidity and certainty resembling an instinct." Indeed, our conceptual understanding of justice not only seems quite uniform within contemporary societies but has also remained surprisingly constant over time (Tugendhat 1992, 366). Our formal understanding of justice still largely resembles the conceptual insights of the ancient Greek philosophers. In his *Republic* Plato provided the oldest known formal definition of justice. Paraphrasing the Greek poet Simonides, Plato states that it is "just to give to each what is owed to him" (Plato 1992, 6, para. 331). Not Plato's original formulation, however, but Ulpian's restatement of his formula as "suum cuique" (to each what he deserves) is still the formal reference point for all contemporary interpretations of justice. John Stuart Mill (2001, 45) praised Ulpian's definition as perhaps the "clearest and most emphatic form in which the idea of justice is conceived by the general mind."

At its core, the concept of justice deals with the fair balance of interests between people. Principles of justice provide guidance on how such a balance can be achieved. Therefore, they are indispensable for the creation and maintenance of any civilized society, that is, any society not ruled by oppression and tyranny but based on the recognition of everyone's dignity as free and equal human beings. Hence, in more general terms, justice addresses the question of how we are to live together under the condition of each of us having different ideas and conceptions about how to live our own good life (B. Barry 1995, 77).

These elaborations already imply the inherently intersubjective nature of justice. Justice always refers to the relation between people. More specifically, it is determined by a moral claim of one person and a corresponding obligation of the other. Hence where relations between people are purely systemic or determined by instinct, there is no room for justice (Höffe 2004b, 28). Where individuals who are capable of acting and reflecting autonomously share and organize their social lives, however, the concept of justice is indispensable. Under the condition of plurality of human values, complete harmony of interests within a society is virtually impossible. Hence the "circumstances of justice" (Hume),[1] that is, the social situations in which justice and thus the fair balance of such conflicting interests are needed, are omnipresent and empirically unavoidable (Gosepath 2004, 69f.). This is one of the basic insights also of Kant's doctrine of rights, developed and formulated in *The Metaphysics of Morals* (1996): "When you cannot avoid living side by side with all others, you ought to leave the state of nature and proceed with them into a rightful condition, that is, a condition of distributive justice" (Kant 1996, 86).

Thus justice is an inevitable necessity in and for any free and civilized society; it is not a luxury but a necessary condition for human coexistence (Höffe 2002b, 25). The Scottish moral philosopher Adam Smith (2002, 101) warned that if the pillar of justice is removed, "the immense fabric of human society [...] must in a moment crumble into atoms." Against this background, it is safe to say that justice claims the highest priority on the moral spectrum. It is, as John Stuart Mill (2001, 59) stated, "the chief part, and incomparably the most sacred and binding part, of all morality." Justice, as Plato's definition made clear already, is the part of morals that is not merely desirable but morally owed.

Justice, as the fair balance of conflicting claims and interests, is, at its core, a distributive problem. It deals with the fair distribution of social benefits and burdens and of rights and obligations among the members of a society. This explains why in modern philosophy *social justice* is normally used interchangeably with *distributive justice* (D. Miller 1999, 2), which is counter to the more detailed categorization one can find in Aristotle's *Nichomachean Ethics*, for example (see Aristotle 1980, 106ff.; Höffe 2003, 155ff.). Aristotle's taxonomy further distinguishes social justice and political justice. While social justice refers to the distributive state of people, political justice deals with the legitimacy of political institutions. In other words, political justice refers to the governing structure and institutions of society. It aims at providing the basic principles for just and collectively binding decision making. The scope of social justice, on the other hand, is wider and includes the entire institutional structure of a society (and thus also political justice), as well as the social structures determined by it (Hinsch 2002, xi). Thus the primary concern or subject of social justice is the distributive effects of what John Rawls called "the basic structure" of society (Rawls 1971, 7; D. Miller 1999, 11; see also B. Barry 1989, 355).

The basic structure of a society, according to Rawls, includes its major social institutions. It contains a society's "political constitution and the principal economic and social arrangements" (Rawls 1971, 7). Thus distributive (social) justice refers to the influence of these major social institutions and practices on the distribution of benefits and burdens among people. This focus on institutions is characteristic of the modern perspective on social justice. In our heavily institutionalized and differentiated societies the institutional structure largely determines the starting positions of individuals and predetermines to a large degree the scope and range of their actions or transactions (Beitz 1999a, 201). The major social institutions are, as Rawls argued, no less than defining for the life prospects of human beings (Rawls 1971, 7). Thus, although ancient accounts of justice focused predominantly on human action, putting the main emphasis on institutions certainly makes sense in the modern context. However, this does not mean that our individual choices taken within this structure are not subject to ethical scrutiny as well. Gerard Cohen (1997) justifiably insists that the principles of justice that apply to the basic structure also apply to the individual choices taken within it. Precisely because institutions are created by human beings, their just constitution is dependent on critically thinking individuals who assess and possibly revise them according to changing circumstances and societal perceptions. A "well-ordered society" (Rawls 1971, 453) thus is ultimately feasible only with citizens who are willing to accept responsibility beyond mere (uncritical) compliance with existing rules and institutions. Rawls himself certainly showed tendencies to commit precisely the fallacy of understanding the focus on institutions as a limitation rather than an extension of the scope of justice, and he was rightly criticized for it (see, e.g., G. A. Cohen 1997).

The self-explaining empirical importance of justice pointed out earlier is usually taken as sufficient to prove the basic validity and rightfulness of the concept of justice in general. Thus scholars and writers dealing with questions and issues of justice seldom feel a need to provide a normative justification of the perspective of justice. As a consequence, their theories often remain incomplete and vulnerable to criticism. Such justificatory nonchalance in the contemporary literature on justice seems reason enough to begin the following explorations with a more thorough look at the normative justification of the justice perspective.

Justifying Justice: The Rightness of the Justice Perspective

Ulpian's definition of justice as what we morally deserve can be restated as what we have a moral claim for. Stating a moral claim is inevitably connected to the assumption of intersubjective validity insofar as it prescribes certain actions for other moral subjects. Therefore, moral claims always demand an intersubjective justification (Tugendhat 1992, 315). Unjustified claims remain irrelevant for moral practice; they cannot have binding power. Thus justice deals with the appropriate fulfillment of morally justified claims of people (Gosepath 2004, 45).

The question is, then, when are claims morally justified? We have a tendency to rely simply on the generally accepted moral perceptions, traditions, and norms within our moral community to settle this question in a particular case. However, it is evident that a thorough normative justification must reach beyond "common sense." Unquestioning acceptance of the status quo or blind reliance on the alleged absoluteness of values prescribed by higher authorities of any kind—whether religious, political, or the authority of moral traditions—conflicts with the critical nature of modern ethics. Acceptance does not necessarily imply ethical rightness or legitimacy at the outset. "Because I said so" and "we have always done it this way" are insufficient responses to those who are questioning our established ways of settling moral claims. In other words, rather than being the standard for ethical justification, such norms and values are themselves subject to it. Therefore, in order to have normative legitimacy, statements of justice must be able to pass the test of critical reflection and public deliberation; they must be based on intersubjectively justifiable standards of justice derived from a nonmetaphysical, universal moral principle.

Especially in the context of our rapidly globalizing world, in which our own moral traditions and perceptions are increasingly exposed to and challenged by different worldviews, the question of the intersubjective and thus universal foundations of morals is of growing importance. Certain moral norms may claim validity in one culture but not in others. Different cultures, societies, and people may derive their judgments from different moral standards and come to different conclusions regarding what ought to be considered good or bad, just or unjust. This might not cause any problems in a fragmented world with low intercultural interaction, but it poses one of the foremost challenges in societies in which people with different cultural backgrounds share a common societal life. In other words, under the condition of pluralism, reaching a moral consensus becomes increasingly difficult. However, in our contemporary, irreversibly heterogeneous societies, conflicting moral judgments even within certain well-defined cultural and moral communities are the norm rather than the exception. Against this background, the question of the intersubjective justification of our moral norms and judgments is not only of philosophical but also of immanent practical importance. Beyond potentially exclusive traditionalistic and metaphysical accounts of morals, the only thinkable starting point for the search for such cross-culturally valid principles must be our shared humanity. Modern ethics is humanistic ethics; it is aimed at and derived from what we all have in common as human beings. Its ultimate reference point is the human condition, that is, the normative core that unmistakably defines all of us as human beings.

The Human Condition

Human action can be characterized as autonomous action. Our behavior is not determined by nature (instinct) but takes place to a large extent as willful action (Ulrich 2008, 13). We are reasonable creatures defined by our capability to reflect upon our relation to ourselves, to other individuals, and to our general environment (Kaiser 1992, 64). The ability to generate our own reflective standpoint from which we assess our own behavior, as well as the behavior of others, that is, the capability "of reflectively standing back" (Williams 1997, 96), defines us as principally autonomous moral subjects, that is, as free and self-determined human beings and hence as moral "persons" (Werhane 1985, 6). This status as persons gives us both a moral claim to self-determination and a basic responsibility for the actions we freely choose. The concept of justice and of morals as a whole is located precisely within this tension between entitlement and responsibility. Thus our freedom and our capability to act are both prerequisites for and enabled by moral action. Human nature is thus essentially moral nature; the human condition is defined by the inherent and undeniable morality of all human beings, that is, by our potential as self-determined creatures to choose to act morally, or, in other words, to reflectively or reasonably choose to act "good." It is this ability to use reason that is "peculiar to men and shared by no other animal" (MacDonald 1984, 28).

"For practical purposes," Kant (1997, 59ff.) argued, "the footpath of freedom is the only one on which it is possible to make use of our reason in our conduct." The practical use of reason, in other words, is aimed at human freedom. However, as the early Hegel added, reason is not only aimed at freedom, but, even more important, evolves from the practical interest of human beings in their liberation from heteronomy and dependency. It is thus not the emancipatory interest that is inherent to (some predetermined account of) human reason, but reason that is inherent in the practical, emancipatory interest (Habermas 1978, 287; Ulrich 1986, 65). Therefore, reason is not a metaphysical characteristic of human beings, as Kant wrongfully assumed, but evolves within and from the practical interplay between the human subject and its natural and social environment—what Hegel called the "dialectics of rationality" (Ulrich 1986, 56). Thus reason denotes the human interest in autonomy under the conditions of social life and coexistence; it is nothing else than human beings' fundamental interest in being human.

Our morality, that is, our basic capacity to use reason, defines us as principally autonomous human beings. As human beings, we all have an unconditional moral claim to freedom and self-determination. Freedom is the ultimate condition for the possibility of being human. Avishai Margalit (1997, 159) refers to freedom simultaneously as "a constitutive element of the good life and a necessary condition for achieving such a life." This constitutive role, he continues, makes freedom "a good thing in and of itself." Thus the claim for freedom does not need further justification; freedom is justified by nothing else than freedom itself. Therefore, freedom, understood as autonomy or self-determination, is the ultimate principle underlying all justifications of moral judgments and norms. Thus our autonomy, that is, our morality, is both the foundation of morals and itself dependent on moral practice. The reason to commit to moral practice is its vital importance for human autonomy and hence for morality itself (Pieper 2003, 44f.). Moral practice thus both evolves from human autonomy and is at the same time aimed at human autonomy. It is this undissolvable, dialectical interrelation between morals and morality that, according to Annemarie Pieper (2003, 46), builds the foundation of human practice as a humane practice.

Free Will and the Foundation of Morals

As autonomous beings, we can only choose to act morally; there is no absolute must to do so. If we are to be understood and defined as self-determined persons, moral obligation cannot be something that is imposed on us externally but must derive from our own free will to obligate ourselves. It derives from our own autonomous insight into the inherent necessity of morals for human practice. This reference to and reliance on our free will should not be confused with a state of ethical "anything goes" in which we are free to do whatever we please. It merely leaves open the (rather theoretical) possibility for us as self-determined creatures to opt out of being a part of any moral community and, therefore, to deny the validity of morals per se (Tugendhat 1993, 89ff.; Korsgaard 1996, 100). However, once we accept our social identities and commit to the communities in which we are embedded, that is, once we build our moral consciousness on the basis of the "self-understanding of moral persons who recognize that they *belong* to the moral community" (Habermas 1998, 29)— and according to Habermas this applies to all individuals who have been socialized into any communicative form of life at all—this option has vanished, and we willingly subordinate our actions to the requirement of justification. Justification in a nontraditionalistic sense means subjecting all our actions to good, that is, universally comprehensible, reasons. Hence it is the will to act upon good reasons that ultimately establishes the binding power of morals. As free and self-determined creatures, we all have the undeniable basic capacity to choose to base our actions on good reasons and thus to act reasonably. This will alone, as Kant claimed in the famous opening sentence of his *Groundwork of the Metaphysics of Morals* (1997), establishes an action as good or bad, as moral or immoral: "It is impossible to think of anything at all in the world, or indeed even beyond it, that could be considered good without limitation except a good will" (Kant 1997, 7).

Kant's "good will" is not to be interpreted as an isolated phenomenon referring to certain specific decisions and actions of a person; rather, it is linked to that person's general motivation that guides all of his or her decisions. In other words, the notion of "good will" refers to the general maxims upon which an individual acts (Kant 1996, 152f.). Hence, according to Kant, the moral worth of an action does not lie in the purpose of the action itself but in the principle on which the agent acts. This insight leads Kant to conclude that the highest moral worth must be attributed to those actions that are carried out from duty (Korsgaard 1997, xii–xiv). In other words, a person can be said to act morally in those cases where, on the basis of these guiding maxims and principles, she feels an inner obligation to do so, as opposed to cases in which she acts in a certain way simply because of her preferences or interests. Moral obligation, in Kant's words, can thus be defined as "the necessity of a free action under a categorical imperative of reason" (Kant 1996, 15).

Like Kant, Aristotle also claimed that justice, which he understood as a personal virtue, does not merely enable one to be just and to perform just actions but makes one want to be and act in line with the requirements of justice (Höffe 2003, 156). In contrast to the virtue-based foundation of Aristotle's claim, however, a Kantian explanation of a person's inner duty refers to the insight that a certain action is morally required simply because it is the right thing to do, that is, because it can be justified by intersubjective reasons. Hence moral obligation derives from nothing else than the imperative of good reasons; our free will to subordinate our actions to the principle of justification establishes their binding power. The validity of moral obligations is thus based on the cognitive and affective ability of human beings reasonably to recognize them as morally valid. In other words, it is our human autonomy that gives us the ability to obligate ourselves (Korsgaard 1996, 91). Hence moral obligations have binding power if, on the basis of reasonable choices, free human beings could generally (and hypothetically) want them to do so. Therefore, what we as reasonable human beings ought to do is nothing else than what we are reasonably able to want to do (Ulrich 2008, 54f).[2] Again, this does not mean that we decide from case to case whether we want to accept certain moral norms as binding; the decisive element is not our concrete decision but our general ability, that is, the inherent potential of all free and reasonable human beings to choose to act morally. We are thus morally obliged not merely in those situations in which we effectively want to act morally but in those situations in which we, as members of the moral community, could reasonably choose to want to act morally.

The ultimate foundation of moral norms and claims in the postmetaphysical age must thus necessarily be our free human will (Tugendhat 1993, 96), that is, the will to act upon the principle of rational justification of our actions based on good reasons. This follows from nothing else than the constitutive importance of human freedom and self-determination for humanity. Consequently, to come back to the central theme in this book, the concept of justice as a justifiable principle and orienting ideal for human practice, as an ethical category, and thus as a notion and concept rooted in human rationality also must ultimately rely on human autonomy. In other words, what we as human beings deserve derives from our justified moral claim to freedom and self-determination. Because the perspective of justice is by definition intersubjective, such a justification must necessarily be framed in impartial terms. An impartial justification of moral claims that does not favor the freedoms of one over those of another must necessarily be based on the ideal of equal freedom for all human beings. Moral claims that are justified on the basis of equal human freedom, as we will see, are nothing else than moral rights.

Equalizing Justice: The Egalitarian Foundation of the Justice Perspective

The Rawlsian claim stated earlier for the largest amount of equal human freedom derives from the constitutive importance of self-determination for a human life. The basic condition for justice is thus the inherent equality of human beings in regard to their fundamental ability and freedom to act. All major ethical theories, as Amartya Sen (1992, 3; see also G. A. Cohen 1989, 906; 1993, 9) points out, are egalitarian in terms of some focal variable. This insight derives from the impossibility of providing a foundation of the moral point of view in general without referring to the basic equality of all human beings. Any nontraditionalistic, nonauthoritative justification of the moral point of view must, as shown earlier, necessarily refer to the defining and therefore shared parameters of humanity and thus to the human condition itself. There is no plausible alternative to this humanistic foundation of morals. Consequently, any ethically sound conception of justice must necessarily be egalitarian at its core.

Dignity, Vulnerability, and the Principle of Equal Respect and Concern

Our morality, as I showed earlier, refers both to our ability to create our own conceptions of the good life and to our basic disposition to reflect upon our life scripts and their impact on the lives of others and the moral communities in which we are embedded. Thus it enables us to assign value to our personal life and to recognize and respect the equal value of the lives of all human beings around us. It is this basic disposition that constitutes an equal moral claim to consideration for all human beings, that is, a claim not to be instrumentalized by other people but to be respected and treated as ends in themselves. This "absolute command" was most famously formulated in Kant's "categorical imperative": "So act that you use humanity, whether in your own person or in the person of any other, always at the same time as an end, never merely as a means" (Kant 1997, 38).

It is important to emphasize that the justification of this fundamental claim for respect is based on our disposition to be reasonable beings and not on our actual achievements or failings in the past. In other words, it is based on our inherent capacity to reevaluate and change a potentially destructive direction of our lives at any given time. "Even the worst criminals," Avishai

Margalit (1996, 70) points out, are thus "worthy of basic human respect" simply because of the possibility of radically reevaluating and, if given the opportunity, changing their lives for the better. This inherent possibility of changing, that is, our ability to live a life that is discontinuous with the past, denotes nothing else than our disposition to act upon "good will" and hence our inherent morality as human beings. This leads us back to the initial insight: our actions are not determined by nature; we are not instinct-driven creatures but self-determined, reflective, and thus autonomous persons. It is this aspect that builds the ultimate foundation of the respect we unconditionally deserve as human beings, and it is this aspect that can be referred to as human dignity. Thus our inherent dignity is the very expression of being human. It is what inevitably identifies us as human beings and what distinguishes us from the nonhuman. The awareness of our own humanity provides us with self-respect, of which dignity is the external expression or representation. In other words, our human dignity "consists of the behavioral tendencies that attest to the fact that one's attitude toward oneself is an attitude of self-respect" (Margalit 1996, 51).

The awareness of our humanity, that is, our capacity of self-respect, however, renders us not only dignified but also inherently vulnerable. Our dignity is both the constitution of our being human and the source of our inherent vulnerability as human beings. Feeling violated in our dignity and self-respect, the capacity to suffer (Williams 1997, 92f.), is thus itself a distinctively human trait. It is expressed in the concept of humiliation. Humiliation can be defined as the denial or rejection of a human being's status as a human. It is attached to the loss of basic control and self-determination and to a person's rejection from the human commonwealth, that is, the degradation of a human being to the nonhuman (Margalit 1996, 3ff.). If we are all equally vulnerable in our humanity, however, our claim for respect and protection of our dignity must necessarily apply to all human beings in an equal manner as well. Thus our equal vulnerability as creatures of inherent dignity must necessarily lead us back to the principle of equal concern and respect on which all morals must necessarily be based.

The concept of justice is not an exception in this regard. Justice too is rooted in this most fundamental moral principle. It was again Immanuel Kant who combined human autonomy (which he defined as positive freedom) and its inherent vulnerability within the concept of justice. For Kant, the circumstances of justice derive from the combination of human agency and vulnerability. "If human beings were not vulnerable and needy," Onora O'Neill (2000, 138) concurs, "they could not damage, destroy, coerce and deceive so successfully (or perhaps at all), and the need for justice would be gone." The foundation of morals in the principle of equal moral concern and respect constitutes the inevitably egalitarian foundation of justice as a concept.

The Egalitarian Foundations of Nonegalitarianism

In this book I will argue that the primary "distribution" of people's fundamental rights is what secures their status as equals (see the section " 'Equal Freedom' as the Substance of Moral Rights" later in this chapter). All distributions of other goods are mere derivatives of this primary distribution and can thus be unequal if, but only if, they serve the claim of equality at the primary level of rights. Most scholars who claim to belong to the school of so-called nonegalitarians fail to make this crucial distinction. They interpret justice exclusively in terms of the distribution of material goods and, as a result, often overlook that their own (not so nonegalitarian) claim for unequal distributions is itself based on the egalitarian presumption of equal moral concern and respect. The same limitation also characterizes the popular but wrong assumption that distributive justice is merely about the redistribution of wealth, that is, of the material results of cooperative social processes. A well-understood interpretation of distributive justice refers to the prior conditions of equal participation within these cooperative processes and not merely to the redistribution of its (unjust) outcomes (Scanlon 1984, 142). Fair and equal participation would in fact render a large part of such redistribution unnecessary.

Thus understood, egalitarianism is not at all a claim for uniformity, as nonegalitarians often suggest (e.g., Lucas 1997, 111). If strict equality of all possible outcomes were the goal of egalitarianism, the nonegalitarian critique would indeed be justified. However, defending equality at the level of rights and opportunities for participation is not a call for uniformity but the very foundation of any equitable and well-understood pluralism, because the recognition of our differences as individuals can be based only on our respect for all human beings as equals. Well-understood egalitarianism, from this perspective, is essentially to be understood as liberal egalitarianism.

Most nonegalitarians who opt for an unequal distribution of material goods are thus themselves—wittingly or unwittingly—committed to the egalitarian position at the first level. Egalitarianism does not per se exclude unequal distributions; in many cases they may even be morally required if they are supported by good reasons. Good reasons for distributive inequality, however, must themselves derive from the fundamental equality of human beings (Tugendhat 1993, 377). Thus unequal distributions are justified if they are warranted by the principle of equality. It was Ronald Dworkin (1977, 273) who pointed out this crucial difference between treating everybody strictly equally and treating everybody as equals.

Thus even distributive inequality must rest on this "presumption in favor of equality" (Gosepath 2001, 140; 2003, 291; 2004, 200ff.) of all human beings. Unequal distributions that refer to an alleged fundamental inequality of human beings, for example, in terms of race or gender, are discriminatory and therefore unjust. Any distribution that is based on the disregard of the presumption of human equality violates the requirement of intersubjectivity and must inevitably be considered arbitrary. From this point of view, the burden of proof or justification is not on the side of the egalitarian position. Equal distribution can prima facie be assumed as justified for all distributable goods unless there are good reasons for distributing unequally (Tugendhat 1993, 374f.).

Sufficiency or Equality? Dismantling Nonegalitarian Humanism

Despite the evident egalitarian core of nonegalitarianism, there are still non-egalitarians who deny the constitutive importance of equality for the justification of moral claims. They claim that the most fundamental standards of justice are not relative, as the concept of equality suggests, but nonrelational, that is, absolute. Justice, as they understand it, deals with the prevention of human misery and suffering and thus with the fulfillment of minimum standards for a decent human life. Such standards, they claim, are not relative; our moral duty to assist people in states of misery does not derive from the fact that others are better off but from the mere humanitarian untenability of their situation (Krebs 2003, 240). Hence nonegalitarians accuse egalitarians of confusing equality with the concept of generality. Equality, they claim, is at best a result of the general fulfillment of minimum standards for everybody (e.g., Westen 1990, 71ff.; Frankfurt 2000; Krebs 2000, 2003; Raz 2000). As such, it is seen as a mere side product of, but by no means as a fundamental principle for, the general fulfillment of these absolute standards (Krebs 2000, 17ff.; 2003, 243). Thus nonegalitarians deny any inherent or underived moral value of equality (e.g., Frankfurt 1997, 3).

In cases where human beings suffer from obvious physical harm due to severe deprivation of food, for example, the argument of such "nonegalitarian humanism" (Krebs 2003) seems plausible, at least intuitively. But human misery comes in many different forms and is often less visible and manifest than in the case of severe starvation. Hence the problem of nonegalitarian humanistic positions is how to adequately determine what is to be considered as human misery, or, positively formulated, what it is that characterizes a decent life and, accordingly, how to justify the respective absolute standards.

Evidently, absolute standards cannot be based on the satisfaction of subjective needs or wishes of human beings. Subjective moral feelings provide insufficient justification for moral claims. That is why even Margalit, whom nonegalitarian humanists often claim as one of their own (e.g., Krebs 2003, 243), defines humiliation not as a subjective, psychological concept but as an inherently normative one. Thus he bases the concept of humiliation on good, that is, intersubjective reasons for a person to feel humiliated and not on that person's actual subjective state in the specific situation (Margalit 1996, 9; 1997, 157). A person can feel humiliated even though objectively there is no sound reason for him or her to feel that way. Similarly, not every person who would have good reasons to feel humiliated actually does feel humiliated subjectively. Victims may identify with their aggressors and accept their humiliation as deserved, for example, or blame themselves and suffer in silence. "Many victims learn to be helpless," writes Judith Shklar (1990, 38), "which allows them to evade the conscious status of victimhood but at an awful cost to themselves." Any normative justification that relies on sound reasons rather than on the subjective state of human beings, however, must inevitably refer back to the presumption of equality. We will look at this connection in more detail in the following paragraphs.

First Reply to Nonegalitarian Humanism: The Inseparability of Fairness, Impartiality, and Equality   Moral norms are said to be just if they derive from a fair process. The basic condition of fairness is commonly seen in the concept of impartiality (Scanlon 1984, 141). This insight does not cause much controversy. Both egalitarians and nonegalitarians agree that the requirement of impartiality is a constitutive element of justice, not only in the application of norms but also in their justification.[3] Hence the standpoint of justice can essentially be understood as the standpoint of impartiality. It is the standpoint from which principles and statements of justice and hence moral claims must be justified in order to be able to claim normative validity. "It is," John Stuart Mill (2001, 45) argued correctly, "by universal admission, inconsistent with justice to be *partial*."

The question then is how we are to specify this impartial standpoint, from which derive the statements of justice and thus the allegedly nonegalitarian standards of sufficiency. Several suggestions have been made. The most famous one in modern political philosophy is without a doubt John Rawls's theory of justice as fairness. For Rawls, the conditions of fairness are those that derive from a hypothetical "original position" in which the people of a moral community decide over their governing rules and norms behind what he calls a "veil of ignorance." The veil of ignorance withholds all knowledge about the future positions of anyone. Hence the contracting parties do not know how the different alternatives will affect their own situation in the future. Therefore, they are obliged to evaluate norms and principles solely on the basis of general and thus impartial considerations (Rawls 1971, 136ff.). To ask about the just constitution and hence the impartiality of norms and principles in a society thus means to assess whether these principles would be agreed upon by free and rational individuals under the conditions of fairness, that is, under the condition of ignorance about anyone's future position in life.

The idealized conditions of Rawls's original position provide a questionable basis for deriving adequate moral judgments in real-life situations (Nagel 1973; 1979, 120ff.; Sen 1980, 201). Statements of justice cannot adequately be derived from a hypothetical agreement of idealized, fully rational, and entirely independent individuals without being emptied of their practical substance at the same time. Human beings are not fully rational creatures and have, as a result, limited capacities to act entirely autonomously (O'Neill 1986, 159). They are by definition needy creatures who depend on the capacities of others for the realization of their life plans. A plausible and thus practically relevant theory of justice must take the limitations and dependencies of human beings into account. It is no coincidence that the shortcomings of such idealized conceptions of justice as that of Rawls are surfacing most distinctively in the context of the modern market economy: The idealization of human beings as fully rational and mutually independent subjects underlying today's contractarian economic theories obscures the role of economic power in market transactions, which might render weaker parties unable to oppose unfair arrangements proposed by the strong (O'Neill 1993, 319). The real test of the legitimacy of certain norms, principles, and statements of justice is thus not whether fully rational and mutually independent people would have agreed to them under the conditions of ignorance, but whether actual human beings with all their flaws and limitations could reasonably agree to them as the persons they are under actual circumstances. It is against this background that Thomas Scanlon (1982; similarly, B. Barry 1995, 67ff.) opts for an alternative construction of the original position based on individuals who do have knowledge of their interests, preferences, and identities. Their moral motivation, accordingly, is not self-interest under the condition of ignorance, as is the case in Rawls's position, but the justification of their actions on the basis of reasoned argumentation between all involved and affected parties. The fact that human beings have interests that may conflict, as Scanlon (1982, 124) rightly argues, is precisely what gives substance to questions of justice.

Hence the required consent that establishes the impartiality and thus the validity of moral norms and claims is one achieved through practical reasoning rather than ideal contracting. Those norms and claims are impartial to which all potentially affected human beings could reasonably agree under actual circumstances within a hypothetical, undistorted deliberative process. Such an understanding of justice, which is based on the reasonable agreement of all affected human beings, resembles what Brian Barry (1989, 255ff.; 1995) aptly called a conception of "justice as impartiality." Thus a norm or principle passes the test of impartiality if it cannot be reasonably rejected by anyone affected by it (B. Barry 1989, 372). Therefore, the impartial standpoint essentially is the standpoint of universality. Universality understood as impartiality or, in other words, as nondiscrimination and thus as inclusion of everyone, however, evidently refers back to the presumption of the fundamental equality of all human beings. Principles of justice that satisfy the conditions of a theory of justice as impartiality, as Brian Barry (1995, 7; see also Nagel 1991, 64) claims, are thus impartial "because they capture a certain kind of equality." The very idea that fairness requires agreement of everyone affected is based on a deep commitment to human beings' fundamental equality (B. Barry 1995, 7).

Thus any violation of the principle of impartial justification constitutes a violation of the principle of justice in general quite simply because people are not treated as equals (Gosepath 2004, 295). The claim here is that fairness and equality cannot reasonably be separated; the impartial justification of nonegalitarian humanists' allegedly absolute standards of justice also necessarily presumes the equality of all human beings.

Second Reply to Nonegalitarian Humanism: Universal Humanity as Universal Equality

This last argument corners nonegalitarians but does not yet quite trap them. As mentioned earlier, nonegalitarians do agree to the constitutive role of impartiality for the concept of justice. However, confronted with this argument, they argue that it does not derive from human equality but from morals of respect (e.g., Frankfurt 1997, 11).

Evidently, they are not entirely wrong in this insight. What they seem to overlook, however, is that the justification of a morals of respect also must ultimately refer to the inherent equality of all human beings. The nonegalitarian humanist claim for fulfillment of absolute standards of sufficiency presumes that every suffering human being can doubtless be recognized as being human in the first place. Therefore, it inevitably presupposes our essential shared humanity. This claim is not denied in the humanitarians' argument; they do acknowledge that "something follows from the fact that men are men, and that all men share a common humanity" (Lucas 1997, 106). Hence they do confirm that all human beings are entitled to respectful treatment and that this "entitlement derives from their possession of certain features [. . .] which are characteristic of the human species" (Lucas 1997, 106). Nonegalitarian humanists do support the idea of equal respect, but they claim that it has little to do with equality. Rather, they claim that it is "an argument of Universal Humanity, that we should treat human beings, because they are human beings, humanely" (Lucas 1997, 106). Even though its implication is correct, the argument itself is incomplete. The mere acknowledgment of our universal humanity, that is, the simple fact of being human, does not yet establish a normative claim for equal respect. The fact of universal humanity constitutes a universal normative claim for respect only on the basis of moral reciprocity. Without reference to the concept of reciprocity, the notion of "being human" remains an empty and meaningless formula, unable to give rise to any normative implications.

Where else than from our own experienced humanity should we derive the meaning of being human and the inherent claim for respect that comes with it? Our respect for other human beings is inherently and inevitably tied to our own status as human beings. It is based on our cognitive capacity to switch roles, that is, to put ourselves in another person's shoes and to "bring his case home to ourselves" (Adam Smith 2002, 128). This capability of mental role taking is the source of our human morality (Ulrich 2008, 33). It gives us, as Adam Smith stated in his *Theory of Moral Sentiments* (2002), the capacity to "sympathize," to understand what the other person might feel and therefore to critically reflect on our own actions in light of their impact on others. Smith stated that we approve or disapprove of our own conduct by looking at it through the eyes of another person. We cannot assess our own sentiments and motives or form any judgments about them without removing ourselves "from our own natural station" in order "to view them as at a certain distance from us" (Adam Smith 2002, 128). The superior range of sympathy, John Stuart Mill (2001, 51) stated, is one of two defining differences between human beings and "other animals." Human beings, he claimed, are "capable of sympathizing, not solely with their offspring, or, like some of the more noble animals, with some superior animal who is kind to them, but with all human, and even with all sentient, beings." The other defining difference, according to Mill, is a human being's superior intelligence, which renders it "capable of apprehending a community of interest between himself and the human society of which he forms a part." Taken together, these two elements lead to the basic reversibility of human perspectives described by Smith.

This reversibility of perspectives leads to the inherent reciprocity of moral claims. We are undeniably capable of recognizing another human being as a human being similar to ourselves. Therefore, any attempt to argumentatively deny his or her human status must necessarily end in self-denial, because one can logically reject an equal as nonhuman only by denying one's own human status. By recognizing another human being as human, we must inevitably acknowledge her same vulnerability, which makes it impossible to deny her same legitimate claim for respect that we claim for ourselves. Hence we cannot but award the same moral worth to her that we do to ourselves. This fundamental reciprocity of moral claims builds the core of the concept of human equality.

The claim for equal respect that nonegalitarians derive from the "universality of humanity" is ultimately based on the universalization of the principle of reciprocity. If we cannot deny a concrete person's status as a human being, we logically cannot deny this same status for all other human beings either. Universalization in this regard is the rational process of abstraction of our concrete relationships with other persons to the general, that is, universal, level of humanity as a whole. The affective or emotional process of concrete role taking thus transforms into a rational process of universal or "ideal role taking" (Kohlberg 1981, 199). It is based on what South African novelist Nadine Gordimer (quoted in Shklar 1986, 26) aptly termed our "rational empathy," and it forms the core of Kant's categorical imperative.

Hence universalization derives from an impersonal standpoint (Nagel 1991, 11), which is just a different way to describe the impartial standpoint or, in Adam Smith's (2002, 183) words, the imaginary standpoint of the ideal impartial spectator. The general concern for all human beings must thus be thought of as an aggregate of all separate equal concerns for every individual person (Nagel 1991, 66). Thus the nonegalitarian suggestion that egalitarians confuse equality with universality is misguided; it is based on a false dichotomy between universality and equality. The truth of the matter is that both concepts are inherently and inseparably connected. The reciprocity of moral claims denotes neither only equality nor simply universality but universal equality of human beings in what Kant (1997, 41, 66) called "the universal kingdom of ends."

Third Reply to Nonegalitarian Humanism: The Social Foundations of Human Dignity   The insight into the constitutional role of reciprocity for moral claims and our human morality as a whole builds the basis also for rejecting the last objection of nonegalitarian humanists. This objection is based on the nonegalitarian understanding of human dignity as absolute (Krebs 2003, 241). Again, this understanding is not entirely wrong insofar as the inherent dignity of human beings indeed deserves categorical, that is, absolute respect and protection. However, even apart from the insight that this absoluteness of human dignity is constituted through the principle of equal respect and concern, which is itself based on the universal reciprocity of moral claims and thus on the universal equality of human beings, it seems that the foundation of dignity itself cannot be expressed fully in absolute terms.

First, the essence of human dignity is its commonality among all human beings. Human dignity distinguishes the human from the nonhuman. Therefore, it can be derived only on a comparative basis. Furthermore, human dignity refers to the inherent quality of human beings as autonomous moral subjects and therefore to their individual identity as persons. Our identity and personality, however, are crucially dependent on our social relations to other human beings. Our self-respect (of which dignity is the external expression) is based on our awareness of deserving the respect of others (Habermas 1991,

150). Therefore, it is inseparably connected to our capacity to reflect on our actions from the perspective of the people around us. A reasonable degree of distributional equality might thus play a crucial role in building self-respect and what we consider a decent, dignified life. If our self-image depends on our reflective relation to other human beings and the environment as a whole, extreme inequalities will inevitably lead to feelings of inferiority. Poverty, as Avishai Margalit (1997, 149) points out, weighs less heavily on people in an egalitarian society where everybody is poor than in an inegalitarian one. The material suffering is the same in both societies, but the humiliation inherent in living in a state of poverty is predominantly connected to inequality. "Manifestations of inequality," Margalit (1997, 148ff.) goes on, may sometimes be "prime examples of humiliation" because "in general, inequality symbolically expresses an attitude of downgrading—the view that the other is inferior in the social hierarchy." What is humiliating for the so-called untouchables in the Indian caste system, for example, is their social status "and not only their terrible suffering." Thus even seemingly absolute standards of justice cannot be justified convincingly without implicitly referring to the presumption of the fundamental equality of all human beings. Any attempt to do so must necessarily be based on an incomplete notion of human dignity.

Defining Justice: A Rights-Based Perspective on Egalitarian Justice

So far, I have shown that the concept of justice is indispensable for the viability of any society. This holds not only empirically but also normatively. The justification or rightness of the justice perspective establishes the primacy of justice as a normative ideal for society. Furthermore, I have shown that any plausible account of justice must inevitably be egalitarian. Hence, after clarifying the formal contours of the concept of justice, we are now able to systematically fill it with content. In this section I will show that the most plausible substantiation of the concept of justice derives from a rights-based perspective.

From Moral Claims to Rights-Based Justice

A moral claim that can be justified from an impartial perspective constitutes a moral right. The general formula "A has a right to X against B by virtue of Y" outlines the four constitutive elements of a right (Gewirth 1984, 93). A right consists of a right holder as the subject of a right (A), the object of a right (X), the respondent of a right as a correlative duty bearer (B), and the justificatory basis of the right (Y). Taken together, these elements constitute the content of a subjective right. A subjective right is a moral relationship between a person and a thing, an action, or a state of affairs (Edmundson 2004, 9). The right holder is in direct control of this relationship (Donnelly 1985a, 12; 2003, 8).

Moral rights are prepositive and prepolitical rights; they are a priori to positive law and institutions. Feinberg (1973, 84) applies the term *moral rights* to all rights regarded as existing prior to or independent of legal laws or institutional rules. Hence in Feinberg's terms moral rights range from claims derived from mutual agreements to the most fundamental human rights. Others have rejected the notion or existence of prepositive moral rights altogether. Jürgen Habermas (1996a, 104ff.), for example, claims that legal and moral rules simultaneously appear "side by side as two different but mutually complementary kinds of action norms." Hence there is no such thing as moral rights existing a priori to positive law. The notion of "a higher law," for Habermas, belongs to the premodern world. Accordingly, even the most basic human rights must be conceived from the start as rights in the juridical sense.

This book adheres to a narrow definition of moral rights, limiting them to those prepositive rights that claim universal validity. A moral claim is universally valid and thus normatively binding if it can be justified from the standpoint of impartiality and thus can "survive open and informed scrutiny" (Sen 2004a, 320). Implicit claims deriving from mutual contracts, promises, or the common law will thus not be included in the catalogue of moral rights because their legitimacy depends on their correspondence with more fundamental moral claims. In this narrow definition moral rights must be stated in a general way; they must be valid for any human being and not just for the parties within a specific cooperative relationship. They derive from and must not violate the inherent equality of human beings. Therefore, moral rights are universal and equal rights (Werhane 1985, 12ff.; Donnelly 2003, 10), as well as rational rights, justified by nothing else than good reasons; they provide the rational basis for an urgent and justified demand (Shue 1980, 13).

The importance of rights stems from human beings' inherent need for protection and thus "from the claim that this protection is justified as being *owed* to persons for their own sakes" (Gewirth 1996, 9; emphasis added). The most basic moral rights can thus essentially be described as human rights. Human rights, in other words, are the rights we enjoy simply by virtue of being human adults. They are independent of our membership in particular communities such as ones defined by nationality, class, sex, religion, ethnicity, or sexual orientation (Nussbaum 2002, 135). Their moral status is the essence of human rights. Human rights are "quintessentially ethical articulations, and they are not, in particular, putative legal claims" (Sen 2004a, 321). Moral rights, understood as human rights, as Gewirth pointed out correctly in the above quote, are the essence of what we, as human beings, owe to one another. This is, not coincidentally, precisely what the concept of justice is concerned with. Hence human rights must build the normative core of any plausible conception of justice: "The language of moral rights is the language of justice, and whoever takes justice seriously must accept that there exist moral rights" (G. A. Cohen 1988, 297).

Mackie takes this insight a step further by claiming that morals per se must be inherently rights based (Mackie 1984, 176; see also Tugendhat 1992, 1993). Mackie's position is ethically appealing. However, it runs the risk of overlooking that the moral principle of equal concern and respect might well lead to duties that do not necessarily derive from moral rights (Wildt 1998) or to ethical requirements that do not amount to full-fledged duties (Raz 1984, 184). Whether such ethical requirements ultimately are rooted in the existence of moral rights as well is a question I will leave open for now. What seems evident, however, is that in those cases in which rights-based duties do arise, we are inevitably dealing with the concept of justice.

Egalitarian distributive justice, to summarize these last paragraphs, is an inherently rights-based affair. (Human) rights are the most fundamental and most important part of any moral theory and are thus the foundational concept of justice. Hence at its core justice deals with the equal respect, protection, and realization of moral rights. Consequently, as Vlastos (1984, 60) argued in his famous essay on equality, an action is to be considered as just "if, and only if, it is prescribed exclusively by regard for the rights of all whom it affects substantially."

What Is Wrong with Contractarianism?

A rights-based conception of justice that derives from the universal principle of equal moral concern and respect is fundamentally opposed to contractarian understandings of justice, which are commonly used to justify market relations and the outcomes resulting from them. The roots of contractarian theories can be found in the moral philosophies of Thomas Hobbes and David

Hume. While Hobbes provided a contractarian justification of government as a generally advantageous institution for lifting people out of their natural state of war, Hume limited the scope of his conception to the domain of property as the object of justice. Thus justice in a Humean sense refers to mutually advantageous rules that govern individual possession (B. Barry 1989, 135; 1995, 44). The focus on mutual advantage is characteristic of contractarian approaches to distributive justice in general (see, e.g., Gauthier 1986). In other words, from the contractarian perspective, the conflicts between different life plans that constitute the circumstances of justice in any pluralistic society are not to be resolved primarily on the basis of equal concern and respect but on the basis of mutually beneficial agreements.

Egoism, Mutual Advantage, and the Kantian "Good Will"   Conceptions of justice as mutual advantage suffer from severe shortcomings. It is even questionable whether agreements that people enter and adhere to only on the basis of their advantageousness to themselves are to be considered a reflection of the standpoint of justice at all. It seems that the moral element, which is constitutive for the justice perspective, is missing in a theory that is based entirely on the instrumental rationality of purely self-interested people.

Proponents of contractarian accounts of justice might respond that the core of moral behavior in general is provided by the voluntary constraint of unfettered self-interest, and because the claim to *mutual* advantage in fact is such a constraint (Gauthier 1986, 2ff.), contractarianism is logically to be considered a genuine theory of justice. This is, at least partly, a valid argument. However, it becomes problematic when one looks at the motivation underlying individuals' willingness to restrain their own interests. In the contractarian view, they are willing to do so because it is beneficial to them (Gauthier 1986, 2), which renders the moral standing of such restrictions questionable. This becomes even more evident when one asks whether purely self-interested individuals would actually still abide by the restraining rules once they became a burden or when breaking them might yield a personal benefit. Thus rules that are enacted by purely self-interested individuals and abided by on a merely instrumental basis suffer from an inherent free-rider problem: if everybody else sticks to the rules, one might be better off breaking them. For a conception of justice as mutual advantage, this problem ultimately proves irresolvable without contradicting its own premises. Brian Barry (1995, 46ff.), for example, suggests a "hybrid theory" that combines mutual advantage as the criterion for the generation of rules with what he calls "fair play" for keeping them once they are enacted. Gauthier's book *Morals by Agreement* (1986) is designed similarly, and Allen Buchanan (1990, 1993) also suggested such an approach, which he termed "justice as self-interested reciprocity" [*sic*]. Such switching back and forth between different premises and foundations, however, hardly makes for a convincing theory of justice. It inevitably leads to a patchwork approach that exposes rather than fixes the inherent flaws of justice as mutual advantage. A better and more consistent approach would certainly be to base the theory on genuine moral reasoning from the beginning, rather than merely fighting the symptoms of an inherently flawed conception. The genuinely moral motivation, that is, the "good will," that according to Kant is a necessary condition for moral behavior is missing in an understanding of justice as mutual advantage. This is why Tugendhat (1992, 324; see also Frankena 1973, 19) refers to contractarianism as a mere substitute for morals.

Moral behavior is normally associated with "inner sanction," that is, with the feeling of guilt, shame, or regret when one breaks a moral norm or rule. A conception of morals that is based on pure self-interest, on the other hand, lacks the foundation on which to develop such sentiments; it does not have a real concept of good or bad. Lacking a concept of inner sanction, however, the contractarian perspective is able to define justice only in terms of rules and regulations that are effectively in place. A person can claim to be treated unjustly only relative to existing norms and rules, but there is no ethical basis from which to assess whether the rules themselves meet the requirements of justice. That is why contractarianism fails the test of universality; a person has rights only to the extent that effective contracts are in place, but not by virtue of her being human per se (Tugendhat 1992, 331). Pure egoism is by any standard the antithesis of moral behavior; and if contractarianism is a mere substitute for morals in general, its theory of justice cannot be more than a substitute for the concept of justice either.

There is a fundamental difference between the quality of an agreement reached on the basis of a conception of justice as mutual advantage and one that is based on a conception of justice as impartiality as it is represented in this book. In the latter case people reach agreements on the basis of reasoned argument and their mutual recognition as human beings of equal worth. In the former case, however, they reach agreements solely on the basis of their self-interest. This is the core difference between a truly Kantian contractualism and a conception of morals based on mutual advantage. The relations between self-interested people are purely instrumental (Tugendhat 1993, 93). Respect for other people is based entirely on strategic premises: others' opinions count only as far as they are beneficial to one's own goals and intentions. Others are perceived as mere means to one's own ends. Such a conception fundamentally clashes with the Kantian claim for categorical recognition of all human beings as ends in themselves. Justice is about the *unconditional* recognition of morally justified claims; an understanding of justice as mutual advantage fails precisely in this aspect.

Voluntary Agreement, Pareto Efficiency, and the Problem of Unequal Starting Positions   Closely related to contractarian conceptions of justice is a concept that economists are similarly fond of and that is most commonly used to assess the "ethical" quality of market transactions: "Pareto efficiency" or "Pareto optimality." Pareto efficiency is the economists' actual concept of justice. At its core, however, it is nothing more than a restatement of justice as mutual advantage; as such, it suffers from the same inherent flaws that I discussed earlier. A transaction is said to be Pareto efficient if it leaves at least one contracting party better off while not hurting any other party involved. Hence the Pareto concept focuses exclusively on the transaction in question and turns a blind eye on the distributional starting position of the contracting parties. From this perspective, preexisting inequalities and the resulting imbalances in bargaining power seem not to play a role in the fairness of a transaction. On the contrary, the concept aims to eliminate the need for such distributional judgments (Sen 1973, 6).

The Pareto condition is normally regarded as met if rational human beings enter a transaction on a voluntary basis; it assumes that no rational person would voluntarily agree to an unbeneficial exchange. This leads to the somewhat contradictory image of the market mechanism as inherently amoral while being praised as the epitome of fair interaction at the same time:

> The first conception central to our theory is therefore that of a morally free zone, a context within which the constraints of morality would have no place. The free zone proves to be that habitat familiar to economists, the perfectly competitive market. [...] Our argument is that in a perfectly competitive market, mutual advantage is assured by the unconstrained activity of each individual in pursuit of her own greatest satisfaction, so that there is no place, rationally, for constraint. Furthermore, since in the market each person enjoys

the same freedom in her choices and actions that she would have in isolation from her fellows, and since the market outcome reflects the exercise of each person's freedom, there is no basis for finding any partiality in the market's operations. Thus there is also no place, morally, for constraint. The market exemplifies an ideal of interaction among persons who, taking no interest in each other's interests, need only follow the dictates of their own individual interests to participate effectively in a venture for mutual advantage. (Gauthier 1986, 13)

What remain systematically unaddressed in such a conception of justice are potential exploitations that may arise from unequal bargaining positions, as well as the fact that desperate conditions often force people with weak starting positions into "voluntary" agreements. Thus the exclusive focus on the transaction itself renders the concept blind to preexisting injustices and inequalities. The conditions of Pareto optimality may be fulfilled even in the face of the most egregious human tragedies, such as poverty, disease, and starvation (Scherer 2003, 78f.). Hence, rather than subjecting agreements to normative-critical scrutiny from the standpoint of justice, contractarians make the standpoint of justice itself dependent on those agreements (see, e.g., J. M. Buchanan 1985, 126). Thereby, they systematically overlook the asymmetric nature of contracts between those who have much and those who have little or nothing. Even though contracts might be formally free, they can be systematically distorted by power imbalances and dependencies (Tugendhat 1992, 359). The Pareto perspective has no concept that would allow for the identification of such cases.

The cynics who defend exploitative working conditions and sweatshops in the Third World with the argument that those workers are still better off than without any work at all are a prime example of the defective logic of this position. The voluntary agreement of workers to work under inhumane conditions is indeed based on the immediate increase of their personal utility—the few cents of salary per day might save their children from starving to death—but from an impartial perspective such transactions must be considered inherently unjust despite this questionable advantageousness. Real justice demands conditions that enable these people to make a living for their families and to be treated humanely. A status quo that institutionalizes a trade-off between justice and survival is ethically indefensible by any means. Furthermore, the voluntariness of such contracts often holds only for the initial agreement. People working in sweatshops are often lured into debt traps by their employer that prevent them from being able to quit the contract and provides the employer with an even more effective exploitative measure. "Induced indebtedness," the International Labour Office's (ILO) 2005 report on forced labor states, "is a key instrument of coercion, backed by the threat of violence or other sanctions against forced workers or their families" (International Labour Office 2005, 2). Sweatshops are set up and run by human beings who have the ability to think reasonably and to choose to treat their workers humanely. Alleged increases in utility are an insufficient justification of the choice not to do so.

Hence Pareto efficiency and with it the entire concept of justice as mutual advantage turn out to be systematically incapable of unconditionally protecting the most basic rights of precisely those human beings who need it the most: the world's poor. In a contractarian world of purely self-interested people, the rights of human beings are respected only as a result of an accidental coincidence of interests (Donnelly 2003, 9). This, however, undermines the whole purpose of the concept of justice, which is to provide a moral foundation for the protection of the relatively powerless (B. Barry 1995, 46).

The most prominent "victim" of these general shortcomings of contractarian theories is arguably John Rawls's theory of justice as fairness. The agreement reached in Rawls's original position is not based on genuine ethical reasoning and mutual respect but on the self-interest of "rational and mutually disinterested" (Rawls 1971, 13) individuals, whose driving motive for entering the contract is not to be put at a disadvantage by the norms and rules under consideration.

Rawls's egalitarian conception of justice focuses on equality of "primary goods." In other words, Rawls assumes that there are certain things of general nature—primary goods—of which a rational human being would prefer more rather than less because they are regarded as beneficial to any human being irrespective of what his or her concrete life plans are. These primary goods include rights and liberties, opportunities and powers, and income and wealth and can be extended to include health and vigor, intelligence and imagination, and all other bases of self-respect (Rawls 1971, 62ff.). Rawls's theory demands that in order to be legitimate, any inequalities in terms of primary goods are to be arranged to the greatest benefit of the least advantaged (Rawls 1971, 302). Thus he essentially aims at the Pareto optimum himself (B. Barry 1989, 214). By subsuming all these different categories of "goods" under the one term *primary goods*, Rawls sets aside the crucial difference between moral rights, on the one hand, and (material) goods in a conventional sense, on the other (Habermas 1995, 114ff.; Ulrich 2008, 234f.). Therefore, he not only ends up eliminating the very differentiation he claimed was the core of justice but potentially legitimizes the trade of certain rights and life chances for economic goods if this is perceived to lead to a situation that leaves everybody "better off" than before. This promotes precisely what the recognition of equal rights is supposed to prevent: a situation where the poor and disadvantaged are forced to give up their rights and freedoms for short-term enhancement in material welfare.

It should be mentioned that by assuming prima facie equal distribution as a starting position, Rawls at least theoretically avoids some of the shortcomings of the Pareto principle discussed earlier. However, because in real life people do not start from equal positions, the practical implications of his theory remain problematic. Rawls does prohibit trade-offs between basic rights and economic or social gain in his theory—basic liberties have priority over other primary goods of lesser importance—but his very narrow list of basic rights makes his position a weak compromise that provides little protection in this regard. In *A Theory of Justice* (1971) Rawls explicitly includes the elementary liberty rights, political rights, and the right to property in the category of basic rights. In *The Law of Peoples* (1999a) he interprets the right to liberty as the right to freedom from slavery, serfdom, and forced occupation and the right to a sufficient measure of liberty of conscience to ensure freedom of religion and thought. Furthermore, he adds the right to formal equality to the group of basic rights (Rawls 1999a, 65). All other rights, especially socioeconomic rights, however, are not interpreted as basic rights in Rawls's conception. They are to be understood as alienable and freely "tradable" in principle.

Some might claim that it is inappropriate to deny a starving child the possibility to trade some of its freedoms in order to ease its hunger. However, this objection misses the point, which is, to reinforce the earlier sweatshop argument, that a child must never be put in a position where he or she faces a trade-off between food and his or her fundamental rights at the outset. Such situations must be eliminated before the necessity of such a trade arises. To give a somewhat more illuminating example, a single mother should never be put in a position where she faces a choice between letting her children starve or working 18 hours a day in unbearable and slavelike conditions. She is entitled to be able to make a decent living for herself and her children without sacrificing her own fundamental freedoms. The key insight here is that she does not have to trade her rights and liberties for the possibility to earn a sustainable wage because she has a right to subsistence at the outset. This is where Rawls commits his categorical mistake.

A Brief Look into the History of Thought

The 17th-century Dutch philosopher Hugo Grotius was perhaps the first to explicitly make the connection between justice and rights as its foundational concept. Although the ancient Greeks surely debated the concept of justice, the notion of "a right" did not enter the (Western) philosophical vocabulary until the close of the Middle Ages (MacIntyre 1981, 67) and started to draw major attention only at the dawn of the Enlightenment period. Grotius was the first prominent figure of this period, and arguably one of his major innovations was to interpret the whole subject of justice as a matter of respecting and exercising individual rights (Edmundson 2004, 18ff.). Grotius believed that moral principles are not to be based on mutual advantage alone but on sociability and mutual respect. What makes a society just, according to Grotius, is the equal fulfillment of basic entitlements, derived from the inherent dignity and sociability of human nature (Nussbaum 2006, 36f.). Nevertheless, Grotius's conception of rights-based justice does not stand the test of closer ethical scrutiny. It ultimately collapses under his problematic interpretation of rights, which he understood as principally alienable. For example, Grotius saw no conflict between people selling themselves into slavery and his principles of justice. The contemporary libertarian thinker Robert Nozick notably adopted this perspective in his influential book *Anarchy, State, and Utopia* (1974, 331).

Somewhat surprisingly, then, it was utilitarian philosopher John Stuart Mill who, in the astonishing fifth chapter of his essay on utilitarianism, outlined the basic implications of what we could call a modern rights-based conception of justice. Although his elaborations take a utilitarian turn toward the end of the chapter—it was, after all, Mill's intent to refute criticisms that utilitarianism was incompatible with the concept of justice (Rinderle 2006)—and overthrow the general validity of his overall conception,[4] this does not reduce the quality of his insights regarding the basic conceptual connection between justice and rights.

Connecting injustice to the violation of people's rights, as Mill claimed, makes intuitive sense because, etymologically, the notion of justice has been closely connected to ordinances of law in most languages (Mill 2001, 47). However, the etymological root of the word did not lead Mill uncritically to reduce the essence of justice to mere abidance by the law. He did acknowledge that laws can themselves be the root and the cause of injustice among people, a claim that was stated perhaps most fiercely in Jean-Jacques Rousseau's *Discourse on Inequality* (1984) a hundred years earlier. In the postmetaphysical age where the revealed faith in God-given, absolute laws is being replaced by the acknowledgment of the fallibility of the human mind, (man-made) laws, as Mill rightly noted, are not self-justifying but are themselves subject to critical evaluation: "When [...] a law is thought to be unjust, it seems always to be regarded as being so in the same way in which a breach of law is unjust, namely, by infringing somebody's right, which, as it cannot be in this case a legal right, receives a different appellation and is called a moral right" (Mill 2001, 44f.). Thus injustice, Mill (2001, 45ff.) concluded, "consists in taking or withholding from any person that to which he has a *moral right*." Accordingly, justice "implies something which it is not only right to do, and wrong not to do, but which some individual person can claim from us as his moral right." In other words, justice leads to a positive moral "obligation of giving to everyone his right."

Mill's insight is astonishing because it conflicts with the dominant utilitarian stance that it is the needs of society as a whole that ought to determine what the rights of individuals should be. In opposition to Mill, the founding father of utilitarianism, Jeremy Bentham, adhered to an entirely positivistic interpretation of rights. For him, the idea of prelegal and therefore moral rights was ethical nonsense, or, in his own words, "nonsense upon stilts" (Bentham 2002, 317). Real rights, in his opinion, can derive only from real laws, while from imaginary laws come imaginary rights (Bentham 2002, 400). Thus a corresponding concept of justice must be limited to the mere violation of positive law as well. Relative to Mill's perspective, Bentham's position appears doubly flawed. First, it conceals the fact that legal law must itself be ethically justified. Any positive law that is not based on justified moral claims and thus moral rights is necessarily and inherently arbitrary. Second, because the ethical claim deriving from rights in general is independent of their legal standing, their incorporation into legal systems must not necessarily be the only way in which rights can be advanced and implemented (Sen 2004a, 327). A conception of justice that is limited to compliance with legal laws and regulations must thus necessarily remain incomplete.

Prepositive, moral rights belong to the tradition of natural rights. The use of the notion of natural rights or natural law in the modern age is not unproblematic and often leads to "disqualifying metaphysical associations" (Dworkin 1977, 176). Traditionally, natural rights were interpreted as entitlements given by God or as somehow genetically instilled in the nature of human beings (Werhane 1985, 8). However, modern natural rights thinking, as it developed in the early 17th century and throughout the Enlightenment period, is secular and antidogmatic. It needs to adhere neither to the moral authority of God nor to that established by nature. Hugo Grotius (1925, 13) was once again among the first to disconnect the ethical standing of moral rights from divine authority and thus to contemplate the possibility that they might have "some degree of validity even if we should concede that which cannot be conceded without the utmost wickedness, that there is no God." The subsequent natural law theories of Hobbes, Locke, and Rousseau, as well as Kant, were the first ones to rest fully on a secular basis, understood as rights that human beings enjoy simply qua human beings (Fields 2003, 10ff.).

Hence modern natural rights are derived neither from the authority of God nor from a deterministic account of human nature. Self-determination, as the constitutive characteristic of human beings, rests precisely on an image of human beings as creatures without a fixed nature. Thus our human nature is a moral nature; it must be understood as a social product rather than a presocial given (Donnelly 2003, 15). Modern natural rights thinking, from this perspective, must be thought of as rational rights thinking; it is human reason itself that provides the basis and justification for such rights (MacDonald 1984, 29).

As rational (that is, antidogmatic and nontraditionalistic) rights, moral rights are inherently critical in their intent (Höffe 2002b, 92f.). They provide the rational perspective for the critique of positive law and human practice in general and thus represent nothing less than the standpoint of justice. Hence the normative-critical foundation of rational rights does nothing less than rehabilitate natural rights thinking within the perspective of justice (Höffe 2002b, 92f.).

"Equal Freedom" as the Substance of Moral Rights

An egalitarian conception of rights-based justice demands equality of human beings in terms of their most fundamental moral rights. Equality of rights must be interpreted not merely as equal possession but essentially as equal recognition and realization of rights. When we speak of realizing a right, we are referring not merely to the right itself but to what a right is a right to. In other words, the phrase "enjoying a right" does not actually mean that we enjoy the right itself but that we have a right to enjoy something else, such as food or liberty. Thus what we really mean is that we are enjoying the substance of a right (Shue 1980, 15f.).

This insight sheds some light on the ongoing discussion about the proper understanding of the relation between rights and distributive justice. The question whether rights can in fact be distributed or not is subject to controversial discussions. Those who argue against this view commonly claim that rights are not basic goods and therefore cannot be distributed. Opposing this view, Gosepath (2004, 231f.) claims that rights must be understood as basic goods in a broad sense. He argues that rights denote goods of the second order because they establish claims to a certain distribution of first-order goods. From this perspective, rights indeed cannot be distributed in a literal sense. However, by distributing first-order goods justly, we automatically also distribute moral rights. In this book I take a third perspective on the issue. This third perspective holds that a just distribution of first-order goods does not constitute moral rights but merely contributes to their practical realization. Hence, although moral rights themselves are not subject to distribution, their practical realization is indeed a distributive affair. In other words, rights determine certain distributive outcomes but are technically not subject to distribution themselves. If justice as a concept is not to be reduced to mere rhetoric, however, the recognition of a moral right cannot be detached from the distributive claim for its realization. Thus if moral rights are the determining parameters of a just distribution, they must be at the core of every conception of distributive justice. Any material distribution, whether equal or unequal, that is in violation of the moral rights of people is ultimately not justifiable and therefore is to be considered unjust. This is a fundamental condition of rights-based justice.

Having clarified this basic relation, let us now look at what the substance of moral or human rights really is. Human rights, as pointed out earlier, are those rights we enjoy simply by virtue of being human. As such, they are necessarily connected to our self-respect and dignity. Dignity and self-respect derive from our moral nature, that is, from our basic capacity to live a reflective and self-determined life. Thus human rights are essentially those rights that secure the conditions for living a life in dignity, that is, the basic freedoms that constitute us as self-determined human beings (Sen 2004a, 319ff.). Hence the most fundamental substance of moral rights, the substance to which all moral rights ultimately refer, irrespective of their concrete content and the issue they address, is the concept of freedom. This does not mean that we have one particular right to freedom, as some scholars have suggested (see, e.g., Shue 1980; Werhane 1985), but rather that freedom is the essence of all our rights. Rights, in short, constitute human freedom.

Thus moral rights derive from the constitutive importance of freedom for a human life and are justified on the basis of human beings' inherent equality. Some might find this statement contradictory because, as a popular (predominantly libertarian) argument claims, there is an inherent trade-off between equality and freedom. Thus they might object that we can have either equality or freedom but not both. Freedom and egalitarian justice, from that point of view, do not go together, because the claim for greater equality is always connected to the constraint on our individual freedom and the other way around (e.g., Lucas 1997, 111). However, the perceived trade-off between equality and freedom is based on a rather problematic notion of freedom as the principally unconditional and unrestricted pursuit of personal interests, that is, as "natural freedom" in the Hobbesian sense. The nature of such unrestricted freedom is inherently arbitrary; it boils down to a Darwinist law of the strongest, because the uncompromising pursuit of one's own preferences must inevitably collide with the legitimate claims for a fair share of freedom of other, potentially weaker human beings.

This is why in a modern, pluralistic society the very notion of freedom, that is, its very definition, must be formulated from the justice perspective. Thus justice and equality are not to be interpreted as a constraint on human freedom but as its constitutive foundation. The notion of freedom, from this perspective, always refers to general freedom, that is, to the highest attainable amount of freedom under the condition of equal freedom for all (Rawls 1971; Ulrich 2008, 228). Our own personal freedom naturally ends where the same legitimate freedoms of our fellow human beings start. Hence human equality is not the enemy of liberalism, as is perceived by libertarians, but its constitutive foundation. In a truly liberal society freedom on its own is inadequate as the highest moral and political ideal; it must necessarily be connected to the concept and the perspective of justice (Gosepath 2004, 292).

Thus justice and human equality are constitutive elements of any civilized liberal society. Without justice, there is no real freedom; freedom without justice is a contradiction in itself. If freedom is the substance of moral rights and human beings are to be regarded as fundamentally equal in terms of their basic rights, then freedom can reasonably be thought of only as equal freedom. For Kant (1996, 30), "innate freedom" necessarily involves "innate equality"; the two are to be thought of as inseparable. Hence freedom is not an independent political ideal conflicting with the ideal of justice and equality but is itself an aspect of it (Gosepath 2004, 294).

The inherent connection between freedom and equality is such that equality determines or expresses the form of our commitment to freedom, while freedom indicates what it is that we aim at equalizing. In other words, the relation between the two concepts is complementary rather than based on a trade-off. Well-understood liberal politics is not about striking a balance between these two allegedly competing concepts, as is often perceived, but about realizing equal freedom for everyone (Dworkin 1985, 188ff.; Waldron 1993, 428).

Human Rights as Principles of Minimal Justice

If we define human rights as moral rights of the highest order (Donnelly 2003, 11), then the question is how we are to identify the rights that belong to this category. What makes certain moral rights genuine human rights? Alan Gewirth (1984, 96f.) claims that the distinction between "regular" moral rights and genuine human rights is based on their degree of specification. Human rights, from this perspective, are those moral rights whose subject cannot be broken down any further than to the human race in general. In other words, in the case of human rights there is no justifiable specification of the subjects that ought to enjoy the right. This leads to the formula stated earlier of human rights as those rights we enjoy simply by virtue of being human.

This insight is connected directly to a second criterion, which refers to the importance of the underlying freedom. Referring to one right as more fundamental than another one means that the freedoms they protect are of different importance to a human life. Thus human rights can be defined as those rights that protect our most fundamental human freedoms, that is, the freedoms that are constitutive and thus inevitable for being human.

A third "threshold criterion" has been added by Amartya Sen (2004a, 329). Sen claims that in order for a moral right to qualify as a human right, its underlying freedom must be not only of utmost importance but also sensitive to the actions of other people; that is, it must in principle be influenceable by others. "In principle" means that the mere empirical impossibility of fulfillment is not sufficient to deny certain human rights to people; the impossibility Sen refers to is normative. Let me illustrate this with an example. The mere empirical fact that we have not yet found a way to secure universal access to clean water does not imply that there is no moral right to water at all, because in principle securing universal access is not at all a matter of impossibility—after all, there is enough water on this planet to accommodate all human beings sufficiently. To proclaim a human right to be loved, on the other hand, seems more problematic. Despite the fact that being loved and giving love constitute one of the truly valuable and perhaps even defining aspects of human life, their principal influenceability seems very limited. Therefore, it is questionable whether they can qualify as a genuine human right.

Henry Shue (1980) defined human rights as the most "basic rights" in the spectrum of moral rights. Two connotations can be attributed to the word "basic" in this regard. First, the violation of basic rights leads to basic consequences in terms of deprivation or destruction of basic needs, freedoms, and capabilities (Galtung 1994, 71). Second, basic rights are those fundamental rights that build the basis for all other rights (Shue 1980; Werhane 1985).[5] Hence without the realization of those "basic rights," no other, derivative rights can be claimed or realized. This follows as a logical conclusion from the fact that such basic rights refer to the human condition, that is, from the fact that our humanity is constituted through those rights. The realization of basic rights, as a consequence, must claim the highest ethical priority.

Basic or human rights are inalienable rights of equal and universal validity. They are equal rights because one either is or is not human, inalienable because one cannot stop being human, and universal because they must logically refer to all human beings in the same manner (Donnelly 2003, 10).[6] Therefore, human rights are often referred to as prima facie rights (e.g., Vlastos 1984, 47). Their validity is presumed a priori for all human beings, which means that only special circumstances can justify an infringement on them. Thus prima facie rights claim priority over other moral or social goals and interests in ordinary circumstances but can be overridden in special cases that are justified by good reasons (Werhane 1985, 11). Where no such special reasons apply, they are, at least within the limits of their defined scope, absolute.

The use of the term *prima facie* in connection with rights can be misleading, and it needs to be applied with caution. It could lead to the false conclusion that human beings lose their rights if special circumstances warrant an infringement. This is not the case. Even if special circumstances justify an infringement on a person's rights, it remains, after all, an infringement. It remains a wrong to the person whose rights are infringed, no matter what. The notion of the prima facie right tends to turn an infringement into a noninfringement because the very existence of the right is only presumed. A justified infringement, then, would imply that the presumption of the right's existence has been overcome. The term *prima facie* can thus be fatal to the very existence of established rights (Feinberg 1973, 75). Human rights are unforfeitable and irrevocable (Feinberg 1973, 88). As such, they are not necessarily to be considered categorically exceptionless, but they are more than just prima facie—they remain rights even in the case of justified infringement.

Cases in which basic rights of people are justifiably (partially) restricted include, for example, punishments of criminals who must be considered a danger to the rights of other persons or limitations on the rights of people who lack a minimal degree of rationality of adult human beings. The developed capacity to reason is constitutive for "rational" rights. Thus people who lack this minimal required degree of rationality are not able to recognize either their own rights nor those of other people to their full extent. Therefore, their rights remain restricted partly in order to protect them from themselves and partly because human rights are based on the concept of reciprocity, that is, because one's own rights are constituted by one's capacity to recognize the equal rights of others. Common candidates in this regard are children or mentally challenged people (Gosepath 2004, 301). Evidently, this does not mean that these human beings automatically lose all their rights. Children or mentally ill people can be denied access to political rights, for example, but their increased vulnerability must lead to an even higher degree of protection in other regards. Similarly, there are justified reasons to imprison a murderer, but there is no justification for humiliating this individual. On the contrary, imprisonment includes the duty to guarantee the possibility of self-respect even under the circumstances of restricted freedom.

As a basic rule, the restriction of basic rights can generally be justified only to the extent that is necessary to protect and guarantee equal basic rights and freedoms of all persons in a just societal order (Gosepath 2004, 302). In specific cases a restriction of self-determination or autonomy of a person based on consideration of that person's own well-being can be justified. However, this applies either to persons with reduced rationality, as pointed out earlier, or to situations in which a person chooses to act in a way that is potentially detrimental to that person's own well-being to the extent that it undermines her very basic rights, that is, to the extent that it would effectively eliminate her capability of self-determination altogether. Thus moral rights generally can be overridden only by considerations of equal moral rights of all people, but not by other competing moral considerations of lesser strength. From this perspective, moral rights can be considered, if not categorically absolute, then at least moral "trumps" (Dworkin 1984). This holds especially when they are pitched against considerations of aggregate welfare. It is the aim of a rights-based account of justice to provide an ethically more sound framework for the resolution of conflicting claims than the utilitarian principle of aggregate utility does. The principle of aggregate utility, in fact, aims at avoiding rather than at resolving the issue of conflicting claims.

Against this background, human rights emerge as actual principles of minimal justice (Shue 1980, 13f.; Tugendhat 1993, 363, 389ff.; Wildt 1998, 124). They trump all other moral considerations and serve as a universal basis for the derivation of legitimate moral norms and claims. Therefore, they are to be understood simultaneously as subjective moral rights and objective, universal principles, that is, as individual entitlements ("having a right"), as well as objective standards ("the right thing to do"). In Donnelly's (2003, 16) words, they are "constitutive no less than regulative rules." As constitutive rules, they refer to the constitutive aspects of human beings as moral subjects. As regulative ideals, they establish general principles of how one ought to act.

A conception of justice based on human rights is a conception of minimal justice from two perspectives. First, it is limited to the most basic moral rights and does not further specify any derivative justified moral claims of lesser urgency. Second, it is not dependent on a specific distributive rule other than the equal realization of those basic rights.[7] Demanding the fulfillment of minimum standards rather than proposing a complete distributive rule takes the argument in this book close to the one of nonegalitarian humanists. The decisive difference, however, is that I do not believe that such standards can be derived without referring to the inherent equality of human beings.

A minimal conception of justice in these two dimensions seems especially compelling for the global context, both from a philosophical and from a practical perspective. Its attractiveness derives precisely from the fact that it covers the minimum necessary condition that must be respected by any plausible theory of justice. Therefore, it provides the moral foundation on which all more advanced conceptions and theories of justice must ultimately be based.

Equalizing Freedom Through Basic Capabilities

In the previous section I argued that human rights are principles of minimal justice. The notion of freedom—the substance of human rights—is at the very core of these principles. Given this centrality of freedom, it is striking that most contemporary conceptions of distributive justice predominantly focus on the means to achieve freedom rather than on freedom itself. In their well-intended goal to find measurable or even quantifiable parameters for determining human equality, they have removed freedom from the center of attention and focused exclusively on the means that help us secure it. Some authors have even gone so far as to conclude that social justice per se is predominantly about the means to certain ends rather than about the ends themselves (e.g., D. Miller 1999, 7).

There are a great variety of suggestions about what means to focus on as adequate approximations of human equality. Despite its evident shortcomings, the focus on income is perhaps the most prevalent one. An exclusive focus on income, however, fails to acknowledge that human autonomy depends on many additional variables and circumstances besides the income level. Furthermore, it conceals the fact that the same amount of income will benefit different persons differently. Persons with special needs such as disabled people or people with chronic diseases, for example, need more financial means to achieve similar social states than people without such handicaps. This shortcoming is notorious in all means-based conceptions of justice, for example, Dworkin's (2000) wider approach to equality of resources, Rawls's interpretation of equality in terms of primary goods, and to a certain extent also the more advanced approaches to equality of opportunity, equality of life chances, or, as G. A. Cohen (1989) suggested, equality of "access to advantage." These latter conceptions are closer to a rights-based conception of justice than the ones that focus exclusively on material goods and income, but they too are susceptible to the trap of focusing on the mere existence of opportunities rather than on the actual ability of human beings to make use of them. People can have the same opportunities as others but still end up impoverished because of a lack of capabilities to capitalize on them. After all, this is precisely why we need basic rights that secure basic subsistence for everybody (Caney 2001, 117).

Thus the problems arising from an "overconcentration on means" (Sen 2004a, 332) are twofold. First, by normatively overstating means and turning them into ends themselves, we risk replacing the substance of rights, that is, freedom, with unsuitable approximations. Second, even in regard to those means that are indeed critical for achieving justice, an equal distribution ignores that there can be substantial interpersonal variability regarding their conversion into actual freedoms (Sen 1990, 112). For example, an equal distribution of food does not necessarily translate into equal nutrition levels for people who have different personal characteristics, who live under different external circumstances (e.g., hot or cold climates), or who pursue different lifestyles. This is why the very equality of resources, income, or primary goods can lead to severe and unjustified inequalities in the freedoms that are actually enjoyed. Hence, rather than focusing on the means themselves, we should ask what different people can obtain from these means (Sen 1990, 115). This, as Amartya Sen pointed out, must shift our focus to a person's capabilities. Our capabilities capture the extent of the freedom we enjoy. Thus capabilities are not to be understood as mere means to freedom; capabilities are freedom. The so-called capabilities approach, which has been developed by Amartya Sen and with slightly different, Aristotelian, connotations by Martha Nussbaum, essentially restates human freedom and thus the substance of moral rights in different terms. It renders more precise the conditions under which human beings can be regarded as truly free and autonomous and provides an alternative measure for aiming at equality of freedom among human beings.

A good life, that is, a self-determined, autonomous life free from dependency and heteronomy, is, as Sen (1985a, 70; 1993, 39) explains, at least partly "a life of genuine choice." The freedom to live alternative conceptions of "the good life" has been described by Sen as the freedom to choose from alternative valuable combinations of human functionings. Different combinations of human functionings in this sense are "alternative combinations of things a person is able to do or be" (Sen 1993, 30). Some of them are as elementary as being well nourished and maintaining good health, and others are as complex as being socially integrated (Sen 1993, 31). The opportunity to achieve different valuable combinations of functionings, according to Sen, is a function of human capabilities. Capabilities do not merely mean personal traits such as talents or personal strengths, as is often (and intuitively) perceived (e.g., G. A. Cohen 1993, 20), but crucially depend also on "external" social arrangements (Sen 1993, 33). This is of particular importance for a justice perspective because social arrangements can make up, at least to a certain extent, for inequalities arising because of personal disadvantages. Most capabilities must therefore be understood as "combined capabilities" (Nussbaum 2002, 132), consisting of a combination of personal capacities and social arrangements.

Thus in Sen's terminology, capability "reflects the alternative combinations of functionings over which the person has freedom of effective choice," or, in other words, "it refers to the extent to which the person is *able to choose* particular combinations of functionings" (Sen 2004a, 334). Therefore, capability "stands for the actual freedom of choice a person has over alternative lives that he or she can lead" (Sen 1990, 114). Sen's emphasis on the ability to choose is crucial. A theory of justice must not focus primarily on people's achieved living, that is, on the combination of functionings people have actually achieved, but essentially on their freedom to choose from alternative combinations and hence their freedom to realize different life scripts (Sen 2004a, 335).

If the extent of freedom enjoyed by a human being is defined by his or her capabilities to achieve different combinations of functionings, then capabilities essentially provide an alternative way to express the substance of rights. Hence the basic equality required by egalitarian justice can in its substance best be expressed as equality of basic capabilities. A rights-based egalitarian conception of minimal justice thus requires equality of those most fundamental capabilities that are necessary for living a decent human life.

Both Amartya Sen and Martha Nussbaum stressed the need to combine the concepts of rights and capabilities very early on (e.g., Sen 1982, 1985c, 1985d, 2004a; Nussbaum 1990, 2002; 2003, 36ff.). However, their conceptual relation remains underexplored and subject to further clarification. Where do the two concepts supplement each other, and where are the tensions? In one of her most recent works, Nussbaum (2006) denotes the capabilities approach as a "species" of the (human) rights approach. Although this might indeed be a way to express their relation, it seems not to capture its essence fully. It is suitable to the extent that both approaches state the same claim but in different language. In other words, rights can be understood and expressed in terms of capabilities. From this perspective, the capabilities approach is one possible and perhaps the most plausible interpretation of the human rights approach. Nevertheless, to call the capabilities approach a "species," that is, a subgroup of the human rights approach, seems to conceal the fact that capabilities are not only an interpretational but also a foundational concept of the human rights approach.

Capabilities are both the conceptual basis for the derivation of moral rights and practical manifestations of social and societal mechanisms that enable their realization. Thus there are two interrelated connections between rights and capabilities. First, when we speak of having a right to fundamental capabilities (that is, freedoms) (Sen 1982, 3; Nussbaum 2002, 136), we are referring to capabilities as the conceptual basis of human rights. In the second relation, however, the realization of a particular right is itself dependent on the availability of certain capabilities (other than the one this particular right secures). Hence it is not only rights that secure capabilities, but at the same time capabilities that secure the realization of rights. This provides a capability-based explanation of Henry Shue's (1980) notion of basic rights: basic rights are basic because they secure the capabilities that are necessary to realize further rights.

Both interpretations are of constitutive importance for the rights approach. When we talk about a certain human right, we implicitly refer to its underlying, foundational capabilities at the same time. Additionally, granting a right does not simply mean granting a right on paper but includes the circumstances and conditions, that is, the capabilities, necessary effectively to realize that right; it is not formal freedom but real freedom (see the section "Basic Needs, 'Real Freedom,' and the Claim for Socioeconomic Human Rights" later in this chapter) that ultimately counts for human beings to live a fulfilled and autonomous life. From this perspective, "the language of capabilities," Nussbaum points out correctly, "gives important precision and supplementation to the language of rights" (Nussbaum 2006, 284).

This does not mean that the language of capabilities can simply replace the language of rights. On the contrary, in one particular aspect the language of capability will always be inherently dependent on the language of rights. A moral right expresses a justified moral claim. The language of rights stresses this claim, as this section has shown, with the normative urgency drawn from the concept of justice (Nussbaum 2006, 290). Capabilities, however, do not have any normative power unless they are connected to the concept of rights and justice. Thus rights express the normative conclusions we draw from the fact of capabilities (Nussbaum 2002, 139). In order to make a strong normative statement, the language of capabilities must necessarily rely on the language of rights. In order to specify its normative claim, however, the language of rights must refer to the language of capabilities. Only the simultaneous use of both languages is capable of explicating the concept of justice in the space of rights.

The Problem with Equality of Utility

In chapter 1 of this book I argued that the utilitarian perspective not only is the antithesis of rights-based justice but also, even more fundamentally, systematically excludes the concept of justice. We can now render this insight more precise. Despite the severe and evident shortcomings of utilitarian thinking, a distinct egalitarian stance underlies it. Therefore, the utilitarian perspective does in fact entail something like a concept of justice. The egalitarian stance of utilitarianism manifests itself in the claim for equal consideration of preferences. People are seen as being treated as equals when their preferences are weighed and balanced in the same scales (Dworkin 1984, 154). In other words, even though the utilitarian "distribution" is biased in favor of the highest utility, this bias is based on equally weighted preferences. The highest total utility is reached when the marginal utility gains of all members of society are equal. Thus utilitarianism and its central demand to maximize social welfare require equal marginal utility. As long as the utility gains of one group are higher than those of another group, redistribution is warranted.

Instead of merely attaching equal weight to preferences, a slightly modified version of this utilitarian egalitarianism promotes equality of total utility (as opposed to equality of marginal utility) as a policy objective. Such "welfare egalitarianism" (G. A. Cohen 1993, 13) or "welfarism" (Sen 1979) contrasts with utilitarianism insofar as it promotes equal fulfillment of preferences, while utilitarianism aims at the highest possible total or average fulfillment of preferences. Therefore, the equality notion of welfare egalitarianism goes a step further even than the one of the capabilities approach. While the latter promotes equality of capabilities to choose from different combinations of functionings, the former claims that even the utilities of the effectively chosen combinations must be equal. From this perspective, welfare egalitarianism might be seen even as an advancement of the capabilities approach and its quest for basic equality of human beings. However, three main objections lead to the refutation of this argument.

First, there is what G. A. Cohen (1993, 12) called the "offensive tastes criticism." The very utility that we aim at equalizing might, in certain cases, derive from the satisfaction of illegitimate preferences, that is, from preferences that discriminate against others or compromise and restrict their freedoms (Rawls 1971, 30). Utilitarianism fails to provide any criteria that would allow for the identification of such illegitimate interests and preferences. On the contrary, for welfare equality to prevail, such preferences would strictly have to be satisfied irrespective of the illegitimate premises on which they are based. This demand, however, runs counter to the requirements of any plausible conception of justice (G. A. Cohen 1993, 12).

Second, people who live in states of deprivation often adapt their expectations and preferences to their social situations (Elster 1982, 1983; Sen 1985a, 22; Nussbaum and Glover 1995; Nussbaum 2000, 2001). The very depressed and downtrodden, as MacDonald (1984, 29) explains, do not dream of life, liberty, and the pursuit of happiness, for they do not question what is customary. An exclusive focus on equal utility would thus potentially legitimize the dire conditions of the disadvantaged rather than promote their improvement.

> The most blatant forms of inequalities and exploitations survive in the world through making allies out of the deprived and the exploited. The underdog learns to bear the burden so well that he or she overlooks the burden itself. Discontent is replaced by acceptance, hopeless rebellion by conformist quiet, and—most relevantly in the present context—suffering and anger by cheerful endurance. [...] Quiet acceptance of deprivation and bad fate affects the scale of dissatisfaction generated and the utilitarian calculus gives sanctity to that distortion. This is especially so in *interpersonal* comparisons. (Sen 1985c, 131f.)

Third, a similar claim derives from what Gerard Cohen (1993, 12) termed the "expensive tastes criticism." Because well-off people might develop more sophisticated tastes, their high demands and expensive preferences would have to be compensated accordingly in order for them to achieve the same utility level as people with modest preferences. This can lead to the paradoxical conclusion that meeting rich people's strong preferences for luxury takes priority over the urgent needs of the poor (O'Neill 2000, 124). Thus equal utility does not at all imply a similar standard of living or well-being of people. On the contrary, it might even perpetuate existing inequalities. Welfare egalitarianism is, by the standards of justice, an inadequate policy objective. People have the ability to reflect reasonably upon their own preferences and can, accordingly, be held responsible for them. Preferences are not unchangeable but can be controlled, shaped, and changed. Therefore, it seems unreasonable to make the subjectivity of personal preferences the yardstick for a just distribution.

Basic Needs, "Real Freedom," and the Claim for Socioeconomic
Human Rights

Libertarian theories in the tradition of Hobbes and Locke and later Nozick and Hayek, among others, interpret freedom predominantly as individual liberty, that is, as noncoercion and noninterference in personal affairs. This purely negative interpretation of freedom is mirrored in a corresponding negative understanding of rights. In other words, rights are perceived as instruments to protect the personal spheres of individual freedom from outside interference. Hence while one's own rights secure one's own personal sphere of liberty, the rights of others constitute side constraints to one's freedom (Nozick 1974, 28ff.). Therefore, the libertarian perspective limits the scope of rights-based justice to mere noninterference.

A focus on freedom as capabilities exposes the inadequacy of the libertarian view and enhances it in two interdependent dimensions. First, referring to the "two concepts of liberty" coined by Isaiah Berlin (1969; see also Feinberg 1973, 12ff.), it extends the scope of justice from negative to positive freedoms. Freedom interpreted in terms of capabilities cannot be limited to its negative dimension. Capabilities do not merely express freedom from interference but emphasize a human being's freedom to achieve certain ends. "All the basic liberties," Martha Nussbaum argues, "are defined as abilities to do something" (Nussbaum 1996a, 290). Mere freedom from interference does not necessarily mean that people are able to secure a decent living. A person might be free in a negative sense, that is, live without any major formal restrictions, but still be incapable of taking advantage of this freedom in a productive way because of personal, structural, or socioeconomic constraints. Hence equal negative freedom from certain restrictions does not imply also equal positive freedom to achieve beneficial outcomes. Consequently, if justice is to be interpreted in terms of rights and freedom, it must include both concepts. They are two sides of the same coin (Waldron 1993, 1ff.).

Second, the focus on capabilities moves the scope of justice from merely formal freedom to the concept of "real freedom" (Van Parijs 1995, 21ff.). This second shift is closely related to the first one. From the perspective of capabilities, we are systematically unable to reduce freedom to an exclusively formal concept, that is, to a space secured by (negative and positive) formal rights. Capabilities ultimately refer to human beings' "real freedoms." Hence, analogous to the difference between a human being's negative freedom and his or

her ability to convert it into positive freedom, there is a similar difference between a person's formal or nominal rights and his or her power to secure those
rights (Williams 1997, 97). Hence whether a formal right effectively translates
into real freedom crucially depends on the social and societal mechanisms
and the economic arrangements in place.

Thus understanding freedom in terms of capabilities militates in favor of
"complementing" classical liberty rights with economic and social rights. However, such rights are controversial not only in regard to their actual content or
the extent to which they may claim validity, but much more fundamentally
regarding their very justification as human rights. Robert Nozick's property-
rights-based argument formulated in *Anarchy, State, and Utopia* (1974) has become the standard libertarian objection to social and economic rights as human
rights. According to Nozick, the realization of socioeconomic rights is principally impossible. The resources that would be required to do so, he argues, are
owned by private individuals. Hence we cannot fulfill the socioeconomic
rights of some without violating the fundamental right to property of others.
For Nozick, the redistribution necessary to realize socioeconomic rights leads
to an irreconcilable conflict between the existence of such rights and the institution of private property. There can be either one or the other but not both
(Nozick 1974, 238).

This position is evidently not compatible with an egalitarian understanding of freedom unless we interpret social and economic rights as categorically
subordinate to the so-called noninterference rights. The right to noninterference regarding private property would thus be considered as more basic than
the right to subsistence and thus "trump" the respective social and economic
claims of deprived individuals. How plausible is this claim? The perception of
socioeconomic or so-called second-generation human rights as subordinate
to and of lesser importance than classical liberty rights is not uncommon. The
mainstream of liberal political philosophy today defends such a view on the
basis of Rawls's lexical priority of first-generation liberty rights over second-
generation economic and social rights, and this view corresponds to the common
interpretation of existing human rights conventions. However, the popularity
of this perception cannot remedy its inadequacy. More thorough reflection on
the issue suggests that socioeconomic rights are not subordinate to but, in
fact, a basic condition for liberty rights. Any claim for liberty rights and noninterference remains unsubstantial and empty without the realization of human
beings' most basic socioeconomic rights. A minimal standard of subsistence

is a condition for the very agency in regard to which libertarians demand noninterference. If the conditions for subsistence are not secured, agency itself must fail, and claiming liberty of action becomes meaningless (O'Neill 2000, 134).

Henry Shue (1980) argued very compellingly that socioeconomic rights are not mere add-ons to liberty rights but are to be regarded as prerequisites for their realization. Even Rawls, whose position in *A Theory of Justice* (1971) was rather skeptical, revised his stance in his later work *Political Liberalism* (1996). Specifically, he claimed that people's most basic needs might be lexically prior to their basic liberties "at least insofar as their being met is necessary for citizens to understand and to be able fruitfully to exercise those rights and liberties" (Rawls 1996, 7). Isaiah Berlin, a champion and generally a strong defender of negative freedom and classical liberty rights, also concurs in this insight:

> It is true that to offer political rights, or safeguards against intervention by the state, to men who are half-naked, illiterate, underfed, and diseased is to mock their condition; they need medical help or education before they can understand, or make use of, an increase in their freedom. What is freedom to those who cannot make use of it? Without adequate conditions for the use of freedom, what is the value of freedom? (Berlin 1969, 124)

Thus, quite contrary to common intuition and the predominant doctrines, socioeconomic rights seem to be more rather than less basic than liberty rights. If even the classical liberty rights are trumped by the importance and urgency of social and economic rights, however, it seems rather questionable how property, which is itself a social institution that depends on positive enforcement and protection (Tugendhat 1992, 361), can claim lexical priority over them. Furthermore, Nozick's redistribution argument is self-defeating. The definition, assignment, interpretation, and protection of property rights are government services financed by the public at large and for the benefit of those who own property (Holmes and Sunstein 1999, 29). Thus if redistribution is a valid argument against socioeconomic rights, as Nozick claims, then it delegitimizes property ownership at the same time. Hence Nozick's hierarchy between property rights and other social and economic rights not only fails but must be turned upside down. Socioeconomic rights build a basis to call "property arrangements themselves into question" (Waldron 1993, 20). In other words, they are not conditioned by the status quo but must serve as its critique. Property, in Waldron's (1993, 20) words, "must answer at the tribunal of need, not the other way around."

This brings us to the important distinction between basic freedoms and basic needs. Socioeconomic rights are often claimed to derive from basic human needs rather than basic freedoms. Some scholars even developed entire theories of human rights based on some commonly shared basic human needs (R. H. Green 1981; Bay 1982). Others endorsed a basic needs approach without connecting it to human rights at all (Streeten 1979). The importance of human needs as an ethical category is undeniable. In order to be prescriptive, however, they must stand the test of intersubjective justification. An intersubjective justification, as shown earlier, can derive neither from the assumption of some kind of fixed human nature in a biological sense nor from a subjective utility-based perspective but must be based on the moral nature of human beings. Therefore, any intersubjective justification of basic needs, that is, any justification derived from the impartial standpoint, must itself refer to human freedom and autonomy. The crucial difference between rights and needs, as Johan Galtung (1994, 66) argues, is that needs are located inside individual human beings (subjective), whereas rights are located between them (intersubjective). Therefore, there can be interpersonal moral claims that do not correspond any needs, while certain needs might not translate into interpersonal claims. Thus human needs, on their own, are systematically unsuitable as a foundational concept for human rights. In order to exercise normative power, they must ultimately be connected to the basic capabilities necessary to realize human autonomy.

Hence there is nothing wrong with connecting socioeconomic rights to basic needs; however, in order not to fall into the trap of subjectivity, on the one hand, or dogmatism, on the other, these needs must ultimately be justifiable on the basis of freedom and capabilities. Economic and social human rights are thus no less claims for autonomy (nondependency) than classical liberty rights (Tugendhat 1992, 362ff.), because the lack of essentials such as food and water puts people in a position of lethargy rather than agency and leaves them in a state of helplessness that undermines the very possibility of living a truly free and autonomous life.

> If [. . .] the autonomy of the person is something that everyone aims at but that is unattainable for most people because of the prevalent conditions, the rights must be rights not only to the protection but to the realizability of autonomy.

[. . .] Autonomy is endangered not only by interference but just as much by the lack of favorable conditions. Human dignity suffers both ways. (Tugendhat 1992, 366)

To focus on freedom and autonomy rather than on needs for the definition of second-generation human rights is not only of formal but also of inherently practical importance. A needs-based perspective does not distinguish between active and passive fulfillment of subsistence rights; what counts is the mere fact that the need is being met. However, moral-psychological arguments formulated from the stance of Hegelian ethics of recognition have pointed to problematic implications precisely of the resulting charitable focus of respective conceptions of distributive justice. This focus may lead to potentially humiliating dependencies and a resulting lack of recognition of human beings as full and productive members of society (see, e.g., Fraser 1997; Fraser and Honneth 2003). A perspective on human autonomy addresses this concern and is able to remedy this shortcoming that indeed characterizes many conventional approaches to distributive justice. It does not settle for meeting human needs by mere redistribution of material goods but stresses the importance of a right to self-sufficiency and the demand for conditions that allow everyone to live the productive life connected to it. A right to subsistence is not merely a right to receive certain material goods but essentially a right to participate in the productive and political processes of society.

Globalizing Justice: Exploring the Philosophical and Political Bounds of Justice

The political unit within which a particular conception of justice is normally perceived to be valid is the modern nation-state. Modern theories of justice and political philosophy in general have predominantly focused, whether implicitly or explicitly, on the nation-state. The decreasing distance to suffering in other parts of the world, however, raises doubts about the adequacy of limiting the scope of justice to the political boundaries of the state. The indispensability of the justice perspective, paired with rapid global political and economic integration, requires us to adopt an equally global perspective on the concept of justice. In other words, the circumstances of justice have become a permanent given also at the global level.

John Rawls claimed that the basic structure of society largely determines the life prospects of people and must therefore be the main focus or subject of justice. Although Rawls himself was not fond of the idea of global justice, the features of his definition of the basic structure certainly are emerging at the global level today. The way people and countries are interlinked and profoundly influenced by and dependent on the workings of global institutions today leaves no doubt about that. Not only does the international realm resemble the domestic one in the aspects relevant to the concept of justice, but their interpenetration renders it increasingly difficult to clearly distinguish one from the other (Beitz 1999a, 198ff.).

A specific stream of counterarguments against this view comes from the school of "cooperative justice." This stream of thought claims that problems of distributive justice arise only within cooperative or collaborative social relationships or arrangements. Such cooperative interconnections between people, however, are not regarded as strong enough to fulfill the conditions or circumstances of justice at the global level (e.g., W. Nelson 1974, 425ff.; Taylor 1985, 285; Kersting 1996, 197ff.). These objections seem highly implausible; not only are they based on an overly narrow definition of the circumstances of justice, but they also understate or even trivialize the degree of today's global interconnectedness. National boundaries are not coextensive with the scope of social cooperation anymore. Therefore, they cannot plausibly be the criteria for marking the limits of social obligations (Beitz 1999a, 151).

Nevertheless, even if we are skeptical about the degree of cooperative interdependence at the global level, reliance solely on a shared framework of social and economic cooperation as the basis of justice is insufficient. The exclusion of certain nations and groups of people from beneficial cooperation is one of the main moral shortcomings of the global economic system. A conception of justice that derives moral obligations only from existing cooperative relationships suggests that affluent societies have special, cooperation-based obligations only toward one another but not toward those who are marginalized and excluded from such cooperative frameworks (Scheffler 1999, 88ff.). By focusing on the benefit of the rich and turning a blind eye on those in need, however, such a suggestion turns the very purpose of justice inside out.

The idea of extending the scope of justice to the global level is not entirely novel but goes back at least to classical Stoicism. Cicero, for example, was fond of the cosmopolitan ideal and reflected on the conditions of global citizenship, while Diogenes the Cynic was a self-proclaimed "citizen of the world."

Plutarch urged his readers that "we should regard all human beings as our fellow citizens and neighbors" (Plutarch, quoted in Nussbaum 1996a, 7). Our first allegiance, according to the Stoic cosmopolitan thinker's claim, is to the moral community made up by the humanity of all human beings (Nussbaum 1996a, 7). Following those early cosmopolitans, Hugo Grotius also formulated his conception of justice from an international perspective (see, e.g., Bull 1966). Today Grotius is often referred to as the father of international law and is known for his contributions to the field of international relations. Many other Enlightenment philosophers included at least a few elements of a global justice focus in their works. Most notably, Kant's (2001b) compelling elaborations on eternal peace have remained highly influential even in contemporary thinking on global citizenship and justice.

The reason that the claim for global justice seems, despite its long history, relatively novel and controversial today is that the emergence of the Westphalian order temporarily removed it from the agenda of political philosophy. Not only the world order but also the way we think about justice, as a consequence, subsequently were framed in the categories of discrete nation-states. The profound transformations in this seemingly rigid state system from the early 1970s onward, however, brought the issue of global justice back to life. Today, not only is there an established debate on global justice, but also it is arguably among the most dynamic and diverse debates in moral and political philosophy.

In the following paragraphs I will trace some of this debate and extend the egalitarian, rights-based conception of justice to the global sphere. More specifically, I will develop an inherently cosmopolitan account of rights-based justice that builds on the rights-based foundation laid in the previous section. I will first provide a positive argument for cosmopolitanism, followed by its defense against claims formulated from the perspective of communitarianism and nationalism. Specifically, I will refute the interpretation of principles of justice as culturally contingent and argue against the ethical significance of national (political) boundaries for their general validity.

Global Justice as Cosmopolitan Justice

Any plausible rights-based conception of justice must essentially be cosmopolitan at its core. Broadly defined, moral cosmopolitanism is the attempt to extend principles of distributive justice beyond the domestic context (generally of a nation-state) to the global level (Beitz 1999b, 519f.). Cosmopolitan approaches to global justice must be distinguished from conceptions adhering to the primacy of domestic justice, which merely consist of some distinct principles for regulating (international) relationships among different societies. In other words, cosmopolitan justice does not provide principles for just relationships between societies or states but aims directly at the regulation of interpersonal relationships between all human beings as members of the human commonwealth.[8]

Moral cosmopolitanism must be distinguished from institutional cosmopolitanism (Beitz 1999a, 199; Cabrera 2004, 28ff.). Institutional, or, in Pogge's (1992, 49) terminology, "legal" cosmopolitanism refers to the political implications of moral cosmopolitanism. It is committed to a concrete political ideal of a global order that grants equal rights and duties to all human beings. As such, it adheres to the ideal of world citizenship and ultimately to the formation of some kind of global republic or world state. Institutional cosmopolitanism can thus be seen as a critique of existing economic and political structures because it refuses—as opposed to realist or neorealist accounts of statism— "to regard existing political structures as the source of ultimate value" (Brown 1992, 24). Although my elaborations on the duties of justice for global corporations can well be interpreted as institutional conclusions from the moral cosmopolitanism put forth in this section, I will reflect on institutional cosmopolitanism somewhat more holistically in the concluding chapter of this book.

There is no single approach to cosmopolitan justice. On the contrary, different conceptions can be very diverse regarding content and implications; they range from utilitarian to contractarian to rights-based approaches. Nevertheless, all of them share three defining formal elements (Pogge 1992, 48f.). First and most distinctively, cosmopolitan approaches are individualistic; that is, the ultimate units of concern are individuals. This is the decisive element that distinguishes cosmopolitan approaches from conceptions of international justice that commonly focus on states or, as in John Rawls's (1999a) case, on a wider notion of peoples as the central subjects. Thus conceptions of international justice take the prospects of states or peoples as central to the derivation of principles of global justice, whereas cosmopolitanism aims at providing principles of justice that take each person's prospects into account. This focus on the individual as the ultimate unit of concern is not to be confused with individualism in a libertarian sense but must be interpreted in a "republican-liberal" (Ulrich 2008, 276ff.) way, or as what we could call a kind of embedded individualism. This "civic" perspective on the individual will be explained more clearly in the following sections.

Second, cosmopolitan approaches are universal. The status of the individual as the ultimate unit of concern applies to every human being equally (Pogge 1992, 48). It is not dependent on what a particular person has done in her past, or where she comes from, or what she looks like. The inherent and equal moral worth of human beings is independent of any other valuable qualities that may determine our (moral) merit. As such, it is indivisible and inalienable; it attaches to every human being equally qua being human. Thus, ideally, everybody should be born with the same starting position in terms of rights and capabilities. The "accident of birth" (Mill 2005, 232) must not predetermine one's life chances and prospects at the outset. Evidently, our contemporary global society, where roughly one in seven enters life severely undernourished (Cabrera 2004, 61f.), is far from meeting this condition.

Universality can be understood as universality in scope, on the one hand, which means that certain principles are meant to include the entirety of the human commonwealth. This "weak" interpretation, however, must be distinguished from the stronger claim of universality of justification, on the other hand, which means that those principles can be reasonably justified to anyone. For example, if human rights were regarded as uniquely Western principles with universal scope but no universal justifiability, we would perceive ourselves as obliged to treat anyone, that is, friends, compatriots, or distant foreigners, with the same decency.[9] We could not, however, claim the same respect from people with different cultural origins. Only universal justifiability can result in universal normative power and provide a foundation for universal moral obligations. True cosmopolitan justice must thus be universal both in scope and in justification.[10]

Universal justification of a rights-based account of justice derives from the undeniable universality of the human condition. For us, seeing our fellow human beings in their human aspect, that is, in their inherent humanity, is not an act of choice or decision but an inevitable fact (Margalit 1996, 95). We cannot but recognize the universality of our shared humanity. However, if we accept the human condition as universal, then the normative claim for unconditional respect and protection of everyone's dignity must be universal as well. This derives from the universal reciprocity of moral claims, as explained earlier in this chapter (see the section "Sufficiency or Equality? Dismantling Nonegalitarian Humanism"). Because of the inherent reciprocity of moral claims, the denial of another person's status as an autonomous subject of equal worth inevitably leads to the revocation of one's own corresponding claim for moral personhood (Ulrich 2008, 35). Hence we cannot claim moral personhood for ourselves without granting it to every rational adult human being at the same time. With Habermas, we can explicate the undeniability of this claim on discursive ethical grounds. Earlier I stated that moral norms and claims are justified and valid if they are formulated from the impartial standpoint. I defined the impartial standpoint as the standpoint from which all rational adult human beings could reasonably agree to these norms within an all-inclusive and uncoerced moral discourse. Discursive ethics thus translates the criterion of universalizability into communicative agreement and makes argumentative practice the reference point for impartiality (Maak 1999, 130).

Habermas concludes that the recognition of the other as a moral person is contained in the formal presuppositions of rational argumentation.[11] These presuppositions, understood as rational norms, can be summarized as inclusivity (nobody who could make a relevant contribution may be excluded), equal opportunity (all participants are granted an equal opportunity to make contributions), honesty (participants must mean what they say), and noncoercion (communication must be freed from external and internal coercion, so that the stance taken by the participants is motivated solely by the rational force of the better reasons) (Habermas 1998, 44). Thus an argumentative validation process is based on the constitutive assumption that all participants in a potentially unlimited discourse are capable of rational argumentation. This makes it logically impossible argumentatively to deny someone else's status as a human being of equal worth because the argument itself implicitly presumes her very status as a rational person. Hence in order to reject someone as nonhuman, we must, paradoxically, presume her humanity at the same time.

This insight essentially reflects Hegel's master-slave dialectic and what Margalit, on the basis of Hegel, called the humiliation paradox: any form of degradation and humiliation of human beings, that is, their rejection as non- or subhuman, inevitably presupposes their humanity at the outset. In other words, humiliation is dependent on the humanity of the humiliated because the very act of rejection presupposes that we are dealing with a human being in the first place. Thus degrading human beings means treating them as if they were objects, machines, or animals; we cannot, however, treat them as objects, machines, or animals. As rational adult human beings, we cannot deny their status as human beings—"human-blindness" is an inherently pathological condition—but only disregard their person (Margalit 1996, 91ff.).

The third defining element of cosmopolitanism is its generality. The aspect of generality refers to the global force of the status of the individual as the ultimate unit of concern. Thus moral obligations deriving from this status arise potentially for everyone and not just for compatriots, fellow nationals, or people of the same gender, religion, or culture. Therefore, cosmopolitanism strictly refutes the existence of any categories of people of more or less moral weight (B. Barry 1999, 36). Our first allegiance and respect, as Onora O'Neill (1996, 7) claims, is to humanity as such, wherever it occurs. This third claim is arguably the most far-reaching and most controversially debated implication of cosmopolitan justice. The degree of acceptance of this condition creates a continuum from "weak" to "strong" (D. Miller 1998, 164ff.) or "mild" to "radical" cosmopolitanism (Cabrera 2004, 29). Weak cosmopolitanism expresses the mere view that all human beings are of equal moral worth but does not draw any implications for the generality of the corresponding obligations. Strong cosmopolitanism, on the other hand, holds that on the basis of the universality claim, all human beings have an obligation to treat all other human beings strictly equally; that is, all particularities and special obligations are per se regarded as illegitimate. The following elaborations on nationalism and patriotism will locate my approach in an intermediate position between these two extremes.

The essence of moral cosmopolitanism, in Thomas Pogge's (1992, 49) words, is that "every human being has a global stature as an ultimate unit of moral concern." The foundation of this global stature, as I argue in this book, can best be expressed in terms of rights and capabilities. Moral rights, in other words, are the essence of moral cosmopolitanism. Caney (2001, 115) rejects the idea of rights-based cosmopolitanism as insufficient. He claims that granting equal rights alone cannot eliminate the fact that some have worse prospects in life than others simply because of their nationality. This objection, although correct in its substance, is based on a deficient understanding of the concept of rights. Understood in terms of capabilities and real freedom, equality of rights includes the concept of equality of opportunity and life chances. Caney's objection is valuable because it shows the dangers of an incomplete interpretation of the concept of rights. Indeed, rights-based approaches to cosmopolitan justice, despite their commonality of being based on rights, can yield large differences in their implications, depending on how broadly the justificatory basis of rights is interpreted. The range of different interpretations can reach from ultralibertarian conceptions such as Robert Nozick's (1974) property rights approach to much more generous interpretations of basic rights like the one of Henry Shue (1980) or intermediate positions such as Pogge's human-rights-based cosmopolitanism. Although Pogge's conception reaches far beyond conventional libertarian interpretations, it remains restricted to a "rather minimal conception of human rights" (Pogge 1992, 49). It seems pragmatically right not to morally overload a global conception of justice. However, the conclusion that we must therefore cut human rights to a minimum is flawed. Human rights are the ethical minimum. Therefore, any further limitation of human rights automatically puts us below the ethically acceptable threshold. Evidently, the chances for realization increase the lower we set our standards and expectations; but making the normative ideal dependent on the ease of its realizability is a classic naturalistic fallacy. Hence Pogge's account of cosmopolitan justice does not go far enough. Its evident weakness is that it is too narrowly focused on negative causalities in the determination of obligations of justice (Pogge 1992, 51). Therefore, it is not bold enough to direct the global economy in a fundamentally new direction.

In the following paragraphs I will defend the cosmopolitan perspective against some popular objections. These objections can be categorized according to the three defining elements of cosmopolitanism. There are objections against the universality claim, against the generality claim, and against the individualism claim of cosmopolitanism. The objection against the universality claim will be called the "communitarian objection," the objection against the generality claim will be addressed as the "nationalist objection," and the individualism claim will be confronted with an objection derived from international justice that I will call the "Rawlsian objection."

The Communitarian Objection: There Is No Such Thing as Global Justice

The communitarian objection to global justice can be interpreted as a combined critique of the individualism and universalism claims of cosmopolitanism. The communitarian movement evolved as a powerful critique of the increasing individualization of Western societies in the 1980s, influenced and directed most notably by writers like Charles Taylor, Alasdair MacIntyre, and

Michael Walzer. It represents a counterposition to radical individualistic liberalism, which has dominated the Western political landscape since the mid-1970s.

The main communitarian concern is that the overemphasis on individual liberty undercuts the cohesion of communities. Liberalism, communitarians argue, promotes a society of "unencumbered subjects" (Sandel 1982, 175), that is, of unattached, purely self-interested and instrumentally related individuals, incapable of achieving genuine community. The constitutive liberal (or, more precisely, libertarian) assumption of mutually disinterested individuals and its contractarian notion of obligation and commitment are perceived as inherently flawed.[12] In opposition to the libertarian view, communitarians claim that human beings are not abstract individuals composed only of general powers and capacities. Rather, they are fundamentally committed to certain persons, groups, practices, institutions, and other social structures and organizations (D. Miller 1988, 649). The communitarian self is a socially embedded self; it is at least partly defined by its relationships and social commitments that form an important part of our personal identity.

Communitarians relativize the liberal claim for individual self-determination in a distinctive way. For them, the individual is at least partly constituted by communal commitments and values that are not up to the individual's free choice (A. E. Buchanan 1989, 853). Individuals are thus at least partly directed by values and ends they cannot freely choose but only discover through their inherent embeddedness in the community. The goals and values of the communitarian individual are the ones it appropriates from the community (Sandel 1982, 54ff.); the community is regarded as the ultimate source of identity and moral value. A community in the communitarian sense is thus not merely an association of individuals with congruent interests (as libertarians interpret contractual relationships) but is constituted by the common ends and values of its members. Individuals think of themselves primarily as members of the group and of their values as values of the community. The difference between "mine" and "ours" in their conception of community recedes into the background and eventually breaks down completely (A. E. Buchanan 1989, 857).

A rights-based cosmopolitan perspective, in contrast, holds that the inherent moral worth of individuals is independent of the community to which they belong (C. Jones 2001, 16). In its most radical form, communitarianism rejects the existence of individual rights. At best, it acknowledges certain rights held by groups. Individual rights are seen to subvert and atomize community and to alienate persons from one another by preoccupying them with the protection of their own interests rather than those of society at large. More moderate views acknowledge the existence of individual rights but deny the prominent status they enjoy in liberal theories. They criticize the "missing dimension of sociality" in contemporary rights talk (Glendon 1991, 109ff.) and on this basis opt for infringements or limitations of individual rights by certain appeals to the common good (A. E. Buchanan 1989, 855). With his work *The Community of Rights* (1996) Alan Gewirth provided perhaps the most powerful refutation of the communitarian claim against individual rights. Gewirth showed that rights and community are not antithetical to each other but have a relation of mutual support:

> Because this principle of human rights entails the requirement of mutual respect (and of mutual aid when needed and practicable), it is a principle of social solidarity, as against exclusive preoccupation with personal interest. This solidarity requires institutions whereby hitherto deprived groups can be brought nearer to equality. By the effective recognition of the mutuality entailed by human rights, the society becomes a community. So the antithesis between rights and community is bridged. (Gewirth 1996, 6)

Thus we are not to confuse individual rights with mere enablers of unfettered market liberalism. On the contrary, they need to be seen as a protection from the potentially harmful consequences such radical libertarian interpretations of society might indeed have on the viability of genuine communities. Therefore, individual rights protect rather than undermine community (see also Raz 1986, 253f.; Feinberg 1988, 81ff.; A. E. Buchanan 1989, 858ff.). Judith Shklar (1986, 25) asserts that "rights have never been demands only for more shares of whatever pie was available, nor are they inherently hostile to social conscience." Rights, she argues, have an inherently social meaning; their assertion and defense are not aimed only at the particular individual but always denote protest against social injustice at the same time (Shklar 1986, 26).

The communitarian limitation of rights to group rights is dangerous not only to the protection of individual dignity but also to the viability of communities. If rights to freedom of expression, thought, religion, and association were to be perceived exclusively as group rights, they would protect existing communities from intrusion but would provide no protection to the possibility of forming new communities, which most often originate in the beliefs and actions of an individual or a minority (A. E. Buchanan 1989, 862). This is not to be misunderstood as an argument or a statement against the existence of group rights per se. However, it is unlikely that there are any group rights that do not ultimately derive from individual rights. This insight is important first of all in those cases where perceived group rights constitute a threat to the moral rights of individuals. Such potential group entitlements must be considered strictly illegitimate.

Communitarians claim that social integration cannot be achieved on the basis of atomistic concepts of personal lives but only through an orientation to shared moral values. Therefore, they cling to Rousseau's (1968) ideal (or utopia) of communities so homogeneous that a single conception of the common good or "general will" indeed becomes possible. Evidently, this has far-reaching consequences not only for the relation between community and rights but similarly also for the perceived role of justice in society. The more individual conceptions of the good life converge on a shared common good (that is, the more pluralism is replaced by uniformity of values and goals), the more justice loses its constitutive purpose for society. Where pluralism is nonexistent, individual conceptions of the good life do not conflict with one another, and hence there are no circumstances of justice. In communitarian thought, all individual life scripts and consequently the whole concept of justice are a derivative of the historically and morally grown conception of the good within a particular communal discourse and tradition that represents the normative ideal for the arrangement of both personal and social life. Justice, from that perspective, turns into a mere remedial virtue (A. E. Buchanan 1989, 853). It is needed only when the higher virtue of community breaks down. Thus communitarians conclude that liberal societies value justice so highly precisely because they suffer so grievously from this defect (A. E. Buchanan 1989, 876). The shared conception of the good replaces the justice focus as an orienting societal ideal because, as Sandel (1982) pointed out, any conception of a just societal order must necessarily refer back to a shared value basis. Theories of justice that disregard this categorical primacy of the culturally traditionalized vision of the good, according to communitarians, will inevitably lead to societal disintegration and alienation.

To the extent that communitarians refer to specific attachments as the basis for the derivation of ethical principles, they argue from a position of ethical particularism or relativism (as opposed to ethical universalism). Ethical relativists hold that ethics and thus justice are subject to community-relative standards.

Intercultural comparisons of ethical standards are perceived as impossible (C. Jones 2001, 111). From the communitarian perspective, any conception of justice must thus necessarily be dependent on the specific conception of the good upheld by a particular community, whether political or cultural (Ulrich 2008, 239). In their eyes, there is no such thing as a neutral, that is, impartial and therefore universal, standpoint of justice. The ideal of equality of opportunity, for example, is regarded as inherently misguided because of the great cultural variety of different concepts of the good life and thus the impossibility of defining universally what are to be considered equal opportunities in the first place (Boxill 1987, 143ff.). Equality of opportunity, they claim, presupposes a certain degree of cultural consensus. Hence what can be considered just or unjust can be formulated only against the background of the valid practices of a specific community. This resembles the core message of Walzer's (1983) communitarian theory about the spheres of justice:

> A given society is just if its substantive life is lived in a certain way—that is, in a way faithful to the shared understandings of the members. [. . .] Justice is rooted in the distinct understandings of places, honors, jobs, things of all sorts, that constitute a shared way of life. To override those understandings is (always) to act unjustly. (Walzer 1983, 313f.)

From this perspective, global justice is not merely utopian but a downright illusion—it is conceptually and substantively meaningless. It is against this background that MacIntyre (1981, 67) refutes human rights as historical fiction and mocks them as a mere belief in witches and unicorns.

A reply to the communitarian attacks on cosmopolitanism must address two endemic flaws in the communitarian argument. The first flaw is the wrong normative conclusion communitarians draw from their justified objection to the defective libertarian conception of the self. The second flaw derives from confusing a justified cultural relativism with an illegitimate stance of ethical relativism. The refutation of these two inconsistencies will ultimately lead to the collapse of the communitarian position. Let us have a brief look at both of them.

The communitarian critique in general is valuable insofar as it uncovers some of the inherent weaknesses and flaws of radical economic liberalism. However, the rejection of these libertarian assumptions does not mean that we must give up on liberal ideals altogether. My earlier elaborations on the foundations of contractarian thought should have rendered clear that we can be on the side of the communitarians in regard to the critique of the radical liberal self without giving up the liberal stance. The liberal political thesis, as Allen E. Buchanan (1989, 853) summarizes, "can survive the abandonment of those views which communitarians rightly criticize." Thus a well-understood liberal cosmopolitanism does not at all deny the constitutive role of social embeddedness in the development of our personal identities. On the contrary, defining human nature as an inherently moral nature means referring both to its self-determination and its sociability. The self-conception of the individual thus derives from a balance between personal and social identity (Ulrich 2008, 280) rather than from its reduction to either libertarianism or communitarianism. Therefore, human beings can be understood as inherently social creatures but with an undeniable ability for critical reflection and autonomous self-determination. Thus well-understood political liberalism does not at all reject but, in fact, crucially relies on the premises concerning the critical importance of community (A. E. Buchanan 1989, 860).

The cardinal error of the communitarian critique is its overstatement of the aspect of sociability at the expense of individual identity. Furthermore, it confuses the constitutive importance of community for personal identity with a normative claim for categorical conformity to traditional communal norms and values (Ulrich 2008, 281). Therefore, communitarianism robs mature adult human beings of their critical perspective and undercuts their individual autonomy and indeed their status as moral agents by holding on to a dogmatic account of role conformity. It is against this background that feminist thinkers have (rightly) objected that the communitarian conception of the self as a derivative of given roles and values is especially prone to trap women in traditionalistic, male-dominated role patterns. Thus communitarianism lacks the critical perspective from which closed value systems based on potentially unjust and exclusionary traditions could be ethically assessed. In the global context this turns well-understood cultural diversity and pluralism into a dangerous ethical relativism that calls into question even the most basic humanitarian minima.

This takes us to the second argument. It is a common and widespread neglect that cultural relativism is not sufficiently distinguished from and is often confused with ethical relativism. While cultural relativism denotes the recognition and acknowledgment of different cultural and moral practices and traditions and thus refutes the legitimacy of one dominant global moral practice, ethical relativism additionally refutes the existence of superior universal ethical principles. What is often overlooked is that ethical universalism does not contradict cultural relativism. Universal ethical principles can be interpreted in culturally specific ways and lead to a variety of different moral norms and practices. The claim against moral paternalism, imperialism, cultural oppression, or forced assimilation and the like does not have to lead us into a position of ethical relativism. The cultural diversity of which communitarians are justifiably fond can be achieved without compromising ethical universality. On the contrary, it is precisely the universal principle of equal moral concern and respect that protects cultural diversity and its legitimate interpretation within and between countries. Tolerance of different cultural practices and traditions, in other words, presupposes equal respect at a universal level. Ethical universalism is thus not at all the enemy of, but a necessary precondition for, a well-understood cultural pluralism.

Against this background, the communitarian account of ethical relativism is counterproductive from two perspectives. First, it expresses a dangerous nihilism and "anything goes" mentality in the global context and lends justification to any ideologically driven attitude, no matter how harmful and oppressive it may be. It covers its own ignorance with a false call for tolerance and opens the door to inhumanity, oppression, and gross violations of human rights. Second, it undermines its own ideals by turning pluralism into dogmatic conformism at the domestic level by subjecting everybody to a fixed account of moral norms and values. It makes a big difference for the lives of free and equal human beings whether we understand their inherent sociability merely as empirical observations or as conformist normative claims. There is no doubt that community is important and even constitutive for human beings. However, emphasizing its importance on a nondogmatic basis does not contradict but presupposes the critical focus derived from an impartial and thus universal standpoint. From this perspective, global justice is not a contradiction but the very foundation of any legitimate "communitarianism" in a globalizing world.

The Nationalist Objection: The Ethical Significance of Boundaries and Citizenship

The nationalist critique can be regarded as a special case of communitarianism because most commonly it is the nation that builds the communal reference point for communitarian arguments. Thus communitarian arguments usually deal with the ethical significance of nationality for our identity (D. Miller 1988; Tamir 1993). The nationalist objection aims at refuting the claim of generality of cosmopolitanism. The worldview of modern human beings is profoundly shaped by the political boundaries that demarcate the territories of discrete and mutually exclusive nation-states. The image of a world organized through and divided into territorial states predetermines the range of concepts and solutions we perceive as feasible and worth taking into consideration in order to respond to novel social and societal problems. It is this dominant worldview that prompted Edmund Burke (2003) to formulate his powerful critique of the French Revolution to which Thomas Paine famously replied with *The Rights of Man* (1985). Burke attempted to refute the existence of universal rights held equally by all human beings. In his opinion, only citizenship within a particular political community and thus within the nation-state could constitute the rights of human beings. In Burke's view, the "rights of man" were not rights of human beings per se but rather the rights of Englishmen, the rights of Frenchmen, and so on. Ultimate ethical significance, from that point of view, must be derived from the political boundaries of the nation-state.

Burke's view still lingers in our dominant perceptions of people's rights. Even though human rights are almost universally accepted, their realization is still closely connected to the concept of citizenship. Giving special ethical significance to citizenship and accordingly to the territorial boundaries to which citizenship is tied does not necessarily deny either the possibility of a global scope of justice (e.g., D. Miller 1988, 647f.; 1999, 19f.; Scheffler 1999) or that of universal ethical principles and human rights. What it does deny, however, is that these global or universal principles lead to strong universal or transnational obligations. Thus foreigners are perceived as having the same rights as we do, but their rights give rise to moral claims only against their own compatriots and their own government, not against us and our government. The political boundaries of the state are perceived to mark the legitimate limits of moral obligations deriving from universal rights. Our obligations to our compatriots are regarded as more extensive than obligations to strangers (D. Miller 1988, 647). Even the less urgent needs of compatriots are often perceived to take priority over the more urgent needs of strangers. Hence, on the one hand, we agree to the existence of universal human rights, on the other hand, we hold that their realization must predominantly depend on the state of which we are citizens (O'Neill 2000, 170).

Depending on which community is perceived to be relevant—the nation or the state—this strand of criticism of cosmopolitan justice usually carries the label of either nationalism or statism. Statists argue that states are the appropriate units of moral concern; nationalists emphasize the nation as the bearer of moral value. Both of them, however, claim that we have special relationships to those with whom we share a state or a nation (Satz 1999, 68f.), and both defend their claim with an array of different but interconnected arguments.[13] What all those arguments have in common is their emphasis on the alleged ethical significance of political boundaries for the circumvention of the universal applicability of principles of justice and the corresponding moral obligations. In the following, I will examine the most significant of these arguments in more detail.[14]

Compatriot Favoritism Based on Special Relationships?   "Compatriot favoritism" (C. Jones 1999, 127ff.; 2001, 111ff.) is usually based on the argument that we share special relations with our fellow countrymen. It is argued that special relationships generally lead to the derivation of special rights (H. L. A. Hart 1984, 87), which in turn lead to special and deeper obligations toward compatriots. It is irrefutable that in certain cases special relationships indeed do encompass special obligations. There are forms of ethical particularism that we intuitively perceive as legitimate. For example, it is a commonsense assumption that the relation between parents and their children leads to special obligations on both sides. Even members of the wider family circle or close friends might fall into this category of special relationships. It is commonly assumed that it is the intimacy of these relationships that implies special moral concern. The ethical significance of this intimacy derives from the constitutive importance of these relationships for a fulfilled human life. A more general perspective suggests that certain special ties are legitimate if they can serve as a principle for everyone. Hence in order to be legitimate, the partiality deriving from special treatment must itself be justifiable and universalizable from the impartial standpoint. Some forms of ethical particularism certainly fulfill this condition—for example, those intimate relationships that form the personal sphere for each of us (Nussbaum 1996a, 13)—but do they include also special obligations to compatriots?

Compatriot favoritists draw an analogy between their own claim and the special ties we maintain to our intimate friends and family. However, it is hard to see to what extent we really share an intimacy with compatriots that resembles the one of such special relationships. We all know the cozy feeling of meeting a fellow countryman far from home—the shared language, history, and culture build an immediate connection and conversation starter that we might indeed not share with foreigners. However, it seems that it is rather the special circumstances than the special relationship that make us feel connected in this situation; after all, the same person would be a foreigner like any other on our "home turf." Hence, although we immediately recognize our friends and family irrespective of the context we are in, most of our compatriots remain complete strangers to us, just as distant foreigners are (C. Jones 1999, 139; Cabrera 2004, 22f.). From this perspective, intimate relationships make a weak foundation for patriotism.

Rather than in meaningful ties, patriotism roots in plain collective self-interest (Pogge 2002a, 124). Indeed, it is a common realist assumption that governments have an overriding (special) obligation to act strictly in the national interest. Accordingly, political realists claim that there is little room for international ethical principles that constitute similar obligations across national borders. The main motives in international politics, they argue, are competing national interests. But even if competing national interests factually were the sole motives in world politics, this does not mean that they should be. Self-interest cannot be a legitimate reason to disregard universal ethical principles and to restrict the claim of justice to the boundaries of the nation-state. Governments are the agents and representatives of their citizens, but that in itself does not establish a general permission to give unlimited and unconditional priority to their interests. If, as I showed earlier, it is not morally permissible for individuals to strictly and unconditionally act according to their own self-interest at all times, then it must be equally illegitimate to appoint an agent (the government) that does so on their behalf (Pogge 2002a, 126; see also Goodpaster 1991, 68). In domestic affairs it seems common sense that people must not have others do for them what they are not allowed to do themselves, so why should this be any different in the international or global sphere (Beitz 1999a, 24)?

This same conclusion can be reached through a different argument. We acknowledge that certain close relationships to family members or friends are associated with prioritizing their moral claims over the moral claims of strangers, but we generally oppose such preferential treatment where it distorts the playing field (Pogge 2002a, 118ff.). The claim for a level playing field marks the limit of such commonly accepted partiality insofar as special ties are not supposed to play a role, for example, in public decision-making processes of state agents and officials (Cabrera 2004, 24). This leads us to an interesting perspective that allows for a concise argument in favor of cosmopolitanism and exposes the inherent inconsistency of compatriot favoritism at the same time:

> How can we despise those who seek to slant the national playing field in favor of themselves and their relatives and yet applaud those who seek to slant the international playing field in favor of themselves and their compatriots? How can we ask our officials to put their own family's finances out of their minds when deliberating about the domestic economic order (e.g. the tax code) and yet expect those same officials to have their own nation's finances uppermost in their minds when deliberating about the global economic order? (Pogge 2002a, 124)

In other words, it seems highly questionable and at least inconsistent to argue for equality of opportunity within national borders and at the same time to deny the validity of those same arguments at the global level. How can we consider it discrimination if people enjoy fewer life chances because of ethnicity, class, and social status on national territory, but see no problem if this is caused by nationality or citizenship at the global level (Caney 2001, 114f.)? If we accept that the moral worth of people is independent of the community they live in, we cannot reasonably defend inequalities in life chances deriving from where they come from. To regard people as moral equals, as Nussbaum (1996b, 133) rightly states, "is to treat nationality, ethnicity, religion, class, race, and gender as 'morally irrelevant'—as irrelevant to that equal standing."

The case for a level playing field can be made even stronger by looking at the global order as downright harmful to the poor (Pogge 2001a). It seems evident that our (negative) duty not to harm or even kill others holds without distinction for compatriots and foreigners. Therefore, Pogge (2002a, 133ff.) is right in claiming that changing our perspective to such a negative duty in the justice of the global order makes a momentous moral difference because focusing on the duty not to harm would make a strong case for global justice even against those who deny transnational obligations to help. After all, how can we consistently accept a negative duty not to maintain national economic institutions that cause extreme domestic inequalities and poverty but reject exactly the same argument for the global economic system?

Some might oppose such insights on the basis of the closely related argument that cross-border moral obligations conflict with the claim for national sovereignty. Thus political realists often accuse cosmopolitanism of not pay-ing sufficient attention to values like national autonomy and sovereignty (see, e.g., D. Chandler 2003). The sovereignty of states, they argue in the sense of Jean Bodin (1962, 84ff.), is absolute; that is, it cannot be subjected to higher (ethical) standards and rules. The argument that cosmopolitan justice con-flicts with state autonomy or sovereignty, however, is based on a categorical mistake. Because justice is the part of morals with the highest binding power, state autonomy and sovereignty can at best be derivatives of more basic principles of justice (Beitz 1999a, 69). That is, state autonomy is not valuable in itself but only insofar as it enhances the equal (real) freedoms of human beings. Hence where the rigid claim of national sovereignty creates illegiti-mate exclusions and unjustified deprivations among human beings, we do not face a case of irresolvably conflicting values but one that calls for a re-allocation of political authority in the name of justice. Thus state autonomy must be connected both to considerations of domestic justice and to princi-ples of global justice (Beitz 1999a, 179). And because global justice is best defined in terms of cosmopolitan principles, the adequacy of a concentra-tion of sovereignty at one particular level must indeed be questioned. Rather, cosmopolitanism demands the vertical dispersal of authority both above and below the state level to aim at the best possible achievement of global justice (Pogge 1992, 57ff.).

Compatriot Favoritism Based on Shared Identity?   The analogy to the special relationships we maintain with friends and family, as we saw earlier, fails for the case of compatriots. This leaves open the somewhat more general claim that our special obligations to compatriots derive from our shared national identity (see, e.g., D. Miller 1995, 49). This identity argument is more plausi-ble than the one based on special relationships, but as I will show, it remains problematic.

Identity is usually perceived as being connected not so much to a state as to a nation. Statism as a doctrine that defends the status quo among states is dependent on nationalism if it is to draw upon the identity argument. Thus nationalism can provide an explanation why states may have value for their members; pure statism, however, cannot (B. Barry 1999, 38). Without nation-alism as a basis, statism has no theory about how state boundaries should be drawn. It simply takes them as given (B. Barry 1999, 25). Despite the roman-ticizing or even misleading notion of the nation-state, the boundaries of nations and states are often not congruent in reality. This removes the potential justificatory basis of nationalism from the statist argument and leaves state boundaries with a stance of arbitrariness.[15]

Let us ignore these insights for a moment and simply grant some validity to the general argument that a shared identity can be a reason for special obligations. Does this make a case for compatriot favoritism? Most likely it does not. If shared identity were indeed a valid criterion for the foundation of special obligations, then the relevant boundaries could be drawn in many different ways. Nationality is certainly not the only factor that defines the identity of human beings. In the same way human beings might feel as part of a nation, they can also be members of religious groups, professions, academic societies, and other groupings. All of these are equally—in the cosmopolitan age (see Beck 2006) perhaps even more—important and constitutive for the multiple identities of human beings. Many of them, however, cut across the boundaries of states and nations. Thus making a case for compatriot favoritism based on identity involves more than simply refuting cosmopolitan generality; it includes the positive demonstration that the ethically primary group is indeed the one defined by political boundaries rather than by religion, sexual orientation, or some other characteristic (Shue 1980, 138). However, there is simply no obvious reason that our national identity should override all other identity-building factors and groups that do not necessarily coincide with given territorial boundaries. For example, it is doubtful that a young French black woman identifies more with a retired French white man than with a young black woman who happens to be from the Netherlands (see Shue 1980, 137). At the very least, the identity argument is not as clear-cut and exclusive as the nationalist account would suggest.

Moreover, there seems to be an indissoluble contradiction between arguing for special ties arising from a shared national identity and the realization of justice for ethnic minorities within state borders. One could argue that this is what the institution of citizenship is for. By granting citizenship to minorities, we can effectively integrate them into the circle of compatriots. This strategy, however, would defeat rather than support the identity argument. De facto citizenship and identity are not the same thing (D. Miller 1988, 657). In cases where granting citizenship means subjecting minorities to policies of cultural, religious, and traditional assimilation, the identities of minority groups might even be destroyed (O'Neill 2000, 173). Hence replacing identity with de facto citizenship, that is, granting equal rights qua citizens instead of qua human beings, as suggested, for example, by Harris (1987, 147), turns the special-ties argument into an entirely arbitrary affair. After all, what are the morally justifiable criteria for inclusion and exclusion in this regard?

Appiah (1996, 28), who is himself a defender of moral cosmopolitanism, claims that because human beings live in political orders that serve as a platform for arguing and debating questions of public right and wrong, the fact of being a fellow citizen is not morally arbitrary. This insight is true but misses the point. Nobody denies that factually such communicative or deliberative processes do create moral significance for those who are a part of them. Being a citizen of one country rather than of another does indeed have moral significance. But these deliberative processes evolved as a consequence of given state boundaries rather than providing a normative justification before drawing them. Relying on the moral significance of the processes that result from given boundaries in order to justify those same boundaries is a logical fallacy or petitio principii. The question of who gets to be included and excluded in the initial process of drawing boundaries remains open and subject to justification. "To say that relationships matter to equality," Debra Satz (1999, 76) rightly notes, "is not to regard current relationships as givens, without need of justification."

One could counterargue that shared identities evolve over time. Granting citizenship could thus be considered a part of a "nation-building" (Anthony Smith 1986, 200ff.) project that at least in the long run leads to some form of territorially bounded identity among de facto compatriots. If we leave the earlier argument regarding multiple identities aside, this could potentially reestablish a case for at least a moderate form of compatriot favoritism. This argument also, however, is circular and inherently self-defeating. If we justify special obligations to compatriots on the basis of our shared identity, we cannot at the same time define this shared identity by referring to de facto compatriotism; something has to give at one point. Furthermore, the implicit confession that national identity is in fact not a "given reality" in the sense of a "blood and soil nationalism" (B. Barry 1999, 18) but is socially constructed or even "manufactured" to suit specific political interests (D. Miller 1988, 654) makes it per se subject to critical reflection and justification. After all, the "nation" could have been constructed differently. From that perspective, there seems no a priori reason why the same thing could not be done at the supranational level; a case in point is the European Union, which can be interpreted as a real-life attempt to redraw political boundaries at the regional level. Evidently, drawing moral boundaries based on identity is a slippery slope; however we turn the argument, there is no evident reason why nationality should be the one dominant determining factor.

This means neither that political boundaries must per se be regarded as illegitimate nor that nationalism is per se incompatible with cosmopolitanism. People do have a right to self-determination and self-government, and this right can certainly be achieved best through decentralization of sovereignty. After all, human beings are not only Stoic moral citizens of the world but also Aristotelian political animals. Political boundaries—however we end up drawing them—are not simply obsolete but are a necessary part of the cosmopolitan goal of human autonomy and self-determination (see Beitz 1999a, 105ff.). Accounts of nationalism that are designed with the intent of realizing these goals in an equal manner for all human beings, such as Brian Barry's (1999, 53ff.) "civic nationalism" and Kwame Anthony Appiah's (1996) "rooted cosmopolitanism" (or "cosmopolitan patriotism"), may very likely advance such cosmopolitan ends. After all, cosmopolitanism is not at odds with us acknowledging and living our local identities, but it requires us to critically reflect upon their implications in light of the overarching criterion of equal moral worth of all human beings worldwide. Rather than having to give up one's local roots, being a world citizen means to be critically aware of them in light of humanity at large.

Under no circumstances, therefore, is there a reason that boundaries should be designed as impermeable or fixed at the outset. On the contrary, if arbitrariness, discrimination, and ethical dogmatism ought to be averted, boundaries must be regarded as porous and principally changeable. State boundaries can never have more than derivative ethical significance. The only thinkable defense of statism is to show that it is superior to any alternative arrangement in advancing equal rights for all human beings (B. Barry 1999, 38). However, if it turns out that boundaries hinder rather than further the equal realization of human beings' most basic rights—and a mere glance at existing inequalities and exclusions between and within states suffices to confirm that this is currently the case—then we seem to have a strong argument for redrawing or reconfiguring them in a more favorable way.

Compatriot Favoritism as a Mere Result of Excessive Demands of Global Justice?

After showing the ambiguity of the identity argument in regard to the boundaries of the nation-state, one might still argue that the claim for cosmopolitan justice is morally and pragmatically too demanding both for individuals and for states. Fletcher (1993, 21), for example, considers it utopian to assume that our loyalty is limitless. Our "natural limits of sympathy," he claims, prevent us from showing concern for all people living on this planet. Similarly, Richard Miller (1998, 215) claims that there is "a psychologically inevitable limit on trust and respect," and Nathan Glazer (1996, 63) also raises the question of "how far bonds of [. . .] loyalty can stretch." Let me make three short points in response to these objections.

First, the attempt to refute cosmopolitanism on the basis of human beings' limited capacity of loyalty rests on a misinterpretation of its normative claim. Cosmopolitanism does not ask us to be loyal to all human beings but rather to grant equal consideration to justified claims of all human beings despite the fact that our sense of loyalty is naturally limited to less inclusive groups (C. Jones 2001, 137). It is precisely because our natural sense of loyalty is limited that the claim for global justice is important. Thus global justice is not dependent on people's limitless loyalty but rather on their global sense of justice (Rawls 1971, 496ff.; Beitz 1999a, 155; Höffe 2002c, 341ff.). A global sense of justice derives from a global sense of community. Insofar as the scope of communal identity, as seen earlier, is not a natural given but socially constructed, there is no reason why the development of a global sense of justice should be impossible. Second, arguing in favor of compatriot favoritism on the basis of the limits of loyalty implies that our natural psychological limits of loyalty coincide precisely with state boundaries, which seems rather absurd. The existence of tremendous differences in size and populations of countries—China versus Liechtenstein, for example—renders the concept of given psychological or natural limits to the human capacity of loyalty problematic (Beitz 1999a, 164; Cabrera 2004, 19). Third, although loyalty indeed plays an important role in the development of our subjective moral sentiments, these sentiments build only one part of our human morality. The other part is constituted through our capacity for abstraction, that is, for generalizing these sentiments to an abstract level and putting ourselves in the shoes of any given human being within a fictitious universal role change. While loyalty restricts our affective sympathy to the people with whom we share an emotional connection, our rationality gives us the undeniable capacity to generalize this sympathy to any given human being, as well as to critically assess it from an impartial standpoint. It is the very essence of the moral standpoint that it generalizes these sentiments in order to overcome the "natural limits" of our capacity to sympathize. The limits of our affections do not coincide with the limits of our moral obligations. Rather than affections limiting the scope of justice, it is the principles of justice that constitute the limits of the legitimacy of our immediate affections.

This does not yet refute the argument that cosmopolitanism poses pragmatically excessive demands for individuals and thus lacks realizability. Therefore, let me add three short replies also to this objection. First, global justice is a normative ideal that makes its basic claim independent of any pragmatic considerations. To reject a normative ideal on the basis of the pragmatic objection of feasibility is a categorical mistake. Compromises in this regard must not affect the normative ideal but rather the specific design of the implementation process. Second, implementing and achieving global justice are indeed step-by-step processes. However, even a step-by-step approach to global justice remains at its core an attempt to realize global justice from the beginning on. Hence the popular argument that we should start with realizing justice within our own countries before caring about its global scope is inadequate even if we take an iterative approach. Such a conception of "lofty nationalism" (Pogge 2002a, 129ff.), which rests on "simple coordinational rules," does not make sense even for devoted communitarians like David Miller (1988, 652). Giving priority to compatriots solely on the basis of coordinative considerations makes sense, he argues, only if each person is equally in need of help and each is equally able to provide it. However, this is a poor reflection of reality. Third, some argue that realizing global justice is a utopian endeavor. The sheer dimensions of human suffering on this planet simply overstrain the available capacities for alleviation. However, even if their basic claim were correct, they overlook that the entirety of human misery consists of countless individual claims. It is precisely the essence of cosmopolitanism that the individual is the center of moral concern, not specific aggregates of individuals. Even if it is impossible to relieve all the suffering on this planet at once, the capacities to secure the particular basic needs and rights of any given deprived individual are clearly available (Waldron 1993, 207). As long as this is the case, that is, as long as we are able to improve the situation of at least one deprived human being, the claim for global justice retains its normative power.

The Global Focus of Liberalism   Any form of compatriot favoritism that conflicts with the basic rights of noncitizens without being justified by the protection of higher-ranking rights of compatriots must be considered illegitimate.

This follows from the status of basic rights as of highest ethical priority by virtue of justice. And because rights-based justice at its core can be thought of only as global justice, the favorable treatment of fellow citizens must stop where it endangers the realization of other people's human rights. In other words, human rights are the "minimal constraint on the scope of acceptable partiality" (Pogge 2002a, 124). It is impossible reasonably to defend liberalism and argue against global justice at the same time. If we accept this claim, moral cosmopolitanism seems the only alternative because it is the very essence of liberalism to value people over collectivities (Appiah 1996, 24). A true cosmopolitan, that is, a true citizen of the world, is thus one "who puts right before country and universal reason before the symbols of national belonging" (Nussbaum 1996a, 17).

The "Rawlsian" Objection: Morality of States over Cosmopolitan Individualism

Cosmopolitan individualism has been criticized by scholars who adhere to a more state-centric view of global justice. A state-centric understanding of global justice focuses on justice between states rather than between individuals (Beitz 1999b, 515). Therefore, it can be defined as international justice. It limits principles of "global" justice to international relations and promotes legal and political equality among states (Beitz 1999b, 518; Satz 1999, 69). Justice between individuals, within such an account, is perceived as a purely domestic affair and entirely up to the respective governments. Against the background of our commonly unquestioning acceptance of the state system as a quasi-natural given, this perception intuitively appears as common sense and reflects the majority view also among political philosophers. On the one hand, it resembles the political realist claim of state autonomy and moral priority of compatriots. On the other hand, however, it refutes the realists' resulting skepticism about international ethics (Beitz 1999a, 7f.; 1999b, 519ff.).

Rawls's original theory of justice as fairness was designed with an exclusively domestic focus. He initially formulated his theory for a closed, self-contained, national community with only minor relations to other societies (Rawls 1971, 457; 1996, 68). Accordingly, in *A Theory of Justice* (1971) he developed a "law of peoples" only for the limited purpose of addressing questions dealing with just war (Rawls 1999b, 529). In his later chapter and subsequent book *The Law of Peoples* (1999a, 1999b), however, he complemented his theory with a somewhat broader range of principles of justice governing international relations. However, he held to his basic suggestion that there is only very limited applicability of principles of justice in the global sphere.

In *The Law of Peoples* Rawls applied his original position experiment to the international sphere. This experiment, which he conducted also in *A Theory of Justice*, can be thought of as a hypothetical international conference consisting of representatives of states or peoples (Rawls 1971, 378f.; 1999b 534) who negotiate behind the veil of ignorance. Therefore, they must be perceived as being deprived of any information about the particular circumstances of their societies. Surprisingly, despite the close analogy between the domestic and the international original position, Rawls concluded that only the first of his two principles of justice applies to the international sphere. Thus he promoted international principles such as nonintervention, self-determination, or self-defense, but not an international difference principle.

Rawls's conception of international justice remains limited to the absolute minimum, and his hesitation to apply his theory fully to the global sphere was rightly criticized. Rawls's understanding of international justice is explicitly anticosmopolitan insofar as he confirms "the state's right to do as it likes with people within its own borders" (Rawls 1999b, 534). It was Charles Beitz (1999a), who, in his normative political theory of international relations, revised the Rawlsian law of peoples along statist lines. Most notably, Beitz argued, against Rawls, in favor of the application of a global difference principle. Even though Beitz claimed that a global difference principle must ultimately refer to persons, he designated states as the primary subjects of international distributive responsibilities (Beitz 1999a, 152f.).

Beitz's conclusion that the difference principle must apply also to the international sphere certainly makes sense. Analogous to the earlier insight that the realization of classical liberty rights is dependent on the realization of social and economic rights, national autonomy and nondomination depend not only on nonintervention by other states but also on economic self-sufficiency. Thus the viability even of Rawls's minimal conception is dependent on conditions that demand a much broader approach to international justice. Securing the conditions of self-determination, which is one central criterion of Rawls's conception of international justice, requires substantial redistribution of international resources (Satz 1999, 80). In agreement with this insight, Beitz points to the necessity of a global resource redistribution principle and consequent transfers from richer states to poorer ones. The claim for a global resource dividend is echoed also by Thomas Pogge (1989). However, for Pogge, an international difference principle does not go far enough. "Realizing Rawls" to the full extent, he claims, would necessarily lead to a full-blown cosmopolitan account of global justice (see also Richards 1982; B. Barry 1999, 34ff.), which includes extensive transformation of the global economic and political system and a shift and reconfiguration of authority to different loci both above and below the state level.

Thus designing global justice as international justice is a less common-sense conclusion than it might seem at a first glance. On the one hand, the roots of our philosophical reflections on global justice, as seen earlier, are in fact cosmopolitan. For the classical Stoic philosophers, global justice was intuitively and inherently connected to the concept of world citizenship. On the other hand, the perception that the effects of the contemporary global (economic) system are relevant only to distribution between but not within states seems highly counterintuitive (Shapiro and Brilmayer 1999, 2). Referring to this latter point, Beitz rightly argues that if, as the Rawlsian conception suggests, we take the worst-off group as a reference point for global distributive justice, there is no a priori reason why the membership of this group should coincide with that of any existing state (Beitz 1999a, 152f.). This insight corresponds to Scheffler's (1999, 105) argument that the decisive justice-relevant divide occurs less and less between rich and poor nations and more between an affluent, technologically sophisticated global elite and a growing number of poor and undereducated people worldwide. Consequently, a global difference principle between human beings would not necessarily imply mere intercountry transfers from rich countries to poor countries. On the contrary, rather than being the primary concern of genuinely cosmopolitan justice, intercountry equality emerges as a mere side product of remedying impermissible interpersonal inequalities.

Despite these evident inconsistencies, Beitz does not necessarily consider these insights incompatible with a perspective on states as the primary subjects of international justice. However, he clearly emphasizes "the plausibility of a more cosmopolitan and less state-centered perspective" for future inquiries and labels intercountry redistribution "a second-best solution in the absence of a better strategy for satisfying a global difference principle" (Beitz 1999a, 6, 152; see also 1999b). However, if the reason for opting for international rather than cosmopolitan justice is indeed merely pragmatic, and hence if we advocate interstatal redistribution on the basis of the belief that this might further the achievement of cosmopolitan ideals, then the current global justice debate is clearly trapped in a dead end because empirically the adherence to the statist world order has rather hindered than furthered the achievement of cosmopolitan justice. From this perspective, even Beitz's own argument for international justice seems to advocate new strategies with much more explicit cosmopolitan content.

Irrespective of this lack of empirical support, Beitz's argument that a focus on interpersonal inequalities is not necessarily inconsistent with an international perspective on justice seems questionable at the outset. Evidently, justice between states can at best constitute some negative nonintervention and autonomy rules as outlined by Rawls, possibly accompanied by some international redistributive principles targeting the interstatal distribution of resources and material wealth. However, these principles can never cover the full scope of a rights-based account of justice, whose focus, as seen earlier, reaches far beyond the mere distribution of material products and resources. An account of international justice that falls short of fully realizing people's rights, however, is problematic because a morality of states can never be a self-contained morality but can be defended only by showing how the interests of states conduce to the interests of individuals (B. Barry 1999, 14). If this condition is not met, the justificatory basis of principles of international justice is severely weakened.

Quite independent of these arguments, Onora O'Neill (2000, 134) rightly questions the realizability of a global difference principle. The complexity of the global structure might make it too difficult to estimate the specific effects certain changes in the structure might have on the position of the worst-off. After all, neoliberal supporters of a global laissez-faire doctrine still believe that their approach will serve poor people's interests best—a promise, however, that has been largely unmet so far. Thus a maximin criterion at the global level constituted by the difference principle might leave too much leeway for interpretations that serve special interests rather than the interests of the worst-off. Therefore, it simply seems wiser to settle for a position that aims at ensuring equal realization of basic human rights and a certain level of human well-being for everyone.

The state-centric perspective on international justice idealizes the agency and mutual independence of states (O'Neill 2000, 154). Accordingly, it obstructs our view of those global systemic factors that cause and contribute to poverty and inequality on a worldwide scale rather than providing effective strategies for achieving global justice. It reduces the claim for global justice to the mere transfer of financial assistance from rich to poor countries and fails to recognize the negative global systemic effects that counteract such development philanthropy day by day. Therefore, if true progress in global justice is to be made, we must give up, at least partly, the normative and methodological nationalism that has dominated the pattern of modern thought processes (Beck 2003, 454; 2006) and start thinking about pressing problems like poverty and inequality in truly global, that is, cosmopolitan, terms.

Global Justice as Human Development

A conception of cosmopolitan justice as specified so far puts people and their justified moral claims—that is, their moral rights—to equal access to human functionings at the center of attention. This claim is of universal validity and thus quite independent of any geographic, cultural, religious, or racial differences. Access to different functionings, as seen earlier, is dependent on a person's capabilities. The capabilities to choose effectively from different valuable functionings determine a human being's freedom to live a self-determined human life. Justice, therefore, does not aim merely at formal, negative freedom but at real, positive freedom. In other words, what matters to human beings is not merely having a right but the ability to realize it. Thus achieving justice through the enhancement of human capabilities, freedoms, and rights can essentially be understood as a process of development. The reverse perspective on such an account of justice as development suggests that development itself essentially is a rights-based process.

Hence an account of rights-based development does not merely promote respect for human rights in the process of developing something else (whatever it might be that we consider worthy of developing) but interprets the whole development process in terms of the progressive and ongoing realization of human rights. In other words, development and the realization of human rights are not two separate, divergent processes, nor are they parallel or somehow complementary (see, e.g., Donnelly 1985b; Shepherd and Nanda 1985, 3) processes that call for harmonization. In fact, development and the realization of human rights are one and the same. This inherent interconnectedness between human development and human rights has long been overlooked. Historically, as Mary Robinson (2005, 27) observes, there has always been a distance between those in the field of development and those who work on human rights. While the issue of development has been largely dominated by economists, social scientists, and policy makers, human rights have been the traditional domain of political activists, philosophers, and lawyers (UNDP 2000, 2).

This book suggests that these two seemingly separate fields can and must be united in the concept of global justice. Development must essentially be understood as a process of achieving equal real freedom for all through the continuous realization of people's rights. It is from this perspective that development is essentially to be interpreted as human development.

From Economic to Human Development

It is thanks to the United Nations Development Programme's (UNDP) annual *Human Development Report* and the committed internal and external contributors to it that human development has become an established term in development-related fields and a powerful counterweight to conventional, mostly neoliberal approaches that have dominated the last three decades of development policy. The first report was released in May 1990, when neoliberal economic globalization was in full swing. Since then, the *Human Development Report* has gradually become the flagship and main platform for the ongoing development of this promising approach.[16] Conceptually based on Sen's capabilities approach, the reports made significant contributions to its operationalization and measurement, as well as its application to different areas and challenges of public policy over the years. Of special importance in this regard is the report's Human Development Index, updated yearly, which is a comparative measure of factors that determine individuals' well-being in different countries rather than focusing on their aggregate wealth.

Evidently, the term *human development* can be specified in many different ways, one of which is the rights-based interpretation. However, all these specifications are ultimately based on the idea and aim to correct two blatant shortcomings of conventional, neoliberal development approaches. First, human development is focused on human beings rather than on countries as the primary subject of development. People, not a country's gross domestic product (GDP), must be the ultimate end of development. Therefore, it is an inherently cosmopolitan concept. GDP growth and any other strategies or policies are perceived as desirable only insofar as they benefit human beings and contribute to the improvement of their lives.

This takes us to the second shortcoming of conventional development approaches. Especially the neoliberal development orthodoxy embodied in the Washington Consensus and enforced by the so-called Bretton Woods institutions is based on "developmental economism" (Ulrich 2004a, 9ff.), which perceives development as an almost exclusively economic problem and portrays the generation of economic growth and national income per se as the panacea for its solution. Earlier I have provided the reasons that such an exclusive focus on income fails from a justice perspective. First, people vary in their possibilities of converting income into desired achievements. Second, the trickle-down effect of economic growth is anything but a proven reality; in fact, reality rather suggests that a majority of the poor remain unaffected by it. Accordingly, GDP growth alone does not necessarily lead to an enhancement of people's standard of living and may well worsen rather than improve inequality within countries.

Economic growth falls short as an indicator of human development simply because it fails to provide any information about how deprived people are actually doing (Nussbaum 2003, 33). Whether economic growth benefits the poor depends on the public policy and development priorities that a country pursues—for example, the infrastructure it builds, the availability of social and health services, or the quality of the education system (Haq 1999, 14f.). A focus on the mere quantity of economic growth fails to disaggregate such important elements of the development process and is systematically unable to take their different effects into account (Nussbaum 2003, 34). Furthermore, it conceals that poverty is an urgent problem also in industrialized nations and thus overstates their status as "developed" countries in general. From a rights-based perspective, the dichotomy between "developed" and "underdeveloped" countries is misleading. The process of enhancing and realizing rights is ongoing not only for what we tend to describe as "developing countries" but also for wealthy and powerful ones. To an increasing extent, industrialized nations also regularly fall short of granting even the minimal requirements in regard to the realization of rights to a growing number of people (Donnelly 2003, 15). In short, growth- and income-based approaches to development not only lead to misguided policy making but also promote the false and dangerous perception that development is merely a matter of giving by the industrialized North and receiving by the South, that it is all about us helping them, and that it is of no further concern to the industrialized nations themselves.

If we look at people's actual state of being, we will be better able to understand what barriers exist in our societies—locally or globally—to achieving justice for groups of people who are neglected and discriminated against (Nussbaum 2003, 33). To be sure, nobody denies the importance of economic growth for the poor regions in this world. Substantial and reliable economic growth, as John Kenneth Galbraith (1996, 24) asserted, is essential for the "good society." Mahbub ul Haq (1999, 21), a founding member of the *Human Development Report*, stated eloquently that although economic growth is not the end of economic development, the lack or absence of growth often is. However, rather than exclusively focusing on the quantity of economic growth, we should pay more attention to its quality, that is, to the question of who does and who does not benefit from it and in what regards. In other words, we must bring the ethical dimension back to the development process.

In his important book *Development as Freedom* (2000) Amartya Sen examines this ethical dimension within the constitutive role of freedom for development. He interprets development as a process of expanding the real freedoms that people effectively enjoy or, conversely, as the removal of major sources of unfreedom that in their diversity range from poverty, tyranny, poor economic opportunities, and neglect of public facilities to intolerance and repression (Sen 2000, 3). Interpreting human misery as a lack of freedom draws our attention to the multidimensional roots of deprivations rather than covering them up by concentration solely on the relief of symptoms through income, wealth, and other material goods. It enables us to understand development issues much more holistically and to come up with more adequate and effective solutions. In sum, if human development is interpreted in terms of freedom and freedom denotes the ultimate substance of rights, then the continuous and progressive realization of rights can be seen as the very essence of human development.

Rights as Goals: Human Development as the Realization of Rights

A rights-based conception of human development rests on an understanding of rights as goals. This is implied by the underlying positive interpretation of real freedom as the effective realization of people's rights. Thus rights are considered neither as having exclusively instrumental value for the realization of other goals nor as mere side constraints on human activity. The former interpretation can be found in utilitarian theory, which, as stated earlier, tends to take justice, and thus rights, into consideration only if doing so enhances social welfare. The latter is typical for libertarian theories that are predominantly based on negative interpretations of rights and freedom (see, e.g., Nozick 1974, 166).

An understanding of rights as goals regards rights as inherently valuable in themselves. Their fulfillment or nonfulfillment serves as a reference point for the ethical evaluation of states of affairs, as well as of human actions (Sen 1982, 5f.). After the earlier criticism of the teleological focus of utilitarianism, one could perceive this consequence-sensitive turn as a weakening of my overall theory. If anything, however, its explicit disclosure makes my claim more plausible. After all, even constraint-based theories of rights, if they are not stripped to an untenable minimum, must inevitably rely on moderately consequentialist assumptions simply because potential conflicts of rights can be resolved only by referring to an implicit hierarchy of rights (Sen 1982, 6; 1985c, 136f.).

Take a hypothetical situation in which my emergency call to the police could spare someone from being assaulted by another person. However, in order to place the call, I would have to break into someone else's apartment. From a strictly constraint-based perspective that prohibits the direct violation of any rights, the break-in could not be justified. Hence I could not use the violation of the assaulted person's rights as a justification for the infringement on the apartment owner's right. For most of us, this solution seems unsatisfying; the moral claim for physical integrity of the one in immediate danger is perceived as more urgent and important than the claim for the integrity of the apartment. Hence any acceptable resolution of the conflict inevitably involves a value statement that gives priority to the right not to be physically harmed over the one not to have one's apartment invaded. This, however, presupposes a moderately consequentialist assessment of the emergency situation.

If we apply this example to the larger context of global social inequality, it becomes clear that a consequence-insensitive understanding of rights, that is, an interpretation of rights claims as absolute side constraints on human action, would force us to tolerate an unacceptable level of human misery on this planet (Nussbaum 2002, 142). Our hands would be tied because we would lack any basis to resolve the rights conflicts that inevitably occur in the process of development. Radical libertarians like Robert Nozick would block any redistribution of resources or goods because this would violate the property rights of their owners. But can this really be a satisfactory final answer to the persistent problems we face on this planet today? For Onora O'Neill, the case is quite clear. All serious practical deliberation concerning hunger, poverty, and similar global problems must take the results of policies that address them into consideration: "when so much hangs in the balance for so many," she rightly argues, "it would be frivolous to depend on ways of reasoning which are not at all concerned with results" (O'Neill 1986, 97).

In opposition to this insight, Martha Nussbaum (2002, 140ff.) claims that if we do not start with an inadequate list of rights, as Nozick does, there is no reason that we should not be able to use these rights as mere side constraints without running into the difficulties outlined earlier. Nussbaum's suggestion is correct insofar as most positive rights can indeed also be interpreted negatively. Therefore, it is possible to extend Nozick's list considerably without giving up the side-constraint assumption. What Nussbaum overlooks, however, is that this leads to very different implications for a corresponding theory of justice. It removes the element of proactive realization from the focus on rights and thus leads to a statist conception of human rights (see, e.g., Tugendhat 1993, 391). Thus it ultimately removes the aspect of development from the conception of justice.

A theory of justice as development is inherently dynamic. It demands consequence sensitivity but not consequentialism. Consequentialism is implausible because it takes consequences as the only relevant criterion for ethical evaluation irrespective of the legitimacy of the means used to bring them about (Sen 1985c, 135). Scanlon's (1984, 146) rule utilitarianism, for example, holds that rights themselves must be justified by the state of affairs they promote. My position, in contrast, claims that it is the state of affairs that must be justified by rights, not the other way around. Complete consequence insensitivity, on the other hand, is not only implausible but also counterintuitive in a liberal ethical theory. The very fact that we consider freedom important is a value statement. If freedom is valuable, however, it may well have some consequential relevance to our choices and decisions (Sen 1985c, 136). After all, true equality of freedom presupposes that the range of functionings from which different people are able to choose are of somewhat similar value. Evidently, if all combinations of functionings open to a person are worthless, his or her freedom to choose turns into a chimera. Such sensitivity to consequences should not be misunderstood as a concession to utilitarianism, as some critics have claimed (see, e.g., G. A. Cohen 1993, 26f.). The valuation of different freedoms is to be understood as a reflective activity that is based on good reasons rather than on the ultimate reference to psychological measures like "desire" or "being happy." Utilitarianism, from this perspective, does not provide a criterion for valuation; on the contrary, it avoids valuation altogether by replacing it with subjective criteria such as happiness or desire fulfillment (Sen 1985a, 29f.).

A Human Right to Development?

The idea of a human right to development gained increasing support along with the steadily growing attention paid to the concept of human development during the 1990s. A right to development was proclaimed by the UN Commission on Human Rights in 1977 (Alston and Robinson 2005, 2) and was stipulated in the 1986 United Nations Declaration on the Right to Development. It was then reaffirmed at the 1993 World Conference on Human Rights in Vienna (David 2004, 250). The right to development is commonly interpreted as a part of the evolving third generation of human rights. While the first generation consists of civil and political human rights and the second generation of social, economic, and cultural rights, this third generation includes possible solidarity rights (e.g., Galtung 1994, 108f.).

The basis of the right to development is the justified moral claim of each individual to personal growth and advancement. If human beings are regarded as self-determined agents capable of making autonomous decisions and turning their lives in different directions at any given time, then a truly human life must indeed be regarded as one in constant flow. Personal or human development is arguably one of the defining and constitutive elements of a human life.

However, it seems that a general understanding of rights as goals sufficiently secures this claim. If development is to be understood as the enhancement of human freedom through the continuous realization of rights, then a separate right to development, although it arguably does not hurt anybody, seems to be a tautology or at least somewhat redundant. Because development denotes the realization of human rights of all kinds, an additional explicit right to development can be interpreted somewhat circularly as a right to the realization of other rights. Therefore, it merely restates the ethical imperative for the realization of human rights that already derives from the concept of justice. Thus, at least conceptually, the status of a human right to development seems somewhat ambiguous. Development, we may argue, is rather enshrined in the requirements of justice than a right in itself.

Nevertheless, it makes sense to distinguish between this conceptual perspective and the practical value of adding a right to development to the catalogue of human rights. The explicit stipulation of a right to development in the UN Declaration of Human Rights can serve as an effective tool to raise public awareness of the morally binding character of development. Embedded in the highly complex and rather implicit questions of justice, the moral importance of development will likely remain less accessible to the broad public. On the other hand, adding a right to development to the existing list of human rights can falsely imply that development is to be regarded as something separate from other human rights. This runs the risk of falling back into conventional development approaches that are largely detached from the realization of human rights as such. There certainly is a need for further inquiry regarding the adequate view of a potential human right to development. However, because this would clearly exceed the scope of this analysis, I will here give only general encouragement of future research on this topic.

Well-Being and Human Development

Connecting the rights-based conception of justice to human development made its consequence sensitivity visible and explicitly promoted an understanding of rights as goals. After all, development would seem rather pointless if it did not ultimately contribute to the enhancement of the states of being of individuals in one way or another. Human development interpreted in terms of the continuous realization of people's rights, from this perspective, can alternatively be expressed in terms of human well-being.

Well-being, with reference to the earlier discussion about the role of income and economic growth, does not simply denote how well off a person is financially but how well he or she is doing overall. Income, opulence, or commodities in general can be a means to achieve well-being. Well-being, however, is not ultimately a matter of how rich a person is (Sen 1985a, 28); it is not dependent on a person's possessions but rather on the overall actual functionings a person has achieved, that is, on what kind of life a person is able to live (Sen 1985a, 23ff.).

Evidently, how well a person is effectively feeling is a subjective question. Well-being is an "inner" concept; it is of intrinsic importance to a person (Sen

1985b, 204). Therefore, it derives from the subjective valuation a person attaches to the functionings she has achieved. However, the prospect of achieving a high level of well-being is determined by the range of different functionings a person can choose from. The range of functionings, as noted earlier, is determined by a person's capability set, or, in other words, by his or her freedom to act. Hence well-being or the quality of life of a person ultimately derives from the degree of a person's capabilities to choose from (subjectively) valuable functionings (Sen 1993, 31). Conversely, the lack of well-being and thus deprivations of all kinds can essentially be interpreted as a lack of capability and hence a lack of real choices, which is nothing else than a lack of freedom (Sen 2000).

From this perspective, human development aims at the improvement of human lives "by expanding the range of things that a person can be and do" (Fukada-Parr 2003, 303). Thus the goal of human development can be restated as the enlargement of people's options or choices to achieve well-being through enhancing their capabilities (Fukada-Parr 2003, 311). The realization of people's rights, then, is essentially a process of empowerment of human beings through the development of their basic social and productive skills (O'Neill 1986, 160). Again, this is consistent with an active rather than a passive and a dynamic rather than a statist interpretation of rights; rights empower, not just benefit, those who hold them (Donnelly 2003, 8). Claiming a right, as Joel Feinberg (1980, 150) asserts, means "making things happen."

Evidently, enhanced agency of a person leaves open the personal choice to pursue other goals than merely enhancing one's own well-being. It is even possible to promote goals that are detrimental to it. In other words, enhanced freedom or agency is not always congruent with higher levels of well-being (Sen 1985b, 203). A mother with a starving child, for example, will in most cases choose actions that benefit the well-being of her child even if this means giving up some of her own. Within the moral limits of her fundamental and inalienable rights, the mother, as a reasonable and responsible adult human being, is principally capable and entitled to make well-reasoned choices that do not benefit her own well-being. The child's agency, on the other hand, is naturally limited (quite irrespective of the starvation aspect). Therefore, it is its achievement of well-being that commands attention. Thus agency can have a detrimental impact on a person's achieved well-being in cases where his or her agency role is connected to the fulfillment of obligations to others (Sen

1985b, 187). However, the example of a mother facing a trade-off of such magnitude between her own well-being and the well-being of her child implies a situation in which the mother's options are severely constrained by economic unfreedom at the outset.

Especially for interpersonal comparisons and thus for the assessment of questions of justice, "well-being freedom" (Sen 1985b, 201), that is, the freedom to choose to pursue one's own well-being, is a central aspect. It makes a big difference whether a person is starving because she chooses on the basis of religious beliefs or because she has no real alternatives. The well-being aspect of a person must therefore be interpreted in terms of both freedom and actual achievements (Sen 1985b, 203). From this perspective and in correspondence with my elaborations on rights as goals earlier, freedom seems valuable from two perspectives: first, it is valuable in itself, that is, as "agency freedom" that is the basis of an autonomous, truly human life and includes the possibility to make choices that do not enhance one's own well-being. Second, it is valuable as "well-being freedom," that is, in its function to provide options for choosing functionings that are beneficial to one's well-being.[17]

Sen's capability approach in general and his very notion of well-being in particular have often been criticized for their alleged "overemphasis" on freedom (see, e.g., G. A. Cohen 1993, 28; Okin 2003, 292).[18] Even though Sen has elaborated extensively on the relation between well-being, freedom, and agency, their weighting as potentially conflicting goals of human development remains somewhat unspecified. Therefore, his position is indeed vulnerable to the objection that free human beings might choose to pursue detrimental goals up to a point that compromises their own dignity. This objection reemphasizes why we need the rights perspective as a necessary complement to the capabilities perspective. It is the very idea of inalienable individual rights to set the limits also for the pursuance of freely chosen but potentially "self-destructive" goals. The concept of inalienability denotes nothing else than the impossibility to make use of such fundamental freedoms for the purpose of compromising or even eliminating those freedoms themselves. It is precisely in these cases that well-being achievement must take categorical precedence over freedom and agency. The justification of this priority of well-being, however, is itself based on the preservation of autonomy and self-determination.

Making Practical Sense of Human Development

An understanding of human development as outlined earlier raises the practical question of what kinds of capabilities (and rights that derive from them) effectively contribute to empowerment and agency in the development process. The *Human Development Report*—by far the most elaborate platform for such questions about the practical interpretation and implementation of human development—uses two criteria for determining the practical importance of specific capabilities: first, they must be universally valued; and second, they must be basic (Fukada-Parr 2003, 306).[19] Martha Nussbaum (2000, 2003) has put forth an open-ended list of 10 basic human capabilities that, in her opinion, meet these requirements. They are seen as constitutive for a life of dignity and must therefore form part of a minimum account of social justice.

In her 2003 article Nussbaum defines the 10 most basic capabilities as (1) being able to live to the end of a human life of normal length (life); (2) being able to have good health, including reproductive health, adequate nourishment, and adequate shelter (bodily health); (3) being able to move freely from place to place, including being protected against assault and violence of all kinds and having opportunities for sexual satisfaction (bodily integrity); (4) being able to use the senses, to imagine, think, and reason, and to do these things in a truly human way that is informed and cultivated by an adequate education, including, but by no means limited to, literacy and basic mathematical and scientific training (senses, imagination, and thought); (5) being able to have emotional attachments to things and people outside ourselves, to love, to grieve, and to experience longing, gratitude, and justified anger (emotions); (6) being able to form a conception of the good and to engage in critical reflection about the planning of one's life (practical reason); (7) being able to live with and toward others, to recognize and show concern for other human beings, and to engage in social interaction, as well as to have the social bases of self-respect and non-humiliation (affiliation); (8) being able to live with concern for and in relation to animals, plants, and the world of nature (other species); (9) being able to laugh, to play, and to enjoy recreational activities (play); and (10) being able to participate effectively in political choices that govern one's life and to hold property and have property rights on an equal basis with others, as well as to work as a human being (control over one's environment).

Amartya Sen (2004a, 333), the other leading figure in the development of the capability approach, is reluctant to join "the search for such a canonical list." He asserts two reasons for his skeptical stance. First, the lists and weights of relevant capabilities, he argues, can be chosen only with appropriate specification of the context of their use. Second, the framework of the capabilities approach can help clarify and illuminate the subject matter of public deliberation but should not substantively diminish the public domain or even displace public reasoning by anticipating concrete capabilities. Hence people in their particular cultural and societal contexts should be able to come to their own conclusions regarding the relevance of specific capabilities through fair democratic deliberation.

Sen seems overly cautious toward Nussbaum's suggestions. He is right in opposing "a grand mausoleum to one fixed and final list of capabilities" because this would indeed "deny the possibility of fruitful public participation" and neglect "the particular social reality that any particular society faces" (Sen 2004b, 77ff.). However, Nussbaum by no means proposes such a "cemented list of capabilities which is absolutely complete (nothing could be added to it) and totally fixed (it could not respond to public reasoning and to the formation of social values)" (Sen 2004b, 78). In fact, she explicitly calls her list "open-ended" and thus variable over time and cultures. Furthermore, by aiming at capabilities rather than at functionings, such a list can do little damage to societal pluralism at the outset (Nussbaum 2003, 43).

Another aspect that Sen seems not to take sufficiently into account is that Nussbaum (2003, 42) regards her list as "explicitly introduced for political purposes only." Therefore, her proposed capabilities do not preclude political reasoning but encourage it. Both their further specification and their implementation are meant to be left to public deliberation, as suggested by Sen (Nussbaum 2003, 47). Sen acknowledges that even if there were such a list, we could not avoid the problem of determining the relative weights of the capabilities considered (Sen 2004b, 78f.). Hence the mere listing of capabilities certainly does not eliminate the perceived need for public deliberation. On the contrary, having some clues about what categories of capabilities we must specify in certain contexts not only might be necessary for guiding the public deliberation process in a universally legitimate direction but also might well enhance the quality of public deliberation in general. Even in his own writings, Sen cannot avoid acknowledging, at least implicitly, certain broadly defined basic capabilities as universal in scope and justification, for otherwise he would inevitably risk sliding into a relativist position. In *Development as Freedom*, for example, Sen (2000, 36) points to the constitutive role of elementary capabilities like "being able to avoid such deprivations as starvation, under-nourishment, escapable morbidity and premature mortality" or "being literate and numerate" for any human life. This clearly indicates that Sen thinks of them as universally valid. The difference between his elaborations and Nussbaum's list seems to lie merely in the way they are presented to the reader.

Making practical sense of human development, however, means specifying not only the relevant human capabilities but also the arrangements that must complement them in order to achieve equal real freedom for all. Drawing from a framework put forth by Ulrich (2004a), we can systematize human development as a four-dimensional practical empowerment process. Empowerment here denotes the enhancement of human capabilities and freedoms with the intent of securing people's independent access to vital resources and goods.[20]

The first practical dimension of such an empowerment process addresses the continuous enhancement of people's nominal rights and the legal instruments for their protection and enforcement. The positivization and legal protection of rights aim at the enhancement of human beings' equal formal freedom. Sen occasionally mentions the important role of entitlements in the form of nominal rights as determinants of freedoms (e.g., Sen 2000, 3), but he abstains from assigning them a prominent role in his concept. As he rightly argues, there are other ways to implement and enforce justified moral claims than through their positivization in legal law (Sen 2004a; see also Gloub 2005). Whatever importance we assign to the positivization of rights, it is clear that on its own it is insufficient for the protection of people's real freedoms. In other words, rights-based development includes, but must not be limited to, the strengthening of legal laws and entitlements.

The ability of human beings to realize their formal freedom unfolds in the dimension of personal capacities and talents and in the dimension of supporting or compensatory external arrangements. Capacity building, for example, through adequate education, is an inevitable and necessary condition for the enhancement of human capabilities and a key concept for the process of human development. However, capacities transform into actual capabilities only if external circumstances are supportive in putting them to use. My talent for playing tennis does me no good if there are no tennis courts, no tournaments, and no organized tennis culture—it inevitably stays an abstract capacity. That is why capabilities, as noted earlier, are in most cases combined capabilities, that is, combinations of internal capacities and external arrangements. External arrangements essentially consist of public policies and infrastructure, as

well as the provision of public goods and services. Because today's globalization process is compromising and limiting the ability of national governments
to provide adequate external arrangements, however, human development is
becoming increasingly dependent on a fourth, superordinate dimension of
enabling global superstructures.[21]

Poverty, human misery, and social hardship are more than ever expressions of "structural powerlessness" (Ulrich 2001a, 212; 2004a, 14) of people in
a global economic order that systematically works against their basic interests. Paying attention to societal structures is of overarching importance in
and for a participatory development process. Poverty and inequality have become global problems that cannot be adequately understood and addressed
by focusing merely on the national sphere (Pogge 2004). The relevant structures that cause and perpetuate human powerlessness and unfreedom are less
and less confined by the borders of the nation-state but transcend them in
various ways and forms. Food structures, energy structures, health structures, finance structures, security structures, and others are all rapidly expanding to the global level. If human deprivations are the symptoms of structural powerlessness, however, then the practical focus of human development
must be the powerful particular interests that dominate and distort those
structures. The flip side of powerlessness and dependency of some is control
and domination by others. Thus a key insight about human development is
that it must aim at the transformation of global structures with the intent of
realizing people's rights instead of serving the particular interests of their
dominant participants.

Human-rights-based approaches to development have certainly gained
popularity in recent years, but they are still facing enormous challenges to
becoming mainstream (Alston and Robinson 2005, 3). One of the first and
foremost tasks in this regard is to develop a clearer perspective on duties and
duty bearers. Principles alone will not suffice; without the definition of corresponding obligations and agents who are able and willing to meet them, there
will be no real progress. It is precisely this aspect that reveals the true benefits
of talking about development from a justice perspective. It enables us not only
to establish human development as an ethical imperative but also to specify
corresponding moral obligations and obligation bearers. Thus it enables us to
move from mere promises to assigning tasks and responsibilities.

This section has shown that obligations of rights-based development are
essentially to be understood as obligations of justice and that a conception of

(global) justice based on human rights is not only ethically sound but also pragmatically accessible; it is, as Wildt (1998, 124) aptly stated, principled and pragmatic, utopian and anti-utopian at the same time. It is this dual nature of the concept of rights-based justice that creates its extraordinary richness and also—as we will see shortly—its fruitfulness for the derivation of moral obligations, not least for business.

Chapter 3

Obligations of Global Justice

A FTER OUTLINING THE PRINCIPLES of rights-based cosmopolitan justice in the previous chapter, the logical next step is to have a closer look at the moral obligations deriving from them. Any account of justice remains incomplete without an adequate discussion of obligations.

Debating obligations of justice means designating responsible subjects. It means sorting out specific actors and pinning down their particular duties—arguably a task that does not enjoy much popularity. This might explain why most authors in the field of global distributive justice have avoided it so far. However, the lack of attention paid to obligations is not specific to the discussion of global justice but characterizes the justice debate in general. The prominent role that the concept of justice plays in moral philosophy has marginalized the more specific focus on injustice, as Judith Shklar (1990, 15; see also Scanlon 1998) comments. It is simply taken for granted that injustice denotes the absence of justice and that once we know what is just, there is no need for any further investigation in this matter. However, this is far from correct; precisely the question of obligations tends to get overlooked when ethical reflection is limited merely to the question of what is to be considered just. After all, obligations of justice catch our attention first of all in situations where the requirements of justice are not met.

This chapter aims at filling this striking gap in the global justice debate. My earlier elaborations on the moral significance of political boundaries provided some first insights and implications regarding obligations of justice (see the section "The Nationalist Objection: The Ethical Significance of Boundaries and Citizenship" in chapter 2). The following paragraphs will complement them and provide a more complete and holistic conceptual framework for their derivation. The conceptual elaborations on obligations and obligation bearers in this and the next chapter should not be interpreted as mere additions to the earlier "theory" of justice but as an integral and constitutive part of it.

Responsibility and the Scope of Justice

One could wonder whether the identification of social injustices on the basis of the abstract principles outlined earlier is of any practical value or if it is a purely philosophical exercise. In other words, what difference does the mere acknowledgment of injustice make for those who suffer from it? The cynical undertone in this question is well intended. Evidently, any statement regarding the injustice of an action, a situation, or a state of affairs constitutes a strong moral judgment. Accordingly, the identification of injustice always and inevitably contains a moral claim for transformation, given that the situation is changeable in principle. In other words, a justified moral claim of one human being is always matched by a corresponding obligation of others. It is impossible to talk about injustice without making an implicit claim about moral obligations at the same time; moral judgments and thus statements of justice are always prescriptive and never just declaratory (Gosepath 2004, 34, 57).

If statements of justice are inevitably prescriptive, however, the concept of justice itself makes sense only in connection with moral agents who are capable of acting upon the principles it outlines. This condition effectively sets the scope of justice; the concept of justice, in other words, is constitutively dependent on the ascription of responsibility. Thus social conditions can be subject to considerations of justice if and only if they are the consequence of actions or omissions by free and responsible adult human beings. Social states and situations that were neither brought about nor could have been changed or prevented by human action cannot be subject to judgments of justice. Without responsibility, there is no injustice.

Responsibility is connected to the free and willful actions and thus to the morality of reasonable human beings. To take responsibility for freely chosen actions means to be able to justify them with good reasons. However, we can only be held responsible for specific actions if there were reasonable alternatives we could have chosen instead. To choose an action freely means to make informed decisions between existing alternatives (Gosepath 2004, 54f.). If there are no alternatives to choose from, there can be no autonomous action and thus no basis for ascribing responsibility. The concept of justice, in other words, ultimately operates in the realm of freely chosen and accountable human action.

Thus denouncing the bad weather during our vacation as an injustice might sound like a valid statement in a colloquial sense, but it is nevertheless conceptually wrong. There is nobody, not even the weatherperson, who can reasonably be held responsible for the weather. The notion of "natural injustice" is a conceptual illusion (Gosepath 2004, 55); without the ascription of responsibility, the reference to the concept of justice is meaningless. A natural disaster on its own can neither be just nor unjust. What can be subject to considerations of justice, however, are the consequences of natural disasters, namely, in cases where they could have been prevented or at least reduced by adequate precautionary and responsive measures by human beings. Famines, for example, are often triggered by droughts, but their magnitude and distribution are largely determined by the reactions of those affected, that is, by those who hoard grain, those who try to make a profit off the desperation of others, or those who rush to the help of those in need (O'Neill 1986, 16). In these and similar cases human beings can bear a secondary responsibility insofar as they can be or could have been able to prevent or reduce their effects (Gosepath 2004, 56f.). A famine, like many other "natural" events, is always a politically avoidable disaster, and when nothing is done to end it, we are dealing with injustice (Shklar 1990, 70).

The scope of justice can be restated in terms of the justifiability of changeable states of affairs (Gosepath 2004, 56). States of affairs are changeable if feasible alternatives are available. Changeability means choice, and choice, as we have seen, implies responsibility. Hence any assessment of states of affairs from the perspective of justice must necessarily start with the question whether there are feasible alternatives to the current state (Pogge 2004, 275).[1] This connection also holds in the reverse direction: any social and societal state that is changeable through human action must principally be subject to justification against the requirements of justice.

Hence for an institutional order to be unjust, its failure to prevent human misery and extreme social inequalities must be "reasonably avoidable through some feasible institutional alternative" (Pogge 2002a, 88). Wherever this condition is met, our reference to the injustice of an institutional setting inevitably contains a normative claim for its transformation. The interplay between human responsibility and injustice inevitably gives rise to moral obligations.

The Mirage of Social Justice?

The insight into human responsibility as a necessary condition for the concept of justice led libertarians fundamentally to question the appropriateness of assessing the global market from a justice perspective. Their argument derives from the deep-seated belief in a naturally evolving free market that keeps our political maneuverability in check rather than being itself subjected to it. The market, in their view, is a spontaneous order that lies beyond human control. This perception implies not only that we are systematically unable to alter its structure according to the principles of justice, but much more fundamentally that the categories of justice do not even apply to the market in the first place, because the condition of human responsibility is not met for a spontaneously evolving process.

This argument was stated most powerfully in Friedrich August von Hayek's book *The Mirage of Social Justice* (1976). Hayek was not blind to the potentially problematic distributional effects of the market mechanism. However, in his opinion, these effects elude the responsibility of any human being: "The manner in which the benefits and burdens are apportioned by the market mechanism would in many instances have to be regarded as very unjust *if* it were the result of a deliberate allocation to particular people" (Hayek 1976, 64).

The superior coordinating capacity of the market mechanism, as perceived by Hayek, is not determined by deliberate acts of will (Hayek 1976, 62). The spontaneous order is the result of the interaction of countless individuals, none of them with the power to direct the process in a specific direction and to produce particular results for specific persons. Thus the state of affairs resulting from the spontaneous process is beyond human intention and as a consequence, cannot be guided by moral rules (Hayek 1976, 33). The notion of "social justice," Hayek (1976, xi) concluded logically, is "empty and meaningless" in connection with the market. According to Hayek (1976, 63ff.), it is a "sign of the immaturity of our minds" that we still demand from an impersonal and self-ordering process that it conform to "moral precepts men have evolved for the guidance of their individual actions." Thus Hayek's notion of the market mechanism is comparable to the weather; it is a process that can neither be directed nor changed by human beings. It can be judged good or bad, but to demand justice of a process that is beyond our control, in Hayek's opinion, "is clearly absurd."

From a conceptual point of view, Hayek's argument is certainly consistent—without human responsibility, there is indeed no justice—but it lacks a great deal of realistic judgment about the nature of the global market. His market-metaphysical stance is anachronistic (if not backward) and conflicts with a modern, enlightened way of thinking. The perception that our uncompromising surrender to unfettered global capitalism is our only hope and choice for coping with globalization derives from ideology rather than from an informed and balanced assessment of reality. In his tremendously important work *The Great Transformation* (2001) Karl Polanyi rightly claimed that the construct of a naturally evolving free-market society is a stark utopia. The self-regulating capacity of the market mechanism, which Hayek and his fellow neoclassical economists praise as the epitome of desirable social coordination, is, Polanyi argued, nothing but a myth.

There is no doubt that global markets do exert considerable pressure on individuals, companies, and even governments. However, these coercive forces are anything but impersonal. They result from the ambitions and intentions of those subjects that relentlessly strive for the improvement of their financial return and competitiveness. Those who choose to do what it takes to succeed in the competitive system effectively force everybody else to do the same in order not to be eliminated (Ulrich 2008, 131f.). The most powerful market participants effectively set the bar and thus the level of pressure for those who are merely trying to get by; the so-called necessities of the market are inherently partial toward the powerful interests of its successful participants (Thielemann 2004b, 22ff.). Against this background, these "necessities" turn out to be anything but absolute and unchangeable; they are not natural forces that unfold beyond our human control, but exist only insofar as they are tolerated or even wanted within a particular economic and societal order. Hence to argue that the market mechanism systematically leaves no room for considerations of justice means to refrain from critical reflection on existing empirical conditions instead of subjecting them to normative-ethical justification (Ulrich 2008, 130f.).

The political transformation of a highly interconnected global economy lies beyond the autonomous capacity of any one nation-state, but there is no reason that this should not be feasible in a collective effort. The global economic order is chosen by human beings and can be changed by human beings. Globalization is not a predetermined path of history. It must not be thought of in the singular but in the plural: different globalizations are feasible (Cavanagh and Mander 2004; Rodrik 2002). Therefore, demanding its inclusion in the scope of justice is neither impossible nor absurd but an ethical imperative. Globalization has the potential to be a force of destruction or one of improvement; which path it will take is not determined in the stars but depends on the kind of global economic system we build (Thurow 2003, 24).

It is one of the distinct features—and perhaps paradoxes—of late 20th-century globalization that it dramatically compromised the scope of autonomous action of nation-states while simultaneously enhancing in unprecedented ways our possibilities for collective action at a transnational level. Precisely these new possibilities for transnational cooperation provide us with the capacity and the prospect of actually achieving global justice for the first time in history. What traditional societies could not even dream of, Thomas Pogge (2001a, 14) remarks, would be quite feasible today: "to wipe out hunger and preventable diseases worldwide without real inconvenience to anyone." Our persistent failure to do so is not a matter of lacking capacities but one of lacking political will.

This perceived lack of political will, however, raises questions about Pogge's assessment that global justice is achievable without inconveniencing the lives of those who currently enjoy the fruits of economic globalization. If there really were no inconvenience, would there not be more political support for global justice? If there were indeed nothing to lose for anybody, why does its practical realization cause so much resistance in the developed world? Pogge is certainly right in asserting that the redistribution of a small fraction of our economic resources can make a tremendous difference to the lives of hundreds of millions at little cost to ourselves (Pogge 2001a, 14). However, although such redistributional measures are certainly necessary, they do not suffice for the lasting eradication of global poverty and hunger. Achieving global justice must go beyond the easing of symptoms through the mere transfer of material goods and resources to the poor. To really make a difference, we must ensure their full participation in the global economy and in the collaborative design of global political processes. This, however, will require a fundamental shift of the current global economic order in favor of the world's poor.

To be sure, Pogge himself denounces the unmodified continuation of our current global economic structures and policies as a moral failure (Pogge 2001a, 15), and he is one of the most outspoken champions of global institutional change. However, it is hard to see how such profound transformations of the global economic order can be achieved without anybody having to sacrifice anything. If global economic structures are genuinely to serve the global poor, achieving this goal will require incomparably bigger sacrifices from industrialized countries than the mere transfer of financial resources for the fulfillment of the most urgent basic needs in the Third World. This is not to say that those sacrifices would be any less justified; justice is not a venture for mutual advantage but the striving for equality through human development. The difference between *ought* and *is* in this regard has never been larger than today. Working toward a more just and equitable world is a matter of political will. Hiding behind the factual forces of the global market in order to immunize ourselves against the normative claim of justice is not only pragmatically cowardly but also "intellectually dishonest" (Touraine 2001, 21) toward those who are put at a disadvantage by the very global economic system that we built, help maintain, and could change.

Justice or Virtue: Morally Owed or Merely Desired?

For Aristotle, justice as an abstract and general concept of universal scope refers to the entirety of righteous actions, mutual claims, and obligations of human beings. In his view, justice is the perfect and most complete virtue; it is the only virtue of our human character not directed solely toward ourselves but toward our fellow human beings. Accordingly, he assigns the noblest character to those who do not use their virtues for their own benefit but for the benefit of others. Hence, unlike other, self-recurrent virtues, justice can be claimed by others.

From the standpoint of modern humanistic ethics, the claimability of obligations of justice derives from the inherent reciprocity of justified moral claims, which is based on the fundamental equality of human beings. Thus genuine social justice deals with the most acute endangerments to a decent and dignified human existence. This can reach from questions concerning joblessness and issues connected to knowledge and education to the existential threats posed by poverty and hunger (Höffe 2004a, 56). Because of their reference to the foundations of humanity, obligations of justice enjoy the highest binding power; they trump all other moral considerations of less importance. In other words, they are to be considered morally owed (Höffe 2003, 155; 2004a, 55; Gosepath 2004, 73).

Hence we must distinguish between obligations of justice and virtue-based requirements such as benevolence, charity, compassion, or the intermediary concept of solidarity (Höffe 2004a, 55). This does not mean that we do not bear a general duty for such kinds of moral actions as well. Onora O'Neill (1996, 138) pointed out that virtues can also be "judged, praised and criticized" in the light of ethical (that is, universal) principles. Hence they too can be of universal scope and are not constituted by and bound to particular historical and moral traditions. Both justice and virtue, she claims, can be identified independently of any historically specific embodiments. There are at least certain virtues—O'Neill calls them "required virtues"—that can be considered genuine moral requirements; others, however, might remain merely optional.

This, I argue, leaves us with three broad categories of moral requirements. First, and from the moral point of view most important, there are obligations of justice, which can be claimed and are thus morally owed. The failure to meet such obligations is connected to moral blame and condemnation. The second category consists of required virtues. Required virtues can be defined as those virtuous actions that we may reasonably expect from others but that are not obligatory. Hence we can neither claim them nor blame anyone for not fulfilling them. However, because we may expect them from others, their actual fulfillment is not specifically praiseworthy either. Thus actions deriving from required virtues are the ones we ought to but not necessarily must do (see Zimmermann 1996, 3, on this distinction). The third category contains optional virtues that are neither required nor expected. One cannot be blamed for not acting upon such virtues but will earn admiration and praise for doing so. Thus they give rise to supererogatory action that lies beyond the call of duty. Actions that do not fall into any of these categories could be designated as what Kant called "morally indifferent" acts. He defines them as "neither commanded nor forbidden" but merely "permitted" (Kant 1996, 16).[2]

Thus the key difference between the first and the second category is that required virtues can be requested by others, but they cannot be claimed like obligations of justice. Even though they are required, they are not morally owed. We cannot, for example, claim the same amount of compassion from others that we might feel is adequate for ourselves, because they do not owe their benevolence to us. However, we can surely claim the same unconditional respect for our fundamental rights that we owe to others. Thus the decisive difference between obligations of justice and required virtues is that the latter lack counterpart rights (O'Neill 1996, 139). In other words, it is the moral rights of people that constitute morally owed obligations; required virtues, on the other hand, correspond to mere wishes or needs (Kant 1996, 24). Or, as John Stuart Mill argued eloquently, obligations of justice are essentially rights-based obligations:

> It seems to me that this feature in the case—a right in some person, correlative to the moral obligation—constitutes the specific difference between justice and generosity of beneficence. Justice implies something which it is not only right to do, and wrong not to do, but which some individual person can claim from us as his moral right. No one has a moral right to our generosity or beneficence because we are not morally bound to practice those virtues toward any given individual. (Mill 2001, 50)

This does not mean that we do not have a general moral obligation to be generous, beneficent, or charitable. Kant (1996, 201ff.) clearly stated that human beings do have a duty to be beneficent. However, unlike obligations of justice, these requirements are highly unspecific. "Though the act is obligatory," Mill (2001, 49) specifies, "the particular occasions of performing it are left to our choice." We are indeed bound to practice charity and beneficence, he continues, but not toward any specific individual and not at any definite time. For Mill (2001, 50), the difference between justice and beneficence is that justice creates concrete obligations toward individuals, while beneficence can be stated only as a general obligation toward mankind as a whole.

Thus obligations of justice are not a matter of convenience or even opportunity that can be met or not, as the case may be. Neither are they merely required, let alone entirely voluntary. They are morally owed and therefore unconditionally binding and mandatory. This is a far-reaching insight, especially concerning the moral obligations of multinational corporations; the fallacy to limit corporate obligations to mere philanthropy and to interpret them in terms of optional virtues still looms large in the contemporary debate on corporate social responsibility. Defining the responsibilities of multinational corporations from the standpoint of justice, however, will challenge this perception fundamentally.

Perfect and Imperfect Obligations of Justice

All moral rights of individuals constitute corresponding obligations for others. This insight is a logical consequence of the combination of the prescriptive character and the rights-based foundation of justice. Because justice is inherently prescriptive, it inevitably and inseparably connects rights to obligations.

Thus the language of rights is congruent with the language of justice and thus corresponds to the language of obligations. In other words, if we talk about rights, we must necessarily also talk about obligations: "Any single-minded focus on human rights, and not on duties, is like reading one side of an insurance contract, overlooking the small print on the reverse" (Galtung 1994, 9). This relation does not necessarily hold in the reverse direction. Every right leads to corresponding obligations, but not all moral obligations derive from rights. As seen earlier, there might well be moral requirements in the form of virtues that are not morally owed but are nevertheless required.

Perfect and Imperfect Obligations: A First Approximation

The particular obligations corresponding to given rights are not always easy to discover, define, and allocate. Even though the rights of people might be violated quite evidently in certain cases—for example, poverty-related deprivations—it can be highly unclear who bears what obligations for improvement of the situation. This ambiguity is captured in the distinction between perfect and imperfect moral obligations, which is generally attributed to Kant (see, e.g., 1996, 176ff.; 1997, 31) but can, in slightly different form and terminology, be found already in Grotius's work (Grotius 1925, 330f.).[3]

A moral obligation is to be considered perfect if all three constitutive elements, that is, the rights at stake, the corresponding obligations deriving from them, and the respective obligation bearers, are clearly identifiable. Thus "perfect" in this sense can be understood as complete. Imperfect obligations, on the other hand, are incomplete insofar as only the rights at stake are clearly identifiable, while the corresponding obligations, as well as the potential obligation bearers, remain unspecified and contingent.

Perfect obligations are, with the exception of certain special duties that derive from specific acts, events, or relationships (see, e.g., Fishkin 1982, 25ff.; H. L. A. Hart 1984, 84ff.; Shue 1988, 688ff.), commonly associated with negative or passive duties, that is, with duties to abstain from doing harm to others. Thus they are based on the causal connection between certain specific actions and a resulting violation of others' moral rights. Because this causal effect is independent of any specific traits of the person who commits the act (the same action leads to the same result for anybody), the obligations deriving from it are universal and uniform in their reach; that is, they are owed by each to all, to the same extent, and at all times without exception. The universal right of an individual not to be killed, for example, leads to a similarly universal obligation for everyone else not to kill. Hence it applies to everyone to the same extent and at all times. Perfect obligations, from this perspective, are context independent.

Imperfect obligations, on the other hand, are most commonly interpreted as positive. They do not merely demand nonviolation but require proactive, positive action toward the protection and realization of certain rights of others. In this aspect, as we will see shortly, the definition of imperfect duties in this book differs decisively from a strictly Kantian interpretation. Kant defined imperfect duties precisely through the absence of any corresponding rights. The claim put forth here, however, is that imperfect obligations also derive from rights—typically from so-called socioeconomic subsistence or welfare rights. Earlier elaborations have shown that such rights indeed exist as universal human rights. However, it is often unclear what duties they generate and for whom. Thus, despite the universality of the corresponding right, imperfect duties are nonuniversal. They are directed to an undefined number of unidentified potential duty bearers. They are collective duties insofar as they demand "a division of moral labor" (Shue 1988, 689f.), that is, concerted and coordinated actions of a variety of agents, each obliged to fulfill different tasks in order to reach a consistent solution to the problem as a whole. The reach of imperfect obligations is limited and highly specific: not everyone is obliged to act, and potential obligations vary in their degree and content.

Perfect and Imperfect Obligations: A Mirror of Negative and Positive Rights?

Perfect duties are often claimed to derive from negative liberty rights, while imperfect obligations are commonly connected to positive rights, that is, rights whose realization demands not merely nonviolation but the performance of positive action. Although this classification of perfect as negative and imperfect as positive duties holds in most cases, their attribution to the allegedly corresponding negative and positive rights is often not clear-cut. In fact, not even the distinction between positive and negative rights is as evident as it might seem (see, e.g., Holmes and Sunstein 1999, 43). The fulfillment of many allegedly negative rights, for example, often not only depends on people abstaining from doing harm but additionally requires the creation and maintenance of favorable institutional structures and arrangements for their implementation and enforcement. The right not to be tortured not only includes a universal passive and therefore perfect obligation for everyone to refrain from torturing but demands active political measures to set up corresponding institutional structures, for example, for the protection of individuals or the prosecution of violators. The protection of a right to physical security, as Shue (1980, 38) also argues convincingly, is not merely a right to be left alone but a "demand to be protected against harm" and thus a requirement for "social guarantees against at least the standard threats." Therefore, it depends on a plethora of conditions that need to be in place, such as functioning police, criminal courts, and lawyers, as well as the taxes necessary to make a system for the prevention, detection, and punishment of violations possible (Shue 1980, 37).[4] Furthermore, the prevention of direct injury is as much a matter of proactively reducing vulnerabilities of people by securing tolerable levels of subsistence as it is one of direct protection and enforcement through curbing the power of potential perpetrators (O'Neill 1996, 169). Nonetheless, if each and every person, without exception, actually did fulfill his perfect duty to refrain from harmful actions, protection and enforcement would evidently be unnecessary. Hence, at least in an ideal world, rights of exclusively negative character are theoretically thinkable. In the less-than-perfect world we live in, however, it seems that most of the so-called negative rights correspond to both negative and positive duties.

Similarly, positive rights can be interpreted in negative terms. Therefore, they generate not only active but also passive duties. For example, issues like poverty and starvation that are normally connected to positive socioeconomic rights give rise to the genuinely negative duty not to participate in unfair social practices or to impose unjust institutional schemes upon others (Pogge 1992, 52; 1998, 383; 2002a, 70; 2002b, 88). After all, one evident duty arising from basic subsistence rights of people is the obligation not to take actions that deprive others of means that would otherwise have enabled them to satisfy their rights (Shue 1980, 55).

The important and useful distinction is thus not so much the one between positive and negative rights but merely between looking at rights in general from positive and negative angles. There is not only one correlative positive or negative duty for each and every right, but in fact a mix of positive and negative ones. In most cases the protection of negative rights demands positive measures, while the realization of positive rights presupposes certain negative abdications. On the basis of Henry Shue's (1980, 52) work, it makes sense to distinguish three basic kinds of obligations that correlate with each and every basic right, irrespective of whether we commonly regard it as positive or negative: (1) duties to avoid depriving, (2) duties to protect from deprivation, and (3) duties to aid the deprived. It is precisely the lack of acknowledgment of the multiplicity of types of duties correlating with each right that often leads to shortcomings or even fundamental contradictions in their full realization. It is, for example, highly contradictory to opt for extensive transfers of resources and physical goods to the poor while at the same time maintaining an institutional order that reproduces economic deprivations at the same rate and on a global scale. The effective realization of any right requires the fulfillment of all three types of obligations. Shue's balanced typology is perhaps the most thoroughly elaborated and convincing systematization of moral obligations in human rights literature. Therefore, it seems appropriate to make use of it as a basis for my assessment of multinational corporations' duties of justice in part III of this book.

Imperfect Obligations as Duties of Justice

The question of where and how exactly to draw the line between perfect and imperfect obligations is not as uncontested as my elaborations so far might have implied.[5] In fact, differing opinions on this question have their roots in fundamental disagreements in moral philosophy. John Stuart Mill, for example, provides a quite different, at its core Kantian, account of what he considers these "ill-chosen expressions": "Duties of perfect obligation are those duties in virtue of which a correlative right resides in some person or persons; duties of imperfect obligation are those moral obligations which do not give birth to any right" (Mill 2001, 49f.). He believes that the line between perfect and imperfect duties coincides precisely with the line we draw between justice and "other obligations of morality" (Mill 2001, 50). For Mill, only perfect obligations are genuine obligations of justice, while imperfect obligations derive from what I earlier called required virtues.

Not surprisingly, this is also how contemporary Kantian philosopher Onora O'Neill (1996, 139, 147f.) defines imperfect obligations. In fact, her account of imperfect obligations is the precise opposite of the one presented in this book. In her opinion, imperfect obligations are not undefined duties deriving from certain existing moral rights but well-defined obligations that lack counterpart rights. Therefore, they are not claimable by each but not from all but instead are enactable by each but not for all. Hence they require action by each, but it is unclear for whom or to whom that action is to be directed. In agreement with Mill (and Kant), she concludes that such imperfect obligations are embodied not in the relationships between agents and recipients but in agents' characters. Therefore, they must be thought of as required virtues of those agents.

Thus Kant, Mill, and O'Neill remove all cases of imperfect obligation from the realm of justice. This, however, is utterly problematic. I do not deny the existence of moral requirements outside the realm of justice. But by limiting the realm of justice to perfect obligations and defining the realm outside justice as moral requirements without counterpart rights, they evidently erase one crucial constellation from the spectrum of moral obligation: the case in which people do have universal moral rights that, however, lead to nonuniversal and highly contingent obligations, as is characteristic of most socioeconomic rights.

Kantian scholars tend to define imperfect duties as virtue-based requirements that are directed at the good instead of at the rights of other people (e.g., Herman 2002, 229). Hence they perceive imperfect obligations as being aimed at the promotion of "obligatory ends," for example, other people's happiness. What they do not sufficiently take into consideration, however, is that rights can be perceived as ends too (see the section "Rights as Goals: Human Development as the Realization of Rights" in chapter 2). Thus they fail to provide an adequate answer to those cases in which rights themselves must be viewed as goals. Clearly, the fulfillment of such rights cannot be entirely a matter of virtue. The claims at stake are, after all, based on moral rights. However, the obligations deriving from them are not perfect either, because it is unclear who must deliver what for the realization of those rights. Hence they must be considered imperfect obligations of justice. It is important to note that even Kant himself, it seems, was aware of this evident problem when he raised the following question:

> Having the resources to practice such beneficence as depends on the goods of fortune is, for the most part, a result of certain human beings being favored through the injustice of the government, which introduces an inequality of wealth that makes others need their beneficence. Under such circumstances, does a rich man's help to the needy, on which he so readily prides himself as something meritorious, really deserve to be called beneficence at all? (Kant 1996, 203)

Neo-Kantian scholar Barbara Herman (2002, 256) appears not to be free of doubts either. She concludes that where we are indeed dealing with injustices, an account of moral duty based on beneficence might provide "more of an ideal than a sufficient guide to what we are obligated to do now for need we could meet." True moral progress toward a more equitable world presupposes that we overcome this crucial inconsistency in Kantian moral philosophy. For Amartya Sen (2004a, 319), whose position on this question is congruent with the one taken in this book, "imperfect obligations are correlative with human rights in much the same way as perfect obligations are." Therefore, he concludes that "the acceptance of imperfect obligations goes beyond volunteered charity or elective virtues."

Thus imperfect obligations derive from rights too; they are no less morally owed than perfect obligations. The only thing that distinguishes them from perfect obligations is that it is unclear who can legitimately be charged with them and to what extent. Once that question has been determined within a comprehensive public discourse, however, those singled out as (partly) responsible bear genuine duties of justice. Only those actions that exceed the extent of these duties, as a result, belong to the category of virtuous action.

O'Neill (1996, 129ff.) has a seemingly easy solution to this evident problem: she simply eliminates the rights underlying imperfect obligations altogether. Her argument is that as long as these rights are not institutionalized, that is, as long as the corresponding obligations are not specified, properly assigned, and thus turned into perfect duties, they simply do not exist. A right, O'Neill argues, exists only if it is effectively claimable; and it is claimable "only if a system of assigning agents to recipients has already been established, by which the counterpart obligations are 'distributed.'" Hence unless duty bearers and their corresponding obligations are clearly identifiable and specified, "claims to have rights amount only to rhetoric."

Susan James (2005, 79ff.) takes a similar position. She argues that rights in their very existence as practical entitlements depend on correlative obligations. In her opinion, "a right cannot be claimed, and therefore does not exist, when we are unable to find anyone on whom to pin the correlative obligations." In fact, James goes a step further than O'Neill in arguing that not only claimability but also the practical ease with which a right can be claimed, that is, its enforceability, are necessary conditions for a right effectively to exist. Moral claims (and thus the rights themselves), in her opinion, come into existence only if the conditions to enforce them are effectively in place. Otherwise they remain mere moral judgments. Consequently, for such situations she proposes simply to replace the vocabulary of rights with alternative notions such as "beliefs" or "wishes."

Expressing rights claims in terms of beliefs, wishes, or priorities, however, means to give up the normative power of justice. Priorities, wishes, and beliefs can be changed at any time and without major demand for justification; they do not obligate anyone to do anything. Stating priorities means to put things on a to-do list—things that should get done. Stating rights and obligations, on the other hand, means that things must get done. By reducing "statements about unenforceable moral rights" to mere "statements about the moral beliefs of those who make them," James (2005, 83) provides the rhetoric for powerful actors to challenge and disregard the very foundation of humanity according to their particular interests.

A position that makes the very existence of rights dependent on their enforceability inevitably opens the door for even more radical conclusions. The insight that the realization and enforcement of both positive and negative rights depends on extensive institutional structures might lead us to conclude that it will not be possible ever to guarantee the full protection even of basic liberty rights. From there, however, it is only a small step to Raymond Geuss's (2001) conclusion that the existence of any rights must be questioned. Even though Geuss's argument is consistent in itself, his conclusion is nonetheless deeply flawed. It pushes us into a relativist position where rights become entirely meaningless. Geuss's perception that a person is systematically unable to possess a right if the obligations on which it depends cannot be enforced turns the justified moral claims of hundreds of millions of people in the developing world into an arbitrary function of the will of the world's wealthy and powerful. Earlier I argued that ending hunger and poverty and thus the realization of the rights of the world's poor are not matters of lacking capacity but of lacking political will. Political will, however, is itself a crucial part of enforceability. Thus making the existence of rights dependent on enforceability turns them into a function of the political will of those who effectively control the global political structures.

The argument that a right's existence depends on the clear identification of the corresponding obligation bearers or even on its practical enforceability is inherently flawed. It inevitably comes down to giving up the claim for global justice and human equality as a guiding ideal. Unfortunately, a vast number of human beings are still unable effectively to place their rights claims with clearly identifiable institutional obligation bearers. But does the lack of such institutional frameworks really mean that all those people do not even have any rights? O'Neill (1996, 133) is correct in her assertion that proclaiming universal rights without paying attention to the justification and establishment of institutions that identify corresponding duty bearers is "bitter mockery to the poor and needy, for whom these rights matter most." But why, one could ask, would anybody feel obligated to set up these necessary institutions in the first place if there are no rights that establish a claim to do so? If, for example, as Susan James (2005, 80) suggests, "one only has a right to health care if there are nurses, doctors, midwives, and so on, who are obliged to provide treatment or advice," how then could anybody feel obliged to put those necessary structures in place if there are not rights that are violated in the first place? "To deny the ethical status of these claims," Amartya Sen (2004a, 347) points out, "would be to ignore the reasoning that motivates these constructive activities." Onora O'Neill (1986, xiii) herself once claimed that the hope for change will remain an illusion if those who have the power to make a difference to the lives of the poor see no reason to do so.

Hence if the "obligations from which rights flow" really "only emerge within elaborate and interlocking sets of institutions" (James 2005, 87), and if O'Neill's (1996, 190f.) argument held true that positive rights are created by the institutions that allocate responsibilities, then the industrialized world could avoid being held responsible for any human misery in other parts of the planet simply by refraining from setting up effective global institutions. Global justice not only in its realization but as a very concept would be reduced to the industrialized nations' whim in such a scenario.

Rights derive from our inherent and undeniable human equality. Therefore, they exist before obligations. It is the very idea and aim of rights to remind us "that people have justified and urgent claims to certain types of urgent treatment no matter what the world around them has done about that" (Nussbaum 2002, 138). Joel Feinberg (1973; 1980, 153) coined the notions of "claim-rights" and "manifesto rights" in this connection. Although for claim-rights the counterpart obligation bearers are clearly identifiable, this is not the case for manifesto rights. Thus manifesto rights imply a manifesto for political change, a "protest," as Judith Shklar (1986, 27) described it forcefully. They represent "the appeals of the injured and outraged to their all too indifferent fellow citizens or even to humanity in general" (Shklar 1986, 25). This, however, as Donnelly (2003, 12) also insists, does not "make them any less truly rights." It is Feinberg (1980, 153) himself who commits the fallacy of interpreting manifesto rights as mere demands or "permanent possibilities" for rights. This, however, as Pogge (2002a, 67) points out correctly, "would belittle moral rights in just those cases where it is most urgent to assert them."

Poverty, starvation, suffering from easily preventable diseases, lacking access to clean water, and similar ills are violations of the most fundamental rights of millions of people and are thus a matter of justice, no matter what. Hence they constitute an unconditional and universal claim for improvement. Specifying the content and addressees of this claim can indeed be difficult and controversial, but this neither negates its ethical status as a matter of justice nor is a sign of weakness of its underlying principles.

In today's globally interwoven society, perfect duties per se are becoming rare. The specification of duties of justice is entirely evident only in very few cases. Hence to tie the concept of justice to the evident, that is, to perfect obligations, increasingly means to give up the concept of justice altogether. However, this cannot by any means be the right approach to cope with the profound societal transformations of our time. The right answer is to accept the fact that in a modern and open society the specification and implementation of moral obligations in the concrete context remains a matter of public deliberation (Nickel 1987, 32). What is not a matter of deliberation, however, is the moral claim itself. The improvement of their situation is owed to the people whose rights are violated irrespective of whether the duty bearers are known. Thus when Kersting (2000, 395) and O'Neill, for example, define duties of justice by their context independence, they are on the wrong track; it is not the duties of justice that are context independent, but—precisely the other way around—the moral claim of the right holders.

A world in which we recognize, for example, the moral right to health care only for those who effectively have the capabilities to realize it, that is, for those who have access to nurses, doctors, and midwives, is a world in which we have accepted the existing, deep inequalities and have given up the ideal of justice and development. Susan James (2005, 79) objects that the "empty beneficence" of granting rights that have no prospect of practical fulfillment is "insulting" to the disadvantaged people in this world. Compared with this insult, however, the complete disapproval of their moral rights on the basis of the argument that if their rights cannot be realized—or more accurately if there is not political will to realize them—they are not even worthy of having them recognized seems a plain outrage. Finding the solution to the "troubling conclusion that the rights of the poor and needy may be useless to them in practice" (James 2005, 83) in the denial of their rights altogether is ethically unacceptable.

To be sure, constructive critiques aimed at rights-based accounts of justice for not paying sufficient attention to obligations in general (see, e.g., Glendon

1991; O'Neill 1996) are justified and important. However, they do not point to an inherent weakness of rights-based approaches themselves, but rather to a neglect of the scholars engaging with them. Any rights-based account of justice that does not pay due attention to obligations and obligation bearers is systematically incomplete. Taking obligations into account is not a mere add-on to a rights-based perspective but constitutive for it. If we talk about rights, we must simultaneously also talk about obligations. Rights and obligations are inherently and indissolubly connected through the concept of justice.

It is true that rights-based perspectives might not sufficiently capture moral obligations beyond the realm of justice. If rights are taken as a starting point of ethical reflection, as O'Neill (1996, 144f.) argues, such obligations are readily overlooked and can be taken into account only by "an awkward swerve of thought," which would not be necessary, she claims, had we started from the perspective of agency and duties at the outset and then distinguished obligations with rights from those without. However, perhaps we just have to accept this "awkward swerve" as the lesser evil than choosing between two alternatives, rights-based perspectives or duty-based perspectives, both of which on their own cannot cover the full spectrum of ethical reflection and inevitably leave some important questions and considerations unaddressed. After all, the strictly duty-based perspective of O'Neill is able to give adequate weight to virtues only by severely compromising the concept of justice and equality. If justice really is the highest societal goal and guiding principle, however, then the consequences of this alternative are immensely more damaging than the ones of a rights-based perspective. A perspective that takes obligations as prior to rights tends to address as virtues what clearly belong to the category of justice. Instead of stating human equality as the ideal and proceeding with identifying the duty bearers and duties required to achieve it, it prematurely settles for accepting existing ambiguities and the shortfalls in achieving justice that derive from them. Declaring imperfect obligations a matter of virtues brings the search for obligation bearers to an end because the very definition of virtues rules out the possibility to actually succeed with it.

A world in which rights-based claims are replaced by virtue-based requirements is a world ruled by dependency. The weapon of the poor against their untenable situation would not be their rightful claim for decent treatment and consideration but merely their hope for others' compassion and benevolence. Rather than thinking of themselves as inherently deserving and asserting their legitimate rights to a self-determined life, they would come to see themselves as owing great gratitude to those who help them so selflessly. Making use of a right, on the other hand, means to claim what is owed to them. It can be insisted upon without embarrassment or shame, and its fulfillment does not warrant gratitude. It is a key source of self-respect and an assertion of our status as autonomous individuals of equal dignity. The benevolence of others, no matter how genuine it is, cannot make up for these values once they are lost (Feinberg 1973, 59).

The only way out of the alleged trade-off between a consistent interpretation of rights-based justice and the consideration of the full range of moral requirements is to adopt a rights and duties perspective simultaneously. Such a dual argument admits the weaknesses of both approaches and draws from both stances to fill the gaps adequately. This is not an embarrassment for either of these approaches or for moral philosophy itself; rather, it is an acknowledgment of and a tribute to the richness of ethical reflection and an attempt to cope with its complexity adequately and undogmatically.

Shifting the Focus from Causality to Capability

In the previous section I held that human responsibility sets the scope of justice. On the basis of this insight, I designated those situations as relevant to the concept of justice in which injustices either were caused, could have been prevented, or could be changed by human beings. It is, of course, not a coincidence that these three constitutive situations correspond exactly to Shue's tripartite typology of duties, that is, to the duty to avoid depriving others, the duty to protect others from deprivation, and the duty to aid deprived others.

The three types of obligations can be allocated to two basic categories of reasons of justice. First, human beings have a direct obligation not to cause injustice through the direct violation of people's moral rights. This obligation constitutes the "primary reasons of justice" (Gosepath 2004, 56f.). Primary reasons refer to just actions of people and thus to Shue's duty to avoid depriving. People who do not follow primary reasons of justice are actively acting unjustly. In addition to such primary reasons, individuals also bear secondary reasons of justice, which refer to the obligation not to let injustice happen to others and similarly to help restore justice in cases where injustice has occurred. Thus secondary reasons refer to the justice of states of affairs. People who disregard secondary reasons of justice, that is, those who are able to alter the course of injustice or avert its effects, are acting "passively unjust[ly]" if they do nothing about it (Shklar 1990, 3, 6, 40ff., 56). In Shue's typology secondary reasons of justice correspond to the duties to protect others from deprivation and to aid deprived others.

On the basis of this distinction, the immediately evident criterion from which to derive obligations of justice is the causal connection between one's actions and potentially or effectively unjust outcomes. The focus on causality has played a paradigmatic role in shaping the way we think about obligations of justice and frames what we could call the commonsense view of these obligations. In fact, the very meaning of obligation in the realm of justice is often entirely reduced to questions of causality; the question of responsibility in a certain unjust situation is commonly answered simply by asking who caused the outcome. Thus we commonly hold that "agents are responsible for addressing acute deprivations when they have contributed, or are contributing to bringing them about." Christian Barry calls this the "contribution principle" (C. Barry 2005, 135).

The Capability Principle

The exclusive focus on causality that has characterized the common understanding of obligations of justice so far does not cover the full range of justice-relevant situations. It does include primary reasons of justice and those cases of secondary reasons for which we are able to unambiguously allocate the causes to certain specific actors. However, such causalities are not always clear-cut. Especially for such large societal problems as poverty, moral obligations are often imperfect, which means that it is often impossible to connect them causally to specific, clearly identifiable harmful actions or to particular agents. Today's global systems and structures establish a clear connection between the actions of Western countries and the persistence of poverty in the South,[6] but this general causal link is not specific enough to derive a clear-cut allocation of particular obligations to responsible agents. In order to make the contribution principle work for the alleviation of global poverty, we would have to specify the exact share of each specific actor's causal contribution to the problem. Because of the increasingly systemic character of such problems, however, this is an insurmountable challenge. Furthermore, even if we were able to allocate the shares of contribution correctly, the contribution principle does not provide a solution for situations in which the responsible agents turn out to be incapable of remedying the situation. Such constellations would inevitably lead to a moral vacuum in which nobody could be held responsible for the alleviation of existing deprivations or the prevention of future injustices. Thus in the kind of world we live in today, a purely causality-based approach to justice tends to lock in the status quo.

The challenge is to find a criterion for the comprehensive derivation and allocation of obligations for those increasingly common cases in which our information about the causal chains between actions and outcomes is incomplete. What is it, in other words, that connects one agent to a deprived other in a way that gives rise to remedial duties that other agents in general do not have (D. Miller 2005, 96)? Responsibility as a constitutive element of justice, as noted earlier, arises not only from what has been caused by human beings but also from what could be changed by them. The difference between misfortune and injustice, as Judith Shklar (1990, 2) argued, does not merely correspond to the one between human and nonhuman causes but "frequently involves our willingness and our capacity to act or not to act on behalf of the victims." Therefore, she argues further, we should focus less on the search for possible initiators and the immediate causes of disasters and direct our sense of injustice more toward those who fail to prevent them or to aid the victims (Shklar 1990, 56). In other words, (remedial) obligations of justice arise not merely from causality but also, and perhaps even more important, from capability.

This shift from causality to capability extends and makes specific a similar claim raised on several occasions by the late Iris Marion Young (see, e.g., 2003, 2004, 2008). Young argued that in cases of structural injustice we must increasingly replace our common backward-looking focus on blame and condemnation with a forward-looking focus on results. Young's "social connection model of responsibility," or what she calls a concept of "political responsibility" (as opposed to responsibility as liability), "depends on the actions of everyone who is in a position to contribute to those results" (Young 2003, 41). Young sees these challenges as shared responsibilities that require collaborative action. The obligation of each responsible subject, in Young's concept, grows along the parameters of connection, power, and privilege (Young 2003, 42f.; 2004, 385ff.). In other words, the more direct the connection, the greater the power, and the larger the benefit to an institution from particular injustices, the bigger is its responsibility. Young explicitly denotes such obligations as obligations of justice, even though there is no direct relation of responsibility between the obligation bearer and any specific individual whose rights are violated. Rather, and in her opinion more important, there is a direct relation between the obligation bearer and the structural process that leads to those violations (Young 2004, 372). In regard to the three constitutive parameters, Young's concept resembles the one put forth in this book: power and capability, as we will see shortly, are directly linked to each other, while connection, in the form of structural causality, also plays a role in the determination of the intensity of moral obligations in this book; the two elements, power and structural connection, will be merged in the concept of structural power (see the section "Sources of Corporate Power: From Relational to Structural Power" in chapter 6), which will be at the core of my elaborations on multinational corporations' obligations of global justice. Privilege, I would argue, is less of a criterion for obligations of justice in general than one that may give rise to the specific accusation of complicity in cases of human rights violations. Thus in this book it will play a role first of all when I discuss the issue of "beneficial complicity" (see the section "Avoiding Indirect Human Rights Violations: Corporate Complicity" in chapter 9). Young's concept of "political responsibility," in other words, is closely related to and a powerful support of the "capability principle" of responsibility put forth in this book.

In order to illustrate this shift from causality to capability, let us look at a modified and extended version of Peter Singer's (1972, 231f.) example of a drowning child. Person A is running into difficulties while swimming in a pond and is now in desperate need of immediate rescue. There is nobody who could come to her help at that time except nonswimmer B and professional swimmer C, who happen to watch the incident from the shore. Neither B nor C is causally responsible for A's situation. Nevertheless, the conclusion that neither of them must do anything about the situation causes a certain unease. It seems obvious that we cannot expect B to rescue A, because he would inevitably put his own life severely at risk and quite possibly drown himself. B would thus hardly be exposed to moral blame for not jumping into the water. If he tried to rescue A anyway and miraculously succeeded, we would quite possibly praise him for putting his life on the line in order to save someone else's. This is what we normally associate with heroic action. Thus it seems that because of his lack of capabilities, B does not have a moral obligation to rescue A. His actions belong to the supererogatory part of morals.

The situation is quite different for C, for whom rescuing A would be an easy task. Because C evidently has all the capabilities needed to rescue A but decides to stay inactive to avoid some minor inconvenience for herself, she would be exposed to moral blame for not coming to A's rescue. Furthermore, because we clearly expect her to help, we would not find it especially praiseworthy if she did indeed rescue A. Thus the superior capabilities of C imply a moral obligation to rescue A. Furthermore, because we tend to look at it as common sense that she must come to A's rescue, her obligation seems not to be based on mere beneficence. In the absence of causal relations, the criterion of capability establishes much stronger remedial obligations.

This example provides an opportunity to reemphasize the crucial difference between capacity and capability. As pointed out earlier, capability derives from the combination of personal capacities (e.g., talents) and adequate external circumstances and arrangements to put them to use favorably (see the section "Equalizing Freedom Through Basic Capabilities" in chapter 2). If nonswimmer B had a boat, he could compensate for his lack of ability to swim. Thus, despite his lack of capacity to swim, he would still have the capability and thus a responsibility to rescue A. Again, this example shows that moral obligation is attached to capability rather than to mere capacity.

However, let us assume that there is no boat. What would happen if it turned out that B actually pushed A into the pond? In this scenario, B can doubtless be identified as causally responsible for A's desperate situation. However, this does not change anything about B's inability to swim and to rescue A. Thus, despite his involvement in causing the situation, we cannot reasonably ask him to jump into the water at the risk of drowning as well. We can blame him for pushing A, but we can hardly blame him for not rescuing her. However, it is unlikely that we would still praise him as a hero if he rescued A anyway, because without him, A would not have gotten into this situation in the first place. Hence, despite his causal involvement, we cannot hold B responsible for remedying the situation, because he lacks the capabilities necessary to do so. For C, on the other hand, the situation does not change. She is still the only one effectively able to rescue A, and we would reasonably expect her to do so. Hence C's remedial obligation holds even against clearly identifiable causal relations that allocate blame to someone else. Only if B had equal abilities to swim would the primary remedial responsibility shift from C to B.

Remedial obligations are meaningless if those singled out as responsible agents do not have the capabilities to meet them. Nobody can be obliged to do something he or she is by any reasonable account unable to do: *ought* implies *can*. On the other hand, everybody who does have the capabilities needed has an immediate prima facie obligation to offer help. In this sense *can* implies *ought*. Thus capability turns out to be the default criterion for remedial obligations of justice. In both of these cases causality is neither a necessary nor a sufficient condition for establishing a remedial obligation. It merely serves as a criterion for determining the intensity of an established obligation. In other words, a claim against a certain capable agent naturally becomes stronger if he or she was initially involved in bringing the unjust situation about. Therefore, causality, as we will see, serves as a cutoff criterion for remedial obligations rather than as a normative condition for them. Capability, on the other hand, is a necessary and in some cases even a sufficient condition for such obligations. Thus it is a mistake to reserve the realm of justice for those cases in which causal chains are clearly identifiable and to look at obligations deriving from the capabilities of responsible subjects as a mere matter of (required) virtues. Justice is as much about the capabilities to prevent and alleviate misery as it is about not causing it.

Gradation and Cutoff Criteria: Power and Reasonableness

The claim that all agents with suitable capabilities automatically bear a "*prima facie* duty" (Ross 1930: 19ff.; see also Zimmermann 1996, 5ff.) to improve an unjust situation needs further clarification. Like the previously used expression "prima facie rights," obligations also remain merely prima facie until all possible objections and limitations—for example, the causal involvement of an agent with similar capabilities—have been considered. This is of special importance for the capability perspective because an exclusive and unrestricted reliance on valuable capabilities would lead to nearly unlimited remedial obligations for virtually everyone in regard to a limitless number of potential injustices, near and far.

For Peter Singer (1972, 231ff.), such an overly demanding view of moral obligations is not a problem. If one can prevent significant bad from happening without having to sacrifice anything of similar moral importance, he argues, one is morally obliged to do so. From this genuinely utilitarian perspective, one ought to keep giving until one reaches the level of marginal utility at which the suffering caused to oneself is greater than relief provided to others. It is not unreasonable to request that everyone make a fair contribution to the improvement of unjust conditions, even if they occur in other parts of the world. Everyone who is able to make a valuable contribution is, at least up to a certain point, obliged to do so, for otherwise he or she is acting passively unjustly. However, Singer's principle leads to unrealistic and overstraining requirements for any individual. Singer admits that by following his own principle, "one would reduce oneself to very near the material circumstances of a

Bengali refugee" (Singer 1972, 241). This, however, is not only unrealistic but on the verge of turning itself into injustice; it might, as James Fishkin (1982, 3) aptly states, lead us to a point where we are "obliged to be heroic."[7]

In order to avoid such outcomes, we need criteria that allow us to distinguish between stronger and weaker obligations on the basis of the gradation of respective capabilities. Additionally, we need to complement these criteria with principles that limit the respective obligations of any responsible agent to a reasonable level (C. Barry 2005, 137). In other words, we must provide principles that establish a "cutoff for levels of sacrifice" (Fishkin 1982, 16).

The example of the drowning child suggests that obligations of justice grow with increasing capabilities, as well as increasing causal involvement of a responsible agent. The less clear-cut causality relations are, the more weight must be put on capabilities. One of the biggest problems with how we conventionally assign remedial obligations, as David Miller (2005, 102) argues, is that we look too exclusively at the past, that is, at the question of who was responsible for bringing a certain situation about, instead of looking at who is best placed to put it right. In order to gain a clearer picture of who bears superior or only minor obligations for unjust states of affairs, we might thus grade capabilities by their significance or decisiveness to make a positive contribution. Thus the better positioned a relevant actor is to make an effective and significant contribution to the solution of a problem, the larger are that actor's prima facie obligations. Miller calls this "the principle of capacity"; following my earlier elaborations, however, calling it "the capability principle" might be more accurate. The rationale behind the capability principle simply is that "if we want bad situations put right, we should give the responsibility to those who are best placed to do the remedying" (D. Miller 2005, 102).

The significance criterion of capabilities essentially ties the degree of moral obligations to what we normally understand as power. Power, as it will be defined later in this book, is the ability to determine outcomes. Capabilities are the very foundation of power; the more extensive one's capabilities are, the larger is one's freedom to act and thus the bigger one's power to affect and determine outcomes. Power, or at least the exercise of power, is thus a combination of internal capacities and favorable external circumstances. This is why the notion of power as a property of a specific agent, as we will see, is misleading. It depends just as much on an environment that allows for the conversion of such power resources into desirable outcomes. This external dimension of power, as I will show in the second part of this book, must increasingly be thought of in structural terms. Thus we can reformulate the capability principle in terms of power: if unjust situations ought to be remedied, the respective responsibilities should be assigned to those with the biggest power to shape and determine outcomes accordingly. In this regard, growing power leads to more extensive moral obligations.

The relation between power and responsibility can be illustrated best in its negative dimension, that is, in connection with the abuse of power. The more vulnerable individuals are to a certain powerful agent, that is, the bigger its impact on these individuals, the larger is its responsibility to protect them from harm (Goodin 1985, 117ff.; see also Margalit 1996). Power relations can always be reformulated as relations of asymmetrical dependency. This dependency holds similarly also in the positive dimension. Because power essentially is the capability to determine outcomes, vulnerable individuals also depend on powerful agents for the improvement of existing unjust situations. Thus, also from the perspective of the vulnerable, power not only leads to enlarged negative obligations but also to increased positive obligations to use power meaningfully in order to transform unjust situations into just ones. Hans Jonas (1984, 92ff.) speaks of the "positive duty of power," which he calls "substantive responsibility" in this regard. Like Iris Marion Young, Jonas also claims that this "vastly different concept of responsibility" is not concerned with "the *ex post facto* account for what has been done" but with the forward determination of what ought to be done; it is to be understood as "responsibility for the future." "Irresponsibility," in his account, is the exercise of power with disregard of the obligation for the well-being, interests, and fates of those whose lives are under the powerful agent's control and care. It is from this perspective that Judith Shklar (1990, 65) denotes injustice as a "social offense of the powerful."

The gradation of capabilities along the criterion of power mitigates the danger contained in Singer's utilitarian theory that even "regular citizens" would be held responsible for virtually anything to which they might be able to make a small contribution. Hence it separates agents with prima facie superior obligations from the large masses with prima facie minor obligations. Thus it potentially shifts the main focus from individuals to more powerful institutional actors. This mere shift, however, does not yet solve the problem of a "moral overload" even of such well-positioned institutional actors. We still need a second criterion that effectively limits the remedial obligations for which a single actor can reasonably be held responsible.

One such cutoff criterion that intuitively seems to make sense, especially when dealing with questions of global justice, is geographic space or distance. Thus we could divide the world around us into concentric circles that define the strength of our moral obligations to strangers. These obligations are strongest toward our closest circle of friends and family and decrease the further out we move in the concentric-circle model. Eventually they dissolve entirely at the very periphery. There is no need to elaborate on this model at great length because my earlier elaborations should have made it clear that such approaches are hardly defensible from a cosmopolitan standpoint. There certainly is no reason to object to enlarged obligations toward one's intimate friends and family, but to divide the sphere outside this intimate circle into geographically graded circles of decreasing priority seems arbitrary. After all, a stranger living in a neighboring country is just as much a stranger as a stranger living on another continent; one of them is more distant, but they both are strangers, one no more or less than the other (Shue 1988, 692f.). The reason that this approach seems intuitive is that geographic distance once provided a fairly accurate reflection or approximation of causal chains (Shue 1988, 693). This image, however, is far too simplistic in our highly interconnected and globalized world today. The concentric-circle approach is an attempt to hold on to the paradigm of causality in a world that increasingly does not allow for it anymore.

If we look at the example of the drowning child again, the evident aspect to take into consideration for limiting capability-based obligations is not geographic distance but the cost or "normative burden" (Nickel 1987, 41) that is connected to the fulfillment of an obligation. For nonswimmer B, the normative cost attached to saving A's life is tremendous. He would most likely pay for his attempt to rescue A with his own life. For professional swimmer C, however, the cost is marginal. If we judged the situation from a pure causality perspective, this consideration would not play any role (D. Miller 2005, 102); in a situation where B pushed A into the water, he would have to follow him and would likely drown. This shows again the inadequacy of the causality criterion as an exclusive guide for the allocation of remedial duties of justice. Thus the question is: what would be an appropriate measure to determine an acceptable normative burden?

Peter Singer, as seen earlier, suggested marginal utility as the unit for measuring the normative cost. However, this not only leads to unsatisfactory outcomes but also entails all the general weaknesses of utility as a criterion for interpersonal comparisons pointed out earlier. To stay true to the normative foundations of the analysis at hand, any legitimate principle for limiting capability-based obligations must be derived from a rights-based perspective. In other words, the limit to remedial obligations is given by the condition of equal moral rights (Shue 1983, 606). Because, as responsible agents, all duty bearers are at the same time also rights bearers, they may, very much in agreement with the concern raised by Fishkin, "justifiably choose not to be heroes" (Shue 1988, 697). In an understanding of justice as development, remedial obligations are thus ultimately limited by a responsible agent's own legitimate claim for personal flourishing and advancement. According to Kant, one has not only a justified claim but indeed a moral duty to provide "for oneself to the extent necessary just to find satisfaction in living" (Kant 1996, 201). Holding a particular agent responsible for remedying unjust situations, in more general terms, is legitimate only insofar as all justified moral claims, including the ones of the duty bearer herself, are being adequately considered. Obligations can never go so far as to force someone to give up on the idea of a personally fulfilling and satisfying life.[8]

The question of what counts as a legitimate and thus an obligation-limiting claim, or, in other words, where to draw the line between reasonable and overwhelming duties, cannot be answered a priori. Weighting conflicting claims will always remain a matter of ethical reasoning and deliberation in a concrete case; there is simply no way around it. Accordingly, the question about the "reasonableness" (*Zumutbarkeit*) (Ulrich 2001a, 156ff.; 2008, 139ff.) of specific claims, that is, the specification of their reasonable extent and their limitations, or, in other words, what we can reasonably ask or expect from a certain powerful actor, can ultimately be answered only in public discourse. What seems to hold as a basic rule within this public deliberation process is that one's own claims become weightier with decreasing causal involvement and lose weight with increasing significance of one's capabilities. Thus causality serves, as mentioned earlier, as a cutoff criterion rather than as a condition for obligations of justice. The "discourse on reasonableness" (*Zumutbarkeitsdiskurs*) (Thielemann 1996, 288ff.; Ulrich 2008, 141) is indispensable and thus a necessary condition both for widening our focus from a narrow causality-based perspective to a more inclusive capability-based one and for finding the line between actions that can reasonably be considered obligations of justice and actions that belong to the category of beneficence or even heroism.

Hence immediate prima facie obligations can be transformed into "final obligations" (D. Miller 2005, 109) by weighing them against opposing (limiting) claims in public discourse. At least in the short run, however, capability must be the overriding consideration for relieving immediate harm and grievances (D. Miller 2005, 109). Any other approach would inevitably prolong suffering and deprivation, even though they could effectively be prevented by holding those agents accountable who are in the best position to provide immediate relief.

Defining the Line Between Beneficence and Obligations of Justice

My theory of obligations of justice implies that unjust states of affairs must be remedied in a collaborative effort by those agents who have essential capabilities to do so unless they have potentially weightier claims that would diminish or offset their prima facie obligations. These prima facie obligations can be overridden by moral claims that are themselves justified by the moral rights of the responsible agent. The final obligations that result from the deliberative process of weighting moral claims are based neither on beneficence or charity nor on the concept of solidarity but on justice. Therefore, they are morally owed.

This leads us to the ultimate distinguishing aspect between duties of justice and actions performed from virtue. Remedial actions are praiseworthy if they lie beyond the threshold of what we can reasonably expect from a specific agent. Hence the decisive and quite evident difference between duties of justice and praiseworthy actions based on virtue or beneficence is that in the former case duty bearers do not have any justified claims for not meeting their duty, while in the case of beneficence they are offering their support despite justified reasons that would exempt them from doing so. Hence they fulfill their prima facie obligation even though it could be overridden by their own justified and more significant claims.

Chapter 4

Agents of Global Justice

ALTHOUGH THE PREVIOUS CHAPTERS defined principles of global justice and clarified the conceptual basis for the derivation of corresponding obligations, we still do not know for whom these principles must ultimately be prescriptive, that is, who must be held responsible for remedying global injustices and for whose actions human development must be the ultimate guiding ideal. Who, in other words, are the agents that must deliver on the realization of the rights of the deprived masses living on this planet?

Evidently, solving the problem of imperfect obligations once and for all by providing a conclusive list of agents and their corresponding duties regarding global injustices cannot be the goal of this chapter. The shape and extent of obligations of justice are dependent on the specifics of a situation and the agents we hold responsible. Therefore, it is possible only to provide a heuristic, that is, an abstract view of how to identify possible candidates in concrete cases. We cannot, however, specify their concrete obligations a priori. The condition of reasonableness on which such obligations ultimately depend is by definition subject to public deliberation.

At this point there are two basic options for continuing the argument. The first possibility is to develop an ideal theory regarding what agents and agencies would be responsible for achieving cosmopolitan justice under ideal circumstances. Such a theory would deal with equally ideal institutions with potentially little connection to the actual structure of society in the here and now. Examples of such ideal theories are ones that typically deal with the creation of a world state or a world government. The second option is to take existing institutions as the point of departure and reflect on their potentially valuable capabilities for contributing to the achievement of cosmopolitan justice. The book at hand is predominantly concerned with this latter question. However, in the final chapter I will briefly touch also on the first one.

Thus when I identify multinational corporations as potential bearers of obligations of justice, I do not mean to suggest that in an ideal world private corporations should be taking over the role of primary agents of justice. Neither do I propose a world ruled by large corporations. Rather, I argue that in a world in which multinational corporations are de facto operating in governing positions already, their actions must be matched with corresponding moral obligations. We are not dealing with ideal agents in a just world but with actual agents in the here and now.

Power and Moral Obligation: Individuals, Collectivities, and Institutions

Before putting forth a general power- and capability-based heuristic for identifying potential agents of justice, we must have a closer look at the inherent connection between power and moral obligation. Because social power is often connected to institutions today, there is an additional need to clarify the concept of collective, that is, institutional, responsibility. The following general elaborations provide the basis on which to assess the plausibility of holding corporations responsible as moral agents in general and as agents of justice in particular.

The Complex Relation Between Power and Moral Obligation

I concluded the previous chapter with the insight that those agents who are best placed, that is, those agents with superior capabilities to remedy unjust situations, have an immediate prima facie obligation to do so. The abstract gradation of capabilities according to their significance reflects a continuum of power among social actors. This follows from the definition of capabilities in terms of freedom; enhanced capabilities mean enlarged freedom, and enlarged freedom means having more control over one's own actions, on the one hand, and greater power in terms of achieving chosen results, on the other (Sen 1985b, 209). While power refers to achievements or outcomes, control refers to processes. Both are crucial aspects for the assessment of an agent's capabilities and its overall freedom. Hence those who have power and control have more extensive moral responsibilities not only because they enjoy the largest freedom to act (control over processes) but also because they have the biggest leverage in using their capabilities in order to induce change (power to achieve chosen outcomes). As a consequence, the relation between power and responsibility cannot be interpreted in purely negative terms, as notably Morriss (1987, 39) suggested. Morriss's argument that all moral responsibility can be denied by demonstrating an agent's lack of power is correct. However, for Morriss, a lack of power merely means that a certain agent could not have caused a certain outcome or could not have prevented it from happening. This assessment, however, is incomplete. For an agent to be freed from any responsibility, it must additionally be able to prove that it does not have the capabilities necessary to remedy the situation.

It is important to note that moral obligation does not eliminate or reduce power but rather aims at its responsible use. In fact, the relation between moral obligation and power also works in the reverse direction; more responsibility in a certain area of human and societal organization can be connected also to an increase in status and power. Hence power and responsibility are, as Adolf Berle showed in his extensive work on power, inherently interdependent:

> Power is invariably confronted with, and acts in the presence of, a field of responsibility. The two constantly interact, in hostility or co-operation, in conflict or through some form of dialogue, organized or unorganized, made part of, or perhaps intruding into, the institutions on which power depends. (Berle 1967, 37)

The relation between power, capability, and responsibility is arguably a complex one. The notion of power used in this book will become clearer and more distinct as the elaborations proceed. I have pointed out the connection between power and capabilities in the previous chapter. Capabilities, as explained earlier, are to be understood in most cases as combinations of personal capacities and external circumstances. The same holds for the notion of power: specific properties or power resources of an agent make that agent truly powerful only if its external environment is conducive to putting them to use. In the absence of such an environment, however, power remains a latent potentiality. Thus capabilities can be interpreted as actualized power, that is, the favorable interplay between personal characteristics (capacities) and external circumstances. As we will see in part II of this book, the relevant external circumstances must increasingly be thought of in terms of structures. In other words, whether an agent is able to exercise its latent power depends increasingly on its position within certain social structures. It is this scenario that is relevant for the allocation of moral responsibility. Moral responsibility arises in those situations in which an agent is effectively able to actualize latent power (capabilities).

Focusing on capabilities in order to determine the moral obligations of an agent is thus more complex than it might seem at first. It does not merely mean relying on the potentially limitless capacities of an agent but must also take the situational external circumstances into consideration. This, on the other hand, does not mean that the scope of moral obligations is limited to the concrete actions an agent is actually carrying out. It similarly includes the full range of possible actions in the range of an agent's capabilities under given circumstances. Hence a powerful agent's moral responsibility derives not only from the actual influence of its concrete actions on certain states of affairs (causal relation) but also from failures to exercise positive influence in cases where a significant and meaningful contribution based on existing capabilities would be possible.

Institutions and Collective Responsibility

Western moral philosophy has traditionally ascribed moral responsibility predominantly to individuals. The argument has been that only they have the ability to act freely (French 1984, vii; Mellema 1997, 2). This might make sense intuitively, but it creates serious limitations on finding adequate responses to an increasing number of pressing large-scale social problems. Individuals' capacity to take on global responsibilities is naturally limited. Consequently, many global social problems simply cannot be solved by individuals acting as individuals (French 1992, 79). Proposals to remedy global injustices based predominantly on individual action (see, e.g., Singer 1972) are thus not only unrealistic from a pragmatic point of view but also tend to be morally overwhelming and therefore ethically indefensible.

A more promising approach to tackling global problems is to assign moral responsibilities also to institutions (M. Green 2005). Holding institutions morally responsible is usually tied to the concept of "collective responsibility" (Lewis 1991), as opposed to individual responsibility. Collective responsibility means to hold groups of people responsible for their actions as groups instead of each individual member for their respective contributions to those actions. This is possible on the basis of the assumption that such collectivities are able to act, make decisions, and understand the moral nature of their actions, that is, be aware of either the moral import of their actions or the moral value of their consequences (V. Held 1991, 90). Hence for collectivities to meet this condition and thus to qualify as moral agents, they must be minimally organized and coordinated (Feinberg 1991, 61; French 1992, 73; M. Green 2005, 121). Such "organized agencies" (M. Green 2005, 123) are what we normally refer to as institutions.

What distinguishes an organized group from a merely random collection of people is its method for deciding to act (V. Held 1991, 97). It has an internal decision structure, that is, a formalized decision-making process, that constitutes its ability to act intentionally. It is this ability that establishes it as a moral agent (French 1991, 141). Hence there is no contradiction in also judging collective decisions and actions from a moral perspective. Our everyday language is full of moral judgments regarding the actions of institutions; we blame nations for starting wars, for example, corporations for producing harmful products, or political parties for their political programs. In modern societies all major social tasks are performed in and through institutions (Drucker 1993, xvi; 1994). Institutions have become, as Kenneth Goodpaster (1983, 9) expressed it, "the primary actors on the human stage." Their influence on our lives is so pervasive and omnipresent that denying their moral responsibility seems almost cynical.

Even though there is little controversy regarding the moral responsibility of institutions today, it needs to be emphasized that this responsibility is still heavily connected to human beings acting in and through those institutions. Institutions can bear responsibilities only insofar as they are created by, used by, and composed of individuals (M. Green 2005, 127). Ultimately there are individual decisions behind every institutional decision and actions of individuals behind every institutional act. An institution not composed of human beings is unable to make decisions and cannot be subject to moral responsibilities; it is from this perspective that moral responsibilities remain, after all, human responsibilities. However, this does not mean, contrary to the claim of methodological individualists, that all institutional acts and decisions and thus also institutional responsibilities can be traced back to the individual actions of their members. Often, although not always, attributions of collective responsibilities are not reducible to attributions of individual responsibilities (V. Held 1991, 93). In such cases collective responsibility is "indivisible" (Cooper 1991, 39). This means that judgments regarding the moral responsibilities of members of collectivities cannot be logically derived from judgments regarding the moral responsibility of the collectivity itself (V. Held 1991, 93). In this sense, collective responsibility indeed means to assign responsibility to a nonhuman entity; the collectivity is composed of human beings, but in and of itself it is nonhuman (Mellema 1997, 4).

The focus on the moral responsibilities of institutional actors is special because it is located in the intersection between institutional and individual ethics (see, e.g., Ulrich 2008, 269f., on this distinction). The clear-cut semantic distinction between individual and institutional ethics, or, in other words, the difference between microfocus on individual actions and macrofocus on their codification within institutions, blurs precisely in those cases in which we do not look at the abstract constitution of institutions and their role in guiding and organizing social interaction but at the actual behavior of institutional agents, that is, at concrete acts of institutions (Margalit 1996, 1f.).

Both a microfocus only on individuals and an exclusive macrofocus on the institutional structure of a society leave the concrete actions of institutional agents systematically unaddressed. From an exclusively structural perspective, institutions can well be identified as just or unjust, but they do not qualify as agents and thus cannot be bearers of direct responsibilities (Lewis 1991, 28). There are two shortcomings of such an interpretation. First, it overlooks the fact that when institutional structures are unjust, it is often institutional actors themselves who are in the best position to induce the necessary changes. Second, as intentional, goal-oriented agents, institutional actors have not only responsibilities but also justified claims. Therefore, there are limits to obligations for institutional actors, just as there are for individuals. Nevertheless, these limits must be significantly less restrictive than those of individuals because institutional actors normally have much greater leverage, reach, and influence than individuals acting on their own (M. Green 2005).

The Corporation as a Moral Agent

Although the application of institutional and collective responsibility to corporations provoked considerable controversy and opposition in early debates on business ethics (e.g., Velasquez 1991), it is now widely accepted that corporations, as social institutions, can be held morally responsible for their actions. Corporations are social institutions insofar as they are, "like any other institution, [...] instrument[s] for the organization of human efforts to a common end" (Drucker 1993, 20). This common end, Drucker asserts, is more than simply the sum of personal ends of the individuals organized in the corporation; it is not a joint end but a common end. Therefore, the corporation is to be regarded as a goal-oriented and thus an intentionally acting agent in itself.

In the 19th century corporate power was very closely connected to the wealth of the corporation's owner, who, as a consequence, determined the agenda of the corporation. Therefore, corporate intentions were largely congruent with the individual intentions of their patrons. Berle and Means's famous study *The Modern Corporation and Private Property* (1991) and later Alfred D. Chandler's analysis *The Visible Hand: The Managerial Revolution in American Business* (2002), however, showed that in the early 20th century the rise of managerial capitalism led to an increasing separation of ownership and control and shifted power to the managers of the corporation. Today a further alteration seems to be taking place. Corporations are developing institutional agendas that are under the full control neither of owners nor of managers anymore. They are ingrained as imperatives in their structure and nature and essentially center on the pursuit or even the maximization of profits (Korten 1995, 54).

The function of a corporation's internal decision structure literally is to incorporate the actions of individuals (French 1984, 48ff.; 1991, 141ff.). The corporation regulates the decision-making process through its corporate structure and uses its corporate policy to direct it toward the overarching corporate goals. The corporate policy can be seen as a set of principles and a rule of conduct that limit and direct individual actions and behavior within the corporation (Drucker 1993, 36f). It is a set of broad principles "that describe what the corporation believes about its enterprise and the way it intends to operate" (French 1984, 58). These principles are not necessarily laid down explicitly in formal documents but are often embedded implicitly in the corporation's normal practices and operations. In some cases corporations are, as Peter Drucker (1993, 38) noted, "like the man who never realized he spoke prose; they do not know they have a policy." Other corporations may well have written statements, which, however, often amount to little more than "window dressing" for the real policies that are factually embedded within the corporation's operations (French 1984, 62).

Thus the basic function of the corporate policy is to ensure that decisions and acts are performed for corporate reasons (French 1991, 144). It subordinates individual ambitions and decisions to the goals and needs of the corporation and thus warrants the identification of particular decisions and acts as corporate (French 1984, 53). Hence corporate policy decisions made by individuals represent choices made for and in the name of the corporation (Goodpaster 1983, 3). Corporations are capable not only of acting intentionally but also of knowing the moral nature of their actions. Their understanding and knowledge in this respect are often even more elaborate than those of individuals because they have far superior capabilities of gathering and processing the information necessary to understand the full consequences of their actions (Goodpaster 1983, 11). This suggests that their moral responsibilities must be even more extensive than those of individuals (M. Green 2005).

As a goal-oriented, intentional actor, the corporation qualifies as a moral agent and must be distinguished from mere partnerships or crowds (French 1984, 35). As a moral subject, that is, a subject whose actions are based on reasons, it is a bearer both of rights and of duties. This takes us back to the earlier insight that the obligations of institutional actors also are not limitless but naturally stop where they infringe on their own justified claims. However, the relation between rights and obligations of institutional agents is not as balanced as it is for human beings. The enhanced capabilities and power of institutional actors are naturally paired with larger moral obligations. At the same time their nonhuman identity also leads to weaker rights compared with those of human beings, simply because they lack the inherent dignity from which all moral and truly human rights derive. It is our dignity as human beings that makes us inherently vulnerable to mental and physical humiliation. The very idea of moral rights derives precisely from this vulnerability. Institutions, on the other hand, are not dignified creatures; they are not vulnerable in their dignity and cannot be humiliated. As a consequence, they are never ends in themselves, as human beings are. Quite the contrary, they are mere means for achieving human ends. Hence as goal-oriented actors, corporations can well have justified claims, but denoting those claims as essentially the human rights of corporations (e.g., Addo 1999) is fundamentally misguided.

Human dignity, as shown earlier, derives from the human being's reasonable nature. Human beings deserve unconditional respect for their inherent ability fundamentally to turn their lives around at any given time. Human beings are, in this regard, inherently free. Reason both creates and depends on our human freedom. Corporations too may act on the basis of corporate reasons, but can we really consider them reasonable subjects in this sense? For the outspoken corporate critic Joel Bakan (2004), corporations are the precise opposite of reasonable; they are inherently pathological and thus comparable to human psychopaths. If we recall that the institutional agendas of corporations derive from the imperatives inherent in their nature and structure, Bakan's observation seems not entirely wrong. A corporation's policy, that is, its purpose, its goals, and thus its reasons, is relatively rigid and stable over time, and its structure often puts limits on its ability to adapt and change them spontaneously. The history of corporations shows that amendments or alterations to corporate policies are commonly limited to mere peripheral issues (French 1991, 146f.). The narrow range of "permissible" corporate action in the realm of the dominant shareholder-value doctrine indeed turns corporate intentions into something like a "pathological pursuit of profit and power" (Bakan 2004).

In sum, corporations are able to act on the reasons institutionalized in their policies and structures, but they are not reasonable creatures like human beings. Therefore, human beings bear a primary dual obligation, first, to give their corporations reasonable policies, and second, to give them structures that leave enough room for reasonable decisions made by those individuals who decide and act through the institution.

Primary and Secondary Agents of Justice

By basing our reflections on agents of justice on power, control, and leverage of their capabilities, we can divide the large pool of potential agents of justice into those who bear primary obligations and those with secondary obligations of justice. This division derives directly from the earlier distinction between prima facie superior obligations and prima facie minor obligations (see the section "Gradation and Cutoff Criteria: Power and Reasonableness" in chapter 3), which is similarly based on the power of particular agents.

Evidently, the differentiation between primary and secondary obligations of justice cannot be a quantitative one but must in some significant regard be qualitative. A powerful agent that bears primary obligations of justice does not merely have more or larger obligations of the same kind as a secondary agent; more important, he or she has qualitatively different obligations. This follows from an understanding of power as a relation rather than a possession (see the section "From Property-Based to Capability-Based Interpretations of Power" in chapter 6). If we look at power as a relation, the existence of power on one side is always matched with dependency on the other. In other words, those who are said to have power normally have power over certain others, who, as a result, are dependent on their actions and decisions.

This can be formulated slightly differently by saying that those with primary obligations of justice are, in some significant regard, setting the terms for others, who, as a consequence, merely bear secondary obligations of justice. Onora O'Neill (2001, 2004) introduced a plausible preliminary heuristic for the identification of agents of justice that is based precisely on this distinction between those who set the terms for justice and those who merely correspond to them. Primary agents of justice, as O'Neill defines them, have the capacities to regulate, define, and allocate the contributions of secondary agents of justice (O'Neill 2004, 242). They assign and reassign powers, tasks, and responsibilities among individuals and institutions and control and limit the actions of other agents and agencies (O'Neill 2001, 181). In other words, they have the capacity to govern other agents' actions or the contexts and domains in which other agents act. Thus they operate in a position to "determine how principles of justice are to be institutionalized within a certain domain" (O'Neill 2001, 181). Accordingly, all other agents and agencies are secondary agents of justice. They contribute to justice merely by meeting the requirements and demands of primary agents (O'Neill 2001, 181). To be somewhat more accurate, the task of primary agents of justice essentially is to enable secondary agents to discharge their own responsibilities by creating a favorable environment for doing so.

This characterization implies two decisive qualitative differences between the obligations of primary and secondary agents of justice. First, primary agents of justice bear direct obligations, while secondary agents merely have indirect ones. The obligations of secondary agents are derivative; they are determined and allocated by primary agents either directly through laws and regulations or indirectly by shaping the institutional and societal context within which secondary agents operate. This does not mean that the obligations of secondary agents are limited to mere compliance with existing laws and regulations. Their moral obligations might well exceed legal laws. However, the possibilities for secondary agents to discharge such moral obligations are themselves dependent on the institutional and legal context created and shaped by the primary agents. Second, because primary agents essentially determine the context in which other agents operate, they have positive rather than merely negative obligations of justice. From this perspective, the distinction between primary and secondary agents of justice is of pivotal importance especially in those cases in which we deal not with perfect, universal obligations but with imperfect ones whose extent is heavily dependent on an agent's range of capabilities rather than merely on its causal role in the process of rights viola-tions. O'Neill argued that imperfect obligations are not claimable and thus belong to the sphere of virtuous action. However, her own typology of pri-mary and secondary agents of justice provides a basis on which claimability can actually be established and ensured. Identifying primary agents of justice consists of nothing else than pointing out the primary addressees of respec-tive moral claims. Once the claim is launched, we are effectively able to enter a constructive dialogue among all potentially helpful parties in order to allo-cate tasks and responsibilities also to secondary agents.

Typically, in modern societies primary agents of justice are what we refer to as a society's governing institutions, that is, those institutions that exercise a certain amount of authority over other institutions and individuals. Gov-erning or "ruling" institutions are those institutions that are constitutive for a society. As such, they have the biggest potential and leverage to do harm to the individuals living under their authority, on the one hand, and to remedy ex-isting injustices, on the other. This enhanced potential manifests itself either directly through their concrete actions or indirectly through the rules, legal or nonlegal, they impose on society. Thus governing institutions have a prime influence on a society's decency.

Avishai Margalit (1996) defines a decent society as one characterized by the nonhumiliating constitution and conduct of governing institutions, while a civilized society is one defined by nonhumiliating interaction and relationships between individuals. Evidently, these two concepts broadly resemble the dis-tinction between primary and secondary agents of justice and thus the one be-tween institutional and individual ethics. By conceptually separating the decent society from the civilized society, however, Margalit dissolves the dialectic in-terconnectedness between individual and institutional ethics. Hence he elimi-nates the connection between the duties of governing institutions and the ones of citizens. According to Margalit, both of them must abstain from humiliation of individuals. Although he does assign first priority in this regard to governing institutions, he says little about how the role of governing institutions affects and determines the role of citizens and the other way around. Such an approach can be followed as long as we predominantly focus on universal and clearly de-finable negative duties of justice. However, as soon as we deal with imperfect obligations and thus with shared duties, or, in Henry Shue's (1988, 689f.) words, with a "division of moral labor" involving different actors in different roles, it is crucial to look also at the relation between those different agents and agencies.

If deprivations of all sorts can be interpreted in terms of human unfreedom, then power and authority relations naturally move to the center of the analysis both of their causes and of possible ways to alleviate them. Consequently, when we are striving for a just or decent society, our primary focus and attention must be on governing institutions. Once we extend our focus to the global context instead of limiting it to the political borders of the nation-state, however, it is less clear which institutions do or do not count as governing institutions and thus as primary agents of justice. Let us look at this question in more detail.

The Conventional View: Nation-States as Primary Agents of Global Justice

It is a distinctive feature of our contemporary society and a hardly challenged assumption that governing institutions and thus the role of the primary agents of justice are associated with the modern nation-state. All other institutions and individuals operating and living on a given national territory are thought to be acting under the authority of state institutions and are regarded merely as secondary agents of justice.

This intuitive assumption carries over seamlessly to the international sphere. From the perspective of the dominant political "realist" school of thought, the international sphere consists of international relations between discrete and sovereign nation-states. Any international order rests exclusively on state power, and international institutions are perceived as mere instruments of state diplomacy (Höffe 2002a, 26). Accordingly, both domestic justice and international justice are seen as a matter of state action and state obligation. States are perceived not only as the subjects of international justice but also as the sole obligation bearers for it. The very notion of nonstate actors used for all actors and institutions that are not state owned reinforces the assumption that the state is the central actor around which all other entities necessarily revolve (Alston 2005, 3). It implicitly qualifies all agents and agencies other than the state automatically as secondary agents whose very nature and identity are defined solely by their relation to the state.

This dominant state-centric view of political realism is perhaps most pervasive in contemporary human rights legislation. The realist interpretation of international human rights law assigns direct human rights obligations exclusively to states, while all other agents and agencies are seen to have at best indirect obligations. Hence it is the state that bears the primary responsibility to ensure that other agents respect human rights on national territory. Nonstate actors are obliged to comply with human rights law only as far as is stipulated in national law, that is, insofar as those obligations are institutionalized and assigned to them by the state. However, they do not bear any obligations deriving directly from international human rights law itself.

This realist focus on state obligations runs into serious difficulties in cases where states themselves are unjust or too weak to facilitate and enforce justice (O'Neill 2001, 182). States have all too often acted as agents of injustice rather than of justice and have used their powers for other ends than to strive for human freedom and equality. There are many cases in which states shamelessly abused their power for the pursuit of explicitly unjust and illegitimate goals, particularly for oppressing, torturing, and killing people under their authority. Not only do such states fail as primary agents of justice, but they also turn all secondary agents who are acceding to their demands into their accomplices because their compliance automatically contributes to the injustice committed and promoted by the state. In other cases states fail as primary agents of justice simply because they are too weak and lack the capabilities and powers necessary to fulfill their role properly. Both the Universal Declaration of Human Rights and most contemporary human rights thinking have little to say about what happens in cases in which the allegedly exclusive primary agent of justice systematically fails to fulfill its duty. If states fail to allocate human rights responsibilities, there is, from a realist perspective, literally no one who bears any obligations. The problem with our common way of thinking about human rights is that it pairs cosmopolitan claims and aspirations with inherently statist obligations of explicitly anticosmopolitan institutions (O'Neill 2001, 185). Once the state fails to discharge its duties, human rights are in free fall.

There is a third, much more profound and pervasive challenge to the state-centered interpretation of agents and obligations of justice: the emergence of a truly global, that is, a transnational (not merely international), sphere that limits the effectiveness of state action not only beyond national borders but also in the domestic realm. The transcendence of national borders by an ever-increasing number of social, political, and economic processes, practices, and institutions leads to an "unbundling" of territoriality (Ruggie 1993, 165), that is, to the disintegration of the traditional unity of territory, state, and society (Albrow 1997, 43; Beck 2000, 21). It is precisely this unity that has secured the state's exclusive authority over its domestic affairs throughout the modern age. Hence by placing the roots of many domestic problems beyond the borders and outside the reach of nation-states, the current stage of globalization significantly compromises many of the state's capabilities and powers to secure justice even on its own territory. It is the nature of such "inherently global issues" (Rischard 2002, 66ff.) that they overstrain the capacities of any one nation-state and are thus insoluble outside a framework of truly global collective action. Genuinely global problems can only be solved at the global level (Höffe 2002c, 14). Their nonterritorial nature fundamentally clashes with the fixed geography of states and reduces the relative significance of the nation-state as a potential problem solver (Mathews 1997, 65).

The single most important global challenge is global poverty. With more and more social and economic processes transcending national borders, the sources of poverty have shifted beyond any single country's reach. This does not mean that there are no domestic factors that contribute to the persistence of poverty, but even the effects of domestic factors are often dependent on features of the global institutional order (Pogge 2004, 272). Thus the adequacy of looking at states as the exclusive primary agents of justice not only is called into question where they are unjust or notoriously weak but also must increasingly be contested even for the strongest ones (Strange 2000, 154). There is literally no country that can escape the impacts of the emerging transnational sphere.

Against this background, it is not surprising that the global human rights situation has not significantly improved during the last few decades. In many parts of the world it has even worsened. For hundreds of millions of people on this planet, humiliation and systematic violations of their most basic human rights are still a regular part of their daily lives. However, if states are less and less able to tackle this untenable situation on their own, who else must step up and take responsibility for the improvement of such conditions?

Toward a More Realistic View: The Inclusion of Nonstate Actors

In the face of the profound transformations at the global level, the state-centered, realist worldview and its corresponding perceptions regarding agents and obligations of justice appear increasingly implausible. Not only do states increasingly experience serious constraints on their capability to act autonomously, but other powerful institutions are emerging at the transnational level that are at least partly operating beyond the authority of any one nation-state. In many regards their capabilities already exceed those of states. A serious analysis of potential agents of justice must include the powers and capabilities of such actors and institutions rather than dogmatically holding on to state centrism. In a world in which the state increasingly is losing its status of exclusivity concerning societal organization and coordination, holding on to the state-centric paradigm is equivalent to giving up the ideal of justice. The refusal to reflect on the full range of potential obligation bearers in a transnational world will translate directly into an erosion of the fundamental rights of a growing number of people.

It is precisely in this reconfiguration of power at the global level that the current stage of globalization is profoundly different from any other phase of globalization the world has experienced before. Not only are today's transnational institutions increasingly difficult to control by the state, but in certain significant domains these traditional patterns of control and power have even been reversed. States increasingly lack the capabilities to set the context for nonstate actors and often even find themselves adjusting their own domestic policies to the changing environment shaped by institutions over which they have less and less control. It is against this background that the "subtle, silent, and insidious permeation" of our national societies by genuinely transnational actors is increasingly seen as perhaps the biggest threat to the autonomy and integrity of states (Strange 2002a, 198).

Many of these transnational actors are formally appointed and controlled by the collective of nation-states—examples include international and supranational organizations like the United Nations (UN), the World Trade Organization (WTO), the International Monetary Fund (IMF), and the World Bank—but no single nation-state is able to control them on its own. Thus in the newly evolving transnational spaces it is not at all evident anymore who the governing institutions and thus the primary agents of justice really are. Under such circumstances it is questionable whether we can still rely on the formula that all nonstate institutions are automatically to be considered secondary agents of justice. Even for those institutions that have traditionally been defined through their relation to the nation-state, the very notion of secondary agents must be called into question; if an adequate primary agent of justice is absent, the very notion of secondary agent becomes meaningless (O'Neill 2004, 252).

Generally speaking, nonstate institutions assume the role of primary agents in situations or contexts in which they factually operate beyond the authority of any other agent or agency. This logically follows from the insight that any agent or agency that is effectively acting under the authority of another agent can at most be a secondary agent of justice. Thus the main condition for a nonstate actor to become a primary agent of justice is its formal or factual escape from the reach of the nation-state's authority. Only an institution that has at least partially freed itself from the reach of the nation-state can effectively be regarded as a primary agent of justice. I do not claim that these institutions act entirely independently of the state; a partial escape merely means that they are able to exercise certain specific powers of considerable relevance beyond the state's control. It is in regard to these powers that such agents must assume primary responsibility, while in regard to others they will naturally remain secondary agents.

Thus in addressing global injustice it is of foremost importance not to rely solely on formal authority, for it systematically falls short as an adequate criterion for the identification of all those institutions that hold significant power in the transnational sphere. Rather, an adequate distribution of responsibilities must be based on the de facto distribution of power and authority. It is precisely the shortcoming of realist perspectives that they rely exclusively on the formal constitution of authority and thus ignore the fact that institutions that are assigned formal authority are not necessarily in control also de facto. This provides at least a partial explanation of the realists' dogmatic defense of their state-centered perspectives and their image of all other institutions as virtually powerless. Contrary to this perspective, however, authority can be a purely factual concept (Margalit 1996, 21). Hence an exclusive focus on formal authority tends to overstate the responsibilities of formal authorities with little factual power and obscures those of factual authorities without a formal mandate.

Nation-states, if they are not entirely dysfunctional, might still be the most powerful institutions overall. Thus in many cases it might indeed be appropriate to turn to the state as the primary agent of justice despite the state system's general shortcomings concerning cosmopolitan justice—at least as long as we lack better alternatives. However, a growing number of domains, domestic and global, are not under exclusive control of the state anymore. In these domains it is systematically insufficient to rely simply on the overall power of the state, because no agent or agency can be obliged to act in ways for which it lacks adequate capabilities (O'Neill 2004, 250). Hence we must hold those agents accountable that effectively do have the capabilities needed for the transformation of certain unjust situations.

Closely connected to these insights is the debate about the alleged loss of sovereignty of the nation-state. Here too, a focus on aggregate power leads to more controversy than necessary. On the one side, there are realists who still romantically picture the state as the ultimate political, economic, and societal reference point with absolute power. On the other side, there are neoliberals who prematurely announce the demise of the nation-state, stripped of all its powers by the uncontrollable forces of global markets. Such black-and-white pictures, however, contribute little to an adequate reflection of reality. The truth, as often, lies between the two extremes. What we experience today is a loss of power of the nation-state in certain specific domestic domains and a limitation of its reach and scope of action in the global sphere. The "denationalization" (Beck 2003, 458) of domestic domains, that is, the shift of their determining factors to the global level, however, will hardly mean the end of the nation-state as such. Newly emerging primary agents of justice will not replace the nation-state across the board but rather will complement it in the specific areas where it is weakening.

Both realists and neoliberals play down the governing potential of nonstate actors in order to protect their ideological interests tied either to the state (realists) or to markets (neoliberals). Therefore, bringing up the issue of power, sovereignty, and responsibility in connection with nonstate actors is prone to trigger controversy, opposition, or even resentment in both camps. As a result, the topic has been largely neglected so far, and de facto powerful institutions are often treated with kid gloves in defining their moral obligations.

Multinational Corporations: Primary or Secondary Agents of Justice?

A growing number of institutions have at least partially emancipated themselves from nation-state control and might potentially assume the role of primary agents of justice. They play increasingly important roles in organizing international und supranational environments, often with considerable consequences also for national regulatory policies. Besides such formally appointed institutions, the emerging transnational sphere has given rise to the emergence of other transnational organizations—namely, international nongovernmental organizations (NGOs) and multinational corporations—that, despite their lack of a formal mandate to govern, have reached a level of capability and power that in many situations puts them in de facto governing positions. In the realm of neoliberal economic globalization the multinational corporation has at least partly evaded the firm grip of the nation-state and has developed into one of the most powerful institutions of our time.

Against this background, it seems somewhat surprising that multinational corporations have been hardly more than a side note to the global justice debate. On the one hand, this lack of attention can be ascribed to the dominant influence of political realism; on the other hand, however, it might be based on the widespread but nonetheless problematic perception that the multinational corporation is, at its core, a corporation like any other (see, e.g., Wilkins 1997, 34) and thus is to be regarded merely as a secondary agent of justice. There is little doubt that in a strong state domestic institutions operating under the authority of the state must, under normal circumstances, be considered secondary agents of justice. They are subject to national laws and regulations and must comply with the institutional role and responsibility determined and assigned to them within ongoing political deliberation. They are conceptually embedded in the superordinate model of a well-ordered (national) society from which they derive their normative orientation and legitimacy (Ulrich 2002b, 13).

Historically, this normative orientation or raison d'être for the economy in general and its corporations in particular was seen in the promotion of the citizens' well-being. In order to ensure compliance with this given purpose, the economy rested tightly regulated and embedded within society. During the last 150 years, however, this preclassical perception of a societally embedded economy has changed dramatically. Classical liberalism emerged and proclaimed a different view of the relation between markets and society. The market mechanism itself was now proclaimed inherently just, and all regulations and interventions by the government were seen as illegitimate distortions. Corporations, as a consequence, were to be freed from the firm grip of the state and left entirely to the coordination of the market itself. Thus the corporation's direct normative ties to society's needs and values were gradually replaced by its strictly functional adherence to the laws of the market. In other words, the corporation was transformed from a social into a purely economic institution.

This view also regards the corporation as merely a secondary agent of justice—perhaps even more so than the preclassical view—but it is now the market mechanism, escaping the regulatory grip of the state, that assumes the role of the primary agent. Because the market itself is considered inherently just, the corporation, as a secondary agent, is perceived to contribute to the maintenance of a just society simply by following the market's requirements. Moreover, the principles of the market are perceived as prescriptive not only for the behavior of corporations but also for the state, whose proper role is to promote free-market policies and to free corporations from all political constraints.

The globalization of markets and corporations during the last quarter of the 20th century took this process a step further and at least partly reversed traditional authority relations. The state's adherence to market principles is not merely an ideological choice anymore but has turned into an imperative, forced onto national governments by the mechanisms of global competition. If we adhered to the image of multinational corporations as secondary agents of justice, our only normative reference point at the global level would be the mechanisms of the global market. However, the global market has clearly failed to fulfill its social and societal promises. The normative foundations of the market ideology are systematically inadequate to serve as a universalizable account of justice and thus as a guiding ideal for secondary agents of justice. Furthermore, as we will see later, the hierarchy between markets and corporations also has been reversed, at least partly. Hence in the absence of a centralized global governance system, the notion of multinational corporations as secondary agents of justice appears increasingly hollow.

As transnational institutions that are increasingly disconnecting from the grip of the nation-state, the big multinational corporations are increasingly assuming political roles and emerging as political actors on the global stage today (see, e.g., Matten, Crane, and Chapple 2003; Scherer, Palazzo, and Baumann 2006; Scherer and Palazzo 2007; Palazzo and Scherer 2008). They have done so more than any other type of corporation we know and to a more significant extent than at any time before in the history of the modern corporation. The huge chartered companies of the 18th century served genuinely political purposes and often even acted in government-like roles, but they were political instruments that merely served as an extension of their government's reach, whereas today's free multinational corporations are acting as autonomous political agents exercising genuine capabilities of political decision making. For Peter Drucker (quoted in Sampson 1995, 26), the modern corporation created the first truly autonomous power center in hundreds of years, which is located within society but independent of the government.

The normative conclusion of multinational corporations acting as primary agents of justice at the global level is that they have a direct obligation to engage in the proactive realization of human rights. The call to engage proactively in the realization of social justice as political or even quasi-governmental institutions means that distributive rather than allocative considerations must build the core of their responsibilities. Thus operating as political agents in de facto governing roles adds a new dimension to the claim of corporate legitimacy for multinational corporations: the requirements of cosmopolitan justice.

Although this section has opened the discussion regarding the new quasi-governmental role of multinational corporations and has given some first implications and conclusions deriving therefrom, the necessary foundations for this argument have yet to be provided. Thus in a logical next step I will develop a theory of the multinational corporation as a quasi-governmental institution, which will then serve as a basis to theorize it as a primary agent of justice and to derive its moral obligations based on the principles of justice outlined earlier.

PART II

Theory of the Quasi-Governmental Institution
Power and Authority in the Global Political Economy

Multinational Corporations Between Depoliticization of the Economy and Economization of Politics

Unfolding the Neoliberal Paradox

IN HIS FAMOUS POLITICAL ANALYSIS in *Concept of the Corporation*, Peter Drucker (1993, 6) described the large American corporation as an "institution which sets the standard for the way of life and the mode of living of our citizens." The large American corporation, in Drucker's eyes, is representative of "big business" in general; "it leads, molds and directs," and it "determines our perspective on our own society." It is the institution "around which crystallize our social problems and to which we look for their solutions." Hence as early as 1946, when the book first appeared, Drucker attributed all the characteristics we would commonly associate with primary agents of justice to big business. It is not society with its values and principles that deliberates on and determines the role and responsibilities of the corporation, but the corporation that largely shapes and determines the values to which our society adheres. Nearly 40 years later Peter French (1984, viii) was still convinced that "corporate entities [...] define and maintain human existence within the industrialized world." Today, more than six decades after Drucker and two and a half decades after French's statement, the social and societal influence of big business has become even more pervasive. Corporations have grown larger and become more influential economically, politically, and socially. Many of them are now said to be bigger than entire economies of small and medium-sized nations. The sales of General Motors, for example, exceed the GDP of Denmark, Poland, or Norway. By this measure, General Motors was the 23rd biggest economy on this planet in the year 2000, and 51 of the largest 100 economies in the world were corporations (Anderson and Cavanagh 2000).

Size alone is not a sufficient indicator of influence, power, and capability, and comparisons between a corporation's sales and a country's GDP can be, as many critics of Anderson and Cavanagh's study have argued, somewhat misleading, but the mere fact that such studies get so much public attention shows the relevance of their underlying message. The reason that Anderson and Cavanagh's study, first published in 1996, has been quoted over and over for more than a decade is simply that it reproduces and underlines a basic perception that is already prevalent in society: the large multinational corporation is acting in an increasingly dominant societal position.

Therefore, it seems somewhat odd that instead of holding these large corporations accountable for their increasing influence over societal life, it is typically those who raise the topic of corporate power who have to justify scientifically their boldness in doing so. The more visible corporate power becomes in society and the more evident it appears to common sense, the more, it seems, it is being played down or even denied by the ideology of those who fear limitations on and regulation of corporate freedom. This was not always the case; during the 1960s and 1970s critical theoretical, empirical, and normative research built a substantial part of theorizing multinational corporations. Only from the 1980s onwards were critical perspectives removed, if not banned, from mainstream currents (M. T. Jones 2000, 943). This is not a novel tactic; in his compelling study of the rise of the modern corporation, Scott Bowman (1996, 9) observed that also in the 19th century the ascendancy of corporate power was promoted "first by disguising it and then by denying its existence." The oldest and wisest strategy for exercising power, as John Kenneth Galbraith (1973, 5) confirmed, "is to deny that it is possessed."

Today corporate power can hardly be disguised anymore, but it is, at least in its political form, still widely denied among mainstream (political) economists. While neoliberals regard corporate actions as conditioned by the market mechanism and thus obscure corporate power behind the notion of the perfect market, (neo)realist scholars in international relations overemphasize the state's power to condition multinational corporations' activities in the global political economy. As a result, corporate power has not been properly—if at all—addressed in economics and has only just started to play a larger role in political science. Therefore, putting forth a theory of the multinational corporation as a quasi-governmental institution might appear a bold move even to the critical minds among us. Perhaps choosing the term *quasi-governmental institution* to characterize our large multinational corporations is indeed quite daring, and I could likely find a less controversial term to describe the same issue. However, we might just need the controversy of this term to effectively make power relations visible and to put the issue of corporate power on the academic and political agenda. The mainstream theorization of power and governance in the international political economy has systematically focused on the nation-state and has neglected nonstate institutions that are factually operating in governing roles. Addressing the large multinational corporation simply as a corporation like any other involves the danger of once again systematically neglecting or even concealing the issue of corporate power in the global responsibility equation. Thus the notion of the quasi-governmental institution opens a new perspective on the formulation of moral obligations in the global sphere—one that departs from a narrow state-centric view of international relations and allows for taking factual power relations in the global political economy into account.

The emergence of the multinational corporation as a quasi-governmental institution has taken place amid an ongoing, profound transformation of the relation between politics, society, and the market from the early 19th century onward. It was facilitated by the rise of the modern market economy and the utopian ideological attempt to free it from all political influence. More precisely, it can be conceptualized against the background of the classical liberal attempt to depoliticize the economy and its subsequent neoliberal radicalization in the form of an economization of politics. In the following paragraphs I will have a closer look at these two crucial developments and their underlying normative assumptions. These elaborations will provide the conceptual and theoretical backdrop for my subsequent reflections on the emergence of multinational corporations as quasi-governmental institutions. We will see that the classical liberal goal to depoliticize the economy inevitably led to the reverse process of an implicit politicization of powerful corporations in the neoliberal era. This process, which I will call "the neoliberal paradox," is an indispensable prerequisite for the rise of multinational corporations to political power.

Depoliticization of the Economy: Classical Liberalism

Markets existed long before the emergence of an actual market economy. However, premodern markets were naturally limited by human beings' social relationships or, as in the era of mercantilism, by extensive political regulations. Premodern economies were well embedded in and subordinate to the conventional moral norms and rules of society as a whole. Economic activities were an integral part of the established sociocultural context of societal life; there was no such thing as an economic system taking on a life of its own and following its own logics, disconnected from its surrounding social norms and values (Ulrich 2008, 116). The economy itself was a mere function of social organization and integration (Polanyi 2001, 52). The transition to the modern capitalist market economy, on the other hand, is characterized by a shift of control from social norms and values to the functional mechanism of the market itself. It is based on the assumption and expectation that human beings are rational maximizers of self-interest whose lives do not primarily revolve around building and maintaining meaningful interpersonal relationships but around the one-dimensional pursuit of personal income and wealth. In other words, the profit motive provides the fuel and the most fundamental condition for modern capitalist systems, and as long as it was absent within the broad population of traditional societies, a market-driven economy was virtually unthinkable.

For the German sociologist Max Weber, the sudden and tremendously powerful rise of the "spirit of capitalism" (Weber 2002) that turned premodern economies upside down and paved the way for the emergence of modern market economies had its roots in the Puritan-Calvinist religious doctrine. By promising salvation to the economically successful members of the community—economic success was considered a sign of God's favor to the chosen ones—its ideology of determination established the unrestricted pursuit of personal gain and profits as a legitimate and even socially expected normative orientation for individuals. However, although this new cultural climate, which provided a foothold for the profit motive, was an indispensable condition for the rise of the capitalist economic system, it was not sufficient by itself. The Calvinist ethos certainly led to a "moral disinhibition" (Ulrich 2008, 119) of economic activity that delivered the "moral energy" (Giddens 2002, xvii) for an increasing disconnection between individual economic activity and social life, but the establishment of a market-controlled economy was by no means a simple act of cultural or even natural evolution; it was an inherently political project.

It was the political program of classical liberalism at the beginning of the 19th century that broke up the centuries-old socially rooted market structures and "freed" economic life from social and political control (Gray 1998, 1). The transformations implied and induced by this project were epochal, and its political and societal effects were tremendous. The change from regulated to self-regulating markets, the shift from a politically and socially controlled economy to an economy controlled by the mechanism of the market, the "great transformation," as Polanyi (2001, 74) called the process in his homonymous analysis of "the political and economic origins of our time," was in fact "a complete transformation of the society" itself. A market that is self-regulating, Polanyi claimed, "demands nothing less than the institutional separation of society into an economic and political sphere."

Not surprisingly, then, the laissez-faire doctrine of classical liberalism was characterized by a deep suspicion of political intervention into the "natural laws" of market coordination and by an unbending, almost religious trust in the newly emerging discipline of (neoclassical) economics. The "discovery of economics" (Polanyi 2001, 124) as an allegedly pure, that is, value-free, science was not only a result of the disconnection between the economic system and society but at the same time one of its major forces. In premodern, socially embedded economies, that is, in economies controlled by social norms and values, all economic activity was systematically thinkable only as subject to political economy. Therefore, economic reflection was inseparable from ethical reflection (Ulrich 2008, 116). Under such circumstances the emergence of economics perceived as a quasi-natural science was virtually impossible.

The "invention" of neoclassical economics was critical, if not defining, for the classical liberal depoliticization project, for it seemingly replaced the need for political deliberation on economic affairs with the allegedly objective laws of quasi-natural economics. It provided the basis for structuring the economic system according to the purely instrumental logics of a value-free science and thus for disconnecting it from the underlying communicative social processes in which it had formerly been embedded. Jürgen Habermas (1987, 153ff.) interpreted this "particular kind of objectification" as a process of "uncoupling of system and lifeworld," that is, as a disconnection between system integration and social integration. Within this process more and more societal functions are depoliticized and handed over to the purely functional coordination of "nongovernmental subsystems." As a result, the system mechanisms become increasingly disconnected from social structures, norms, and values, that is, from the communicative practice through which social integration takes place. In other words, the lifeworld itself is no longer needed for the coordination of action and is turned into the mere system environment.

The emergence of the capitalist economic system, according to Habermas, marked the breakthrough to this level of system differentiation.

Nevertheless, despite classical liberal economists' antipathy to all political intervention into the coordination mechanism of the market, their project was heavily dependent and built on political enforcement. State intervention increased massively during any of the so-called economic liberal eras, and administrations grew steadily in order to ensure the functioning of the system. Laissez-faire as a complete retreat of politics from the economic sphere is a myth. In other words, depoliticization of the economy in the realm of classical liberalism does not mean the elimination of politics as such; rather, it must be thought of as a retreat of effective politics, that is, of a kind of politics that imposes social limitations on the expansion of free markets. Hence it refers to the function of politics in the economy rather than to its actual presence. Laissez-faire, as argued earlier, does not just happen but is a deliberate political project.

This does not mean that a truly depoliticized economic system was not the ultimate ideal of classical liberals. Evidently, they did believe that once the system was established—although on the basis of heavy political enforcement— laissez-faire in principle would work. What the need for political enforcement of laissez-faire shows, however, is that the widespread assumption of free markets naturally evolving on their own once things are allowed freely to take their course is inherently flawed (Gray 1998, 17; Polanyi 2001, 145ff.).

> In the absence of a strong state dedicated to a liberal economic programme, markets will inevitably be encumbered by a myriad of responses to specific social problems, not as elements in any grand design. [...] Encumbered markets are the norm in every society, whereas free markets are a product of artifice, design and political coercion. Laissez-faire must be centrally planned; regulated markets just happen. (Gray 1998, 17)

Gray's argument makes sense. A complete disconnection between system and lifeworld is virtually impossible because human interaction can never be completely separated from a communicative practice that allows for some sort of mutual understanding (Habermas 1987, 310). The degradation of the lifeworld into merely one subsystem among others will always remain a purely theoretical possibility. This is why a complete depoliticization of the economy necessarily remains a utopia: it would presuppose the dehumanization of human beings.

This tells us something about the general nature of development and societal modernization. Habermas showed that the functional differentiation or rationalization of societal subsystems is, in fact, dependent on the simultaneous communicative rationalization of the lifeworld. In other words, modernization, that is, societal rationalization, cannot be reduced to the one-dimensional expansion of rational-empirical, that is, scientific, knowledge, as notably Max Weber's (1958a, 351) notion of the "disenchantment of the world" wrongfully implies. On the contrary, it is crucially dependent on a second dimension that addresses the continuous improvement of our communicative and thus moral competences. If, as argued earlier on the basis of Kant and Hegel, human rationality evolves from the practical interest of human beings in their freedom, then societal rationalization must be interpreted as a process of human beings' liberation from heteronomy and dependency. While the dimension of technical rationalization aims at the liberation of human beings from the constraints of their external environment, the dimension of moralization and communicative rationalization denotes their emancipation from violent and coercive interaction with one another. In other words, technical rationalization targets the strategies and instruments and thus the use of means to certain ends. It is based and dependent on the scientific, that is, the theoretical, analysis of objective relations between causes and effects. Communicative rationalization, on the other hand, aims at the expansion of possibilities and processes of non-coercive, argumentative communication in which consensus over such societal norms and ends can be reached. Therefore, it is an inherently practical task of rational politics (Ulrich 1986, 58f.). This clarifies further the notion of depoliticization, which, from this perspective, must not be interpreted narrowly as the mere absence of formal political intervention but as the (attempted) elimination or suppression of communicative rationalization within the societal modernization process.

A one-sided societal development dominated by only one dimension of rationalization will inevitably run into crisis at some point because it suppresses the rational interest of human beings in the full account of their freedom. Therefore, it is likely to trigger countermovements, which will eventually enforce a change in the dominant type of rationalization (Ulrich 1986, 76ff.). This is no different in the case of the unbalanced expansion of market principles in society. The permanent existence of such countermovements during any of the liberal eras is undisputed. Even before he turned against economic liberalism, John Gray doubted that "in the domain of political and legislative practice, [. . .] there was any period in which an uncompromising principle of laissez faire was respected" (Gray 1995, 27). He states that "the political consensus o[n] classical liberal precepts was at no time altogether unbroken" (Gray 1995, 28). This shows that even though they have been unequally weighted, both constitutive dimensions—functional and communicative rationalization—have always been present throughout the historical rationalization and modernization process. It is thus not a coincidence that revisionist liberal ideas, which gained influence after 1873 and ultimately led to the fall of classical liberalism, were deeply influenced and inspired by Hegelian philosophy (Gray 1995, 31).

Economization of Politics: Neoliberalism

The previous section showed that a century of depoliticizing the economy and all the social questions and issues naturally connected to it eventually had to lead to a serious backlash. The political disregard for the unsuccessful in the economic liberal order and the soaring inequalities resulting from it inevitably provoked the political radicalization of those very social issues that were so culpably neglected in the economic liberal era (Ulrich 2008, 157f.). It is not a coincidence that both totalitarian ideologies that arose in the 1930s, Fascism and Stalinism, were equally anticapitalist and hostile toward the classical liberal laissez-faire doctrine (Drucker 1989, 5).

Not surprisingly, the identity of the revisionist era after the Second World War was deeply influenced by the horrific consequences of the early economic liberal project. The countermovements and social concerns that had always lingered under the classical liberal surface finally were politically addressed after the Second World War. Consequently, the period between 1945 and the early 1970s was marked by a strong political will to control and direct the market and to address proactively the social issues at stake. The Beveridge Plan in Britain, the "Great Society" that followed in the footsteps of Roosevelt's New Deal in the United States, and the development of the social market economy in Germany were direct manifestations of this renewed political commitment. Furthermore, the "turnaround" from free to mixed and managed economies became not only visible in economic policy but also in economic theory, most notably in the theory of John Maynard Keynes.

Nevertheless, the postwar managed economies, as John Gray points out perceptively, were not based on a broad intellectual conversion from laissez-faire but grew out of the horrific social experiences in the run-up to, as well as during, the Second World War and the resulting resolute refusal of people to return to the interwar social order (Gray 1998, 15). Accordingly, the production of intellectual contributions to economic liberal thought never stopped during the revisionist era (Gray 1995, 36). Thus the eventual "revival of classical liberalism" (Gray 1995, 36ff.) represented by the influential works of a new generation of liberal scholars such as Friedrich August von Hayek, Milton Friedman, and Ludwig von Mises in the 1970s did not come as a surprise. It was based on and triggered by the contractarian revitalization of political philosophy through John Rawls's *Theory of Justice* (1971).

The "new realities" (Drucker 1989) of neoliberalism arrived with a vengeance. The creeds and ideals that molded political economy in the postwar era, the belief in government control and direction of the economy and society as "progressive causes" (Drucker 1989, 7), lost ground rapidly. Once again, the liberation of markets did not just naturally emerge but was connected to heavy political enforcement, namely, through the "Reagan-Thatcher free market doctrines" (Stiglitz 2001, xv) that came to dominate the 1980s and turned neoliberalism into an ideology of unprecedented dominance and pervasiveness and of truly global dimensions. At first glance, these neoliberal doctrines seem like a mere copy of the classical liberal laissez-faire policies. Indeed, "the utopian experiment of a self-regulating market" (Polanyi 2001, 258) forms the core also of the neoliberal project. However, neoliberalism deviates from its classical ancestor in one central aspect (Ulrich 2008, 326ff.): its novelty lies in its explicit acknowledgment of the active role of the state as a facilitator and guarantor of the undistorted working of the "free" market. In classical liberalism the state was regarded as insignificant or as an obstruction to the free-market project, but it plays a constitutive role in neoliberalism (e.g., M. Friedman 1962, 15, 22ff.). It is in this aspect that neoliberalism's roots in postwar ordoliberalism become visible. What distinguishes neoliberalism from ordoliberalism is merely the function ascribed to the government. While ordoliberalism sees the state as a regulator of the market, neoliberals emphasize its role as the market's liberator and enforcer (Ulrich 2008, 320f.).

Thus neoliberalism does not share the deep and fundamental suspicion of classical liberalism toward any political involvement in the economic or societal order (Ulrich 2008, 323f.). Nozick (1974), for example, claimed that free markets work only within an effective political framework constituted by the institutions of the minimal state. Classical liberals, on the other hand, regarded such a political framework as dispensable and even as hindering the free market. To be sure, within such a framework of legal, jurisdictional, fiscal, and infrastructural rules, neoliberals also believe that the market should be self-regulating, and they condemn any further punctual political intervention by the state as an illegitimate distortion. Hence neoliberals also consider the mechanism of the market superior to any other form of social coordination and the deregulation of all restrictions on economic competition as socially desirable.

Thus this ostensible "repoliticization" of the economy in neoliberal thought turns out to be a chimera. The constitutive role of politics is not aimed at the limitation of the market mechanism but, on the contrary, at its active enforcement (Ulrich 2008, 321). At a closer look, neoliberalism even denotes a radicalization of the classical liberal creed by subordinating even the principle of laissez-faire itself to the demands of the free competitive market (Polanyi 2001, 155). Because laissez-faire in the truest sense of the word would inevitably result in social limitations on the market, its liberation had to be politically enforced by subjecting the market frame itself to the requirements of market efficiency. Neoliberalism aims not only at the depoliticization of the economy but much more profoundly at the apolitical interpretation of politics in general (Maak 1999, 24). In other words, neoliberalism does not aim at the depoliticization of the economy but at the economization of politics. What is portrayed as a necessary and even healing process by neoliberal ideologues is in fact the most enhanced and persistent form of economism: the "displacement of politics by the market" (Höffe 2002c, 26; translation by author).

The growing technocratic tendencies that characterize all developed nations, as well as the political processes at the global level today, are direct symptoms of these developments. The very fact that economic policy itself is interpreted as subordinate to the requirements of a functioning market mechanism enhances the dependency of politicians on the judgments and assessments of economists, who are replacing democratic deliberation through the "functional authority" (Ulrich 1986, 152) of their specific knowledge. Symptomatically, economists tend to define the term *political economy* as the mere application of economic methods and concepts to politics (e.g., Frey 1984).

It is these ideological transformations that build the foundation of an adequate understanding of multinational corporations' transformation into quasi-governmental institutions. Paradoxically, the initial classical liberal attempt to depoliticize the economy led to a reverse process of increasing politicization of multinational corporations in the subsequent neoliberal era. The economization of politics did not make politics as such disappear. Rather, it led to the politicization of economic institutions themselves. I will further examine this conclusion, which I will call the "neoliberal paradox," in the following paragraphs.

The Neoliberal Paradox: The Implicit Politicization of the Private Enterprise

Karl Polanyi unmasked the economic liberal dream of a self-regulating market economy as a utopia. Free markets evolve and survive only through political enforcement and protection. Neoliberalism, as argued earlier, drew the consequences of this insight and sacrificed the idea of laissez-faire to the overarching goal of a free market. Thus the neoliberal approach aims not at the elimination but at the instrumentalization of politics in the name of the market. It seeks to place the whole organization of society under the functional authority of the market mechanism. It has promoted not only the uncoupling of the system from the lifeworld but also the "colonization" of the lifeworld by the imperatives of the system (Habermas 1987, 196); its ideal is the seemingly apolitical governance of society by the market and thus the creation of a "total market society" (Ulrich 2008, 113) in which systemic interaction replaces other forms of social integration in all areas of societal life.

What is striking about the neoliberal approach is that its worldwide enforcement indeed brought it closer to the realization of a truly free market than at any time before in history. Breaking up national economies through heavy deregulation and liberalization, combined with the limited political reach of nation-states and the lack of any comprehensive framework at the global level, has created a global regulatory vacuum that is as close as one gets to the global laissez-faire utopia. This represents the core of what Ulrich Beck (2000, 9) calls "globalism," that is, "the ideology of rule by the world market" and thus "the view that the world market eliminates or supplants political action."

However, even the market-dominated global society created by neoliberal policies is not an apolitical society. The vision of an apolitical society will always remain a phantasm. Replacing political spaces and governance through the market mechanism does not eliminate the political altogether; the economization of politics does not make the political space or domain as such disappear. Rather than a complete replacement of politics, it denotes its apolitical interpretation. This, however, does not lead to the depoliticization of political spaces but, on the contrary, to the politicization of the apolitical itself. In other words, the retreat of governments from effective politics in the global economic sphere does not mean the elimination or decline of the political. The political is not tied to one specific actor; rather, the political space will be taken over by those institutions that are next in line. Hence the replacement of politics by markets in fact leads to the politicization of the market itself and thus of the economic actors whose power develops through its mechanism (Zürn 2008, 293, 305ff.).

Adolf Berle (1967, 37) observed that any vacuum in human organization is invariably filled by power. Consequently, the global regulatory vacuum that has opened up between a partial "retreat of the state" (Strange 1996) and the lack of an adequate institutional response at the global level shifts power to new players entering the political carousel—new "geographic or functional entities," as Mathews (1997, 61) puts it, "that might grow up alongside the state, taking over some of its powers and emotional resonance."

The architects of the global free market should have considered this insight. They planned to free the multinational corporation from all political interference and establish it as an apolitical institution. But what they achieved—Berle would have predicted it—was the exact opposite: the multinational corporation itself turned into a genuinely political actor on the global political parquet. By the end of the 20th century, at the zenith of their economic power and influence, multinational corporations had become the dominant institutions and "political key actors" in shaping the global business environment (Vernon 1998, 27; Scherer 2003, 95).

The politicization of multinational corporations comes in two distinct shapes, which we may call implicit politicization and normative politicization. The implicit politicization of multinational corporations that results as a direct consequence of the formal depoliticization of the economy and the economization of politics can be understood in terms of a shift of influence on the constitution of the society and its will-formation processes to multinational corporations. In other words, the notion of implicit politicization captures the transfer of political power to multinational corporations. The notion of the apolitical corporation is but a cynical remnant of the perverted neoliberal idea to create a mechanistic society governed by the law of the market. At a time when politics seems little more than a puppet of "economic necessities," those actors that factually control and command the economic sphere inevitably turn into the politically dominant institutions. Hence instead of creating an apolitical corporation, neoliberalism exposed the multinational corporation as a quasi-governmental institution—this is the essence of the neoliberal paradox. The fact of political power, however, leads to the claim for normative politicization. Normative politicization is the need for multinational corporations publicly to justify and legitimize their actions in the face of direct, that is, unmediated (by either the state or the market), claims and concerns not merely of consumers and with reference to the laws of supply and demand but of the political subjects or citizens of the relevant community within truly deliberative processes. In other words, normative politicization of the corporation means shifting the normative focus on corporate legitimacy from the mere satisfaction of given material preferences in the market to the discursive clarification of claims and concerns in the public and political arena (see, e.g., Palazzo and Scherer 2006, 76ff.; Scherer and Palazzo 2007, 1108). As Michael Zürn (2008, 293) puts it, " 'Governance with and without government' is subject to the same normative claims as 'governance by government.' " The following two chapters will spell out in more detail the implications of the implicit politicization of multinational corporations. Its normative consequence, that is, the notion of normative politicization, will be addressed in chapters 8 and 9 in the form of human rights obligations of multinational corporations and with the claim for democratization in chapter 10.

Chapter 6

Political Power and Authority of Multinational Corporations

THE BRIEF ELABORATIONS on the depoliticization of the economy and the economization of politics in the previous chapter built the train of thought that implies the transformation of the multinational corporation into a quasi-governmental institution today. Polanyi's observation that in the classical liberal era societal life became increasingly subordinated to the requirements of the market holds true even more today. The crucial difference, however, is that today it is the requirements of the global competitive market that shape and dictate the political agenda and organization of our society.

It is under these circumstances that the multinational corporation has acquired vast amounts of power and influence over social and societal life in general. In a market-controlled society the institutions that shape and dominate the global economic sphere inevitably turn into major political forces that affect the organization of society as a whole. While the business of governments seems more than ever to be business, as Noreena Hertz (2001, 169) eloquently stated, the business of business, in contrast, is increasingly turning into that of governments.

An inquiry into the quasi-governmental role of multinational corporations must start with an analysis of corporate power. More specifically, I will start with an inquiry into the public nature of corporate power, which will then lead to an assessment of its historical foundations. In the logical next step, I will examine the sources of corporate power in the global political economy. I will argue that corporate (political) power today is essentially structural. This argument will be supported by showing not only that the structural transformations in the global market have put multinational corporations in commanding positions in the global political economy, but that multinationals were themselves a driving force in bringing these transformations about. I will illustrate these findings with the example of corporate control over the global food system and conclude this chapter with an inquiry into the concept of authority. This will effectively complete the conceptual foundations for theorizing the multinational corporation as a quasi-governmental institution.

The Public Nature of Corporate Power

Mainstream economic thought is based on a sharp institutional separation of the economic and the political spheres. Both the market and its main actors—corporations—are perceived as inherently apolitical. In other words, the goal of the neoliberal ideology is not only to foster the illusion of the corporation as a purely private institution but also to make us embrace its allegedly apolitical nature. This perception of the corporation as an entirely private, economic institution has contributed decisively to obscuring the question of corporate power. The disassociation of corporate power from the political sphere has effectively shielded it from major public scrutiny (Derber 1998, 2ff.).

It is peculiar to the economic liberal ideology that it associates the private sphere with unrestricted personal freedom while denouncing anything public as coercion and interference in our personal lives. The private and the public are seen as mutually exclusive, with the private being the good guy and the public its enemy. The emphasis on "private freedom" is the real reason for economic liberals' affinity for the free market. "Free" in this regard means free of political interference and restriction; a free market is guided only by personal preferences and private transactions. Therefore, it represents the epitome of the kind of freedom that libertarians claim is the essence of a human life. The argument in part I of this book, however, shows that this definition of personal freedom is based on questionable premises. Well-understood freedom, as we saw, must be thought of as equal freedom. In other words, one's own freedom must be defined not in terms of one's own self-interest but in terms of the equal freedom of all others. This notion of equal freedom is inherently public. From the perspective of equal freedom, it is impossible judiciously to separate the private and the public, the economic and the political spheres. The private sphere is inevitably subject to public legitimation insofar as it might be in conflict with the idea of the fundamental equality of human beings. In other words, the private is private only as long as it can—hypothetically—be publicly legitimized. It is against this background that Immanuel Kant (2001a, 136f.) discovered the freedom of man to make use of one's reason, that is, the freedom to form and follow one's own (private) motives and activities, in the *"public use* of his reason in all matters." Hence, according to Kant, it is the public use of man's reason, not the private one, "that must be free at all times." Legitimacy of one's own motives and thus of the sphere of private activities is based on mooting them publicly. Hence the public turns out to be not a restriction to personal freedom but its constitutive basis. There is nothing more public than the determination and definition of what is to be considered private within a society (Ulrich 2008, 298f.). If the public is constitutive for the private sphere, however, then their separation into exclusive and discrete domains logically cannot hold. If we understand as publicly relevant those questions, issues, states of affairs, and actions that affect the way we live as a society, that is, the ones that give rise to the claim for legitimation and justification, then the political refers to the communicative processes for the deliberation of these claims. In other words, issues that are of public relevance are per se subject to political deliberation because they inevitably affect the constitution of our society. It is from this perspective that there are no issues of purely or exclusively economic nature; economic questions are of public relevance and thus by nature and implication notoriously political (Strange 2002a, 202). Hence neither the market nor, consequently, corporations can be considered purely economic, private, or apolitical institutions.

Insofar as corporate actions are of public relevance, their role and purpose are subject to political deliberation. Thus private corporations are anything but purely private and apolitical. They are, in fact, "quasi-public institutions" (Ulrich 1977; translation by author) of inherently political concern. Their publicness naturally increases with the growing impact of their policies and actions on society. In other words, any attempt to separate the private from the public will ultimately fail because of the aspect of power. Power is by nature public; there is no such thing as "private power." This is why economists tend to define corporate power in purely negative terms, that is, as the absence of competition. Only this negative definition allows them to maintain the separation of the economic from the political sphere and thus to exclude the question of power altogether from economic analysis. As long as there is competition, no individual or firm is perceived as dominant, and no economic power is evoked (Galbraith 2004, 7). A positive definition of power, on the other hand, would inevitably lead economists into political evaluations of the question "power over what?" It shifts the focus to those who are subject to corporate power. In other words, it deals with authority relations. Authority, however, is inherently public (R. B. Friedman 1990, 79; Cutler 1999a, 63). It cannot be dealt with from an apolitical perspective.

The perception that the absence of government intervention renders the economic sphere apolitical presupposes an overly narrow understanding of the political as associated exclusively with state actions and institutions. However, politics is not limited to what politicians do (Strange 1996, xiv); it entails more than formal political institutions or processes and includes all the informal communicative and deliberative processes and activities that create and maintain such institutions and processes in the first place. Without such deliberative processes a democratic system is not viable. Thus institutionally bound, government-centric interpretations of the political, which focus exclusively on formal political processes, fail to capture the forces and factors that determine the factual functioning of the governing system of a political community (Ulrich 1977, 18). They fail to account for the profound impacts that allegedly private institutions can have on the public sphere and thus for the politically relevant character of their actions. A. Claire Cutler summarized these connections with compelling clarity:

> Liberalism obscures the political significance of private economic power through the association of authority with the public sphere and its disassociation with private activities. Indeed liberalism renders *private authority* an impossibility by creating the distinction between public and private activities and locating the "right to rule" or authority squarely in the public sphere. [...]
> The public/private distinction renders the political significance of transnational and multinational corporations invisible. (Cutler 1999a, 73)

If we are to understand and analyze international politics properly, and if adequate solutions to current political problems and challenges at the global level are to be found, we can no longer turn a blind eye on the political role of international business (Strange 1996, xiv). The corporation is by no means an apolitical institution and never has been. The history of business shows in many ways how companies have always played publicly and politically significant roles; the modern multinational corporation is no exception. On the contrary, its operations are more politicized than ever before in corporate history. The following section will develop this historical perspective on corporate power in more detail.

Historical Foundations of Corporate Power

The history of corporate power is a history of the ongoing deregulation of the marketplace, combined with the simultaneous and continuous expansion of corporate rights. This process started to gain momentum in the early 19th century and is still continuing today.

What we perceive as a private corporation today started as a genuinely public institution. English law in the 18th century did not make a distinction between private and public enterprises. All of them were equally regarded as an instrumentality of the state (Bowman 1996, 50). Even after the emergence of private business institutions in the first half of the 19th century, corporations were tied to the extensive and tight regulations of public charters. Charters were issued by parliamentary act and were constitutive for the creation of corporations.[1] Thus the corporation, even though privately owned and run, was still regarded as an instrument of the state in its quest to serve the public good. What was private about the corporation was merely its foundation in private property; its purpose and goals, however, remained firmly rooted in the public domain. Concordantly, only those corporations that served the public interest directly by providing a public service had the prospect of receiving a charter, which meant that only a very limited number of charters were issued during the first half of the 19th century. The number of "private" corporations, in other words, remained small.

Corporate charters had a limited duration, typically about 20 years. Often, charters were issued only for the realization of a very specific public project after whose completion the business was terminated. There was no such thing as immortal business as we know it today—a corporation's life was determined by its charter and could be ended by the government at any time. As a consequence, corporations that failed to fulfill their mandate to benefit the public frequently had their charters revoked and were dissolved. The charter's extensive and tight provisions secured close legislative oversight over the company's operations at all times (A. D. Chandler 2002, 82). In sum, a corporate charter defined a company's scope of business and its duration, determined its internal organization and operations, and limited its size by regulating its capitalization (Bowman 1996, 42, 51). Under these circumstances the accumulation of great corporate power was virtually impossible.

However, the more complicated business organizations and their operations became, the more corporations started pressing for more freedom and independence from government regulations. The English Joint Stock Company Act of 1856 and several similar rulings in the United States throughout the 19th century (see Bowman 1996) ultimately created the basis for the corporation's accumulation of economic power. It should be noted that in England the so-called South Sea Bubble Act banned the corporate form almost completely for more than 100 years after the fraudulent collapse of the South Sea Company in 1720. By establishing limited liability for shareholders, the Joint Stock Company Act made it possible for the corporation to issue a larger amount of stock to a much broader public. It enabled, first of all, the booming railway industry to raise the massive amounts of capital necessary to finance its giant projects. Limiting the liability of shareholders to the amount they invested in the company effectively separated the corporation as an entity from the people who ultimately formed and owned it. In other words, business was no longer merely a partnership of individuals, as it had been historically, but was turned into an artificial individual itself—an individual able to act in its own name, on its own behalf, and on its own responsibility.

This status of the corporation as an individual was backed and strengthened by the courts in several rulings in the second half of 19th-century America and ultimately culminated in the landmark ruling of 1886 in which the Supreme Court granted protection to corporations under the Fourteenth Amendment. By the end of the 19th century the corporation was fully transformed into a person (Bakan 2004, 16). It was now to be treated as a free individual enjoying the constitutional rights of real human beings. Granting corporations the rights to property, freedom of speech, and liberty of contract was the basis on which corporate power was created and perpetuated. The Fourteenth Amendment, which was initially intended to protect the equal rights of freed slaves, was reinterpreted to protect the rights of the corporation, that is, of the very creature that often was and today still is at the center of the persistent and ongoing abuse of people's rights, not least through forced labor and slavery-like working conditions (see, e.g., International Labour Office 2005). This is certainly not the only irony in corporate history, but it is without a doubt one of the most striking ones.

Corporate personhood not only was the basis and ultimate condition for the accumulation of corporate power but also provided an ideological means for its justification at the same time. By regarding the corporation as an individual participant in the economic game, the classical liberal creed of the "invisible hand" could conveniently be maintained and used as the ideological basis on which the claim for noninterference in corporate affairs could be defended. In other words, the accumulation of power in and through the corporate form could conveniently be hidden behind the ideological veil of corporate individualism. Even today, as Scott Bowman (1996, 182) concludes, "corporate individualism continues to be the most important ideological weapon in the arsenal of corporate power."

Along with the establishment of the corporation as a free person went the steady decline of charters as a regulatory instrument and safeguard of the public interest. The constitutive parliamentary act that had been necessary for setting up a corporation eventually was replaced by a simplified administrative process. Charters could now be issued more efficiently and in greater number without extensive examination of the corporations' business operations. In Britain the Joint Stock Companies Act of 1844 even established incorporation through simple registration (Micklethwait and Wooldridge 2003, 49). Slowly but surely the private interest of the corporation replaced the public purpose it was originally designed for. Not only did the act of incorporation become less formal, but also the regulation stipulated in the charter was loosened, allowing for longer durations, greater capitalization, and other benefits. Finally, when in 1899 the new General Incorporation Law of the state of Delaware shifted the determination of the scope and purpose of the corporation entirely from the public into the private realm, the corporation broke loose. Delaware's measure was an answer to New Jersey's successful attempts to attract 95 percent of the country's biggest corporations (Derber 1998, 133). Thus New Jersey's favorable incorporation law forced all other states to match its measures, sparking a true race to the bottom in corporate regulation among American states. The abolition of regulations limiting the duration, purpose, and scope of the corporation, the loosening of controls on mergers and acquisitions, and allowing corporations to hold stock in other corporations triggered the first wave of gigantic corporate mergers and heralded the age of corporate capitalism. In the six years between 1898 and 1904 some 1,800 corporations were consolidated into 157 (Bakan 2004, 14), giving rise to larger and more powerful corporations than ever before in corporate history.

The dramatic increase of corporate power was accompanied by its equally blatant abuse. These artificial creations, "the Frankenstein monsters," as Justice Louis Brandeis called them, threatened to overpower even their creators, that is, the people and the government. Increasing opposition and protest were prompted not only by activist judges like Brandeis but also by a growing number of concerned citizens and outraged workers whose rights were trampled underfoot by the fast-growing corporations. It became increasingly visible that the market mechanism, which was so highly praised in the Gilded Age, did not work in favor of all but only for an exclusive handful of wealthy capitalists.

As the social outcry gained momentum in the broad public, the myth of the self-regulating market and with it the utopia of an institutional separation of the economic and the political spheres started wavering. The death of this myth eventually exposed powerful corporations as political agents; the core of their economic activity started to get politicized in the public. The formation of powerful countermovements in the form of trade unions at the beginning of the 20th century eventually spilled over into governmental policies that actively curbed corporate power for decades to come. Only the emergence of the neoliberal ideology and its powerful global aspirations in the last quarter of the 20th century gave corporate history another turn. The trend toward enhanced regulatory control of companies that prevailed during the postwar era until the early 1970s was reversed. Countless national and international rules and rulings reinforced the neoliberal course of economic globalization and strengthened corporate rights. These developments essentially laid the foundation for an unprecedented surge in corporate power during the last decades of the 20th century (Bakan 2004, 20f.).

The late 20th-century economic globalization process has brought about a further push for corporate autonomy. It has enhanced the international mobility of corporations, freed them from the bonds of location (Bakan 2004, 22), and withdrawn them from the grip of governments. It is this aspect of mobility that renders the power of today's multinational corporations even superior to that of the behemoths of the early 20th century. They have entered a new stage of their development. Starting as associations or partnerships among entrepreneurs, they eventually became accepted as "persons," that is, as citizens of a political community with their own personality, constitutional rights, and the ability to perform autonomous actions in the mid-1800s. Today multinational corporations have entered the transformation from citizens into governments. They are increasingly acting not as mere persons but as rule makers; as such, they determine our private and social lives, as well as our public affairs, to an unprecedented and ever-increasing extent.

Ingredients of Corporate Power

"Power is like the weather," says Joseph Nye (2004, 1); "everyone depends on it and talks about it, but few understand it." This seems to hold true especially for the power of corporations. Much has been written about corporate power, but the divide between those who believe that corporations have too much power and those who think that they have too little could not be deeper. While some claim that corporations now rule the world, others feel that their power is still only marginal in comparison with that of governments. What many of these contributions have in common, however, is that they lack a clear idea of what corporate power actually is. While some simply equate power with size, others reduce it to the mere possession of financial resources. This commonly leads to discussions about whether corporations really have become bigger and wealthier, which ultimately divert attention from the real issue of corporate power rather than contributing to its clarification. Therefore, this section aims at enriching the discussion by providing a more nuanced and realistic account of corporations' power, especially in its political dimension.

Corporate (Political) Power Briefly Defined

Before we can analyze multinational corporations' political power and its sources, we must have a broad idea about the meaning of power in general. A suitable starting point for reflection is the basic Weberian interpretation of power as the possibility of one individual to influence the behavior of others. A definition of power solely in terms of influence on others' behavior, however, remains vague. As seen earlier in connection with the communitarian argument, human beings are inherently social creatures whose actions and behaviors are inevitably interdependent. Therefore, all our actions and activities are necessarily conditioned by the fact that we live with other people (Arendt 1998, 22). Because we are in constant interaction with other individuals, however, most of our actions will cause certain reactions. If I drop an empty can on the street, for example, does that mean I exercise power over the person who ultimately happens to pick it up? I clearly influenced someone else's behavior through my actions, but did I really exert power over him or her? Perhaps that person picked up the can because of an inner commitment to a clean environment and even took satisfaction from disposing of it. Or what if this person is a garbage collector who gets paid for picking up my can?

Intuitively, it seems that not all kinds of influence denote power under all circumstances. Thus the reliance on influence alone is unlikely to lead to a consistent understanding of the nature of power.

Two specifications are needed to make more sense of the notion of power. First, if we are to measure power in terms of the change in behavior of other individuals, we must know something about their preferences (Nye 2004, 2). Power can then be interpreted as the ability of A to get B to do something she would not otherwise do. Second, to influence someone or something without accomplishing anything for ourselves seems not to reflect an exercise of power either (Morriss 1987, 30). A more promising way to define power that meets these objections is in terms of outcomes, that is, as the ability of an actor to achieve desired outcomes, possibly but not necessarily (Morriss 1987, 30ff.) by influencing the behavior of other individuals. In other words, power is the ability to direct outcomes in such a way that our preferences take precedence over the preferences of others (Strange 1996, 17). This leads us to Max Weber's more elaborate, final definition of power: "In general, we understand by 'power' the chance of a man or of a number of men to realize their own will in a communal action even against the resistance of others who are participating in the action" (Weber 1958b, 180; 1962, 117).

The previous sections did not merely talk about corporate power in general but more specifically about corporate political power. Social interaction is commonly said to be of a political nature if it is directed toward the achievement of a common end. For Iris Marion Young (2004, 377), the political is the "activity in which people organize collectively to regulate or transform some aspects of their shared social conditions," as well as the "communicative activities in which they try to persuade one another to join such collective action or decide what direction they wish to take it." This is consistent with the notions of politicization and depoliticization developed earlier. Depoliticization, as defined earlier, is not merely the absence of formal political intervention but essentially the suppression of communicative rationalization of social processes. Thus, if we combine the notion of the political with the one of power developed so far, political power refers to an agent's ability to direct and influence such collective organization processes and to "manipulate" (Merriam 1934, 7) its participants to identify with and work toward the ends set and the outcomes desired by the agent who exerts power—political power is "social power wielded for political objectives" (Presbey 1997, 32). Therefore, politically relevant power has a direct influence on the maintenance or transformation of the formal or factual constitution of a society within a particular geographic entity (Ulrich 1977, 19).

Early 20th-century students of corporate power generally still interpreted corporate political power in narrow, institutionally bound ways. The political power of corporations was seen in the ability of corporations to directly control and influence political leaders. Hence they understood political power exclusively in terms of corrupt alliances between business magnates and political leaders (Bowman 1996, 101). Corporations were regarded as unable to act politically on their own terms; the only way for them to achieve political power was through invading formal political channels, that is, through influencing and corrupting the traditional political entities and agents. The ability to do so was perceived to derive from the corporations' economic power, which was usually defined in terms of wealth concentration.

The reality of early 20th-century liberalism was indeed one of heavily enmeshed interests between political and economic leaders. However, such institutionally bound understandings of political power are too narrow and perpetuate the strict separation of the economic and the political spheres. It is precisely this omnipresence of corrupt relationships that might have contributed to obscuring the fact that not only is the use of corporate wealth in order to influence political leaders of political relevance, but also the very corporate decisions made within the prior process of the creation and concentration of this wealth must be interpreted in terms of political control and power. In other words, the separation between economic and political power is largely futile.

Peter Drucker was among the first scholars to spell out the political relevance of corporations' economic activities and processes. Accordingly, his notion of corporate power was not based simply on accumulated wealth; he defined corporate power as corporations' control over access to a society's productive organization (Drucker 1949, 44). Accumulated wealth can indeed be used for influencing political agents—and, as we will see later, is one of the prime instruments in securing corporate authority—but it is only a symptom of an underlying process that is itself highly politicized. In other words, it is an expression, not a source, of corporate power.

What Drucker recognized, in contrast to early 20th-century scholars, was that the decisive aspect of corporate power is the capacity of corporations to influence the structure of society through their business decisions. The politically relevant power of corporations thus arises from their core activity and not just from the political use of the revenues deriving from it. According to Drucker (1949, 203), it is the managerial decisions and policies themselves that determine to a large extent the character of our society. Therefore, they are themselves deeply and inherently political. Controlling access to the productive organization of a society, he claimed, is similar to controlling access to the livelihood of its citizens. Therefore, he concluded, "the enterprise is also a *governmental* institution, inevitably and necessarily discharging political functions." For Drucker, "there has never been any doubt that whoever controls access to the citizen's livelihood exercises political control" (Drucker 1949, 44). This capacity for structural change was later described as the decisive determinant of the new (political) quality of corporate power also in Richard J. Barnet and Ronald E. Müller's influential work *Global Reach* (1974).

From Property-Based to Capability-Based Interpretations of Power

The emphasis of early 20th-century students on corporate wealth implies an understanding of power as a property of a particular actor. The wealthier a person or a corporation gets, the more powerful it is perceived to become. Such interpretations of power are problematic because they tend to disconnect the notion of power from the specific context in which it is generated. Hannah Arendt (1969, 44; 1998, 244), in contrast, claimed that power is generated when people act in concert and disappears the moment the group is dissolved. Arendt's limitation of power to concerted action is not without problems either (see, e.g., Habermas 1977, 15f.; Passerin d'Entrèves 1994, 8), but it contains one major attribute that leads to the rejection of the notion of power as a property: her insight that power disappears the moment a specific group is dissolved implies that it cannot be "possessed" (Presbey 1997, 29) but must ultimately be attributed to relations. If power could be possessed, as Arendt rightly argues, "omnipotence would be a concrete human possibility" (Arendt 1998, 201). In reality, however, power is limited by the existence of other people; it is a function of people's social relations (Merriam 1934, 16). Because it is bound to social relations, it is inherently dependent on the context in which those relations exist. A changing context can thus quickly lead to the evaporation of power even if the properties of a specific agent remain unchanged (Nye 2004, 2).

Power resources are not as fungible as money. What wins in one game may not help at all in another. Holding a winning poker hand does not help if the game is bridge. Even if the game is poker, if you play your high hand poorly, you can still lose. Having power resources does not guarantee that you will always get the outcome you want. [. . .] Power resources cannot be judged without knowing the context. Before you judge who is holding the high cards, you need to understand what game you are playing and how the value of the cards may be changing. (Nye 2004, 3, 4)

Wealth- or resource-based definitions certainly make power appear more predictable and quantifiable, but they are unable to explain or even capture the fact that the mere possession of resources does not always translate into power over outcomes (Strange 1996, 19; Nye 2004, 3). This is where the notion of power connects with the concept of capability. Capabilities can be interpreted as the ability of an agent to convert income, wealth, resources, or opportunities into desired achievements. It is precisely this ability to determine outcomes that is at the heart of the definition of power. Thus power is dependent not only on a specific agent's characteristics and properties but just as much on favorable external circumstances. In the absence of favorable external conditions, power remains an abstract potentiality or capacity. In other words, capabilities denote the ability to actualize latent power.

It should be noted that Susan Strange (1996, 19ff.), whose concept of structural power will be of central importance in this book, was rather skeptical about such capability-based interpretations of power. Strange too warned against defining power as a property of agents rather than in terms of relationships or processes that affect and determine outcomes. Capabilities, in her opinion, are possessed by persons and institutions and thus are properties that are unable to capture the more latent character of power. Her interpretation of capabilities as properties, however, is too narrow; it ignores that capabilities are generated through the interplay between personal characteristics and enabling external conditions. Hence, rather than the connection between power and capabilities, it is Strange's notion of capabilities that is problematic. In other words, it is not our notions of power that are incompatible, but rather our definitions of capabilities. Once we define capabilities in the broader terms of this analysis, however, a combined structural and capability-based interpretation of power is entirely possible.

Sources of Corporate Power: From Relational to Structural Power

In her 1988 work *States and Markets* and later in *The Retreat of the State* (1996), Susan Strange argued that the emergence of a highly interdependent global economic system renders a conventional "relational," or Weberian, understanding of power as the ability of A to get B to do something she would not otherwise do increasingly obsolete. She was dissatisfied with the realist and neorealist tradition of defining and explaining the global economy purely in terms of international economic relations. Instead, she claimed, power must increasingly be understood as structural. Thus she argued that power is not located within the economic relations between states but increasingly within the structures of the emerging global system that spans the entire society of states. It should be pointed out that Weber (1958c, 161) himself was not unaware of the structural nature of power. He explicitly noted that power can be ascribed to political and economic structures and that the "Great Powers" are the ones who "ascribe to themselves and usurp an interest" in these "political and economic processes over a wide orbit." This inherently structural power, as Weber already noticed, is of increasingly global dimension: "Today such orbits encompass the whole surface of the planet." This new perspective opens the methodological space necessary not only to include nonstate actors in analyses of power in the global political economy but also to assess the impacts of the system and changes therein on state policies (Lawton, Rosenau, and Verdun 2000, 7f.).

According to Strange, four main or basic structures are the pillars of the global political economy. Without a central production structure, finance structure, knowledge structure, and security structure, she argues, the global economic system is not viable. All other, secondary power structures—examples include transport systems, the organization of trade, energy, or welfare—are to be considered mere derivatives of and dependent on and molded by these four primary structures. Strange's claim is that these structures are the ultimate sources of power in the global political economy. Commanding them means to make decisions about the four basic societal needs that must be met in the global economy: security, knowledge, production of goods, and the provision of credit and money (Lawton, Rosenau, and Verdun 2000, 8). In other words:

> Power over others, and over the mix of values in the system, is exercised within and across frontiers by those who are in a position to offer security, or

to threaten it; by those who are in a position to offer, or to withhold, credit; by those who control access to knowledge and information and who are in a position to define the nature of knowledge. Last but not least, there is the production structure, in which power is exercised over what is to be produced, where, and by whom on what terms and conditions. (Strange 1996, ix)

Strange's basic argument is that in the highly interdependent global economic system the ability to determine outcomes is less dependent on direct relational influence over other actors than it is on the capability to shape the context in which those relations are embedded. More precisely, she argues that power in the global political economy means to control and determine the structures within which other participants, including states and their political institutions, have to operate and interact (Strange 1988, 24ff.). Her argument resembles Joseph Nye's (1990, 2004) observation of a shift from hard to soft power, occurring against the background of an increasingly interdependent global system. While hard power is similar to relational power and denotes the capacity to coerce, soft power is a more indirect way of determining outcomes through influencing others' interests, attitudes, agendas, and identities. Similarly, structural power "confers the power to decide how things shall be done, the power to shape frameworks within which states relate to each other, relate to people, or relate to corporate enterprises" (Strange 1988, 24ff.). In other words, it is precisely the kind of power that distinguishes primary from secondary agents of justice.

It is important to be aware of two slightly different interpretations of structural power, both of which will be relevant to this analysis. Strange herself had been criticized for not paying sufficient attention to this distinction (Keohane 2000b, xi). They derive from two different interpretations of "structure" as either power in itself or merely as a power resource. In the first case, the determination of outcomes through structures directly constitutes power. Therefore, power itself is to be interpreted as a structure. Control over structures thus constitutes a power position for an agent because he or she is able to affect or determine the relevant outcomes. This interpretation has also been called "locational power" (Caporaso and Haggard 1989, 113ff.). In the second case, the power-relevant outcomes are derivatives of the outcomes produced by the structures. Control over structures is thus used as a power resource in order to achieve higher-valued outcomes for the agent in control. This happens when an agent strategically uses its superior structural position in bargaining processes in order to achieve favorable outcomes. Using structures as a power resource thus constitutes a hybrid position between structural and relational power: the agent uses its structural power position as leverage within direct, relational bargaining processes.

Against this background, multinational corporations that control large parts of the global production structure can be regarded as powerful in two ways. First, they are powerful because of their commanding position over the production process, that is, their ability to determine outcomes in the global production structure. Additionally, they can use the dependencies deriving from this commanding position to influence bargaining processes in their favor. For example, with increasing dependency of states on multinationals' performance in creating and maintaining wealth for their citizens, multinationals can bargain for favorable conditions and treatment in tax and regulation matters. In the following I will use the term *structural power* as a collective term for both interpretations. If one keeps these brief elaborations in mind, it will be sufficiently evident which interpretation I refer to in the specific case.

In a nutshell, corporate political power can be summarized as the capability to determine outcomes by controlling, shaping, and influencing the structures of the global political economy. Hence if corporate political power is to be interpreted as structural power, then an inquiry into its nature must trace the structural transformations in the global economy that ultimately shifted power from states to multinational corporations. Using this insight, let us now look at how the structural transformations of the late 20th-century global economy have systematically increased multinational corporations' political power.

Structural Change and Corporate Power in the Global Political Economy

Susan Strange's central thesis in 1988 was that along with the structural turn, power in the global political economy had shifted from states to markets. The structures that determine outcomes in the global political economy, according to Strange, were not controlled exclusively by governments anymore, but increasingly by the market mechanism and the dominant market actors, that is, first of all by multinational corporations. The shift toward a more integrated global economic system and the ever-increasing significance of markets in allocating resources and outcomes has without a doubt continued and accelerated since Strange's analysis in 1988. In other words, the shift of structural power from states to markets is ongoing.

The insight that economic globalization has shifted power from states to markets is relatively uncontested today (Gilpin 2000, 315; Höffe 2002c, 153). Where opinions clash is about the degree and the desirability of this power shift. Mainstream economists are commonly sympathetic with the enlarged role of markets because, they argue, it frees individual initiative from governmental restraints and creates personal freedom and opportunities for everyone. Their opponents, on the other hand, point to the market mechanism's partiality and its structural asymmetries that create power imbalances and social dependencies. My aim in this section is to show that multinational corporations were and still are key agents in both inducing and reaping the benefits of these ongoing structural transformations. Therefore, they have created and consolidated an exceptionally powerful position within these structural changes. Two fundamental structural shifts are of defining importance for today's global economic system: the globalization of the production structure and the emergence of the knowledge-based global economy.

First Shift: From International Trade to Global Production

The deregulatory revolution that spread throughout the world in the 1980s and 1990s heralded the continuous reduction of barriers to foreign investment and the liberalization of the international money and goods markets. Combined with revolutionary technological innovations that decreased communication and transportation costs and offered new possibilities to do business at a global level, this revolution led to a dramatic increase in numbers and significance of multinational corporations in the world economy (Graham 1996, 9ff.). In 2004 the annual *World Investment Report* released by the United Nations Conference on Trade and Development (UNCTAD) counted 61,000 multinational corporations worldwide with over 900,000 foreign affiliates and more than 50 million employees around the globe. This number of multinationals was a fivefold increase since 1975 (Micklethwait and Wooldridge 2003, 173). In 2007 the number of multinational corporations reached 79,000, employing 82 million people around the globe (UNCTAD 2008, xvi).

These 79,000 multinationals now generate estimated total sales of $31 trillion yearly (UNCTAD 2008, xvi), an amount that greatly exceeds the total value of exported goods at the level of industrialized countries and at the aggregate global level (Vernon 1998, 9; Berghoff 2004, 141). The last three decades have undoubtedly established multinationals as the key drivers of economic globalization (Scherer 2003, 99; Berghoff 2004, 141).

In 1970 growth in foreign direct investment (FDI) overtook the average growth both of the world economy and of world trade. In the 1990s FDI grew four times faster than world output and three times faster than world trade (Micklethwait and Wooldridge 2003, 173), reaching an average growth rate of 25.6 percent in the period between 1986 and 2001 (Berghoff 2004, 141). This trend has also continued after 2001; after four consecutive years of steady growth and despite the accelerating global financial crisis, the year 2007 saw a record growth of 30 percent (UNCTAD 2008, xv). Consequently, multinationals' total FDI stock grew from $211 billion in 1973 to $7 trillion in 2003 and to over $15 trillion in 2007. As impressive as these numbers sound, they do not reflect the full magnitude of multinational corporations' significance in the global economy. Their indirect effects through multiplier mechanisms in the form of employment in supplier industries, for example, or their partnerships with contractors and subcontractors, which are increasingly replacing direct investment in subsidiaries, might be of even more significance than the direct effects expressed by these numbers. Moreover, multinational corporations not only have increased the quantitative dimensions of economic globalization but, more profoundly, have decisively altered its quality and structure. They have responded to the tremendous new opportunities and possibilities provided by new technologies and the liberalization of markets by adopting truly global strategies, splitting up their value chains across borders and countries and organizing their functions in truly transnational ways. Thus they have profoundly and irreversibly changed the logics of international production and allocation of goods and services.

The occurrence of such shifts is not entirely novel. The significance of this "revolution" in the global production structure can be compared with the one in late 19th-century America. In the wake of corporate capitalism, heavy liberalization and deregulation led to the interconnection of formerly local markets, while the spread of railways and new communication technologies offered new possibilities for corporations to expand their operations over large geographic distances. The emergence of an integrated American market offered tremendous opportunities for those corporations that mastered the new challenges of mass production and mass distribution (A. D. Chandler 2002).

Scale became the key success factor of the time, and massive consolidations within the market were the logical consequence. Those corporations that were successful in the new game grew dramatically in size, wealth, and power, and only a few hundred of them were left to dominate the American economy. Thus after scaling up local production for local markets into national production for national and international markets in the late 19th century, multinationals have now entered an entirely new stage of transnational production for global markets.

Just like the integration of the American market, the integration of global markets has led to a tremendous increase in market size. New skills and organizational measures are required to cope with the new challenges and to exploit the new opportunities. At the end of the 19th century large nationally oriented companies changed the logics of production and gained control over local corporations, but it is now multinational corporations that have decisively reshaped the production structure, taken it to the global level, and thus gained tremendous advantages over national companies. In the late 1990s sales of multinational corporations accounted for 20 to 30 percent of world output (Schwartz 2000, 220; Hertz 2001, 34). This ratio has become even more biased toward multinationals today. In 2007 the value-added activity (gross product) of multinationals' foreign affiliates worldwide accounted for 11 percent of global gross domestic product, with sales generally being five to six times higher than value added (UNCTAD 2008, 9f.). In many countries the share of multinational corporations—whether home based or foreign owned—of manufacturing output reaches well over 50 percent (see, e.g., Vernon 1998, 12f.), while the remaining domestic production is heavily influenced or even determined by the sourcing decisions of large multinational retailers (Klein 1999, 163). A similar increase of multinationals' importance is expected soon in the rapidly growing multinational services sector (UNCTAD 2004). After all, the services sector has accounted for by far the largest share of global FDI stocks and flows in recent years (UNCTAD 2008, 9). "The entire world economy," Charles Derber (2002, 71) concludes, "is increasingly a proprietary production of a few giant firms."

It is safe to say that multinational corporations have replaced the centuries-old leading position of foreign trade as the single most important organizational form for the allocation of goods in foreign markets (Scherer 2003, 99; Berghoff 2004, 140). The volume of international production exceeded the volume of international trade for the first time in the mid-1980s

(Stopford and Strange 1991, 14). Multinationals, however, not only have replaced a large part of international trade through global production but also have encroached on a growing fraction of the remaining part. Consequently, they account for about half of the world's trade in goods, two-thirds of which is internalized; that is, it takes place within multinational corporations themselves. This puts multinational corporations in a commanding position also over the overseas business and trade interests of many countries (Vernon 1998, 10ff.).

Multinational corporations have become the "central organizers" of economic activity in the world economy (UNCTAD 1992, 1, 6) and the dominant institution in the global production structure. Although in the 1980s and early 1990s multinationals were regarded as economic "engines of growth" (UNCTAD 1992), they have since advanced to becoming the key "agents of change" (Wilkins 1998b, 104; Story 2000, 26) in the transformation of a trade-based international economy into an integrated and highly interdependent global marketplace (UNCTAD 1998, xvii; Gilpin 2000, 164, 170; Micklethwait and Wooldridge 2003, 174; Berghoff 2004, 144f.). Massachusetts Institute of Technology (MIT) economist Lester Thurow (2003, 1) refers to them as the "actual builders" of a new, privately built global superstructure, and for Peter Drucker (1993, 37), it is one of the defining aspects of the large corporation that it not only is operating in a medium that is subject to continuous change but also occupies a leadership role within this change.

The replacement of traditional trade patterns as the main organizational form of allocating goods in foreign markets means that conventional comparative advantages are rapidly losing significance for nation-states. Michael Porter (1998b) showed that competitive advantage is increasingly replacing the concept of comparative advantage of nations. Competitive advantage of a state in the global economy, however, results from corporate strategies and government policy choices rather than from "given" comparative advantages, as was assumed in traditional trade theories (Gilpin 2001, 213). "National prosperity," Porter (1998b, 155, 161) commented on this fact, "is created, not inherited." Those countries with high-productivity industries or even only industry segments are most likely to succeed in the global competitive game. Precisely these seminal industries and among them especially those that are leading the technological advances of the future are dominated by multinational corporations today (Vernon 1998, 27). Thus the structural shift from a trade-based international economy to an integrated global market has significantly diminished the power of states to control economic events. Although they retain considerable negative power to control trade on their territory, their positive power to harness international resources and to influence and control the parameters of international production in the global market is increasingly limited. In this dimension they have largely lost their power to direct. All they can do is bargain (Stopford and Strange 1991, 14).

Economists have long considered multinational corporations insignificant. The shift from a trade-based international economy to a global competitive market, however, has put these corporations at the very center of attention. Multinational corporations have become the "major operators" (Strange 1996, 53) in the global economy; their prosperity and competitiveness have become a vital concern and priority of governments. For national governments today, economic policy means largely to ensure that their firms perform well in global markets. This reflects the very essence of structural power: multinational corporations have successfully altered the global economic system in a way that conditions other agents, among them most significantly nation-states, to advance multinationals' own preferences and to strengthen their own position. What seems like a harmony of preferences between governments and corporations—both of whom seem to be concerned predominantly with the corporations' economic success—is, in fact, the manifestation of multinational corporations' soft power, that is, their power to have other agents want to work in their favor. The reality increasingly is that governments do not have much choice under the current competitive circumstances. In order to avoid getting caught in a "downward spiral" (Hirst and Thompson 1999, 128), governments must stay competitive, and in order to stay competitive, they must support multinationals in their pursuit of profits. This is the essence of the shift of structural power from governments to large multinational corporations.

Second Shift: The Emergence of the Knowledge-Based Economy

Susan Strange argued that multinational corporations' power derives predominantly, if not exclusively, from their dominant position in the global production structure. She also recognized the increasing importance of the knowledge structure for the distribution of power and even claimed that its significance is "most overlooked and underrated" (Strange 1988, 115) by students concerned with power, but multinational corporations did not play a major role in her analysis of this structure.

Today there is hardly anyone who would disagree that knowledge has become a key factor in the global economy. The shift from an industrial era to a knowledge-based era, the third industrial revolution, as Lester Thurow (2003, 23ff.) called the process, has put the knowledge structure center stage. Knowledge and innovation have become the single most important factors of competitiveness in the global economy. The knowledge and production structures have always been inherently interconnected. However, in the shift to a knowledge-based economy, the knowledge structure has profoundly penetrated the production structure and has even come to dominate it. The capacity to control knowledge now "serves as the dynamic for the cornucopia of corporate production" (Brinkman and Brinkman 2002, 737). Within this process competition shifts to the creation and assimilation of knowledge, and information turns into the key element for gaining competitive advantage over other market participants (Porter 1998b, 155; Porter and Millar 1998, 75ff.). Consequently, for multinationals to keep and consolidate their dominant position in the production structure, they had to gain control also over the processes of knowledge creation and distribution.

Hence as the knowledge structure is taking over the economy, multinationals increasingly turn into the dominators of knowledge processes and thus into the "key actors in today's system of knowledge production" (Mytelka 2000, 39). This not only consolidates their powerful position relative to states but constitutes a far-reaching privatization of knowledge. This is illustrated perhaps most strikingly in regard to open and public access to the Internet, which is already in the firm grip of a handful of exceptionally powerful companies—the five or six global media giants, the main Internet service providers, and the usual suspects of cyberspace, i.e., the three Internet powerhouses Google, Yahoo, and Microsoft—controlling everything from access to applications and all the way to content, often and increasingly with severe implications for the privacy of Internet users (see Steinhardt and Stanley 2005, 245ff.). In other words, private corporations are in the process of monopolizing not only the information highway but also the information that flows through it (Derber 1998, 67). The information highway, as Debora Spar (1999, 352) commented aptly, is more and more turning into a "toll road." It is because of this trend that Charles Derber (1998, 67) compares the power position of today's "masters of the world's information highway" with the one of the "old railway barons." Both of them controlled, in some significant regard, the key distribution channels of their age. This process is not limited to the

Internet. In the United States five global media conglomerates, both competing and cooperating with each other in cartel-like market structures, own and control most of the country's newspapers, magazines, book publishers, motion picture studios, and radio and television stations. Although the media reach more people than ever, they have never been controlled by and concentrated in the hands of so few providers. No despot or dictatorship in history, Ben Bagdikian (2004, 3ff.) comments, has ever exercised more communications power than any one of these five companies. Universities also are increasingly penetrated by corporate interests. Lucrative sponsorship deals with large corporations shape their research focus and their curricula and make publicly funded research exclusively available to private corporations (see, e.g., Angell 2004).

Corporations' efforts to produce and control knowledge are backed by an extensive system of rules for the protection of intellectual property rights. These rules effectively support the monopolization of knowledge and its transformation from a public into a private good (Mytelka 2000, 43). The neoliberal era has heralded a continuous strengthening of these rules, increasing the patentability of knowledge and extending the duration of patents. The Agreement on Trade Related Aspects of Intellectual Property Rights (TRIPs) now grants patent life for 20 years, securing corporations' factual monopoly control even over such highly sensitive areas as lifesaving drugs. The scope of patents has also widened considerably and now reaches from products to processes and even to life-forms (Mytelka 2000, 44). The possibility to patent organisms and even human genes has effectively put corporations in a position to own and gain control over the keys to human life.

In the early 2000s the top 200 multinationals held 90 percent of the world's patents (Derber 2002, 71). In the biotechnology sector 95 percent of the gene-related patents were controlled by only five firms (Mytelka 2000, 43). Hence in order not to lose touch with technological development and thus to jeopardize their competitiveness, states must increasingly rely on alliances with large multinationals (Strange 1996, 7). Their role in maintaining alternatives to multinational corporations for securing the generation of and access to knowledge has been severely reduced (Mytelka 2000, 51).

The shift to a knowledge-based economy, according to Lester Thurow (2003, 30), is driven by six key technologies and their related industries: microelectronics, computers, telecommunications, man-made materials, robotics, and biotechnology. It is not a coincidence that in all these innovation-driven industries that are characterized by short product life cycles, high pace of technological change, and high costs, risks, and uncertainties (Mytelka 2000, 47), research and development activities are highly concentrated in the hands of a small number of large and potent firms. In the United States only 50 corporations out of a total of over 41,000 accounted for almost half of industry-based research and development in 1996. In Switzerland three firms accounted for 81 percent of national research and development, and in the Netherlands four companies were responsible for a share of 70 percent (UNCTAD 1999, 199).

However, knowledge processes not only play a central role in such new industries but also have become a key issue in traditional sectors where corporations have increasingly detected competitive advantages in organizational routines, collective expertise, or individual skills, that is, in firm-specific and highly localized tacit knowledge that is hard for established competitors to copy and thus creates effective entry barriers for potential new challengers (Mytelka 2000, 40f.). Thus production in a wide variety of industries has become more knowledge intensive, which has led to more emphasis on research and development or issues like process engineering, quality control, marketing, and the creation of brands or management skills in general (Mytelka 2000, 47). The notion of production increasingly transcends the narrow concern with material products. Accordingly, institutional and collective learning and mechanisms to create, store, and share knowledge, as well as measures to obtain, appropriate, and secure information, have moved to the center of attention in management studies.

Especially in knowledge-intensive industries the shift from a product-based to a knowledge-based economy is accompanied by the formation of large networks of strategic partnerships between firms trying to protect themselves against competition that arises across industry and sector boundaries. As a consequence, competition occurs increasingly between such networks instead of between individual companies and creates what Mytelka and Delapierre (1999) called "knowledge-based networked oligopolies." These networks shape the global economy and the rules of competition in unprecedented ways and consolidate the dominant position of multinational corporations in the global political economy. It is characteristic of knowledge-intensive, network-controlled industries that competition among industry leaders slows down, which stabilizes the position of large companies (Mytelka and Delapierre 1999, 140). Control over the knowledge structures thus effectively locks in their power positions.

The dependencies created by this increasing knowledge-based power of multinational corporations reach far beyond the implications for states' competitiveness in the global market; the social and societal ramifications of dependencies created in sensitive and essential sectors such as pharmaceuticals and health care too can hardly be overstated. Of symbolic character for this insight was the lawsuit filed by 30 pharmaceutical companies against the government of South Africa in 2001 that aimed at stopping the country's policy of securing access to affordable AIDS drugs for South African patients by breaking international patent laws. Although the lawsuit was eventually dropped in the face of manifest public outrage and protest, it illustrates strikingly the slowly shifting power balance in today's global society. The way multinationals shape the direction of technological change (Mytelka 2000, 42), the way they generate knowledge, and, most important, the way they share it not only change our political economy but also affect the foundation of our social and societal coexistence.

The knowledge structure, broadly defined, determines what knowledge is generated, how it is preserved and stored, how it is shared, by whom it is appropriated, and to whom it is communicated and on what terms. Therefore, it largely shapes the prevailing beliefs, morals, and principles in a society, it determines what is known and perceived as understood, and it defines the channels by which beliefs, ideas, and knowledge are communicated (Strange 1988, 115ff.). Thus control of the knowledge structure implies much more than just power. It also provides the means to create a sense of legitimacy for it, which means that it effectively creates a position of authority. This insight will be of central importance in the paragraphs to follow. Before expanding on it, however, let us have a more detailed look at one concrete example of how the structures of the global economy are increasingly dominated by large multinationals. The global food structure can serve as a representative example for many other similar structures, such as the global health structure and global transportation systems.

Illustrating Structural Power: The Global Food Structure

In his 2006 annual report to the Commission on Human Rights, the former UN special rapporteur on the right to food, Jean Ziegler, expressed grave concern that global hunger will continue to increase. He raised particular concerns regarding the policies of large transnational corporations that now dominate and monopolize "the whole food distribution system." Only 10 corporations, Ziegler reported, control one-third of the entire commercial seed market and 80 percent of the global pesticide market. Monsanto controls 91 percent of the global market for genetically modified seed. Another 10 corporations, Ziegler went on, control 57 percent of the total sales of the world's leading 30 retailers and account for 37 percent of the revenues of the 100 largest global food and beverage companies (United Nations 2006b, 16ff.). In 1994 only two companies, Cargill and Continental, shared half of total U.S. grain exports. The significance of this number increases if one notes that the United States accounted for 36 percent of wheat, 64 percent of corn, barley, sorghum, and oats, 40 percent of soybeans, 17 percent of rice, and 33 percent of cotton traded worldwide (Lehman and Krebs 1996, 125). These numbers seem to confirm the 2003 note of the UN secretary general to the General Assembly raising concerns that large corporations increasingly control the production and provision of food and water and thus the entire global food system (United Nations 2003, 11).

Under these circumstances, small farmers are rapidly disappearing. Those who survive get squeezed between corporate monopolies up and down the supply chain, that is, between those who control seeds and fertilizers and those to which they must sell at an unsatisfactory price (Lehman and Krebs 1996, 122). Often it is one and the same company that is positioned at both ends. Corporate agribusiness, Lehman and Krebs (1996, 123) conclude, has our food system in a "stranglehold"; it exerts increasing control over all stages of the food production process.

> Imagine a system in which a single company sells seed to the farmer, operates the local grain elevator, owns the railroad and the port facility, buys the grain from the farmer, and sells the grain to itself to be processed into food. That's the system we have now in grain production in the United States and, increasingly, around the world. (Lehman and Krebs 1996, 123)

In the United States 95 percent of the food is manufactured and marketed by corporate agribusiness, which is densely linked with the financial community and the corporate networks that control the rest of the economy, as well as the international organizations that craft the rules for the global marketplace; and other countries that are keen on copying U.S. policies are well on the way to replicating this situation (Lehman and Krebs 1996, 124). This means that the 37 out of 53 states on the African continent that are not self-sufficient in food production (Ziegler 2005, 217) effectively depend on the global market and thus on the large food and agribusiness corporations to feed their people.

Eighty billion dollars would be sufficient to provide food for everyone and to give all human beings a perspective by securing their access to basic education and health care, as well as to clean water and sanitation (Ziegler 2005, 45). As a comparison, the 374 largest transnational corporations are hoarding reserves of $555 billion in their safes. Microsoft's share alone is $60 billion and is growing by $1 billion per month (Ziegler 2005, 34). This does not mean that these corporations must donate all their assets to the poor. However, it does raise the evident question why all this money flows into the pockets of corporations rather than being used to secure a decent living for the millions of poor people in this world. The answer lies, not surprisingly, precisely in the structurally powerful position of these large corporations in the global economic system. Structural power, as Susan Strange (1996, 23) defined it, refers precisely to "the way the system operates to the advantage of some and the disadvantage of others, and to give greater priority to some social values over others." The several hundred-billion-dollar government bailouts of large multinationals around the world throughout 2008 and 2009 are another prime example of this insight. The tax money pumped into corporations that have become "too big to fail" would have been enough to effectively put an end to hunger and poverty around the world. Some might interpret the need for government support as a symptom of those companies' ultimate powerlessness. However, the fact that governments hardly have a choice but to keep those companies alive proves the precise opposite; these bailouts are the epitome of multinational corporations' structural power.

These insights conclude my elaborations on the foundations of corporate power, but they do not yet provide a sufficient conceptual explanation of the multinational corporations' quasi-governmental role. An inquiry into quasi-governmental power is concerned not only with the sources of power of a specific agent but essentially with the way this power is exercised. Hence the quasi-governmental position of multinational corporations derives not merely from their power potential but from the concrete expression of this power, which takes us directly to a discussion of the concept of authority.

The Public Expression of Corporate Power: Political Authority

The aim of the second part of this book is to show that multinational corporations are effectively operating as quasi-governmental institutions and thus are in a position that is normally attributed to primary agents of justice. In order to be considered a primary agent of justice, it is not enough for a specific agent to accumulate power; it must at least partially exercise such powers beyond the rule and restrictions of any other agent or agency. The central concept that determines whether a specific actor can be considered a primary agent of justice is not merely its latent power but its authority. Hence we must take the discussion of corporate power a step further and show that multinational corporations assume not only powerful but also authoritative positions in the global political economy.

Debating authority is prone to provoke controversy not only about who does or should have authority but also about the very meaning and definition of the concept. Steven Lukes (1990, 204, 214) is correct in arguing that the process of identifying authority is itself inherently perspectival. There is no objective way of doing so. Our perceptions on authority are always part of an "integrated set of ways of seeing and judging matters of fact and practical questions." Hence, Lukes argues further, "if authority is justified, it is justified from a point of view," and it is the essence of authority that this point of view often is "that of the authority itself, which becomes that of the subject." As we will see later, this is no different for the authoritative position of multinational corporations. The very fact that corporate authority has gone largely unnoticed in our society is based on a dominant public perception of authority that obscures rather than exposes this position. It is not at all a coincidence that this perception is largely shaped by corporations themselves and the "economic class" supporting their ascendance.

The concepts of power and authority are naturally closely related and interlinked and are often used interchangeably (Sennett 1980, 18). Susan Strange (1996, 25) claimed that power must not be analyzed only as power *from* but first of all as power *over*. The perception of an agent having power over someone or something intuitively implies some kind of authority relationship. Power, according to Hannah Arendt (1969, 36), is an instrument of rule. Hence it is not the mere existence of power but its use that constitutes authority. Within the concept of authority, power transforms from a potential into a social fact. Therefore, authority can be interpreted as a manifestation or an expression of power. In the formal political context the expression of power is commonly institutionalized (Hall and Biersteker 2002, 4); it is this aspect of institutionalization that marks the difference between mere influence and governing power.

Political authority is commonly referred to as "a right to command" or the "right to rule" (Raz 1990a, 2) or similarly the "right to decide" (Annese 1978, 6). This implies a further decisive difference between the mere use of power and the concept of authority. Authority, as an institutionalized expression of power with governing intent, is always connected to a claim for legitimacy (Weber 1968, 213). This does not mean that this claim is always justified. As we will see shortly, "legitimacy" can be merely surreptitious. Thus authority claims recognition on the part of the subjects over which power is being exercised (R. B. Friedman 1990, 64). This ultimately means that it creates—or at least claims to create—an obligation for its subjects to obey.

The Matter of Legitimacy: Distinguishing Between Normative and De Facto Authority

The notion of authority developed in the preceding paragraphs was closely tied to the term *legitimacy*. I defined authority in terms of a normative relationship in which one has a right to command and the other a duty to obey (R. B. Friedman 1990, 71). From this perspective, authority as the legitimate use of power "implies that there is some form of normative, uncoerced consent or recognition [. . .] on the part of the regulated or governed" (Hall and Biersteker 2002, 4f.). Accordingly, it is commonly assumed that the recognition of authority must be a public one; hence there must be a public way of identifying legitimate authorities (R. B. Friedman 1990, 69; Cutler 1999a, 62). However, for identifying authoritative institutions this normative definition might be too narrow because it is prone to draw attention only to those agents and agencies whose authority is indeed believed to be legitimized by normative consent. Hence it tends to limit our focus to those agents to which we have formally assigned the "right to rule" and accordingly turns a blind eye on the ones that might operate in authority positions merely de facto, that is, without having a de jure mandate to do so.

Expanding the focus to de facto authority does not change the normative nature of the concept because authority relations always imply corresponding moral obligations for the powerful party. In fact, precisely because authority must always be accompanied by moral obligations, it is important not to confuse its (factual) existence with its (normative) justification. In other words: we must distinguish between its empirical and its normative validity (Weber 1962, 73; 1968, 32), or between a sociological and a normative perspective on the concept. This is not meant to derogate the tremendous importance of justifying authority. On the contrary, precisely because authority must be normatively justified, we must disconnect its justification from the question of its factual emergence and existence. Our tendency to focus merely on the need for and justification of formal authorities has largely obstructed the view of a number of institutions, including multinational corporations, with increasing factual authority and has rendered them invisible for the ascription of adequate moral responsibilities.

Thus it is important to distinguish between authorities that are normatively legitimate and those that are merely de facto (Raz 1990a, 3). Authority in a de facto sense means that an agent might exercise authoritative power without having a legitimate claim for obedience by others. This does not mean, however, that this agent is not "quite capable of eliciting a distinctive kind of obedience, allegiance, or belief, involving [. . .] deference or respect or trust" (R. B. Friedman 1990, 61). Legitimate authorities are in a commanding position by right; mere de facto authorities do not have a right to act as authorities, but they claim such a right nevertheless. Herein lies the difference between the mere use of (influencing) power and de facto authority: "*De facto* authority comes under a mantle of legitimacy. It claims the right of an authority" (Raz 1990a, 3).

De facto authority derives from de facto (as opposed to normative) legitimacy, or, in Max Weber's (1968, 312) terms, from "*de facto* recognition." Such de facto legitimacy, Weber claimed, is based not on recognition through normative consent but simply on factual validity (*faktische Geltung*) (Gay 1997, 23). Hence de facto authorities are those agents who claim a right to rule and succeed in establishing and maintaining their rule. However, their authority is normatively legitimate only to the extent that their claim can be normatively justified and thus generate a duty for others to obey (Raz 1990b, 117).

Countervailing Power: Distinguishing Between De Facto
Authority and Domination

It is a widely shared perception that authority implies in one way or another the "surrender of judgment" by the ones who are expected to obey (R. B. Friedman

1990, 64; Raz 1990b 118). This means that the subjects of authority accept orders or proposals they are being asked to follow not on the basis of their justification through good reasons, but simply because they are prescribed by an agent they recognize as an authority at the outset. The subjects of authority thus refrain from demanding a satisfactory justification as a condition of their obedience (R. B. Friedman 1990, 73). It is on this basis that Hannah Arendt claims that the "hallmark" of authority is "unquestioning recognition by those who are asked to obey; neither coercion nor persuasion is needed" (Arendt 1969, 45).

The absence of a need for persuasion as a characteristic of authority points to a state of nonobjection. From this perspective, we may conclude that the institutional expression of power turns into de facto authority if there is no significant opposition to its claim for legitimacy. Interesting in this regard is Merriam's (1934, 113) observation that "traditionally, the most common reason for obedience is no reason at all." In other words, obedience can derive from mere lethargy and acquiescence, that is, from the simple fact that there is no evident reason to oppose a certain authoritative request. De facto political authority is thus not dependent on explicit normative agreement but rather on mere compliance, that is, on the absence of objection. Hence the prerequisite for power to turn into factual control and authority is, to use the classical Galbraithian terminology, the lack of effective "*countervailing power*" (Galbraith 1952, 118).

It is this element of nonobjection that distinguishes authority from domination. Like authority, domination also can be interpreted as a particular expression or mode of power (P. Miller 1987). However, *domination* has a distinct negative connotation; it is connected to repression and the violation of people's autonomy. Therefore, it is questionable whether domination, in contrast to authority, can ever be justified (Gay 1997, 15ff.; see also P. Miller 1987, 2). In the literature on corporate power it is, perhaps not surprisingly, the term *domination* that is used more often than the term *authority*. However, this raises the question whether there really is enough resistance among people to the corporate use of power to justify the term. It certainly seems that there were times when opposition to corporate power was much more prevalent and outspoken than it is today. The resistance to corporate power that characterized the 1930s, for example, or the 1960s and 1970s largely vanished in the 1980s and 1990s and is perhaps just starting to reappear at present. From this perspective, and as we will see in more detail in the following chapter, the position of multinational corporations today is indeed rather one of authority than of dominance. Symptomatically, our unfamiliarity with using the term *authority* in connection with nonstate actors is precisely one of the reasons that the issue of corporate power has not yet been adequately addressed.

The two constitutive characteristics of authority lead to the conclusion that power transforms into (factual) authority if the claim of legitimacy of its exertion over others remains, at least to a certain degree, unchallenged, whether on the basis of trust, acquiescence, or sheer indifference and apathy. This is why the concept of authority, as stated earlier by Hannah Arendt, is not dependent on coercion or persuasion. The explicit use of coercion might in fact even indicate a loss of authority because it is needed only if those who claim authority start to lose the trust and approval of those who are subject to it. Thus coercion rests implicitly as a mere potentiality within the concept of authority and is used as an instrument for its protection only when emerging countervailing forces start to challenge it (Lincoln 1994, 6). Within this aspect the connection to structural power becomes very evident. Susan Strange also refers to force as a potentiality or capacity implicit within asymmetrical power relations. Noting that relational power, in Strange's definition, is largely based on the explicit use of force and coercion, we can conclude that it is the shift from relational to structural power, as observed and described by Strange, that has actually created a position of authority for the multinational corporation in the global political economy.

To conclude this chapter, let us remind ourselves that this connection between structural power in the global economy and political authority is not at all a coincidence. A. Claire Cutler (1999a, 70ff.) argues that "the nature and locus of authority" has always "changed and shifted with changes in the mode of production," that is, with changes in the political organization of the economy. "The historical specificity of political authority," she claims, "begins to appear with moves from feudalism to absolutism, to mercantilism, and to capitalism." Within all these moves, according to Cutler, definitions of authority were "resting upon distinct modes of production, which generated historically specific social and political relations." Not coincidentally, these insights remind us of the Marxist claim that the power of the ruling class does not rely on violence or force but is defined by the role of the ruling class in the process of production or in society as a whole (Arendt 1969, 11). These insights provide an evident but perhaps an unexpected context for Peter Drucker's claim stated earlier that the power of corporations derives from their control over access to the productive organization of a society. Thus it is within the reconfiguration of the mode of production and the consequent transformation of the basis of political authority from the national to the global level that the multinational corporation is emerging as a quasi-governmental institution today (Cutler 1999a, 72). It is from this perspective that the next chapter will analyze the practical manifestation of this new quasi-governmental role.

Chapter 7

When Multinational Corporations Act like Governments

AFTER COMPLETION OF THE CONCEPTUAL groundwork on power and authority in the previous chapters, it is now time to start the practical inquiry into the quasi-governmental position of multinational corporations. Specifically, we must look at the two constitutive aspects of authority in the corporate context. First, after the previous outline of the multinational corporations' power potential, I need to show how they successfully create a veil of legitimacy around the exercise of their power and how we tend to silently follow their rule without questioning it. Hence I must demonstrate how multinational corporations factually *govern people*. Second, I must show that their authority evolves as countervailing power diminishes. As seen earlier, a primary agent of justice is defined by not being subject to the authority of any other agent or agency, which would make it merely a secondary agent of justice. Besides the absence of opposition from civil society (which constitutes de facto legitimacy), which will be dealt with in the first step, I must look at three additional levels of potential countervailing force. At the first level, I will reject the common argument that multinational corporations are powerless and merely execute what the forces and requirements of the global market ask of them. I will show that multinational corporations have, in fact, outpowered the market mechanism in many respects and *govern markets* today. At the second level, I will analyze the potential countervailing power of governments. National governments have traditionally been the centers of absolute authority in modern societies. Therefore, the rise of corporate authority is possible only when the authority of national governments over them diminishes. Hence I will show how corporations increasingly *govern governments*.

At the third level, I must draw attention to the international political arena. I will show that there is no effective framework of governing institutions at the global level that could compensate for the loss of authority of national governments and thus effectively establish a countervailing force by regulating and controlling multinational corporations. Within this regulatory vacuum multinational corporations increasingly have the authority even to *govern themselves.*

Governing People: Derber's "Corporate Mystique"

Peter Drucker (1949, 44) claimed that corporate control over access to a society's productive organization touches the very livelihood of people. In other words, people have become dependent on the corporation for their ability to make a living. As a result of this power imbalance, as Charles Reich (1995, 29f.) observed, they are willing to accept the dictates of their corporate employer on almost any terms, even if those terms go far beyond anything they would reasonably accept from their public governments. "Private economic government," he concludes, has become even more significant in the lives of people than their public government. For Charles Derber (1998, 54), these systems of internal and at times rigid or even oppressive rules and laws turn the corporation into something like "a nation within a nation."

There is much that is valid in Derber's analogy between nations and corporations. After all, the rules that corporations impose on their employees determine a large part of their active daily lives. The steadily growing pressure on employees, combined with the generally increasing insecurity of employment, has led people to work ever longer and harder (R. B. Reich 2002, 111ff.). This does not hold only for low-skill work; the choice of an increasing number of high-skill career paths is connected to devoting 14 or more hours a day, six days a week, to the job. Accordingly, an increasing number of people spend well over 75 percent of their active time (time that we are not asleep) under the direct rule and supervision of the corporation. Therefore, it is not surprising that our standards of success and failure in life in general are increasingly defined in terms of attaining some corporate status. Our accomplishments and indeed our value as human beings are turned into a mere function of achievements, positions, or ranks within the corporate enterprise (French 1984, ix).

However, multinational corporations' growing control over our lives is not limited to the contractual relationships of employment. The ongoing economization of politics and civil society supports the penetration of the public sphere by the undemocratic power structures of the market. Therefore, corporate decisions touch virtually every aspect of our private and social lives. The daily decisions of a few hundred multinational corporations largely determine where and how people live, what work they are able to pursue, what they eat and drink, what style of clothes they choose or can afford to wear, what they watch on television and read in the newspapers, what knowledge they learn at school and universities, and ultimately what kind of society they live in (Barnet and Müller 1974, 15; Bakan 2004, 5). Today our lives are governed by corporations; "we are inescapably surrounded by their culture, iconography, and ideology" (Bakan 2004, 5).

Although the penetration of corporate influence over people's lives is arguably most profound in the United States, the ongoing process of economic globalization has produced similar tendencies in almost all economically "advanced" nations. The largest 200 corporations on the planet, as the outspoken corporate critic and Boston College professor Charles Derber (2002, 72) comments, "corporatize all aspects of life in *every* nation" and make corporate ascendancy emerge "as the universal order of the post-communist world" (Derber 1998, 3). What we observe today, according to Derber, is the beginning of "a worldwide business civilization" in which the top 200 corporations produce and sell most of the products and services that matter to us on a daily basis. Our food, clothes, cars, and health care are predominantly provided by them, and so are our computers and software, the information that enables us to be citizens, the drugs that save lives, and the arms that end them (Derber 2002, 71).

These corporations govern citizens with the "core market powers at the heart of their being" (Derber 1998, 171). They increasingly have the authority to determine the distribution of work and wealth, the use and allocation of land and natural resources, and the production and distribution of ideas, knowledge, and images that shape our culture (Derber 1998, 171). In accordance with Peter Drucker (1949, 203), who observed that corporate decisions largely determine the "character of our society," Derber concludes that today's corporate decisions have a most profound impact on our lives as citizens. They not only influence and shape us personally but also mold our collective way of life and our values, culture, and identity (Derber 1998, 171). Corporate influence over our personal and communal lives has become so pervasive that Peter French (1984, ix) compares their social positions with those held by the church, the nobility, the army, and the feudal lords in previous eras.

What these authors contemplate is at its core nothing else than the profound impact of multinational corporations' growing structural power on our personal and social lives. The subject of corporate power is thus "deeply personal." It affects us continuously, anywhere and anytime. It determines our opinions, dreams, and images of the good life and our morality and identity as workers, consumers, and citizens (Derber 1998, 4f.). Paradoxically, however, the more profoundly corporate power penetrates our daily lives, the less we seem to be aware of it—the corporate takeover, as Noreena Hertz (2001) suggested, is a silent one.

If we follow the decades of analyses from Drucker to Barnet and Müller to Derber, we can conclude that corporations have steadily enlarged and consolidated their power over time. Interestingly, in an almost synchronous process, critical voices have fallen increasingly silent. This parallel development of increasing power and diminishing opposition is not a coincidence. The absence of large critical movements is a constitutive element of governing or authoritative power. Accordingly, all forms of authoritative expressions of power must ultimately be backed by and rooted in a prevailing way of thinking, in shared beliefs and values (Derber 1998, 119). Adolf Berle (1967, 37) defined this as one of the "natural laws" of power. In the absence of a system of ideas or philosophy, he argues, power ceases to be effective, and those in power will eventually be replaced.

Thus political institutions have authority to the extent to which they are perceived to reflect and embody the shared beliefs of the citizens (R. B. Friedman 1990, 58). The social consent that "legitimizes" corporate power is thus not explicit and normative but rather is implicitly expressed through "a way of thinking that both venerates and disguises corporate ascendancy" (Derber 1998, 119). The key to acceptance and recognition of corporate authority lies in what Derber (1998, 2ff.) termed the "corporate mystique." The corporate mystique is a "set of cherished beliefs and illusions" that dictate how we think about the role and importance not only of corporations but also of government, markets, and democracy, as well as the good life and just cohabitation in general. It is at its core "an ideology" that, according to Derber, has effectively disguised the steadily growing power of corporations for decades. Their control over the knowledge structure not only has enhanced their power but also has simultaneously provided them with the means to render it an accepted and often simultaneously denied feature of public life by shaping the public perception accordingly (Bowman 1996, 149ff.). Thus the knowledge structure is the key to citizens' silent approval of corporate influence and the effective repression of countervailing power.

Corporations have relentlessly fostered a culture of materialism and consumerism. They do not respond to human needs anymore but create and shape them in their own favor, often through fear, invidious comparisons, or inducements to emulate the fashionable (Bowman 1996, 183). These are the effects of a profound transformation that Naomi Klein described in her best seller *No Logo* (1999) as the shift from the production of goods to the production of brands. Thus large corporations are taking power over our consumption while at the same time they promote consumption as the essence of our lives. The striving of large corporations for business opportunities and profits has actively commercialized every aspect of our lives and subordinated them to the logic of the market. People compete for jobs, corporations compete for consumers, consumers compete for bargains, and communities compete for lucrative corporations. This process is enabled and catalyzed by an environment of decreasing loyalty and increasing opportunism.

The silent acceptance of corporate ascendancy is deeply rooted in our ways of thinking, in our values and social practices, and in a lack of imagination how it could be otherwise. The modern corporation, John Kenneth Galbraith (1977, 257) asserts, is the institution that we "seek most elaborately to misunderstand" by assiduously propagating a myth with little relation to reality. The core of this corporate mystique is the conviction—"a collective necessary illusion" (Derber 1998, 135)—that business is a private affair based on private property, individual freedom, liberty of contract, and no reasonable obligation to be accountable to the public. It is this faith in the separation of the private and the public spheres and the profound belief in the corporation as an apolitical institution that keep the illusion alive that we can have both great concentration of power in the private sphere and a true and functioning democracy in the public sphere (Derber 1998, 119). It is in this sense, Scott Bowman (1996, 137) asserts, that "private enterprise is private government."

Thus it is the shared illusion about the corporation's nature as a private institution that shields the corporation from public scrutiny and opposition. The "corporate mystique" has shaped a public perception that uncritically associates all authority with the state. Precisely this intuitive association of authority with formal political institutions obscures the growing authority of private actors. When the state or public authority in general is identified as the only legitimate authority in our society, nonstate and thus private authority is rendered a theoretical and empirical impossibility. As a consequence, we systematically lack the means and the vocabulary to address the issue of private authority properly. We are, in other words, facing a "new problem with no name" (Derber 1998, 1ff.). This leads to a fundamentally momentous problem: as an "ontological *non sequitur*," private authority systematically escapes the radar of the discourse on responsible and accountable governance (Cutler 2002, 24).

The emergence of a position of authority, as seen earlier, can be a result of trust, acquiescence, or even indifference or apathy. All these elements play a decisive role in corporate authority. For example, it is symptomatic of our state-centered perception of power and authority that we automatically blame our governments for economic downturns or other social problems. This systematically obstructs the view of the role that large corporations might play in these conditions (Derber 1998, 174ff.). Corporations have successfully persuaded the public that drastic measures such as massive layoffs are inevitable in order to stay profitable in an environment of accelerating competition and merciless pressure of financial markets. They have done so by creating a climate of job insecurity and anxiety among employees, by transferring competitive pressure onto them, by increasing expectations both regarding qualification and performance, and by forcing them to work longer and harder hours. One would expect such practices and policies to stir increasing opposition, but paradoxically they have fostered a rather strange kind of understanding and often even gratefulness for the "efforts" of allegedly powerless corporations to do everything possible to save the jobs of as many employees as possible in their brave battle against global market powers and ill-conceived economic policies of governments.

It was again Susan Strange (1994, 210) who proved extraordinarily farsighted when she argued that a system of international production that is organized, managed, and planned by corporations will not only compromise the power of states but also affect their legitimacy. The combined control over production and knowledge, that is, over wealth, values, and perceptions in our society, puts multinational corporations in a position effectively to pull the rug out from under the state. Increasingly, in questions and issues concerning the economic strength and wealth of our societies, we seem to turn to corporations rather than to our governments. We trust the economic foresight of large corporations and mistrust political interventions of states. We are skeptical about economic policies crafted by politicians and applaud the recommendations of company bosses to keep our countries competitive.

Along with the increasing insecurity and anxiety that dominate our economic lives, we have developed an odd kind of trust in corporations. We believe that if we just let them do what they have to do, they will keep our world running. Corporations are the source of our wealth and the providers of all the goods and services we depend on in order to keep up our standard of living. Criticism of corporate conduct often appears to be a threat to the foundation of our societal development. We uncritically assume that there are good reasons for corporations to assume such powerful positions in our society. As long as this trust is kept up, the position of authorities will not be challenged; they will not even have to explain themselves, because the tough questions will not be asked (Lincoln 1994, 5f.).

Thus it is not so much that the subjects do not ask for justification of the authority as that it simply does not occur to them that they are capable of evaluating it from any other standpoint than the one given by the authority. How should they, as normal citizens, be competent to judge the corporation's actions in today's complex economy? Is it not the corporations themselves who know best what needs to be done in order to prevail in competitive global markets? "The grip that the established authority structure has over a person's mind," Richard Friedman (1990, 73) argues, "may be so complete that it does not occur to him that that structure could be judged in the light of any standards external to it."

Although some uncritically accept corporate authority as a necessity of our time, it is simply nonexistent for others. Many of us are not even aware of how much our lives are shaped by and dependent on corporations. Accordingly, critics of corporations are often denigrated as defeatist or smiled at as somewhat paranoid activists inflating incidents of minor relevance into fundamental societal problems. Within this environment there is no breeding ground for the development of alternative systems—a system, for example, that does grant a central role and a prominent place to corporations as social institutions in our societies but rejects their corpocratic rule over citizens and their governments.

The global mobility of firms has rooted out large parts of countervailing powers in civil society. It has diminished the effectiveness of unions and similarly of consumer organizations, which have not yet managed to organize themselves in a similarly transnational manner (Scherer 2003, 104). Furthermore, it has undermined autonomous communal decision making and has spread a climate of powerlessness, resignation, and apathy among citizens in the face of the corporate dictate. Today corporations' influence over society is even greater than in the golden age of the late 19th century.

> Nowadays, the influence of this unsettling organization is even more pervasive. Hegel predicted that the basic unit of modern society would be the state, Marx that it would be the commune, Lenin and Hitler that it would be the political party. Before that, a succession of saints and sages claimed the same for the parish church, the feudal manor, and the monarchy. The big contention of this small book is that they have all been proved wrong. The most important organization in the world is the company: the basis of the prosperity of the West and the best hope for the future of the rest of the world. Indeed, for most of us, the company's only real rival for our time and energy is the one that is taken for granted—the family. (Micklethwait and Wooldridge 2003, xv)

However, even the family is on the loser's road today. The trend toward fewer children is evident in almost all economically developed Western countries— children are detrimental to the (corporate) career. Families disconnect and fall apart over job issues, people work longer and harder, and they spend more and more time at the office and less and less at home with their families. The family is not a rival of the corporation anymore but is itself shaped and determined by it. In fact, corporations often present themselves as "large families" in order to display unity, solidarity, and mutual support to the outside. At the same time real family life is becoming a function of work life; family time degenerates into artificially created "family days" introduced by those same corporations that demand more and more of their employees and keep them at their offices in the evenings and on the weekends. Quality family time at home has steadily deteriorated over the past few decades. In the year 2000 half of the United Kingdom's fathers spent barely five minutes per day with their children (Hertz 2001, 49) while working 12 or more hours in their offices. Corporations are slowly but surely about to take over governance even of this last bastion against corporate authority.

Nevertheless, there are signs of change on the distant horizon. The corporate scandals in the early 2000s, the careless culture of risk taking of mortgage lenders and investors exposed in the subprime crisis that started to unfold in 2007, the persistent disproportion of executive compensation packages, and the repeated involvement of corporations in human rights abuses here and abroad have not only scratched the image of corporations as socially responsible institutions but also severely damaged the foundation on which they are built: the public trust in their effectiveness. In Europe multinational corporations are now the least trusted institutions (Hertz 2004, 202), which makes them highly vulnerable to countervailing powers arising from civil society. The last few years have heralded a remarkable increase in scrutiny of large corporations and their business practices by international NGOs, activist groups, and academic initiatives. NGOs have increased their aggressiveness in campaigning against businesses for at least a decade, but they are now starting to be heard in the public. In September 2000 *Business Week* reported that 72 percent of Americans claimed that business had too much power over too many aspects of their lives, and 74 percent claimed that corporations had too much political influence (*Business Week* 2000, 144ff.). The legitimizing foundation of corporate authority is increasingly perishing, and paradoxically "it is their very power [. . .] that makes them vulnerable" (Bakan 2004, 25). The corporate scandals that shook the world economy at the beginning of the new millennium might well be what we will later consider the beginning of the end of corporate ascendancy.

Governing Markets: Networked Capitalism

The influence of corporate values and culture on our daily lives can hardly be overstated. However, a popular argument claims that corporations are far from acting freely in this regard. On the contrary, they are heavily constrained by and bound to the requirements of the market in which they operate. These competitive pressures are claimed to be fiercest at the global level, where market forces remain largely unconstrained and shielded from government intervention. Hence the impersonal forces of the market are regarded as keeping even the largest corporations in check. Their position of power and authority, as a result, is perceived as a myth. The accumulation of power by economic institutions does not fit into the models and mind-sets of mainstream economists, who have demonstrated an astonishing affinity for the classical liberal models of perfect markets and corresponding explanations of trade patterns. While for Justice Louis Brandeis the bigness of corporations was the main evil of his time, today's mainstream economists see little reason to worry. The tight forces of competition, they believe, diffuse power automatically and hold even the biggest multinational firms in check.

The question of size has always dominated the discussion of corporate power (Vernon 1971, 7). It is not a novelty that international business breeds companies of gigantic size. It has done so since the beginning of its history. As a consequence, international companies have always been institutions not only of great economic importance but also of high political relevance. However, recent trends, as some scholars point out, actually show diminishing sizes of multinational corporations. Thus multinational corporations might actually be losing, not gaining, power. This argument overlooks the nature of power, which is, as pointed out earlier, not a property that can be possessed; it derives from control rather than from ownership. Precisely the aspects of ownership and control, however, are disconnecting in today's markets. In other words, it is possible that corporations diminish in size while simultaneously becoming more powerful.

Multinationals have started to disintegrate hierarchies and instead to organize in vertical networks. Many functions are not fulfilled by subsidiaries anymore but by external contractors and subcontractors. This is reflected also in the number of foreign subsidiaries, which decreased from roughly 900,000 to 790,000 between 2003 and 2007 (UNCTAD 2008, xvi) while during the same period the number of multinational corporations worldwide, as pointed out earlier, increased from 61,000 to 79,000. The telecommunications giant Ericsson, for example, reduced the number of its production facilities around the world from 70 to 10 by outsourcing most of its production processes to contract manufacturers and keeping only the knowledge-intensive processes in-house (Berghoff 2004, 144). This outsourcing of production processes does not mean that corporations are losing control over them. On the contrary, contractors and subcontractors are often heavily dependent on multinational corporations and are effectively locked into their value chains. They have little power, and their intermediate goods are of little value outside that production chain (M. T. Jones 2000, 946). Hence despite their nominal independence they are under de facto control of multinational corporations.

Multinational corporations themselves increasingly focus on high-value-added, knowledge-intensive activities and the overall coordination and control of the network (M. T. Jones 2000, 946). However, this trend toward disaggregation of their activities and processes has even increased the concentration of power and profit appropriation (Sassen 2002, 99). Along with the outsourcing of an increasing number of corporate functions to contractors and subcontractors, the reach of effective control of the largest corporations in today's "networked capitalism" has steadily grown (Derber 1998, 57). Although ownership and control were commensurate in vertically integrated forms of business firms, such production networks have extended the control of multinationals far beyond the boundaries of actual ownership (M. T. Jones 2000, 946f.). The widespread perception of big companies giving way to small ones (Micklethwait and Wooldridge 2003, xxii) must thus be put in perspective. The shift to a networked global economy has created an "illusion of small-firm proliferation within a reality of power concentrated among the largest corporations" (Derber 1998, 58). Behind this illusion, market shares of small competitors are gradually eroded by the aggressive "big-box" or "clustering" strategies of large corporations such as Wal-Mart or Starbucks (Klein 1999, 129ff.).

The networks of control of big global corporations do not spread only vertically. Increasingly, large multinational corporations are partnering with one another both within and across the boundaries of their respective industries. Joint ventures, partnerships, strategic alliances, and other liaisons among large multinationals build increasingly interdependent global networks of business activity (Dicken 1998, 201ff.; Hirst and Thompson 1999, 84). In nearly every global industry the largest players maintain partnerships with almost all their competitors and are tightly linked to their equivalents in other sectors, turning global markets into "a planetary network of hundreds of the biggest companies" (Derber 2002, 73ff.).

Most such networks serve the purpose of knowledge generation and knowledge sharing. With the shift to a knowledge-based global economy and the corresponding focus of multinationals on knowledge-intensive processes, collaboration in horizontal and vertical networks has become a fundamental component of their strategies, which has led to a sharp increase in the number and significance of these alliances (Fukada-Parr and Hill 2002, 188). According to Kobrin (2002, 44ff.), such networks are about to replace hierarchies and markets as a basic form of economic organization. Therefore, they herald a profound "change in the mode of organization of international economic transactions" and with it a fundamental shift in the patterns of control over the structures of the global political economy. Thus the power of multinationals increasingly derives from their position within such global networks, alliances, and partnerships. As long as corporations keep their position in the networks, they are a part of the power game; being replaced, on the other hand, can potentially have fatal consequences for any company. In short, these networks are a major new source of structural power for multinational corporations.

To be sure, these alliances and networks have not entirely eliminated global competition, but they have arguably turned any speech of a truly free market into a chimera. Under these circumstances competition is not primarily a means to prevent an undue concentration of power, as mainstream economists like to argue, but, on the contrary, serves as a smoke screen behind which the accumulation of power becomes socially acceptable. "The myth that holds that the great corporation is the puppet of the market," Galbraith (1977, 258) realized, "is, in fact, one of the devices by which its power is perpetuated." Competition in the global networked economy has little in common with the perfect market envisioned by Adam Smith and his neoclassical followers. Their models referred to the economic realities of the 19th century, when smaller businesses operated in predominantly local, relatively slow-paced and stable markets and offered fewer and simpler goods to customers with limited spending power (Jacoby 1973, 139). Today, however, multinational corporations operate primarily in oligopolistic market structures (Bowman 1996, 287; Vernon 1998, 15ff.; Gilpin 2001, 280) in which small groups of well-known companies together constitute the "superpowers" in all the major industries worldwide (Drucker 1989, 129). In the mid-1990s in the automotive, aerospace, airline, energy, electronic components, electrical, and steel industries, for example, the top five corporations controlled 50 percent or more of the global market, while in oil, personal computers, and media they controlled roughly 40 percent (Derber 1998, 61, 89). By 2006 the market shares of the top five companies in these (and other) industries had largely prevailed or even increased (see Lazich 2008). If we consider Smith's outspoken antipathy toward large corporations, it seems ironic that precisely his dearest followers use his arguments to cover up and legitimize the power of large corporations today. In the eyes of David Korten (1995, 74ff.), this amounts to a downright "betrayal of Adam Smith." Hence acknowledging the existence of power in the global marketplace requires us to look behind the mysterious façade of market metaphysics and unmask the market's seemingly impersonal forces as the result of politically relevant decisions of its most powerful actors.

Free-market competition made the big multinationals stronger, not weaker, as is often assumed. Harvard's prominent scholar on competition, economist Michael E. Porter, emphasizes that it is strong competition that makes corporations grow and flourish (Porter 1998b, 155; similarly, Drucker 1993, 220).

This is not at all a surprising insight. It is the core of the "survival of the fittest" logic of the market that the winners of the competitive battle get stronger and stronger while the losers get swallowed or wiped out. This process eventually leads to the elimination of effective competition from within. While successful players keep getting bigger, market entry for new competitors becomes increasingly difficult, and market structures become more monopolistic and less competitive (Korten 1995, 75). As a consequence, multinationals are now perpetuating their competitive advantage not through their superior efficiency or their innovative strength but first and foremost through the use of political power, for example, to demand concessions from governments that bolster their powerful positions (Boddewyn and Brewer 1994; Korten 1995, 75; M. T. Jones 2000, 948).

If the scope of autonomous action is an indicator of power, then the situation seems very clear: while nation-states have seen their scope of action becoming compromised in many areas, multinational corporations have increased theirs and thus have strengthened their powerful position in the global political economy. Multinational corporations are now the dominant institutional form in the global market. They control large parts of the world's resources, hold about a quarter of the world's productive assets (Hertz 2001, 33; UNDP 2002, 10), and determine the market's structure and outcomes. They have become major determinants of the location of industries and services, trade flows, and technological development, as well as major sources of capital and market access (Gilpin 2000, 24, 171). It is up to their decisions which regions or countries receive the investments needed for creating new jobs and production facilities (Scherer 2003, 107). Today a country's entry into global markets must pass the veto of multinational corporations (Thurow 2003, 36).

In today's networked capitalism it is not the market mechanism that governs corporations, but the networks of large multinationals that increasingly govern markets. Multinational corporations have replaced markets as the central organizers of economic activity in the world economy. Through their networking strategies they have successfully brought global markets under their control. They control what is being produced, where it is produced, and for whom it is produced. They control the rules, the intensity, and the scope of competition. In many global industries they control who does and who does not have access to global markets. They control information, knowledge, and a large part of the cutting-edge technologies that decide the boom or bust of a country's competitiveness in today's knowledge-based economy. As more and more countries are opening up their economies and increasing their dependency on global markets, such "economic" decisions of multinationals have an ever-growing impact on those countries' wealth, welfare, development, and progress.

Governing Governments: Sovereignty of States or of Corporations?

There are two distinct perspectives on globalization today. While one notoriously plays down and underestimates its effects on the policy-making capacity of national governments (e.g., Garrett 2000), the other similarly overstates its effects and announces—somewhat prematurely—the unstoppable demise or even death of the nation-state (e.g., Ohmae 1995a, 1995b; Khan 1996). What both perspectives have in common is their inherently state-centered standpoint, which obstructs the view of the much more diverse and complex "new geography of power" (Sassen 1996, 5) that characterizes the global political economy today.

Globalization has not simply eroded the power of nation-states across the board. Rather, it has "reshaped and reconfigured" it (D. Held 2004, 6; similarly, Sassen 1996; Drucker 1997; Mann 2000; Rosenau 2000; Slaughter 2004). Recent incidents such as the conflict between Russia and Georgia, for example, show that states still matter in the global power equation, even in a time of growing global interdependence. Thus it is certainly premature to speak of the death of the nation-state (Keohane 2000a, 116; Willke 2001, 174; Höffe 2002c, 14, 153ff.; D. Held 2004, 6). After all, the question whether or not its end is near will not be determined by some uncontrollable forces of global markets but by the way we respond to them.

Nevertheless, the territorial boundaries of states seem no longer to coincide with the extent or the limits of political authority over economy and society (Strange 1996, ix). In other words, the congruence of territory and authority that has been characteristic of the modern era in general and the Westphalian system in particular is being dissolved by the emergence of "nonterritorial functional space," that is, dimensions of collective existence that are transterritorial in character (Ruggie 1993, 165). This transterritorial space creates what Susan Strange called "no-go areas," that is, areas "where no single political authority is effectively in charge" (Strange 2002b, 235). These areas or spaces both transcend and deeply penetrate national territory. Through their penetration they interfere with, influence, and sometimes heavily compromise the state's authority over its policy-making processes. Through their transcendence, on the other hand, they exceed state authority and move critical issues beyond its regulatory reach and capacity.

To be sure, nation-states have never been completely independent in their policy-making processes, despite their territorial separation in the Westphalian era (Krasner 2000, 124ff.; Malanczuk 2002, 176f.). A world of complete independence between different civilizations existed at best in the ancient past (D. Held 2000, 421). Thus participation in the international economy has always confronted states with the trade-off between efficiency and a loss of autonomy (Kobrin 2002, 58). What is novel is the degree to which nation-states are interwoven today and thus the degree to which they lose the capability to act autonomously. Furthermore, the emergence of a truly global sphere has led novel transnational and supranational actors to enter the global political stage and to claim their share of authority. Some scholars even speak of the emergence of a neomedieval system at the global level (e.g., Kobrin 1997, 1998). According to this view, the global system compares with the Middle Ages, when many different authorities, such as emperors, kings, knights, bishops, or even guilds and cities exercised overlapping power at the same time and over the same territory (Mathews 1997, 61). In the following, let us have a more detailed look at the fundamental changes in the relation between states and multinational corporations heralded by the emergence of this system.

The "Golden Straitjacket"

David Held (2000, 424) notes that with increasing global interdependence "the fortunes and prospects of individual political communities are increasingly bound together." Under such circumstances the boundaries between domestic and foreign affairs, between state-internal and external policy issues, are blurring. Governments face increasing difficulties in fulfilling many of their commonly assumed responsibilities. Protecting their citizens from (economic) insecurities, for example, poses increasing problems because of their growing exposure to the structural forces of change unfolding at the global level.

These structural forces not only are located beyond the reach of national politics but also affect and compromise governments' effectiveness in making and implementing domestic policies (Cerny 1995, 597; Hirst and Thompson

1999, 219). While governments have actively promoted the creation of global markets through the liberation and deregulation of their national economies, they have exposed themselves to forces they cannot control anymore. Hence by supporting the expansion of an unleashed global market instead of controlling its forces through effective collaborative regulation, nation-states are indeed engaging in their (unintended) self-disempowerment (Höffe 2002c, 168). Therefore, nation-states not only give up control over the international economic sphere but also effectively let the forces of the transnational market take control of their domestic economies (Drucker 1989, 115; Strange 1996, 4; 2000, 149; Brinkman and Brinkman 2002, 731).

Perhaps the most striking example of this process is the expansion and transformation of global financial markets. Global capital is the engine behind and the lifeline of national real economies (Ruggie 1993, 141; Drucker 1997, 166; Strange 1998, 179f.). However, throughout the neoliberal era these markets have become increasingly speculative and have rendered global capital flows highly sensitive to changing investment conditions. In this environment, governments, which depend on these markets and enter them as rival borrowers, are forced to make their investment ratings a top priority. This effectively limits the scope of their actions and policies, not only concerning interest and inflation rates but also in areas such as public health and education, to the narrow parameters underlying the financial community's investment decisions (Strange 1998, 180; Garrett 2000, 307ff.; Stiglitz 2003, xvi).

It is important to emphasize that governments still have the formal authority to flout the de facto dictates of the market. However, the economic penalties for doing so can be severe (Mathews 1997, 57). This insight again takes us to the core of the concept of structural power. It is not that governments do not have a choice to opt out of the global economic game, but de facto the consequences of the "no-go" choice are too severe to be taken seriously into consideration. Thomas Friedman (2000, 104ff.) has described this dilemma of national governments as a "Golden Straitjacket." It is, he claims, the defining feature of late 20th-century globalization. Those countries that wear it right can make a fortune more quickly than ever before; those countries who shuck it off, however, will be left behind just as quickly. Wearing the golden straitjacket, Friedman goes on, has two consequences for a country: its economy will grow and its politics will shrink. Participation in the global economic game will increase trade and foreign investment and eventually lead to more growth and higher average incomes, but this will come with decreasing national autonomy and the narrowing of political and economic policy choices to very tight parameters. As a consequence, those countries that put on the straitjacket see their political spectrum erode. Differences between Left and Right turn into mere rhetoric because neither of them can afford to deviate too far from the core rules set by the market. The logic of the golden straitjacket is purely reactive: the more tightly you wear it, the more gold it produces, and the more gold it produces, the more padding you can afford to put into it for those parts of the society that get squeezed by it.

Hence in order to benefit from the promised lands of neoliberal globalization or even only to be a part of it, in Friedman's message, countries must permanently stay competitive in global markets. The more national governments expose themselves to the open markets of the global economy, the more they must subordinate or even sacrifice their autonomy in economic, social, and environmental policy making to the dictates of global competitiveness. Rent-seeking global capital and direct investment reward only the most efficient national economies, and efficiency here means deregulation, privatization, and the continuous reduction of social welfare and labor costs—hence potentially all measures aiming at the reduction of regulation and state intervention. The welfare state, as Philip Cerny (1990, 204ff.) concluded, is transforming into a "competition state."

These insights might appear counterintuitive to many citizens whose practical experience is one of growing influence of state bureaucracies over their everyday lives and of increasing government activity in many areas of the public domain. In many cases, however, this increased activity of governments is itself a symptom of their decreasing effectiveness in balancing the negative side effects of global market forces (Strange 1996, 5; 2000, 149). The prominent German ordoliberal and founding father of the social market economy Walter Eucken (1932, 307) observed early on that the expansion of government throughout Germany's history was, in fact, an indication of the weakening rather than the strengthening of the state. Moreover, I have argued earlier that free markets do not evolve naturally but require increased government intervention to become and remain open. Those who claim that the state and national politics become unimportant and insignificant in the realm of economic globalization are thus severely wrong. National policy making might, in fact, be more important than ever. The problem, however, is that there are no real alternatives for governments regarding the autonomous design of their policies.

Hence in order to understand the decisions made by national governments, we must look behind their policy choices to the structural context in which they are embedded (Stopford and Strange 1991, 57). This structural context suggests that the policy choices that are realistically open to countries are severely limited by the requirements of competitiveness. Not even the largest countries can afford to ignore the need to compete in global markets (Drucker 1989, 128; Porter 1998a, 1). It is against this background that thinkers like Alain Touraine (2001, 9) conclude that the market is about to replace or already has replaced the state as the principal regulatory force in our society. As the principal actors and agents operating in those global markets, multinationals must logically move to the center of attention when we analyze this shift of authority in the global political economy.

This broadly sets the context that increasingly allows multinational corporations to evade the countervailing force of national governments. Three distinct processes illustrate this shifting relation between governments and multinational corporations. First, the increased mobility of production, combined with the need of states to stay competitive, enhances the bargaining position of large corporations. Second, the ongoing privatization of public domains leads to a transfer of control and authority from governments to corporations. Third, multinational corporations increasingly eliminate countervailing power by lobbying public officials and invading political processes at both national and global levels.

Shifting Authority to Multinationals in Production: The Exit Threat

The global structure of multinational corporations' production processes, combined with the increasing dependence of states on their performance, enhances their ability to curb countervailing power of governments in three dimensions. First, it provides them with various possibilities to evade taxes and national regulations. Second, it allows them to press for favorable conditions by confronting governments with the so-called exit threat. Third, it gives them the opportunity to play off different governments against each other in order to enhance their own position.

Evasion of Taxes and Regulations   The increasing incongruence between multinational corporations' sphere of activity and governments' sphere of regulation undermines the capacity of governments to pose countervailing power to the increasing might of multinationals. Thus multinational corporations' mobility puts serious constraints on national governments' possibilities to regulate and control them effectively. Additionally, their increasingly complex network structures start to blur the boundaries of the firm, which severely complicates their supervision and control, as well as jurisprudence over them (Cutler 2002, 32; Kobrin 2002, 50ff.; Masci and Tripathi 2005, 25).

Thus the global network structures of multinational corporations serve as an effective tool for them to evade national rules and regulations. Not only do they allow them to shift certain operations and activities to countries with less restrictive regulations, but they also provide the possibility to evade the regulatory reach of governments by shifting resources within their corporate structures. Because multinationals effectively can evade national regulation while not facing an equivalent at the global level, they are operating, at least partly, in an unlegislated sphere (Scherer 2003, 103).

The practice of evading national regulations is being exploited perhaps most blatantly in taxation matters. To be sure, most states have tax rules or treasury regulations designed to prevent fiscal emigration (Hu 1992, 117). However, the margin for corporations to circumvent these regulations is still considerable (Scherer 2003, 105). Multinationals aim at minimizing their taxes first of all through the use of transfer pricing and other related instruments and practices (Martin and Schumann 1997, 198ff.; Vernon 1998, 39ff.; Garred 2004, 6ff.). They shift taxable profits to offshore subsidiaries or holding companies—often set up as pure letterbox companies—in so-called tax havens while deducting costs in the locations with the highest tax rates. The tax history of the big German automobile company BMW after the mid-1980s, for example, shows very precisely the growing possibilities of multinational corporations to evade national taxation: in 1988 BMW reported profits of 545 million marks to the tax authorities in Germany. Four years later the amount was 31 million, and just a year after that BMW declared a loss in its domestic operations while reporting rising overall profits. As a result, BMW received a tax refund of 32 million marks in Germany. Similar stories can be told also for Siemens, Daimler-Benz, or Commerzbank, among others (Martin and Schumann 1997, 198).

Today corporate tax evasion has become an industry of its own. Offshore tax havens such as the Cayman Islands or Bermuda offer a wide variety of instruments and services that facilitate tax flight. The Virgin Islands hosts 300,000 registered companies, of which only 9,000 have local operations

(Garred 2004, 3). In 1999 Rupert Murdoch's News Corporation maintained 60 of its 800 subsidiaries in such offshore tax havens. Earning $2.1 billion in profits in the United Kingdom between 1988 and 1999, News Corporation did not pay a cent of net taxes in the United Kingdom and paid only 6 percent worldwide (*Economist* 1999). Similar examples are easy to find. Halliburton, to mention another, holds 30 subsidiaries on the Cayman Islands alone, while Enron maintained a total of 662 subsidiaries there (Garred 2004, 6f.).

Tax evasion weakens the state by depriving it of its financial basis for the execution of its social and public mandate. This shortfall of taxes often provokes a two-tiered shift from the taxation of mobile factors to immobile factors and from income to consumption (Garred 2004, 8). Because both income and mobility are privileges of those who are well off, both shifts increase the tax burden of the poor and reduce that of the rich. Hence these shifts effectively constitute a transfer from the poor segments of society to corporations and corporate elites. This is structural power at work.

Exit Threat   Most often, multinational corporations do not even have to make use of their possibility to shift activities, operations, or resources out of a country in order to evade regulation or taxation. They are like the elephants in Nadine Gordimer's *Ultimate Safari* (1989): they are too big to need to run from anybody. The mere possibility of multinationals' shifting their operations abroad, combined with their increasing importance for national economies, leads to an implicit "exit threat" (Ulrich 2001a, 378; translation by author), which is often sufficient to bring national governments to their knees. The spatial dispersion of business operations and their organization in global networks have dramatically weakened the structural bargaining power of national governments and have put other potential countervailing forces such as workers or other stakeholder groups on the defensive (M. T. Jones 2000, 951). The sword of Damocles of the implicit exit threat dangling over their heads often prevents them from articulating and enforcing their claims against the corporations.

There are a handful of concrete examples where corporations explicitly threatened governments with moving their operations abroad and, in some cases, even realized their threat. In 1996, for example, Fidelity Corporation threatened the state of Massachusetts with moving substantial parts of its operations to New Hampshire and Rhode Island if it did not get the very generous tax breaks it had hoped for. The threat was sufficient to make Massachusetts capitulate and comply with the requirements of the corporation (Derber

1998, 168). Similarly, Volvo threatened the Swedish government with moving its headquarters abroad in 1997 (Vernon 1998, 39). Other Swedish companies such as Tetra Pak or Ericsson realized their threats. Ericsson opened large headquarters in London in 1999 (Hertz 2001, 54), and Tetra Pak changed its legal nationality and moved to Switzerland (Hu 1992, 116). Today Tetra Pak is a part of Tetra Laval Group, which calls itself "a private industrial group of Swedish origin headquartered in Switzerland."

The actual number of concrete examples of corporations articulating the exit threat, however, is a bad indicator of its acuteness. Corresponding to the characteristics of structural power, the exit threat is most effective as a latent but omnipresent threat to governments, that is, a threat that need not be expressed explicitly but is silently contained within the structure of the global economy controlled by the big and powerful corporations. "The concern over economic power," John Kenneth Galbraith (1952, 156) asserted, "is always less a matter of the way it is manifested than of how it *might* be employed." After all, it is the nature of structural power that it influences the choices of others not by putting explicit and direct force on them but by imposing risks and costs on them that make it harder for them to make some choices while making it easier to make others (Strange 1988, 31).

Accordingly, the latent exit threat will be stated explicitly only as a last resort that is, in case of real confrontation. In such cases structural or soft power turns into relational or hard power. In accordance with earlier elaborations, however, in such cases of direct confrontation, that is, when corporations explicitly threaten governments with realizing their exit option, their authority is already in question. It is precisely the implicitness of the threat that consolidates multinational corporations' political authority. To come back to Nadine Gordimer's metaphor, the authority of the elephant is in place only as long as it does not have to run away.

Playing off Governments Against Each Other   The structural threat emanating from the exit option allows corporations to strategically play off national governments (and, similarly, workers) against their peers in other countries (Hertz 2001, 52ff.; Scherer 2003, 107f.; UNCTAD 2003, 124). Thus they force governments into so-called bidding wars in which they must outperform their peers by offering better conditions and incentive packages to corporations in return for new jobs, investments in infrastructure, and economic growth (Hertz 2001, 52).

In 2001 no fewer than 250 different European locations competed for a new production site of BMW, which ultimately was built in Leipzig, Germany (UNCTAD 2003, 124). Incentive packages offered in such bidding wars often amount to several hundred million dollars in value. Hence corporations not only evade taxes but often turn into tax collectors themselves, receiving tremendous sums in subsidies and welfare regardless of their own wealth. In fiscal year 2006 the U.S. government's direct and indirect subsidies to corporations, that is, the transfer of money from taxpayers to companies, amounted to $92 billion (Slivinski 2007).

Governments' willingness to reach deep into their pockets to attract corporations is not based merely on their potential to generate jobs and tax money. More important, these corporations are the nation-states' gate to the global economy, the key to their international competitiveness, and their main source of technology, knowledge, and information. The importance for national governments of being able to offer them attractive conditions as potential host countries, that is, of effectively selling themselves as good places to do business (Thurow 2003, 37), can thus hardly be overstated (Underhill 2000, 122).

The factors taken into account in multinational corporations' assessment of potential locations are manifold, for example, education of the potential workforce, infrastructure, and access to markets. In fact, such factors have proved to be the key determinants in corporations' decisions on industrial locations (Vernon 1998, 33). This is not surprising, given the increasing concentration of their focus on knowledge-intensive processes. This might also provide a partial explanation of why the existing tendency of lowering social standards in the world economy has not yet degenerated into an uncontrollable "race to the bottom" (D. Held 2004, 4f.). Nevertheless, first of all in cost-sensitive industries and with tightening global competition and improving mobility of firms also in other sectors, cost arguments and thus locational incentives play an increasingly significant role in multinationals' evaluations of suitable locations (UNCTAD 2003, 125). When corporations compete in the global market, those operating in areas with high social costs have a systematic competitive disadvantage in comparison with corporations operating in "free markets" (Gray 1998, 79). For corporations to survive global competition, as the economist Rudiger Dornbusch stated, "they need a streamlined economic environment, at least as good as their best competitors around in the world" (Dornbusch 2000, 30). Not surprisingly, 70 to 80 percent of multinational corporations in the services sector mention lower costs as the main reason for offshoring (UNCTAD 2004, xxv). As a result, many of them have started to move service operations such as customer care or call centers to India, Malaysia, Singapore, or recently also South Africa (*Economist* 2005, 52), all of which are countries with well-developed telecommunications and information technology infrastructures and good business services, banking, and insurance sectors but low labor costs.

As long as corporations were predominantly operating in national markets, they had an evident interest in high domestic demand, which was linked to a certain concern for the broad determinants of the nation's economy. This link, however, is becoming weaker the more transnational the focus of corporations gets. For a corporation that earns most of its profits on the global market, the interest in low domestic costs outweighs the interest in high domestic demand. There is an increasing tendency for multinational corporations to separate their business interests from the interests of the national community (R. B. Reich 1995, 161; Strange 1998, 181; Derber 2002, 171f.; Ulrich 2008, 363). Hence retaining multinational corporations in the national bookkeeping is less and less a question of corporate loyalty and turns itself into a matter of international competitiveness of the host countries.

According to Vernon (1998, 35ff.), there is considerable empirical evidence that bidding wars have led to an outward drift of multinationals' activities into other countries. Hence the tighter the competition for corporations in the global market, the bigger the pressure on governments to cut their social costs in welfare requirements, pension contributions, and health-care provision, to downgrade social, labor, and environmental standards (UNCTAD 2003, 125), and to implement tax cuts or subsidies in order not to lose the economic race for FDI against other competing states. The *World Investment Report* observes an extended use of such locational incentives and connects it directly to more intense competition between states. Although this competition is most profound among similar and geographically proximate locations (UNCTAD 2003, 124; 2004, 196ff.), it is becoming increasingly global (UNCTAD 2003, 124). With China's entry into the global market, competition has certainly accelerated also among developing countries. The battle for FDI among developing nations is almost entirely cost based, often with devastating consequences. Developing countries are estimated to lose over $50 billion annually from tax competition alone (Garred 2004, 7). Moreover, the abandonment of environmentally sustainable policies, for example, has turned many developing countries into so-called pollution havens (Hertz 2001, 42), posing severe risks to the health of their citizens. Often governments even tolerate illegal practices and human rights abuses in order to attract FDI.

Also in "developed" nations, locational factors not only consist of tax cuts, subsidies, and other financial incentives but also include regulatory concessions and thus the direct erosion of countervailing governmental power. In order to attract foreign multinationals, they create so-called policy enclaves that may be exempt from the normal regulatory rules and practices of the host country in order to reduce investment costs (UNCTAD 2003, 124). According to Raymond Vernon, the 1980s and 1990s were distinctive for such efforts of governments. Between 1991 and 1995 governments all over the world implemented hundreds of changes to their FDI regulations. With few exceptions these changes were all aimed at making the respective countries more attractive in the eyes of foreign companies (Graham 1996, 19ff.; Vernon 1998, 31). Ten years and many hundreds of additional changes later, the situation has changed little; out of 244 changes in laws and regulations affecting FDI on a worldwide scale in 2003, 220 were aimed at more liberalization (UNCTAD 2004, 6), and even in 2007, at the brink of the global financial crisis, 74 out of 100 changes were aimed at a "more favorable" environment for foreign FDI (UNCTAD 2008, xvi).

Hence competition among multinationals breeds competition among states (Stopford and Strange 1991, 1). Therefore, it plays a major role in governments' diminishing scope of action in their regulatory policies and their fading capability to pose countervailing power to large multinationals. By externalizing competitive pressure onto governments and imposing the costs and risks connected to it on taxpayers, multinational corporations have shed their status as subordinates of states and present themselves more as allies or partners. This adds a whole new dimension to diplomacy in the 21st-century global political economy: it includes the bargaining relationship between governments and multinational corporations (Strange 2000, 152; 2002b, 231).

Shifting Authority to Multinationals in the Public Sector: Privatization of State Functions

The takeover by the New Right in the late 1970s and the early 1980s and the consequent spread of neoliberal policies across the world heralded massive privatizations of public domains. Initially, transport, telecommunications, and energy sectors, among others, were sold off to private investors; and after the massive sellout of public assets in these infrastructure sectors, the second wave of privatizations now targets the most sensitive domains remaining under public control, that is, the domains that secure the core of human well-being, such as social welfare and security, health services, education, housing, and even water supply.

The privatization tendencies in the security sector provide a striking example of this trend. The private takeover of public security is particularly pervasive in the complex and tumultuous situation in "postwar" Iraq. An unprecedented number of private military contractors are now handling everything from military logistics to training of soldiers, protecting installations, and escorting convoys (Singer 2004). They even engage in armed combat, where they have proved to be exceptionally trigger-happy. The Blackwater incident that left 17 civilians shot dead by private security guards is the best-known example but certainly not the only one.

Thus an increasing number of key positions in the security structure are shifting to private corporations, which take the form and appearance of "private, for-profit militias" (Barstow 2004). Although the situation in Iraq is exceptional in many ways, this tendency is increasingly general. The privatized military industry is now estimated to have a whopping $100 billion in global annual revenue. Philip Alston (2005, 17f.) calls the privatization of security provision one of the key factors propelling nonstate actors to greater prominence. John Kenneth Galbraith spells out the full implications of this development:

> As the corporate interest moves to power in what was the public sector, it serves, predictably, the corporate interest. That is its purpose. It is most important and most clearly evident in the largest such movement, that of nominally private firms into the defense establishment, the Pentagon. From this comes a primary influence on the military budget. Also, and much more than marginally, on foreign policy, military commitment and, ultimately, military action. War. Although this is a normal and expected use of money and its power, the full effect is disguised by almost all conventional expression. (Galbraith 2004, 53f.)

These elaborations show that multinational corporations' role in the provision (or denial) of security to citizens is anything but apolitical. On the contrary, it seems that we are on a path that leads us straight back to the 16th century, when maintaining armies and fighting wars were normal features of large chartered companies' "business plan."

The education sector too is increasingly penetrated by private corporations. Chartered in 1636, Harvard University is the oldest private corporation in the United States (Micklethwait and Wooldridge 2003, 43). Even those schools and universities that are not yet entirely in corporate hands are becoming more dependent on them. The shift to technology-based, modern education methods, combined with a lack of public funding, has rendered schools and universities dependent on private sponsors. The corporate invasion of schools, as a consequence, has in large part "eliminated the barrier between ads and education," created a "mall mentality" on campuses, and turned students into mere shoppers and consumers (Klein 1999, 88, 98). Corporate influence over the education system is arguably the most effective and unprecedented reinforcement of the "corporate mystique."

It is one of the fundamental beliefs of liberal societies that government has an inherent responsibility to protect the social and economic rights of its citizens and to provide the structures necessary for them to fulfill their basic needs. This is why institutions essential to public health, human progress and development, and public safety, as well as natural resources and domains, were typically placed under public authority and shielded from private exploitation (Bakan 2004, 112). Even within the core of these essentials, however, authority is handed over to private corporations today.

The involvement of "private" corporations in public enterprises and sectors is nothing new. In fact, the roots of the corporation are in the provision of public services. However, in the early days of the corporation, when their charters required them to fulfill narrowly defined public tasks, they operated as public instruments under the authority and the tight control of governments. Today's takeover of public sectors by autonomous corporations that are acting on behalf of private interests is very different. The push of corporations into the provision of essential public goods and services entails the repression of public regulation by private interests in some of the most fundamental areas of our societal organization and coexistence.

The occupation of more and more public sectors by multinational corporations strips governments of their component parts and diminishes the sphere of their influence and authority (Derber 1998, 169). Therefore, it leads to a further strengthening of corporations' bargaining position and a weakening of countervailing force by governments. However, the takeover of public sectors by private corporations has implications that reach much further than the decline of government regulation. At its core it means the partial replacement of governments by corporations for the fulfillment of genuine governmental functions. It turns the legitimacy of governments into a function of corporate interests because no government can claim legitimacy without providing the most essential public goods and services to its citizens. Privatization is thus not simply an expansion of the private sector into the public realm but a transfer of public authority from governments to private corporations. As providers of public goods and services, corporations themselves step into the role of governments, while government itself is transformed into "a creature of private enterprise" (Derber 1998, 170).

Ironically, the increasing dependence of governments on multinational corporations for the provision of public goods and services can be linked directly to these corporations' practices of evading taxes and pressing for extensive financial incentives. The shortfall of tax revenues hits governments hard at a time of constantly rising administration and welfare costs. As a result, the call for more cost efficiency and thus for a stronger integration of and reliance on private actors in the provision of public services has become louder. Thus in order to get the cost explosion in the provision of public services under control, we are increasingly relying on the expertise and financial potency of the very institutions that play an important role in the growing inability of governments to fulfill their mandate in the first place. The same connection holds for the increasing dependence of cultural events and institutions on private funding. Corporate tax breaks have eroded the financial basis of many cultural events and institutions and made them dependent on corporate sponsorship. Instead of creating suspicion among citizens, however, corporations have successfully managed to make people believe that such events and institutions would be impossible without their generous support (Klein 1999, 30ff.). We are trapped in a classical vicious cycle: in an era of expanding market coordination, governments are not only getting weaker but also poorer (Strange 1998, 135); and as they get poorer, they are forced to rely even more heavily on the market that makes them weaker—the golden straitjacket is getting tighter and tighter.

Shifting Authority to Multinationals in Political Processes: Lobbying

The countervailing power posed by governments is not eroding only through multinational corporations evading their tax or regulatory authority or through privatization of traditional public sectors; political processes too have become more susceptible to corporate lobbying and more dependent on their financial contributions to campaigns, candidates, or political parties.

Large multinational corporations are gaining growing influence in and over formal political processes and decisions. They have realized the crucial role of political influence in their success on the market and in the preservation of their power. Accordingly, they have steadily increased their pressure and influence on the political system and have used their financial potency to distort democratic processes and to buy access to political decision making. At a time in which elections are being decided less and less over factual issues and are based on the right marketing strategies and media coverage, the cost of political campaigns and elections has been rising to astronomical heights. The money required to win elections by far exceeds the capacity of membership contributions, and large corporations are more than willing to step in and fill the gap.

By feeding the political carousel with the funds needed, large corporations become the lifeline of political candidates and parties and turn democratic processes into a function of corporate interests. In the almost entirely commercialized election processes of the United States, the two parties raised $393 million in "soft money" during the 2000 election cycle alone (Hertz 2001, 91). In the 2004 cycle donors with business interests contributed an estimated $1.5 billion to politicians and political parties (SustainAbility and WWF 2005, 5). Between 1997 and 2003 the 25 largest pharmaceutical companies spent $48.6 million on election campaigns (Public Citizen 2003, 2); similar amounts can be found for the tobacco industry, which contributed more than $30 million to members of Congress and the two political parties between 1987 and 1996. Even though it is difficult to link certain policy changes to a specific donor company, the general correlation between industry donations and the number of votes in Congress in favor of the respective industries leaves no doubt about the success of such corporate political strategies (Hertz 2001, 96f.).

Corporate attempts to gain an edge over democratic processes and elected politicians become more successful the more tightly a country puts on the golden straitjacket. Not only are governments forced to deregulate their economies, but even those regulations that remain in place are increasingly a reflection of the preferences of the largest and most powerful global market players (Underhill 1997, 43). Regulation, once a central counterforce to corporate power, is more and more turned into the opposite: a manifestation of corporate authority (Derber 1998, 149).

Economic considerations and the struggle for competitiveness are not only turning into the main concern of national policy making but form the cornerstone also in international relations. Relationships between countries are increasingly driven by economic interests, and this effectively puts multinational corporations and their industry associations in a position to dictate foreign policy (Hertz 2001, 70). Caught in the golden straitjacket, governments increasingly evaluate genuine political questions such as human rights issues, humanitarian interventions, and sanctions in purely economic terms. Thus they render themselves more dependent on information and guidance of corporations and their lobbyists. As a result, corporations and their advocates enter political processes increasingly also through the door of experts and policy advisors.

The increased dependence of politicians on the expertise of corporations and their representatives is a direct consequence of their dominance over political-economic structures. Thus Susan Strange's (1988, 130f.) perception in 1988 that such dependence would sooner or later result in increased susceptibility to corporate influence in policy making was correct. The consequence is that more and more regulations are being removed or tilted toward corporate interests. While the state is slowly being deprived of setting the context and the limitations for the pursuit of private corporate interests, it is now those corporate interests that dictate the context for public policy making. Business, as former labor secretary Robert B. Reich wrote in a 2001 *New York Times* article, "is in complete control of the machinery of government" (R. B. Reich 2001).

A look at the statistics suffices to realize the extent of corporate influence over our allegedly democratic political processes. In 2005 the European Parliament's website reportedly listed 5,039 accredited lobbyists working for large corporations (Bianchi 2005). However, Corporate Europe Observatory (2005, 8ff.), a European research and campaign group targeting topics connected to corporate political power, estimates a total of over 15,000 European Union (EU) lobbyists. Two-thirds of them represent big business, while only 20 percent represent NGOs. The remaining 10 percent represent the interests of regions, cities, and international institutions. Big business is believed to spend up to 1 billion euros on lobbying yearly.[1]

The situation in Washington looks no different. After the Republican take-over on Capitol Hill in 2000, the number of registered lobbyists skyrocketed to 34,750 (Birnbaum 2005). The Center for Public Integrity reports that lobby-ists have spent nearly $11 billion between 1998 and 2005 to influence mem-bers of Congress and federal officials on legislation and regulations (Knott 2005). In 2004 expenditures on lobbying Congress and the White House, as well as other federal agencies, amounted to over $3 billion, up from $1.6 bil-lion in 1998 (SustainAbility and WWF 2005, 6). These increased efforts by corporations have paid off: according to the *Washington Post* the number of new federal regulations declined by 5 percent between 2000 and 2005, and the number of pending regulations that would cost corporations $100 million dropped by 14.5 percent (Birnbaum 2005)—not to mention the body of laws and regulations that secure corporate welfare in the hundreds of millions of dollars every year. Hence corporations have strong incentives to increase their spending for having a say in Washington. According to the Center for Public Integrity, the pharmaceutical and health products industry lobbied on more than 1,400 congressional bills between 1998 and 2005 and spent a total of $612 million on lobbying—the Pharmaceutical Research and Manufacturers Association (PhRMA), the industry's lobbying group, alone spent more than $65 million (Ismail 2005). In 2007 the industry spent a record $189 million for its lobbying efforts on Capitol Hill, of which PhRMA spent $23 million (Is-mail 2008).

Calling lobbyists the "fourth branch of government" is neither an exaggera-tion nor an empty metaphor. The boundaries between government and business are blurring. Charles Derber (1998, 119) even sees the melding of government and business as one of the defining features of our time. This assessment is both plausible and somewhat ironic. It is plausible because it is the logical consequence of the ongoing economization of politics. The phenomenon of the "revolving door" is symptomatic of this insight; the Center for Public Integrity found that some 240 former members of Congress and agency heads are now active lobby-ists, and an additional 2,200 lobbyists used to work in senior government posi-tions (Knott 2005). It is ironic, on the other hand, because the melding of govern-ment and business, of private and public, and of political and economic is the result of the attempt of economic liberals to separate these spheres.

While the increasing fusion of business and governments strengthens the position of the corporation, it undermines that of governments, not only in their relation to business but also within the public at large. While we tend to accept silently and unquestioningly the rule of corporate values over our lives, we lose trust in our politicians who increasingly function according to those same corporate principles. Politicians who accept massive corporate donations and turn out to be corrupt and driven by corporate interests lose their credibility and their backing in the public. Consequently, the legitimacy of government and politicians is increasingly being questioned, while that of corporate power is silently accepted. From this perspective, corporations have literally put governments in checkmate. They have secured government support for themselves while at the same time turning the public against their governments, leaving them virtually without a legitimate purpose and thus without the capacity to be a legitimate countervailing force to corporate power.

Under these circumstances corporations are increasingly confronted directly with claims of people who bypass the powerless traditional political channels in order to express their concerns and demands. Addressing corporations directly, they believe, is a more reliable way of being heard (Hertz 2001, 112). Hence corporations are becoming more and more exposed to direct political claims of people without those claims being mediated by governments or markets. They are, in other words, acting in genuinely political roles. However, within this ultimate source of authority also hides its biggest threat, for it is precisely this unmediated exposure to claims for justification and this shifting relation between the corporation and people from primarily economic to predominantly political that provides the breeding ground for society to reestablish effective countervailing power.

Sovereignty at Bay?

Ever since Raymond Vernon published his groundbreaking analysis *Sovereignty at Bay* in 1971, discussions concerning the power of multinational corporations have been connected closely to the concept of sovereignty of nation-states. Using a notion so momentous for modern society to draw attention to the rising power of multinationals is both effective and dangerous because it is likely to lead to controversies and misunderstandings. Twenty years later Vernon warned against using book titles that carry only half the message

(Vernon 1993, 19). Indeed, both the supporters and the critics of the thesis of contested national sovereignty still regularly quote Vernon's work. However, they often refer solely to its title rather than the content of the book. The controversy—and a great deal of the misunderstandings connected to it— does not even revolve around whether multinationals really gained power while nation-states lost some of theirs, but rather around different under- standings of the notion of sovereignty. In other words, the controversy is se- mantic rather than empirical.

While supporters of the sovereignty-loss thesis point to the diminishing autonomous decision-making power of states, critics argue that despite these factual constraints governments still have formal authority over most areas of public concern and still hold the ultimate power to overrule and veto any of the nonstate actors' decisions. The key to solve the controversy seems to take us back to the distinction between the factual loss of governments' capability to make autonomous policy decisions and the revocation of its formal decision-making authority (Thomson and Krasner 1989, 196). This difference ultimately crystallizes in different understandings of power. A focus on tradi- tional concepts of relational power leads to a perspective of uncontested state sovereignty because it isolates the relation between the two powerful actors from the structure they are embedded in. Therefore, it emphasizes only for- mal power and authority. As a result, the state is still seen as the ultimate epi- center of power because it enjoys formal authority over the multinational corporation. An examination of the relation between states and multination- als in the realm and the structures of global markets, however, yields different results. It reveals that de facto the state's authority is often undermined by the workings of these structures. Hence there is incongruence between the state's formal authority and its factual capability to exercise it (Keohane 2000a, 117). For example, even though the state retains its formal right to tax multi- nationals, its capability to exercise it has diminished considerably (Strange 1996, 62).

Thus when we talk about the nation-state's alleged loss of sovereignty, we must distinguish between formal and factual sovereignty. Although factually the nation-state's sovereignty over its policy-making processes seems to be jeopardized, its formal sovereignty is affected only when it willingly transfers also its formal decision-making authority. However, recent trends of corpo- rate rule making, which will be addressed in the following paragraphs, seem to herald a shift of authority even in the formal sense.

Governing Themselves: Corporate Rule Making

The last remaining domain of potential countervailing force is the global political economy itself. We already know that competition in general and specifically at the global level is systematically enhancing, not curbing, the power of the largest multinationals. Although the tight forces of global financial markets are without a doubt one of the most effective disciplinary instruments for multinational corporations' power, they also work very much in their general interest. They promote the same values, provide the most important resource for corporate growth, and create the political space within which many of the key decisions of global corporations materialize. Not least, they are one of the main reasons for the ongoing decline of the nation-state's regulatory autonomy. Therefore, in order to complete the picture of potential countervailing forces, we must analyze the international regulatory landscape in the global political economy.

As I noted earlier, economic globalization systematically overstrains the "regulatory umbrella of the state" (Sassen 1996, 8) and diminishes the relative significance of any one nation-state as a political actor in the global political and economic arena. Again, we can draw an analogy with the situation at the very beginning of the 20th century, when the first wave of corporate mergers profoundly transformed the American economy. The sharp increase in interstate economic relations through corporate mergers, as well as the increasing competition among states for corporate patronage, largely shifted their regulatory responsibility over corporations to the federal government (Bowman 1996, 71). The difference in comparison with today's "global shift" (Dicken 1998), however, is that today there is no central authority at the global level that could step in as the federal government did in the early years of the 20th century. There is no adequate framework at the global level that compensates for the widening regulatory gap between the separate (and thus weakening) national units of policy making and globalizing economic processes and activities (Hirst and Thompson 1999, 193; D. Held 2004, 90). On the contrary, the diffusion of authority away from governments has created a regulatory vacuum or, to use Susan Strange's (1996, 14) words, a "yawning hole of nonauthority."

This aspect is novel in the history of economic globalization. The first wave of global capitalism led to the emergence of an international economy, which merely linked discrete, national economies through cross-border economic relations, as opposed to a truly global economy, which fuses them "into a coherent whole" (Kobrin 2002, 45ff.). Even the postwar international economy that emerged after the Bretton Woods Conference in 1944 was still too tightly regulated for globalizing markets to move beyond the control of states and international authorities (Strange 1998, 1). After all, the postwar international economy was designed with the goal of ensuring domestic policy autonomy and international monetary stability. Hence the agreements made at the global level actually prevented national economies from overexposure to open global markets and explicitly left room for national governments autonomously to pursue economic stabilization and social welfare policies (Gilpin 2000, 57ff.). Thus national regulation remained dominant during the postwar period, and international institutions were designed to complement it where necessary (Hirst and Thompson 1999, 193). John Ruggie (2003, 94) called this the "embedded liberalism compromise," that is, a form of economic liberalism embedded in social community. It allowed national governments cautiously to balance free-trade agreements with their domestic commitment to protect the weaker members of society. According to John Kenneth Galbraith (1977, 225), the time of embedded liberalism, or, in his words, the "Age of Keynes," was the time "when capitalism really worked." It was capitalism with a social conscience, that is, a capitalism that took its critics seriously and, as a result, aimed at balancing the growing inequalities and instabilities that are inherent in any capitalistic system (Thurow 2003, 137).

Lester Thurow (2003, 137) has no doubt that what was possible in the postwar period between 1950 and 1972 could be done also in the current stage of globalization. It is not that global markets are ungovernable by nature. Global economic governance is not a matter of impossibility but one of political will and insight. Both, however, were trampled during the G7's adoption of neoliberal free-market policies in the 1980s and 1990s. The new "consensus" over the proper purpose and aim of international institutions that emerged during the 1980s did not emphasize effective regulation of national and international markets but their subordination to the rule of unhindered competition. Thus nation-states transferred a substantial amount of their domestic regulatory authority to transnational regimes and organizations (Lipschutz and Fogel 2002, 115), which were predominantly concerned with enforcing and furthering free global markets. As a consequence, many of the fundamental responsibilities formerly attributed to the state were no longer adequately discharged by anyone (Strange 1996, 14).

The IMF and the World Bank, two institutions that were created as a Keynesian brainchild, were meant to be instruments for the reconstruction of Europe after the Second World War and for the world's protection from recurring market crises. Today, however, they are promoting and enforcing minimal government throughout the world and have become major engines of the rapid integration of global markets. They often contribute to global instability rather than fulfill their original mandate as a stabilizing force in the global economy. They have put the interests of rich nations over those of the poor and have promoted policies for the strong and to the detriment of the weak. Keynes, as Joseph Stiglitz (2002a, 12f.) contemplates, would be rolling over in his grave if he saw what has happened to these institutions.

A similar story can be told about the World Trade Organization. The 1993 Uruguay Round strengthened the WTO's authority considerably. This increased authority is used predominantly to rule out regulatory and jurisdictional discrepancies between different states. Such discontinuities are perceived as major barriers to global commerce (Rodrik 2002, 3). To be sure, efforts toward creating a more harmonious global regulatory landscape are not to be condemned per se and across the board. What is worrisome about the current approach, however, is that the targets for removal are predominantly social and environmental regulations at the national level. They are considered protective measures and thus unwarranted interventions in the market (Stiglitz 2002a, 216). The current approach aims not at creating harmonious and consistent regulation at the global level but at removing regulation altogether. Regulatory harmonization in fact seeks to eliminate politics from certain contentious domains and issues by shifting regulatory authority beyond the domestic sphere (Lipschutz and Fogel 2002, 119).

Thus the expansion of international cooperation has not significantly enhanced the supranational regulation of multinational corporations (Kahler and Lake 2003, 425). The Uruguay Round did stipulate the need for improving the regulatory framework for FDI, but we are still far from having a holistic system of rules, let alone a specific international law, in place that could effectively govern global FDI flows and the issues connected to them, such as taxation, transfer pricing, or the use of incentives in governmental bidding wars (Gilpin 2000, 183; 2001, 300f.). On the contrary, the efforts so far have predominantly focused on further liberalization of FDI flows rather than on their effective regulation (Hirst and Thompson 1999, 214).

There have been a number of attempts to build an overarching international system for the regulation of multinationals, but they were all abandoned or rejected. In 1974 the UN Economic and Social Council founded the Commission on Transnational Corporations, whose mandate was to develop a code of conduct for multinationals. The negotiations, however, stagnated over conflicting claims between developing and industrialized countries and eventually were abandoned in 1992 (Haufler 2001, 16f.). Other instruments such as the Organization for Economic Cooperation and Development (OECD) Guidelines or the ILO Tripartite Declaration remained of only minor regulatory significance. The most recent initiative to establish a single overarching code for transnational corporations, launched by the UN in 2003, is currently suffering the same fate as those previous attempts. The Norms on the Responsibilities of Transnational Corporations and Other Business Enterprises with Regard to Human Rights (UN Norms) were arguably one of the most promising initiatives so far but ultimately proved too weak to overcome the powerful interests opposing them. I will elaborate on these norms in the section "Remedial Duties at the Global Economic Policy Level: Regulatory Obligations" in chapter 9 of this book.

This leaves the Multilateral Agreement on Investment (MAI) proposed by the OECD in 1995 as a new attempt to create a regulatory system for FDI. Its goal was to establish a new body of international investment laws that would give corporations the unconditional right to buy, sell, and conduct financial operations all over the world (Global Policy Forum n.d.) and to sue national governments that undermine corporations' interests by imposing "unfair" restrictions (e.g., restrictions motivated by the protection of the environment, public health, and the like). Conflicting claims over this controversial proposal eventually left the negotiations in a political deadlock. The treaty was torpedoed by the joint efforts of NGOs and pressure groups, which correctly claimed that MAI was an instrument to lock in the course of liberalization and was likely to weaken rather than improve governmental control over FDI. Furthermore, the negotiations took place with the exclusion of the majority of developing countries, which explains their fierce opposition to the agreement. The antidemocratic MAI was not fit to fill the regulatory gap at the global level, and its rejection was not only the logical but also the right consequence.

Thus, rather than regulating multinational corporations, the global economic system works squarely in their favor. Given this lack of regulatory supervision, multinational corporations have themselves turned into key forces in the global political and even legislative arena. As a result, policy and decision making at the global level is often a direct function or expression of multinational corporations' interests. Private corporations and interest groups such as the European Round Table of Industrialists were tremendously influential in pressuring national governments to open up their economies and adopt the Washington Consensus (Currie 1999, 22; Hertz 2001, 29). Today they are often directly involved in the creation and formulation of policies on the international political stage (Chomsky 1999, 20). Peter Sutherland, the former director general of the WTO, hardly conceals what the WTO stands for. For him, the WTO represents "a forum for the development of economic policy in the interest of corporations all over the world," and for this, he states, "the WTO functions reasonably well" (Sutherland 1999, 55). Thus corporate interests have traditionally been the yardstick for WTO decisions and rulings, even if they went against the wishes of democratically elected governments (Hertz 2001, 82). In 1997, for example, the Indian government had to overrule the upper house of Parliament in order to pass a bill that would ensure compliance with the WTO's TRIPs rules. The reason that the WTO stepped in was a projected loss in the range of $500 million for U.S. companies. The mere threat of WTO sanctions led the Indian government to back down and to circumvent the regular democratic process in order to enforce priority of corporate interests over national democratic decisions (Mytelka 2000, 45).

As much as international agreements were instrumental in expanding the free market, the involvement of multinational corporations in the process was usually critical for pushing them through (Vernon 1998, 143). Thus the integration of world markets, that is, the replacement of the cooperation-based Bretton Woods system by a system of market-based governance, was less a result of cooperative decisions of governments than a process directed by powerful market actors and a small number of rich countries with congruent interests (Sassen 1996, 25; UNDP 1999, 98; Strange 2000, 149; Lipschutz and Fogel 2002, 119). At the global level there are few historically grown formal political processes within well-defined political bodies. This renders newly emerging negotiations, policies, and regulations much more susceptible to corporate influence. Such influence goes far beyond "conventional" lobbying and often puts multinational corporations in a position factually to veto international economic agreements. The active objection of multinational corporations is an almost certain death sentence for any international agreement affecting their transborder business activities (Vernon 1998, 143f.). An increasing number of business representatives enter the political rule- and decision-making processes as experts, consultants, and advisors and are often directly involved in "drafting the fine print" of such international economic agreements (Vernon 1998, 144). They often contain several thousand pages full of technical details that require familiarity with and expertise in all thinkable industries and markets, which makes the advisory services of multinationals and their representatives almost indispensable (Vernon 1998, 145). This puts governments and intergovernmental organizations in an arguably tricky situation: they increasingly lack the expertise necessary fully to oversee the numerous highly complex areas of business and depend on the direct cooperation of the very companies they are supposed to regulate (Currie 1999, 19). As a result, governments increasingly hand over the regulatory responsibility to multinational corporations themselves.

There are three broad areas in which multinational corporations emerge as active policy and rule makers in the global political arena. First, they engage in economic rule making, which involves them directly in the regulation of their own business activities. Second, they are increasingly concerned with creating voluntary standards in order to regulate the social and environmental side effects of their business activities. Third, they enter social and environmental policy-making processes, which target those genuinely global problems that can be solved only by collaborative efforts. The following paragraphs will deal with each of these areas separately. One must keep in mind, however, that the boundaries between them are not clear-cut and are often blurred by extensive overlaps.

Multinational Corporations as Economic Rule Makers

Industry self-regulation is not a new phenomenon. In the Middle Ages it was the dominant form of governance of international commercial relations. International commercial relations were characteristically not subject to local commercial laws and were often left entirely unchecked by public authorities. Hence 16th-century merchants started to develop their own system of rules for cross-border exchange. They created their own law, the so-called law merchant, and enforced it in their own independent merchant courts (Cutler 1999a, 69). The law merchant was essentially custom law. It aimed at the promotion of better business practices, at filling the gaps of each jurisdiction's commercial law, and at harmonizing disparate approaches in different markets and nations (Steinhardt 2005, 221). This uniformity of the medieval law merchant, however, was eroded during the emergence of the Westphalian system. The law merchant ceased to exist as an autonomous legal order. It was gradually integrated into the domestic legal systems of sovereign nation-states and codified as private international trade law (Cutler 1999a, 70; Haufler 2001, 15).

The late 20th-century efforts by governments to integrate their economies into global markets have created a new demand to harmonize and unify these nationally distinct legal systems. Although governments primarily pursue this goal through heavy liberalization and deregulation of their domestic economies, it is again the (transnational) commercial actors themselves who engage in the creation of a "New Law Merchant" (Cutler 1999a, 72). Their aim is to shape a calculable environment favorable to international business by generating soft and optional law that is based on the consent of the commercial actors themselves. Therefore, as Cutler (1999b, 313) specifies, this new law merchant corresponds to the general "neoliberal commitment to regulatory norms that facilitate and supplement the private ordering of commercial relations." Symptomatically, in various international markets the most important rules on access to resources or to markets have been worked out by cartels or small oligopolistic groups of large corporations (Strange 2002a, 205). Multinational corporations and their business associations are increasingly regulating the entire process of transacting, from contracting to transporting, financing, insuring, and even resolving disputes (Cutler 1999b, 316). The International Chamber of Commerce, which consists of companies and business associations from over 140 countries, for example, has been developing self-regulatory rules and tools for facilitating international business transactions for almost a century (Jackson and Nelson 2004, 185).

This "soft infrastructure" is developed in different forums in which private-sector entities regularly play important, if not decisive, roles (J. Nelson 2002, 54). Such forums take place in both international and transnational arenas and vary in their degree of institutionalization (Cutler 1999b, 307f.; 2002, 28f.). They range from informal industry practices and increasing institutionalization through trade associations and self-regulatory organizations to international regimes where "private and public elites [. . .] committed to privatization and deregulation" (Cutler 1999b, 308) share regulatory authority.

Such industry self-regulation is not only enhancing the power of multinational corporations but also contributes decisively to the separation of their activities from governmental and social control (Cutler 1999a, 73). Therefore, it is effectively eliminating countervailing power and consolidates the political authority of multinational corporations in the global political economy. However, multinational corporations are ruling themselves not only by determining the core rules of the game in the global market but also by regulating the side effects that derive from their business conduct.

Multinational Corporations as Regulators of Social and Environmental Side Effects

The WTO's attempts to eliminate regulatory and jurisdictional discontinuities between states show that unification at the global level is often achieved at the cost of social and environmental regulations at the national level. As a consequence, the shift of regulatory authority to the global level increasingly confronts multinationals with a need to expand their self-regulatory efforts also into areas that are commonly not regarded as essential to their core business activities (Haufler 2001, 14). Hence while national governments deregulate their economies, multinationals are increasingly expected to regulate the so-called side effects of their business conduct themselves. They have responded with increasing collective efforts to design and implement a growing number of social and environmental standards. They have developed self-regulatory policies and instruments such as corporate codes of conduct, management, and accounting systems that translate those commitments into specific roles and responsibilities within the company, implementation programs, as well as monitoring, auditing, certification, and labeling programs (Haufler 2001, 12). Today such standards, policies, and instruments are emerging as a significant and important new source of global governance (Haufler 2001, 1).

The rationale for corporations to commit to voluntary social and environmental standards might vary. Some might indeed adopt such standards out of a serious commitment to corporate social responsibility, while others might see them as a strategic defense against growing NGO pressure and its potentially negative impacts on their reputation. Many corporations, however, might simply choose voluntary standards as the lesser evil than regulatory measures that might be forced on them otherwise. Governments, on the other hand, might welcome corporate self-regulation precisely because it provides a potential solution to their dilemma between having to protect society from negative side effects of corporate activity and being forced to stay competitive in the global marketplace (Haufler 2001, 2).

Although industry self-regulation consolidates corporate authority at the global political level, the implications of voluntary social and environmental standards reach even further. Multinational corporations, as we saw earlier, draw their authority from the factual legitimacy created through the "corporate mystique." Voluntary standards in social and environmental domains, however, potentially create a novel form not only of factual but also of genuinely normative legitimacy for their dominant position in the global political economy. These standards often include soft enforcement mechanisms based on public scrutiny and pressure and are thus tied to the corporations' own economic interest in a good reputation. By exposing corporate behavior to public scrutiny, these standards create a sense of democratic legitimacy and turn corporate self-regulation into a quasi-legitimate form of governance. Thus corporate social and environmental self-regulation might well be interpreted as a first attempt of corporations to reach a morally legitimate status as governing institutions.

What is striking about corporate self-regulation, whether in the areas of corporations' core activities or in the realm of their side effects, is that corporations not only "legislate" the rules for their own conduct but simultaneously also perform the executive and judicial functions in regulating themselves because none of the prevailing standards are endowed with formal enforcement and monitoring systems. It is one of the defining features of self-regulation that its subjects both design and enforce the rules (Haufler 2001, 8). From this perspective, multinational corporations execute powers that under the rule of law and the separation of powers are not even granted to governments. Hence self-regulation is probably the most effective way imaginable for multinational corporations to curb countervailing powers, as well as the most explicit form of shifting authority away from elected authorities to private institutions.

Multinational Corporations as Public Policy Makers in the Global Political Arena

The two forms of self-regulation discussed in the preceding sections are not the only way multinational corporations are entering the policy- and rule-making processes at the global level. As public budgets are getting tighter and the call for efficiency louder, managerial expertise is turning into a valuable asset also for public policy making and problem solving in broader social and environmental domains. Many of the present social, economic, and environmental challenges are, as mentioned earlier, inherently global and characterized by highly interdependent causes and effects. As such, they have simply become too complex to be solved by any one actor alone (J. Nelson 2002, 2ff.; 2004, 24). Thus by increasingly integrating corporations into social, environmental, and economic policy making, public bodies hope to gain access to information, new ideas, and solutions that may be more viable for implementation (Rondinelli 2002, 404). This leads to the emergence of new forms of public-private partnerships, many of which grant considerable influence to the partnering corporation over the policy decisions of the public body.

It is against this background that not only the Bretton Woods institutions but also a growing number of UN agencies have intensified their collaborative efforts with the private sector and have established new and innovative types of partnerships with business. These partnerships are qualitatively different from earlier forms of collaborations that the UN maintained with corporations for procurement purposes or philanthropic resource mobilization. In contrast to those earlier forms, the defining features of these new types of collaboration include shared processes of decision making and problem solving. The partners literally work together "at all levels and stages" (J. Nelson 2002, 47).

Jane Nelson (2002, 43ff.) distinguishes two main types of relationships involving business in the broader policy- and rule-making processes of the UN. First, business corporations may participate formally or informally in intergovernmental processes, that is, in official intergovernmental deliberations, as well as in the institutional governance and the normative and standard-setting structures of the United Nations system (Nelson 2002, 63ff.). Such involvements may include full participation of business in UN governing bodies and in formal consultative relationships through advisory bodies, formal commissions, committees, task forces, experts' meetings, or working groups. Also, business involvement in UN processes may be established through observer status or ad hoc participation at General Assembly proceedings, invitations as members of national delegations at UN conferences, or accreditation for specific conferences and events. In addition to such formal business involvement, there are a variety of informal mechanisms for business participation in intergovernmental processes. Generally, the private sector is represented by its officially accredited business and professional associations, but it is not uncommon for individual business leaders or private-sector experts to enter the policy-making process directly.

The second type of relationship is established through so-called global public policy networks (see, e.g., Benner and Reinicke 1999; Reinicke and Deng 2000; J. Nelson 2002). Such partnership-based governance networks and policy dialogues aim at bringing together actors from the public sector, civil society, and business in order to inform and influence intergovernmental processes and to achieve "cooperative policy solutions to common global or cross-boundary problems" (J. Nelson 2002, 73). Therefore, they engage in the development of standards and norms, in the provision of global public goods, and in the implementation of international agreements. They often also play critical roles in putting issues on the global political agenda (Reinicke and Deng 2000, xiii; Benner, Reinicke, and Witte 2004, 196f.). Global public policy networks exist in a variety of areas. They are most prevalent in the global environmental and global public health domains (Streck 2002); however, as we saw earlier, they play important roles also for the creation of the new law merchant.

Global public policy networks have developed mainly during the last two decades. They can be interpreted as a response to the constant need for policy solutions to an increasing number of complex global problems arising within the persistent governance gap that is opening between the limited reach of national politics and the lack of centralized governmental and rule-making structures at the global level (Benner, Streck, and Witte 2003, 63; Benner, Reinicke, and Witte 2004, 192f.). Especially the last decade heralded an increase in the number and scope of such networks, and their importance and impact are likely to increase further in the near future.

Multinational corporations have become major players in global politics not least by playing important roles within such networks. In their attempts to tackle prevailing global problems, states and international organizations are no longer in a position to bypass the concerns of powerful transnational actors who have mobilized around many global issues and strengthened their bargaining position around much-needed moral, financial, and knowledge resources (Benner, Reinicke, and Witte 2004, 195). The agenda that drives corporate involvement in such problem-solving networks and partnerships is unclear. Is it their genuine commitment to finding sustainable solutions to prevailing societal problems or an opportunistic strategy to serve their own interests? In our increasingly knowledge-based economy such relationships between business, public agencies, and NGOs enhance corporations' access to information and knowledge, which could prove to be crucial for achieving a competitive edge over their competitors. Irrespective of the corporations' rationale for engaging in such partnerships, there is no doubt that they do provide potential platforms for them to shape the global public sphere and to eliminate countervailing power by expanding their authority into the provision of global public goods.

These new kinds of problem-solving partnerships, as well as the trend toward extended self-regulation of multinationals, add a completely new dimension to the public and political role of multinational corporations. These partnerships, which integrate corporations directly into the formal political decision-making processes at the global level, alter their factual governing position into a more formal governing status. Thus these trends send a rather ambiguous and dilemmatic message. On the one hand, they can indeed provide effective answers for the increasing number of complex global challenges and have the potential to take global business activities to a new level of social and environmental sustainability. On the other hand, however, they consolidate the governing power at the global level of multinational corporations as actors that are not democratically legitimized. I will come back to these normative questions in connection with multinational corporations' obligations of justice, discussed in part III of this book.

In sum, it seems clear that multinational corporations have become key players in shaping the international legislative and political environment. They heavily influence and often even determine national and global regulatory policies and are a crucial part of the emerging new landscape of global governance. They overpower people, markets, governments, and international institutions and thus operate in positions of increasing political authority. Any analysis of global justice that ignores these new constellations of authority and governance in the global political economy and the role of multinational corporations in them will necessarily remain incomplete. This conclusion can be stated also from the reverse perspective: an account of corporate responsibility that fails to take multinational corporations' new role as primary rather than secondary agents of justice into consideration is systematically incomplete. The basic principles of global justice have been outlined in the first part of this book; it is now time to develop a framework for corresponding obligations of multinational corporations that match their quasi-governmental role as presented in this second part.

PART III

Multinational Corporations as Primary Agents of Justice

The Duty to Respect, Protect, and Proactively Realize Human Rights

Chapter 8

Challenging Common Perceptions

Some Preliminary Conceptual Reflections on Multinational Corporations' Obligations of Justice

POWER, AS PETER DRUCKER (1994, 101) stated correctly, "must always be balanced by responsibility; otherwise it becomes tyranny." Obviously, the question whether power is exercised formally or merely factually is of minor importance in this regard. It is quite evident that the quasi-governmental position of multinational corporations must result in substantial corresponding moral responsibilities. Hence this final part of this book will shed light on the normative implications of multinational corporations acting in the position of primary agents of justice. Thus part III provides an examination of the quasi-governmental position explicated in part II in light of the rights-based principles of cosmopolitan justice and the corresponding conceptual notion of moral obligations developed in part I.

If we consider the pivotal role of justice in the viability of any society, as well as the increasingly powerful position of multinational corporations in the global political economy and their profound influence on people's lives, it is surprising that especially the booming debate on corporate social responsibility has not yet paid major attention to the concept of (global) justice. In fact, there is hardly any systematic analysis, let alone a complete theory, of the corporation's role from a genuine justice perspective. The dominant perception still holds that the place to pursue justice in society is the political realm, not business (see, e.g., Streeten 2004, 72). What such statements conceal, however, is that multinational corporations themselves have become major players in the political arena.

There are a few notable exceptions in the literature on corporate responsibility that take the justice perspective into account. First and foremost, Iris

Marion Young's concept of "political responsibility," which I discussed earlier in this book, is, according to her own view, squarely located in the realm of justice (see the section "The Capability Principle" in chapter 3). By analyzing the problem of sweatshops (see Young 2003, 2004, 2008), she explicitly ties the concept to corporate obligations. Hsieh's (2004) inquiry into the obligations of transnational corporations from the perspective of the Rawlsian "Law of Peoples" is another example. Symptomatically, however, it suffers from the same inconsistencies and exclusions as Rawls's theory of justice in general. Hsieh does show, on the basis of Rawls, that wealthy peoples have a duty of assistance to burdened societies, but he does not provide an explanation why this should create derivative obligations for multinational corporations in those cases in which governments fail to do so. Hence the question of the foundation of such corporate obligations remains rather obscure. Logsdon and Wood's (2002) human-rights-based conception of "business citizenship" explicitly aims at taking the conventional programs of corporate citizenship a step further by institutionalizing "a process of experimentation with the aim of arriving at a just distribution of benefits and burdens" (Logsdon and Wood 2002, 176). In agreement with the position taken in this book, they argue that many of the programs currently regarded as voluntary and community-oriented elements of corporate citizenship are in fact social-justice-related duties (Logsdon and Wood 2002, 176). Hence they clearly recognize the potential contribution that the social justice perspective can make beyond conventional approaches to corporate social responsibility. However, as "a process of experimentation," their concept opens up an explorative frame for thinking in terms of justice rather than putting forth a comprehensive theory. This is the void that the book at hand attempts to close.

My elaborations in this chapter aim at drawing the corporation-specific conclusions from the general conceptual elaborations on the nature of obligations of justice in part I. I will draw these conclusions in the form of a critique of three existing perceptions and debates about the role and responsibilities of corporations in society: the neoclassical business model, conventional approaches to corporate social responsibility and corporate citizenship, and the newly emerging debate on business and human rights. This critique will clarify the conceptual features of corporate obligations of justice; at the same time, it will provide a solid foundation for the rejection of the neoclassical perspective on business and make valuable suggestions for the improvement of the last two debates. On the basis of these preliminary insights, I will then inquire into the systematization and specification of different categories of multinational corporations' obligations of justice in the next chapter.

Refuting the Neoclassical Business Model: From Wealth Creation to Just Distribution

The theorization of multinational corporations as primary agents of justice must lead to the rejection of the neoclassical business model that has dominated economic theory and thought for more than a century. In the following paragraphs I will first outline very briefly the basic presumption of profit maximization that underlies the neoclassical business model. I will then test its legitimacy in light of the justice-based perspective developed in part I. Finally, I will briefly inquire into the feasibility of alternative, more suitable interpretations of the nature of the corporation.

The Presumption of Profit Maximization: Measuring Societal Health Through Corporate Profits?

The neoclassical concept of the corporation is a reflection of neoclassical market metaphysics. It rests on the utilitarian goal of maximizing society's aggregate wealth and the belief that this can be achieved by relying on the allegedly superior coordinating capacities of the free market. Therefore, "good" corporations are thought to adhere strictly to nothing else but their self-interest. Without having to make this one of their explicit goals, economically successful companies are perceived to be acting in the interest of society as a whole simply by generating large profits.

This position has been stated most radically in Milton Friedman's classic *Capitalism and Freedom* (1962) and his subsequent, very famous 1970 *New York Times* article on the social responsibility of corporations. Corporate social responsibility, Friedman (1962, 133) claims, is a "fundamentally subversive doctrine" with an inherently collectivist core. Its widespread application, he argues, would ultimately destroy the foundations of a free society (Friedman 1962, 120). On the basis of this position, Friedman draws his famous conclusion, which has become the battle call of the conservative libertarian opposition to the corporate social responsibility movement: "There is one and only one social responsibility of business—to use its resources and engage in activities designed to increase its profits so long as it stays within the rules of the game, which is to say, engages in open and free competition without deception or fraud" (Friedman 1962, 133).

In a 2005 survey of corporate social responsibility that received wide attention in the business community, the *Economist* devoted twenty-two pages to a restatement of Friedman's argument and an attempt to defame the demand for corporate social responsibility as an ill-conceived fad of wretched do-gooders. This survey argues that the market achieves its most desirable outcomes best when it is left alone. All morally motivated interventions, even if they are well intended, will inevitably lead to ethically inferior results, that is, to a reduction of societal welfare. After all, as Adam Smith illustrated in his famous example of the butcher, the brewer, and the baker (Adam Smith 1985, 16), by pursuing his own interest, the individual "frequently promotes that of the society more effectually than when he really intends to promote it" (Adam Smith 1985, 222). At least for those who interpret Smith's *Wealth of Nations* detached from his holistic moral philosophy, it might indeed seem that it is the purely economic, that is, instrumentally rational and thus strictly amoral, pursuit of one's own interests that leads to the ethically most desirable outcomes for society. From this perspective, corporate profits might even serve as a guide to how well society's interests are served. If what people are willing to pay for a good, and thus the value they attach to it, exceeds the cost of producing it, society has gained, and the corporation has made a profit. The logical conclusion is that the bigger the profit of the corporation, the bigger the gain for society at large (Crook 2005, 15).

From this neoclassical perspective, the claim for corporate social responsibility is inevitably perceived as self-defeating. It reduces not only corporate profits but also societal welfare. Hence profit maximization turns out to be not merely an economic but a genuinely moral imperative. Evidently, however, this normative assumption behind the neoclassical business model is severely at odds with the understanding of a just society put forth in this book. Despite the lengthy elaborations on justice and the economy in part I, let me very briefly make these contradictions explicit again.

The Normative Argument: About the Alleged Moral Obligation to Maximize Profits

The logical conclusion from the previous elaborations on the nature and principles of justice is that the neoclassical perspective on business must be rejected as deeply and inherently flawed. Both the perception that generating profits is the only social responsibility of business and the interpretation of profit maximization as a social and thus moral duty are mistaken. Egoism and morality are located at opposite ends of the moral spectrum. The contractarian argument, on which the demand for the self-interested pursuit of maximum profits and the neoclassical business model are based, is a substitute for morality rather than an adequate interpretation of it. Thus what Friedman promotes is a rather strange kind of "ethics without morality" (Cortina 1992; Ulrich 2008, 95) that promises ethical outcomes without having to think and act morally. On the contrary, morality or integrity is replaced by mechanical compliance with the dictates of the market. This position is inherently misguided. From any reasonable standpoint, a moral responsibility to maximize profits, that is, a moral obligation for egoism, does not exist.

An alternative or rather derivative justification of profit maximization based on utilitarian ethics fails equally. By subordinating justice to the maximization of social welfare, utilitarianism simply excludes potential distributive injustice from the realm of ethical reasoning. Therefore, it has nothing to say about either the legitimacy of corporate goals or the means by which these goals are pursued. Utilitarianism legitimizes any kind of self-interested behavior simply by referring to the alleged net increase in the value of aggregate utility.

However, it is unnecessary to make an in-depth analysis of such neoclassical "ethics without morality" to reject its underlying business model as inherently flawed. The very trust in the superior coordinating capacities of the free-market mechanism on which the neoclassical business model ultimately rests is based on a flawed and rather peculiar metaphysical belief rather than on empirical, let alone logical, fact. As I made sufficiently clear earlier, there is no such thing as a self-regulating market that coordinates self-interest in a way that benefits everyone. Competition always creates winners and losers by definition; and its intensification in the realm of ongoing market liberalization and deregulation, as well as its aggravation between entire national economies, has meant that the share of losers has steadily increased while fewer and fewer winners have come to share the growing cake among themselves. The "Creative Destruction," as Joseph Schumpeter (1976, 83) famously characterized the virtues of the capitalist market process, occurs in anything but a balanced manner. An ever-increasing share of people are confronted with its destructive potential, while the fruits of its creations benefit not only different people but also a decreasing number of them. It is virtually impossible for the (free) market to achieve just outcomes on its own because it systematically reproduces the preexisting inequalities and asymmetrical power relations entailed in the starting positions of its participants. The notion of market neutrality is thus an illusion; the market mechanism is inherently partial and slanted toward the basic configurations and predispositions of its strong participants. Therefore, the success of some is planting the seeds for the misfortune of others. This is what Sandra Waddock (2007) described as the dark side of corporate success. It denotes the hidden social costs of corporations' enhanced financial performance; the better they perform, the more worried we must be about our quality of life, the environment, and the values that are driving our societies. "Something must be dreadfully wrong with the system," she concludes, "when successful corporate strategies result in social ills just by virtue of their success." In other words, corporate profits are anything but a good measure of societal well-being; in some cases they can be the reason for its opposite.

From a rights-based perspective, the categorical maximization of self-interest cannot be a legitimate goal for any corporation, irrespective of whether it is big or small, domestic or international. The uncompromising pursuit of maximum profits rejects all potentially opposing claims of human beings a priori and by definition (Ulrich 2002a, 145; 2008, 379ff.). It is systematically unable to differentiate between morally justified and unjustified claims of human beings and takes them into consideration, if at all, only insofar as they are themselves instrumental for the generation of profits. This attitude may lead not only to the toleration of deliberate human rights violations but even to their legitimation by reference to the profit motive. Corporate history is full of examples in which corporations have done just that.

This argument against profit maximization as a legitimate corporate goal is closely related to the rejection of Nozick's property-rights-based claim against social and economic rights. Libertarians tend to argue that corporations owe the maximization of profits to the shareholders who own the company. Milton Friedman (1962, 135) even denoted the corporation as a mere instrument of stockholders. Therefore, every decision of management to use funds for purposes other than the maximization of profits is seen as an infringement on shareholders' property rights. Not surprisingly, the survey of the *Economist* mentioned earlier argues along the same lines. The argument is that giving away money for charitable purposes happens at the direct expense of the company's owners. The fact that Robin Hood stole from the rich to give to the poor did not make him any less a thief; "he might have been a good corporate citizen," it concludes, "but he was still a bandit" (Crook 2005, 8).

The property-rights-based argument must fail because it inevitably relies on the flawed assumption of absoluteness of shareholders' property rights. Within a consistent framework of rights, as shown earlier, this position cannot reasonably be maintained (see the section "Basic Needs, 'Real Freedom,' and the Claim for Socioeconomic Human Rights" in chapter 2). Rather than being absolute, the existing distribution of property in society is always subject to ethical scrutiny and must be able to stand the test of reasonable justification. The justified claims of the poor constitute a critique of the status quo that puts the fairness of existing distributions into question. A distribution that leaves large parts of the population without anything while a small minority lives in lavish luxury can hardly be considered legitimate. However, if existing distributions turn out to be unjust, redistributive measures deriving from it cannot be qualified as mere charity. A charitable contribution implies giving up one's legitimately held resources in order to make someone else better off. Insofar as the existing distribution is unjust, however, we are not holding our resources legitimately, because this would imply a legitimate right to an unjust distribution. Moreover, if the corporation is understood primarily as an instrument for serving society, then the shareholders' claims cannot be separated from the fulfillment of this purpose. In other words, shareholders are investors, not owners, and they invest their money under the prior assumption that the corporation is an instrument not primarily to maximize their profits but to serve a social purpose. Hence their prior decision to invest money in the corporation is a decision to invest in a social institution that fulfills a societal cause. This fundamental premise about the purpose of the corporation is thus systematically and even logically prior to the profit expectation of shareholders. This does not mean that the property rights of shareholders count for nothing, but they are not moral absolutes, as presupposed by the claim for profit maximization; they are but one of many legitimate claims the corporation must try to balance—no more and no less.

If we take the principles of rights-based distributive justice rather than those of utilitarianism or contractarianism to be prescriptive for the global economy, then it cannot be the maximization of wealth that exercises normative power for corporate conduct but rather its just distribution. In other words, the ultimate guiding ideal for corporations can no longer be efficiency but must shift to social justice (Fukada-Parr 2003, 308). This insight is of great momentousness, especially for those institutions that we consider primary agents of justice. The large multinational corporation faces a particular challenge in this regard. It does not merely have to take on responsibilities as a citizen within the institutional framework of the state but must, as a quasi-governmental institution and primary agent of justice at the global level, directly respond to global injustices by providing adequate (positive) distributional answers.

The Empirical Argument: About the Alleged Factual Necessity to Maximize Profits

For a corporation to be socially responsible means to pursue a meaningful business idea by legitimate means (Ulrich 2008, 408ff.). Some might argue that in the face of ever-intensifying competitive pressure in globalizing markets, this is easier said than done. Even if corporations were willing and ready to take on responsibility beyond the mere generation of profits, they might not be able to do so in their struggle to stay competitive.

This argument is indeed relevant. However, the empirical realities of current market conditions cannot override the normative validity of what a just economy should look like. This logically implies that in order to be able to meet their individual moral obligations under market conditions, corporations bear a derivative responsibility to aspire to a suitable regulatory framework that effectively enables them to do so (Ulrich 2008, 414ff.). Thus truly responsible corporations do not uncritically point to given "necessities" of the market in order to legitimize their moral failures but subject the empirical conditions of the market to ethical reflection and justification. Corporate responsibility, in other words, does not stop at the boundaries of the corporation but extends to the market conditions in which it is exercised. The reference to given market structures as an argument for not being able to take on social responsibility might achieve some credibility if it were used by small and medium-sized corporations with little economic power. However, it appears almost cynical when it is voiced by large and powerful multinationals because it is precisely large multinationals that largely control the structures that generate the competitive pressures in the first place.

Furthermore, as Ulrich (2008, 131ff., 385ff.) showed, it is not least the corporations' own profit motive (and the investors' expectations behind it) that subjects them to the alleged "necessities" of the market. The more strictly corporations formulate their goals and projections in terms of maximum profits, the more profoundly they deprive themselves of leeway for the consideration of potentially conflicting claims. Thus the forces of the market are created by the corporations' desire to maximize their economic success. Hence the less the daily struggle in the market is aimed at mere survival than at the actual maximization of profits, the less the perceived "necessities" of the market are in fact imposed on corporations externally and the more they derive directly from the narrow and restrictive definition of their own goals (Ulrich 2002a, 37). If power is a function of capabilities and thus of the freedom to choose, then it is precisely the large and powerful corporations that actually have the capacity to choose their goals in a less restrictive way. Hence it is within their own power to formulate goals for themselves that leave room for the consideration of broader societal claims and demands and thus effectively to take pressure off the market mechanism. The room to maneuver that large multinational corporations actually have is thus not simply a matter of given external market conditions but to a large extent is determined by the more or less restrictive margins they impose on themselves through the goals they deliberately choose. In other words, beyond the struggle for survival, the so-called necessities of the market largely turn out to be psychological imperatives of the market participants themselves. Therefore, the claim about the empirical impossibility of social responsibility under market conditions mirrors the myth of the normative necessity of profit maximization. From this perspective, let us now have a critical look at how contemporary interpretations of corporate social responsibility correspond to and integrate the claim of rights-based justice.

Challenging "Corporate Social Responsibility": From Beneficence to Obligations of Justice

Concepts like corporate social responsibility and corporate citizenship received growing attention in practice, academia, and the larger public throughout the late 1990s and onward. This growing popularity can be interpreted as an initially defensive reaction to the growing contradictions and shortcomings of one-dimensional neoliberal policies and the inability of the neoclassical business model to cope with an increasingly complex world. The concepts themselves are nothing new. In fact, corporate social responsibility has been known as a concept at least since the 1950s. However, it did not receive broad academic attention before the 1970s. What is novel about today's approaches is rather the force with which they are able to challenge mainstream economic thought, as well as their breadth and depth in theorization and practical application.

Although the notions of corporate social responsibility and corporate citizenship are often used with slightly different implications and connotations (see, e.g., Matten, Crane, and Chapple 2003; Waddock and Wettstein 2005, 41; Wettstein 2005), they both aim at the same goal: to define the purpose and responsibilities of business in much broader terms than the neoclassical paradigm does. Trying to find one "binding" definition for these terms, however, is a hopeless endeavor; there are perhaps as many different suggestions and proposals as there are articles, papers, and books on the topic. There is, in fact, not even agreement on the correct use of the terms themselves.[1]

Nevertheless, a common denominator of the different definitions and terms is their general reference to the necessity for businesses to integrate and examine societal expectations and demands more directly in their normal business strategies and practices. It is precisely because all societal expectations and demands are naturally in a constant state of flux and because their reasonableness and justification can be determined only discursively that any attempt to define the content of corporate social responsibility and corporate citizenship must necessarily remain very broad (Lunau and Wettstein 2004, 22f.). Therefore, Jan Jonker (2005, 20f.) suggested that we must think of corporate social responsibility rather as a "sensitizing concept," that is, as an "umbrella term" that helps identify all those issues and aspects that need to be debated in order to specify the position and function of the corporation in contemporary society. The term itself, he concludes, has no other function than to heighten our sensitivity to the complex debate that challenges the role of companies today.

What distinguishes corporate social responsibility from corporate citizenship is not their underlying idea—both concepts equally aim at the redefinition of the role of the corporation in society—but the starting point from which they reflect on it. Corporate citizenship evidently aims at creating an analogy between human beings and corporate actors as members of a political community. It claims that the same expectations we have regarding the adequate conduct of fellow human citizens are valid also for corporations operating as members of our communities and societies. Therefore, it may help emphasize the new political mandate of multinational corporations that go beyond the traditional interpretations of social responsibility better than the term *corporate social responsibility*, which lacks this immediate political-philosophical element in its initial premises (Palazzo and Scherer 2008, 578). For the purpose of this analysis and because the same general limitations and confusions can be found in the conventional use of both concepts, I will use the two terms largely interchangeably, referring to and critiquing their shared elements, goals, and argumentative frames rather than their conceptual differences. In other words, the following critique largely applies to both concepts. One must keep in mind, however, that in certain aspects they are conceptually different.

The increased attention that the concepts of corporate social responsibility and corporate citizenship enjoy today is certainly a welcome development overall. However, it is not a new insight that the inflationary use of catchwords and concepts often leads to the slow dilution of their content and meaning. Accordingly, today's conventional interpretations of corporate social responsibility and corporate citizenship are also characterized by some major shortcomings. A consequent justice focus, as we will see shortly, will be the key to move past such misinterpretations.

Justice, Not Charity

Obligations of justice enjoy the highest priority among moral responsibilities. Therefore, one would think that assessing moral responsibilities of corporations must logically start with defining and outlining their obligations of justice. Surprisingly, however, the current debate on corporate social responsibility hardly ever refers to the concept of justice. Instead, it predominantly interprets corporate social responsibility as a virtue-based concept.

Such virtue-based interpretations give rise to two interconnected, fundamentally flawed, but surprisingly persistent premises regarding the character of corporate responsibilities. First, in most cases social responsibilities of corporations are interpreted as mere philanthropy and charity. Thus they are, second, predominantly perceived as voluntary. Although there certainly are signs that the debate is ready to move beyond these narrow interpretations, these two premises still enjoy wide popularity today both in practice and in academia. In more general terms, the two premises reflect misperceptions regarding both the sphere and the nature of corporations' moral or social responsibilities. While the critique referring to their sphere is of general ethical character, the one referring to their nature derives directly from a justice-based perspective. In the following, let us have a brief look at both of them.

Misperceptions About the Sphere of Corporate Responsibility: Profit Genera-tion and Profit Distribution   Reducing corporate social responsibility or cor-porate citizenship to mere philanthropy, as conventional thinking about eth-ics in business often does, means to limit its sphere to the distribution of profits while exempting the whole process of profit generation from ethical scrutiny. Corporations are perceived to have a responsibility to donate some of their profits to "good" causes, but the way they generate those profits, that is, their concrete business policies, strategies, and practices, seems to be of no ethical concern (Ulrich 2002a, 147f.; 2008, 402ff.). Such approaches evidently are based on a divided, some might say somewhat schizophrenic, understand-ing of corporate social responsibility. The corporation is perceived to be free to maximize its profits by whatever means it chooses. In return, however, once the profits are made, they must partly be given to social causes.

Corporate social responsibility, thus understood, works as some kind of indulgence strategy in which the donation of a share of the corporation's prof-its serves as a compensation for the potentially harmful or even ruthless tac-tics pursued for their prior generation. Potentially, this leads to entirely ab-surd constellations in which corporations donate some of their profits to precisely those social causes that they helped undermine through their busi-ness practices in the first place. This evident contradiction culminates in the insight that profit maximization itself turns into the ultimate condition for corporate social responsibility: only those corporations that generate enough profits can afford to do good—after all, the more money a corporation gener-ates, the more it can donate for good causes.

It is precisely this incomplete understanding of corporate social responsi-bility that Joel Bakan attacks in his widely noticed critique *The Corporation* (2004). He argues that corporate social responsibility serves as a mere smoke screen for corporations to conduct business as usual while maintaining a clean public image. Even if some good can result from such concepts, they do not change anything about the nature of the corporation as an inherently self-interested institution (Bakan 2004, 50). Bakan's critique is justified. For many companies, corporate social responsibility indeed serves as mere window dressing. Bakan is also correct in claiming that the (current) institutional form of the corporation contradicts a serious interpretation of corporate so-cial responsibility. This does not mean, however, that socially responsible business is per se impossible, as Bakan wrongfully concludes, because this would essentially imply that we take the current neoclassical form of the corporation as an unchangeable fact. From this perspective, we would—as Bakan does—enforce social responsibility solely through an external regulative framework while again freeing the corporation itself from all moral responsibility. This approach, however, is a reassurance of rather than a challenge to the neoclassical business model. It implicitly acknowledges the righteousness of the uncompromising pursuit of corporate self-interest. Bakan is correct that regulative frameworks in favor of corporate responsibility are of tremendous importance, but they can never fully discharge corporations from adopting their fair share of individual moral responsibility (Ulrich 2008, 349).

The image of the responsible corporation is not an illusion. Institutions are created by human beings and can be transformed by human beings. To deny the possibility of responsible corporations means to claim victory of the machine over human reason. Thus, instead of rejecting the whole idea of corporate social responsibility across the board, we should rather engage in promoting, both in academia and in practice, a consistent interpretation of it, that is, an interpretation that holds what it promises.

Misperceptions About the Nature of Corporate Responsibility: Justice, Law, and Voluntariness   Reducing corporate social responsibility to mere beneficence is based on a confusion regarding not only the sphere of corporate responsibilities but also their nature. The concept of corporate social responsibility is often perceived to refer to those responsibilities that corporations adopt on a voluntary basis beyond mere compliance with positive law. Hence compliance with legal law is taken as the minimum threshold, that is, the floor of morally acceptable corporate conduct, while all social responsibilities adopted beyond legal rules and regulations are regarded as virtuous and thus particularly praiseworthy. In other words, the realm of justice is reduced to legal laws, while everything else is a matter of (voluntary) beneficence and is up to the goodwill and discretion of the corporation. The latest report of the European Commission on the issue of corporate social responsibility, for example, asserts that the concept is essentially about the integration of social and environmental concerns into business operations and is thus, "fundamentally about voluntary business behaviour" (Commission of the European Communities 2006, 2). Twelve references to the concept of voluntariness in the 13-page report leave no doubt about the continuing dominance of this perception in the contemporary practical discussion of corporate social responsibility.

Evidently, such a combined voluntaristic and positivistic interpretation of corporate social responsibility is severely at odds with a rights-based account of justice. Rights-based justice is based on moral rights that are systematically prior to legal rights. Hence the realm of justice extends far beyond positive law. Justice is not the essence but the critique of legal laws. In a society of constant and profound development and change, formal laws always lag behind foundational ethical insights and moral practices. Therefore, positive law never addresses all the issues that should be addressed (Carroll 1998, 4). In some cases existing legal regulations might even conflict with the requirements of justice. Thus to limit obligations of justice to compliance with legal law is a serious categorical mistake. As a consequence, there must be corporate responsibilities that reach beyond mere compliance with positive law, but without automatically losing the moral urgency of the justice concept.

An early approach that considered this insight is Archie B. Carroll's framework of economic, legal, ethical, and discretionary responsibilities (Carroll 1979, 1998; Carroll and Buchholtz 2003, 35ff.), which still serves as a standard and basis for many contemporary approaches to corporate social responsibility. Carroll fills the identified gap between compliance with positive law and mere charity with the category of "ethical responsibilities." The problem that evidently arises from such a categorization is where to draw the line between ethical and discretionary responsibilities. In this regard Carroll and most of his contemporary successors stay conservative. They predominantly limit the category of "ethical responsibilities" to some narrowly defined negative duties within the sphere of profit generation. Hence, although they cover some of the negative implications that doing business may entail, they fail to include any of the positive responsibilities that address broader societal issues and problems. Those are commonly still attributed to the category of discretionary and thus voluntary responsibilities of the corporation. Thus a corporation's decision to assume certain social roles and to engage in providing solutions to such societal problems is assumed to be "purely voluntary" and guided only by a corporation's desire rather than being mandated, required, or even only generally expected in an ethical sense. In other words, a corporation's nonparticipation in such matters is "not considered unethical per se" (Carroll 1979, 500). It is not perceived as an integral part of ethical business conduct but merely as an add-on to it, that is, a matter of beneficence and charity.

The problem with Carroll's position is that by shifting the entirety of positive action associated with the corporation's assumption of "social roles" into the realm of discretionary responsibilities, we eliminate the question about the general purpose and the larger societal role of the corporation from the realm of ethical reflection. In other words, we take the purely economic function of the corporation as a given and shield it from ethical scrutiny. Furthermore, Carroll's position leads to the somewhat paradoxical situation that precisely those issues and concerns that must be attributed to the category of social justice, that is, the issues of foremost moral and social urgency, are considered of only minor and discretionary concern to corporations. This seems rather odd if we consider that large multinational corporations are the dominant societal institutions and often even operate in quasi-governmental roles. How can we exempt the most powerful social institutions, that is, precisely those institutions with the biggest leverage in providing solutions to societal problems, from all responsibility for active participation and engagement in the creation of a just society? The misinterpretation of the nature of corporate responsibilities as a mere matter of virtues, with its consequent attribution to the realm of voluntariness, is the most capital and fundamental flaw of the current debates on corporate social responsibility and corporate citizenship. Furthermore, it threatens to undermine the whole concept and moral urgency of human rights in general by shifting all obligations deriving from them into the realm of supererogation.

This critique is not to be misunderstood as an all-out assault on virtues. Virtues still play an important role in the concept of corporate social responsibility. When we refer to obligations of justice, we focus on actions, that is, on the aspect of doing. Virtues, on the other hand, emphasize the aspect of being. It is the aspect of being just that Aristotle called the highest and most complete virtue, which contains all other virtues. This means that being just is based on and includes virtues like fairness, honesty, integrity, truthfulness, benevolence, and nonmalfeasance. Taken together, these virtues build our moral character and thus provide an important predisposition for acting upon principles of justice. A virtuous character is thus the foundation of moral leadership regardless of whether we talk of individual or corporate leaders (Carroll 1998, 5). Hence those corporations that have successfully internalized the "cardinal virtues" in their organizations and practices and thus have built strong moral characters will be most likely to prevail as leading corporate citizens. Our ability to distinguish between just and unjust and to direct our actions accordingly is based on our moral character. Hence acting justly, that is, doing justice, depends, after all, on a virtuous character and thus on being just.

Starting our reflections on corporate social responsibility from the standpoint of justice broadens the scope of potential issues that fall into the range of genuine corporate responsibility. A perspective of justice takes the moral rights of people as a starting point. A focus on rights claims of human beings, however, cannot be confined to potential harms that might be connected to corporate misbehavior but inevitably includes the question of what contributions corporations may be able to make to the realization of unfulfilled rights. Therefore, social and societal aspects of human development become as much a potential part of corporate responsibility as economic ones, and addressing them is not merely a matter of corporate altruism but one of genuine and thus morally owed obligations of justice. Shifting the focus of corporate social responsibility to obligations of justice means to abandon the common paradigm of voluntariness and beneficence that has largely dominated its conventional interpretations. It does not mean that virtue-based responsibilities, both required and entirely voluntary, are eliminated entirely from the realm of corporations' social responsibilities. But a corporation's responsibilities cannot be reduced to voluntary beneficence or philanthropy. Any account of corporate social responsibility that fails adequately to address the most fundamental moral responsibilities, that is, genuine obligations of justice, is systematically incomplete. Unfortunately, this is the case for almost all current interpretations.

The Case Against the "Business Case"

The assumption of voluntariness underlying most conventional interpretations of corporate social responsibility creates the no-less-problematic need for those approaches to formulate and promote a so-called business case for corporate responsibility. In other words, precisely because corporate responsibility is perceived as voluntary, it cannot be encouraged by stressing its moral imperative but must be incentivized by showing that it is in the best financial interest of the corporations themselves. Concordantly, a host of empirical studies have suggested that being socially responsible can indeed have a positive impact on a corporation's balance sheet (e.g., Wood and Jones 1995; Pava and Krausz 1996; Waddock and Graves 1997; Margolis and Walsh 2001; see also the metastudy by Orlitzky, Schmidt, and Rynes 2003). Explanations of this impact vary from positive effects on the corporation's reputation and recruitment of better and more motivated employees to increasing customer loyalty. However, the considerable body of literature that tries to prove this so-called business case in order to make the concept of corporate social responsibility more attractive to corporations does not answer the much more fundamental question of why corporate social responsibility actually ought to be profitable in order to be of concern to business.

For Credit Suisse Group, the large multinational banking institute headquartered in Switzerland, economic success seems to be the prime motivation for engaging in social responsibility. In its 2004 sustainability report, for example, it leaves no doubt about the necessity of corporate social responsibility for globally active corporations "if they are to achieve long-term business success" (Credit Suisse Group 2004, 1). The generation of "sustained corporate value," the argument continues, requires a business policy that takes the needs of society into consideration. Credit Suisse Group is not alone in its instrumental interpretation of corporate social responsibility. For many, perhaps most, self-proclaimed "good" corporate citizens, the ultimate reason for adopting social responsibility is not, as one might think, their interest in doing the right thing but rather the prospect of economic success that supposedly comes with it. Somewhat ironically, even Heinrich von Pierer, the former chairman of the ethically troubled German multinational Siemens AG, asserts that "a corporation should simply act morally because immoral behavior does not pay" (Pierer 2003, 11; transl. by author). "Corporations that neglect ethics," he goes on, "ultimately hurt their own bottom line" (Pierer 2003, 11; translation by author). Finally, Kraft Foods' CEO Roger Deromedi also seems more interested in the economic potential of corporate social responsibility than in its ethical quality. Responsibility, he stated on Kraft's website, is "essential to our long-term success." Indeed, the demonstration of corporate responsibility, according to Deromedi, is one of Kraft Foods' "core business strategies."

This instrumental view of corporate social responsibility is not limited to practitioners. Much of the academic debate also sings from the same hymn sheet, emphasizing the alleged harmony between increasing profits and social responsibility and proclaiming that "sound ethics is good business." The win-win euphoria of Chris Marsden and Jörg Andriof, for example, went so far as to proclaim corporate social responsibility as consistent even with the claim for profit maximization: "Corporate citizenship [. . .] should also be seen not always as a business cost, a trade-off against additional profits, but more often as a significant contributor to long-term business success and entirely consistent with the goal of profit maximisation" (Marsden and Andriof 1998, 330).

Love is blind, some might say; it finds harmony where none exists. Marsden and Andriof's statement is quite evidently self-contradictory; profit maximization, as I made sufficiently clear earlier, excludes all potentially conflicting claims per se and across the board, irrespective of whether they are morally justified. Therefore, there is by definition no such thing as harmony between profit maximization and corporate social responsibility. After all, where corporations with true ethical awareness are needed the most is not in situations in which their drive for profits allegedly goes hand in hand with social responsibility but, on the contrary, precisely in those situations in which it conflicts with human beings' morally justified claims.

In an increasingly complex and diverse world, such conflicts are the rule rather than the exception. In other words, in a pluralistic (world) society, the circumstances of justice are a permanent given. To proclaim unconditional harmony between profit maximization and social responsibility not only is empirically unrealistic but also resembles at its core nothing else than Smith's metaphysical account of the invisible hand of the market; it does not correct but reaffirms the neoclassical business model. The market itself is perceived to be responsible for directing corporate behavior in socially and ecologically sustainable directions simply by endowing even moral responsibilities with a potential for economic profit. Hence in order to do the right thing, corporations do not need to be concerned with anything else than following their own self-interest.

It can hardly be denied that the win-win rhetoric of business-case enthusiasts has contributed a great deal to today's popularity of the notions of corporate social responsibility and corporate citizenship. Furthermore, it might indeed have increased corporations' awareness of their social responsibilities. However, this neither changes nor diminishes the fact that at its core it is fundamentally flawed. A purely instrumental interpretation of corporate social responsibility as a mere strategic success factor inevitably raises one central question: what happens in situations in which the consideration of legitimate stakeholder claims does not yield any profit potential for the company (L. S. Paine 2000, 327)? Or negatively formulated, what if the ignorance of these claims happens beyond the public screen and, accordingly, does not lead to a loss of reputation or to any other negative impact on the corporation's bottom line?

It is precisely the cases that occur out of the public eye that form the touchstone for the genuine commitment of true corporate citizens. Not surprisingly, this is exactly where such a conventional "business-case ethics" systematically falls short. It is these cases that separate corporations with a genuine interest in the legitimacy of their business conduct from pretend-to-be corporate citizens who merely strive for public acceptance.[2] A corporation that merely strives for social acceptance considers moral claims only to the extent necessary to avoid public scrutiny and opposition. Hence it will seriously engage only with those stakeholders that are powerful enough to be a potential danger for the corporation's reputation and image (Ulrich 2008, 400). Therefore, it is not surprising that the previously mentioned Roger Deromedi of Kraft Foods merely refers to "*demonstrating* corporate citizenship" as one of its core business strategies rather than, for example, to its "genuine commitment to corporate citizenship." Genuine commitment to corporate citizenship crystallizes around cases of little public attention, cases, that is, in which social responsibility is being pursued for its own sake. A focus on the mere demonstration of good corporate citizenship, on the other hand, aims first and foremost at the corporation's positive public image: ethics only matters if it pays.

Promoting responsible business conduct solely on the basis of its functionality for economic success rather than as an end in itself conflicts with an understanding of justice as put forth in this book. Considerations of justice enjoy unconditional and categorical priority over self-interest and cannot be subordinated to the profit principle. The business world is no exception in this regard. On the contrary, it is the pursuit of profits that is to be subjected unconditionally to ethical scrutiny and the criteria of just human coexistence (Ulrich 2004b, 12). Hence businesspeople too should do the right thing simply because it is the right thing to do rather than because there might be a financial payoff for doing so (Bowie 1999, 130). Again, this does not mean that there cannot be cases in which morally responsible business conduct indeed leads to better financial performance; on the contrary, where it does so, it is highly welcome. But this empirical link must not be instrumentalized and turned into a normative condition for deciding whether we ought to act in a morally responsible manner. It is very likely that exactly those corporations that subject their profit orientation unconditionally to the criterion of its legitimacy will (and should) in the end also be successful with it precisely because they conduct their business with genuine integrity and because, as a result, they indeed earn their enhanced reputation on this basis.[3] In other words, those corporations that merely pretend to be socially responsible in order to make a profit will be figured out by the critical public sooner rather than later and will lose their undeserved goodwill. The bottom line is that an increase in profits can always be only a welcome by-product of conducting genuinely moral business but never a requirement or a normative condition for it (Waddock 2002, 6f.; Ulrich 2004b, 7; 2008, 401).

Moving Beyond Corporate Social Responsibility: Toward Rights-Based Justice

Examining multinational corporations' societal role from the perspective of rights-based cosmopolitan justice implies that we move beyond the premises of conventional interpretations of corporate citizenship and corporate social responsibility. It suggests that we expand our discussion of corporate responsibility beyond the realm of virtues into the sphere of social justice and that we abandon the assumption of voluntariness commonly associated with the concept of corporate social responsibility. Obligations of justice are neither voluntary nor dependent on a potential economic payoff. They are morally owed and thus unconditional and mandatory.

This claim does not spark much controversy in connection with governments' obligations. No one considers a government's responsibilities for the well-being of its citizens merely voluntary or its corresponding actions particularly virtuous and praiseworthy. Therefore, it seems reasonable to apply the same standards also to those institutions that de facto operate in governing positions. From this perspective, the notion of corporate citizenship can be misleading. It implies that large multinationals enjoy equal status as human citizens in regard to both rights and responsibilities. However, their governing position rather suggests that they must bear more extensive responsibilities while enjoying a more restrictive set of rights (Wettstein 2005).

A holistic framework of corporate responsibility can be developed along the lines of the tripartite categorization of moral responsibilities outlined earlier. In the first and most important category are those obligations, that is, obligations of justice, that are morally owed and mandatory. In the second category are required virtue-based duties, that is, duties that are not morally owed but that corporations can reasonably be expected to meet. Finally, there are optional and thus voluntary responsibilities that go beyond what is reasonably expected and are thus highly appreciated and praiseworthy.

More precisely, a corporation can be said to have morally owed and thus mandatory obligations of justice where it has unique and superior capabilities for the realization of people's moral rights. These obligations are most evident where the respective capabilities merely refer to the abdication of directly harmful actions and become more complex and ambiguous when they move toward obligations to protect from or even to remedy existing or potential rights violations. Such obligations of justice hold up to the point where they are trumped by the corporation's own justified claims according to the cutoff criterion of reasonableness. Beyond this point corporate responsibilities become a matter of virtues. In some cases we might reasonably expect the corporation to adopt certain responsibilities even beyond what justice demands. Such responsibilities can be regarded as required. A corporation might be expected to support certain cultural and societal events, for example, or make very general donations (as opposed to specific contributions based on unique capabilities) to good causes. In other cases, however, the engagement of the corporation might even exceed such reasonable expectations and be entirely optional, that is, voluntary.

It is not surprising that corporations tend to focus their effort on the second and third categories of responsibilities because such virtuous and thus praiseworthy action has the largest potential for positive publicity. Thus a stronger emphasis on obligations of justice requires a shift both in corporate focus and in public perception. It is precisely such obligations of justice that are hardest for corporations to cope with because they involve the way and context in which they conduct their business and not merely their willingness to donate some of their profits to good causes.

Thinking about corporate social responsibility and corporate citizenship from a justice perspective means adopting a consequent focus on people's moral rights. This is precisely what the newly emerging debate on business and human rights does. From this perspective, this new stream of thought in corporate ethics is the most promising platform from which to expect major contributions to the clarification of corporations' moral responsibilities. However, the business and human rights debate also is not free of shortcomings and misinterpretations. An assessment of these shortcomings from the justice perspective and some subsequent proposals for improvement in the following paragraphs will end the preliminary conceptual remarks in this chapter and enable me to proceed to a systematic assessment of the multinational corporation's obligations of justice in the next chapter.

Advancing Business and Human Rights: From "Do No Harm" to Human Development

The relation between business and human rights remained largely unexplored until the mid-1990s. This is surprising, considering the long history of concepts like corporate social responsibility and corporate citizenship. Despite their practical roots in the workers' rights movements of the early 20th century, these concepts have seldom inquired systematically into the conceptual and substantive clarification of human rights obligations of businesses. Concordantly, there are only a small number of early approaches to corporate responsibility with a rights focus. Furthermore, in most cases they focus almost exclusively on the evident context of employment relations and workers' rights and seldom take a broader perspective on the corporation's impact on human rights in a larger societal context (see, e.g., Werhane 1985). Thus human rights were of rather marginal concern both to corporations themselves and to their critical observers throughout nearly the whole 20th century.

This changed dramatically in 1995. Royal Dutch Shell's questionable role in the execution of the Nigerian environmental activist and playwright Ken Saro-Wiwa and eight of his followers led to a worldwide public outcry that suddenly put human rights on the corporate agenda. Saro-Wiwa and his fellow activists in the Movement for the Survival of the Ogoni People (MOSOP) led a peaceful campaign against environmental damage in the Niger Delta caused by multinational companies in the oil-extracting industry. They were arrested in 1994, charged with incitement to murder, and tried a year later by a specially convened tribunal. The tribunal found them guilty and sentenced them to death. Saro-Wiwa and his eight followers were executed by hanging on November 10, 1995, despite vehement protests by human rights groups and organizations accusing the tribunal of violating international fair trial standards. In his perceptive closing statement Saro-Wiwa asserted that Shell was really on trial. He warned that the day for Shell would surely come when the "ecological war" it had waged in the delta and against the Ogoni people would be publicly condemned and punished (Greenpeace n.d.).

Saro-Wiwa was right. On October 7, 2008, 13 years after the execution of the Nigerian writer, Judge Kimba Wood of the U.S. District Court for the Southern District of New York set February 9, 2009, as the trial date for the case *Wiwa v. Royal Dutch Shell*. The case was filed in 1996 and charges Shell with complicity in the hanging of Ken Saro-Wiwa (EarthRights International

2008). After the Wiwa incident the human rights record of the private sector indeed came under much closer public scrutiny. Especially the last few years have heralded increasing numbers of mainly practice-driven efforts both from international institutions and NGOs and from corporations themselves to address the evident impact of their activities on human rights. Human rights advocacy groups and organizations such as Oxfam, Human Rights Watch, and Amnesty International have systematically and prominently put the topic of business and human rights on their agenda and have increased their pressure to hold corporations accountable for violations of human rights. Furthermore, we have witnessed the development of an increasing number of human-rights-related standards for corporate conduct, most prominently the UN Global Compact or, in earlier years, the OECD guidelines for transnational corporations and the ILO Tripartite Declaration. The UN Norms as the most recent initiative in this regard provided new and valuable impulses to the debate despite their ultimate failure to generate broad-enough support. Last but not least, some corporations have launched innovative new initiatives, projects, and partnerships for the promotion of human rights. Exemplary in this regard is the Business Leaders Initiative on Human Rights (BLIHR), a collaborative effort among currently 12 corporations under the auspices of Mary Robinson, aimed at finding "practical ways of applying the aspirations of the Universal Declaration of Human Rights within a business context and to inspire other businesses to do likewise" (BLIHR 2003, 6).

Academia picked up on these practical efforts after some delay but has recently started to engage in the systematization and conceptualization of the discussion from a more theoretical perspective. This emerging theoretical debate is characterized by a great diversity of involved scholars from a wide variety of different disciplines. On the one hand, there are scholars who have traditionally been concerned with questions of corporate social responsibility who are slowly starting to inquire more into the human rights conduct of business. On the other hand, traditional human rights studies located in the broader fields of law and political science also are expressing growing interest in corporations' impact on human rights. This overlap of various disciplines in questions about the role of business in human rights has certainly added much to the dynamic and fast-paced development of the debate and provides a promising basis for making further progress in finding new approaches and solutions in the foreseeable future—solutions that the relatively closed discussions on corporate social responsibility and corporate citizenship have not been able to provide so far.

The human rights approach is arguably the most substantive and promising approach to making sense of the moral responsibilities of multinational corporations. It grants first priority to those urgent claims for which corporations have an obligation of justice rather than to the ones that are a mere matter of benevolence. Taking human rights as a starting point for reflection on corporate responsibility, however, raises two main challenges. First, the dominant view of the relation between business and human rights still holds that only states can have direct human rights obligations, while the obligations of corporations are, as a result, merely indirect. Second, the debate on business and human rights has been largely limited to negative responsibilities of corporations concerning human rights. In other words, it has mainly focused on corporations' obligations not to violate human rights rather than to make positive contributions to their realization. Both of these common perceptions, however, do not fit into the account of rights-based cosmopolitan justice outlined in this book. It is precisely the shift from indirect to direct and from negative to positive obligations that characterizes primary agents of justice. Hence in order to consider the quasi-governmental role of multinational corporations adequately, these common perceptions must be adjusted in these two dimensions.

From Indirect to Direct Human Rights Obligations

The doctrine that officially underlies current legislative and judicial international human rights practice holds that international human rights legislation applies directly only to the public sector. Human rights claims, in other words, have normative power only for governments, and because there are no additional or complementary international human rights instruments or standards that specifically address also companies' impact on human rights, corporations have largely remained immune from any obligation to protect human rights (Steinhardt 2005, 178). Thus human rights claims are perceived to be prescriptive for corporations only insofar as governments translate them into national laws and regulations. In other words, it is the state that is perceived to be ultimately responsible to ensure corporations' compliance with human rights principles and to protect its citizens from corporate misconduct (Muchlinski 2001, 32). Human rights obligations of corporations, as a result, can at best be indirect.

At least two stringent objections show that this official doctrine is too narrow to reflect adequately the complexity of the contemporary global context.

These two objections summarize precisely the main arguments developed in the previous two parts of this book. This is not a coincidence. After all, the rejection of the premise that corporations have only indirect human rights obligations is the core assumption on which this whole book is ultimately based.

The first objection, that is, the moral case against the dominant (legalistic) doctrine, derives from the nature of human rights as moral rights rather than purely legal rights. Human rights are enjoyed by human beings simply by virtue of being human. Therefore, they make their claim a priori and not only through their legal codification. Thus human rights naturally lead to genuinely moral rather than merely legal obligations for responsible actors. Therefore, it seems an almost trivial insight that it is not the existence of legally binding instruments that determines human rights obligations of corporations, but, exactly the other way around, the moral obligations of corporations that determine whether legally binding instruments must be put in place. Even the conventional assumption that governments are responsible for corporations' compliance with national human rights rules is implicitly based on this premise. After all, we can judge the failure of the state to do so only if we know the sorts of obligations that these private actors actually owe to individuals (Clapham 2004, 56). If corporations did not have prior moral obligations to individuals, the state's derivative responsibility to hold them accountable would be empty and meaningless. For the victims of human rights violations, it is irrelevant whether they are committed by the state or by a private institution. Human rights violations are human rights violations irrespective of the perpetrator. If we understand human rights as moral entitlements inherent in and constitutional for every human being, then they logically make their normative claim for unconditional respect not merely vis-à-vis governments but against everyone.

The second objection, the legal case against the dominant doctrine, is connected to the multinational corporation's status as a quasi-governmental institution. It is true that existing international legal instruments for the protection of human rights are primarily, some might say exclusively, directed at states. Today multinational corporations still have no clear legal obligations concerning human rights other than mere compliance with domestic laws of the states in which they operate (Alston 2005, 36). The global regulatory vacuum described in part II of this book renders multinational corporations and their actions systematically "invisible" under international law (Cutler 2002, 32).

However, a consistent contemporary interpretation even of existing international human rights legislation can hardly ignore the changing roles both of governments and of large corporations. International human rights law was originally developed for an international society in which the only relevant and powerful players were seen to be national governments. Global economic interdependence was not nearly as dense as it is today, and multinational corporations played a much less prominent role in the global political economy. As I made sufficiently clear earlier, however, today's global realities look different. We are in the midst of a profound transformation of an international society of states into a truly cosmopolitan world (Beck 2006). Accordingly, the interpretation of international law must also change and adapt to the different context and circumstances.

The purpose of human rights law is to hold powerful institutions accountable for their impacts on people's lives. At the time it was enacted, these powerful institutions happened to be almost exclusively nation-states. Had there been a different institution with similar power, human rights law would almost certainly have been written differently. What sense would a statist law have made in a world in which states did not play a major coordinating role in society? If international law is meant to serve as an instrument for establishing and upholding justice in society, and I believe that it is or at least should be, then it seems that its underlying intention is not merely to hold states responsible but much more broadly to address all institutions that have the capacity to act as primary agents of justice. My earlier elaborations leave no doubt that multinational corporations count as one of these institutions today.

The mere fact that the issue of business and human rights is on the table today shows that the dominant positivistic and thus statist view of human rights obligations is losing some of its appeal in the broad public perception. After all, the current discussion of corporate human rights obligations rests on the premise that it is at least thinkable that institutions other than the state may bear a fair share of direct responsibility for human rights. From this perspective, the mere existence of the business and human rights debate is a critique of the state-centric perspective. Its growing momentum can be taken as a sign of the weakening of the (neo)realist paradigm in human rights studies. This does not diminish the fact that we are still far from actually realizing the inherently cosmopolitan claim of human rights. However, the first step in doing so is indeed to expand the range of responsible agents to the transnational and global levels.

From Negative to Positive Human Rights Obligations

The current debate on business and human rights still largely focuses on corporations' (negative) potential to violate human rights. Accordingly, its main emphasis is on measures to prevent corporations from directly or indirectly inflicting harm on others. Part I of this book designated direct contributions to harmful activities as primary reasons of justice. Equally important, however, are secondary reasons, which involve a moral agent's capabilities to contribute in some significant way to the improvement of unjust states of affairs. In fact, it is not, as commonly assumed, the focus on causality that is constitutive for the justice perspective, but the one on capability. Precisely this constitutive focus on capabilities, however, has been neglected almost entirely in the business and human rights debate so far. Even though the current debate shows certain signs of slowly changing perceptions in this regard (Marsden 2000, 10), its general tenor still holds that it is not corporations' task to engage actively in remedying existing injustices unless, of course, they were directly involved in bringing them about. Symptomatic of this general stance is the most recent report of the UN special representative on business and human rights, which explicitly contends that companies cannot be held responsible in cases of human rights violations "in which they were not a causal agent, direct or indirect, of the harm in question" (United Nations 2008a, 20). Its companion report at least acknowledges the danger that such restrictive interpretations might "wrongly limit the baseline responsibility of companies to respect rights" (United Nations 2008b, 6).

The reason for this neglect, at least in business practice, is evident. To date, corporate human rights policies have been formulated predominantly from a defensive stance of corporations that came under public attack for their potentially harmful business practices. Consequently, most of those companies take a rather minimalist approach and address only those problems and issues for which they have been criticized (Avery 2000, 48). So far, very few corporations have started proactively to assess their human rights obligations without being pressured into doing so by external forces. Because the business and human rights debate is still very much practice driven, these defensive policies dominate a large part of the debate in general.

From a more conceptual and theoretical angle, another reason is that the business and human rights debate has not yet been systematically connected to the concept of global justice. Therefore, also corporations' human rights obligations have seldom been formulated from a genuine standpoint of justice. Connections between justice and human rights obligations of business have at best been drawn implicitly and without any specific and significant normative implications for the debate. In other words, human rights have at best served as a yardstick for assessing the legitimacy of existing stakeholder relations; they have not been integrated into a political philosophy of the corporation's fundamental role and purpose in society.[4] A political philosophy of society—in our case global society—from which to derive the basic purpose of multinational corporations, however, is not normatively viable without a sound underlying conception of justice (see the section "Establishing Justice: The Indispensability of the Justice Perspective" in chapter 2).

Lacking a stringent political-philosophical foundation and thus a systematic reference to the concept of justice, the current debate on business and human rights has been systematically unable to integrate capabilities as a basis for the consistent formulation of corporations' obligations to engage in the proactive realization of human rights. It has exclusively relied on causal rather than genuinely moral responsibilities. Therefore, it has connected corporate obligations merely to potential violations rather than to the proactive realization of human rights. In other words, human rights have been perceived merely as side constraints rather than as goals of corporate conduct, and this perception has naturally limited the focus of the debate to the harmful potential of business activity instead of broadening it to include the corporation's fundamental role and purpose within society. It is perhaps the main weakness of this young debate that it has not yet been able to systematically and stringently connect the purpose of business to human rights and their constitutive role for human development.

A comparison of the shortcomings of the corporate social responsibility and corporate citizenship debate with those of the business and human rights debate reveals some evident complementarities. So far, the two debates have developed largely parallel to each other: the former lacks the constitutive focus on people's rights, while the latter lacks its connection to the social purpose of the corporation. Thus there is great potential for creating synergies and bringing both discussions forward by integrating them into one consistent approach.

On the one hand, a resulting human rights perspective on corporate social responsibility or corporate citizenship can provide the foundation for a stringent categorization of corporate responsibilities along the lines of the corporation's ability to contribute to the realization of people's rights. I have outlined a proposal for the basic shape of such a categorization in the section "Moving Beyond Corporate Social Responsibility: Toward Rights-Based Justice" in this chapter. Furthermore, a stronger focus on human rights would help place the dispersed interpretations of corporate social responsibility and corporate citizenship on a common value basis and provide the desperately needed set of common foundational principles for the overwhelming number of different practical standards, codes of conduct, and other initiatives in these areas (Wettstein and Waddock 2005, 307ff.). On the other hand, the broader focus of the corporate citizenship concept would effectively connect the business and human rights debate with the ongoing discussions about the basic social purpose of the corporation. This broader focus would not only complement human rights obligations of business with the non-rights-based categories of moral responsibility but also provide the necessary context for reflecting on and weighing the corporation's own justified claims against the demands it faces from various stakeholder groups every day.

Chapter 9

Making Sense of Multinational Corporations' Obligations of Justice

A FTER CLARIFYING THE CONCEPTUAL STATUS of corporate obligations of justice and their relation to existing debates and interpretations of corporate responsibility in the previous chapter, it is now time to assess what those obligations actually look like. Evidently, both the extent and the content of obligations of justice cannot be defined a priori (Kaplan 1976, 184); capability-based obligations are by definition dependent on actual circumstances and the characteristics of each individual company. Therefore, their specification must always remain a matter of public deliberation. We can, however, provide a systematization of the general features of such obligations, that is, an abstract framework or taxonomy that can serve as a guideline or at least as a conceptual basis for their specification in concrete cases.

Shue's tripartite typology of basic rights obligations outlined in part I of this book forms a promising basis for such a framework. Shue claimed that no clear-cut distinction between negative and positive rights can be made; on the contrary, all rights necessarily give rise to both negative and positive obligations. This insight suggests that there are three basic categories of duties corresponding to each right: the duty to avoid depriving, the duty to protect from deprivation, and the duty to aid the deprived. Thus making sense of multinational corporations' obligations of justice means to clarify their role in these three categories of general human rights obligations. Using a slightly adjusted terminology, we can define and specify them in terms of *respect, protection*, and *realization* of human rights. They unfold within the context of avoiding injustice by respecting human rights, preventing injustice by protecting human rights, and restoring justice by proactively realizing human rights. In short, multinational corporations' human rights obligations derive from their capacity to violate, protect, and realize any potential right at stake, both separately and in their interdependence. Evidently, the first category contains perfect obligations of negative character. The obligations of the second and third category, on the other hand, are positive and imperfect. Concordantly, causality will be of decreasing importance when we move from the first category to the second and third and will be replaced by capability as the primary criterion for determining the intensity of the corporation's obligations.

Avoiding Injustice: The Duty to Respect Human Rights

The obligations of multinational corporations as primary agents of justice start with the general and all-embracing duty to respect human rights. Thus multinational corporations have a direct obligation to refrain from all actions that might be in violation of human beings' basic rights, whether directly through their normal business conduct or indirectly through their complicity in human rights violations committed by a third party. Concordantly, the duty to respect human rights unfolds at these two systematic levels.

Avoiding Direct Human Rights Violations

It is safe to say that the most intuitive of all human rights obligations for the multinational corporation is the one to refrain from all activities that directly undermine people's basic rights. Just like any other institution, multinational corporations have an unconditional general obligation to respect human rights within their operations.

As emphasized earlier, this obligation does not depend on legal requirements in the countries in which multinationals operate. Some states might have little interest in enforcing human rights; some are even repressive and actively disregard human rights themselves. In other cases they might be too weak to enforce them. Furthermore, because of the powerful position of multinationals, certain states might simply believe that their hands are tied and tolerate corporate human rights violations in order to avoid the exit threat. As a result, multinational corporations often enjoy de facto immunity from human rights claims. To make matters worse, this immunity is growing precisely along with the increasing capacity of multinational corporations to abuse human rights. However, because governing positions, whether formal or merely de facto, always create dependencies and thus contain an inherent potential for exploitation and abuse, they must necessarily give rise to extensive moral obligations.

A corporation's employees and workers are naturally at the core of such direct dependencies. Thus workers' rights and issues concerning workplace discrimination and freedom of association have traditionally and justifiably been of major concern in corporate human rights violations. Forced labor is certainly one of the most urgent and troublesome examples of these violations. Forced labor or even slave labor is not a thing of the past, as some might (choose to) assume. The 2005 ILO report on forced labor estimates that some 12.3 million people are victims of forced labor worldwide, 9.8 million of whom are exploited by private agents (International Labour Office 2005, 10). Furthermore, forced labor is a problem of truly global dimension; it is present on all continents, in almost every country, and in every kind of economy at all stages of development (International Labour Office 2005, 1). The problem of forced labor, according to the ILO, is one of unclear legislation, of few or no resources for prosecutions, and of limited awareness and publicity. This does not eliminate the unconditional obligation of any corporation to refrain from such coercive practices. Forced labor is the antithesis of human autonomy and thus is in deep conflict with almost any human rights norm one can think of.

Even though the duty not to violate workers' rights is at its core a negative one, its proper fulfillment requires extensive positive measures. Avoiding human rights violations within complex organizations like multinational corporations presupposes adequate protective mechanisms and standards and their proper enforcement. Such mechanisms may include training of employees in human rights issues, codes of conduct, or effective whistle-blowing mechanisms. It means paying living wages and providing decent, that is, safe and healthy, working conditions for everyone. Such seemingly perfect duties are often much more complex in their realization than they might appear to be. Take the example of child labor. A perfect negative duty to abstain from child labor would require that a corporation immediately shut down all affected factories. Although there is indeed no justification for *exploitative* child labor, the sudden and complete eradication of child labor as an institution would likely lead to further and potentially more severe deprivations of families and entire villages that have traditionally depended on it. Thus radical responses to very legitimate problems may actually be counterproductive from a human rights perspective. Bruce Klatzky, a former chairman and CEO of Phillips–Van Heusen Corporation and a leading member of various human rights organizations and initiatives, warned about the negative effects on villages when companies shut down their operations. Problems like child labor, as he illustrates with the example of one of his factories in Guatemala, require more sensitive solutions, like the collaboration of the company with local schools for the improvement of the physical infrastructure, the training of teachers, and the improvement of students' nutrition (Harvard Law School Human Rights Program 1999). Similarly, Levi Strauss developed a model of shared responsibility with suppliers that were discovered to employ children in Bangladesh. The suppliers agreed to pay the children's regular wages while they attended school, while Levi Strauss paid for their tuition and the school material. Additionally, all the children were offered a job at the age of 14 by the respective suppliers (Donaldson 1996, 62).

Hence for corporations that face the problem of child labor within their organizations and operations, withdrawal requires time and substantial flanking measures that secure the well-being of the families and communities behind the children. Where we are confronted with human rights conflicts—in this concrete case the conflict between the right of the children to be children, to go to school, and to play instead of jeopardizing their mental and physical health and the right of a family to subsistence—solutions are never black-and-white; ideal solutions unfortunately often fail in a nonideal world.

Facing such dilemmas does not imply moral failure; on the contrary, their acknowledgment is a sign of a corporation's serious effort and interest in clarifying its human rights obligations. Corporations that claim to be free of moral dilemmas are likely to be hiding something. It is crucial to create awareness of this fact both among corporations and within civil society at large. Corporations must start to realize that publicly acknowledging moral dilemmas—for example, in their annual reports—is not a weakness but a crucial step in improving the global human rights situation. Civil society organizations, on the other hand, must not take this as an opportunity to blame corporations but as an invitation to work on collaborative solutions that deserve goodwill and credit.

Another example in this first category is environmental damage and degradation. Companies in the extracting industries are especially notorious in this regard. Oil companies, for example, cause tremendous environmental damage not only through oil spills and pollution of air and water but also through the extensive infrastructure required for their operations. Environmental degradation caused by oil exploration and production can have a devastating impact on human rights. It may render land unusable for farming, deplete biodiversity, or destroy fishing grounds (see, e.g., Human Rights Watch 1999b), which undermines the local people's right to food, to health, or, in cases in which parents are unable to pay school fees because of their destroyed livelihoods, even to education of their children. Large companies in the water and beverage industry are another example. They dehydrate whole communities and deprive local farmers of their ability to irrigate their lands properly. Coca-Cola, the largest beverage company in the world, uses almost three liters of fresh water for the production of one liter of Coca-Cola. According to the India Resource Center, the ratio in India even reaches 4 to 1, which means that 75 percent of the extracted water is eventually turned into wastewater (Srivastava 2006). Coca-Cola's total water consumption adds up to 283 billion liters a year. It seems highly questionable whether there are good-enough reasons to justify such numbers, considering that 1.1 billion people on this planet do not have access to clean water (UNESCO 2003, 10; UNDP 2004, 1), 6,000 people, predominantly children under the age of five, die every day of diseases that are directly related to the consumption of unclean water, and 25,000 human beings die daily of malnutrition induced in large part by water shortages (UNESCO 2003, 4).

A look into corporate history confirms that there have always been corporations that shamelessly spurned and abused the most fundamental rights of human beings in order to make a buck. Yet, as I mentioned earlier, cynics might still argue that even though undesirable, such sacrifices might be necessary in order to bring the least developed countries onto a track of sustainable growth and progress. If societal development itself is understood as a rights-based process, however, corporate practices that are based on the systematic abuse of human rights must per se be considered counterproductive. Economic development is desirable only insofar as it furthers societal development and thus the realization, not the abuse, of human rights. Hence corporate profits and economic growth can only be beneficial to societal development if they are achieved on the basis of unconditional respect of human rights.

Even though they are two of the most persistent and highly visible examples, corporate human rights abuse is not limited to issues of employment relations or environmental damage. Human rights violations occurring within the broader communities or societies in which corporations operate are often even more pervasive than the ones committed behind their own doors. Such violations, however, are predominantly committed indirectly, that is, through active or passive complicity with or support of third-party perpetrators. Let us have a closer look at them.

Avoiding Indirect Human Rights Violations: Corporate Complicity

The duty to respect human rights refers not only to direct but also to indirect human rights violations. Indirect human rights violations are not committed by the corporation itself but by a third party with significant connection to the corporation. The collaboration with the perpetrator turns corporations into accomplices, that is, into active or passive supporters of the human rights violation. Such indirect cases of corporate complicity are equally as widespread and persistent as cases of direct abuse, but they are often much harder to detect and to cope with. The concept of complicity is highly ambiguous not only in its practical implications but also in its conceptual definition. Symptomatically, its clarification has been one of the core tasks of the mandate of the UN special representative on business and human rights.

The concept of complicity derives from criminal and tort law. However, because human rights must essentially be understood as moral rights, an interpretation of complicity from the perspective of existing legislation must inevitably remain incomplete. Because I am analyzing corporations' moral rather than legal obligations, the concept of complicity must also be analyzed from a strictly moral perspective. Thus even where legal complicity is absent, there might still be reasons for attaching moral blame (ICHRP 2002, 121).

Complicity is generally defined in terms of two constitutive elements: the intensity of participation in the human rights violation and the underlying intention of the alleged accomplice. Participation in the rights violation can take place in the form of practical assistance, encouragement, or moral support. In regard to the underlying intention, it is commonly considered sufficient that the alleged accomplice acted under knowledge that his or her actions would assist the commission of the offense (Clapham and Jerbi 2001, 346). Hence for a specific case to qualify as complicity, a corporation does not need to share the malignant intent of the perpetrator. All that is required is that the company knew or should have known that its actions might assist, support, or encourage human rights violations.

Once a corporation is identified as an accomplice, it is of minor importance whether the human rights violation at issue would have taken place even without the corporation's support. The assistance given does not need to be indispensable for the violation; however, it must have a substantial effect on it. This does not mean either that the effect must be causal or that the assistance given must necessarily be tangible (Clapham 2004, 63f.). In other words, the substantiality of a corporation's assistance might not always derive from individual actions that are of great magnitude and scope, but can arise from ongoing support that becomes substantial by virtue of its duration (Ramasastry 2002, 150). A corporation's actions might thus merely facilitate human rights violations rather than directly contribute to them (Clapham 2004, 68).

Therefore, corporate complicity in human rights violations can broadly be understood as the knowing facilitation of, participation in, encouragement of, and contribution to human rights abuse committed by another, principal perpetrator (Clapham and Jerbi 2001, 345). Different kinds of complicity are normally distinguished by the kind of involvement of the corporation, as well as by its relation to the principal perpetrator. The most common categories of complicity in this regard include direct, indirect, silent, and beneficial complicity. We will look at these categories in more detail shortly.

The mere acknowledgment of corporate complicity as a valid concept in human rights discourse does not yet constitute a full departure from the conventional state-centric view. In fact, the very notion of corporate complicity is usually interpreted in largely state-centric terms insofar as it is commonly perceived as relevant only if the principal perpetrator is the state. Symptomatic of this insight is Human Rights Watch's definition of complicity as a corporation's facilitation or participation "in government human rights violations" (Human Rights Watch 1999a, 105). This interpretation is crucially based on the assumption that corporations do have direct human rights obligations, but it still adheres to the rather traditional worldview of the state as the sole, unchallenged authority in the international sphere.

A more plausible interpretation of complicity must acknowledge the plurality of authority in the global political economy and refer to the harmful collaboration of corporations not only with the state but also with other powerful institutions at the global level. For the secretary general of the International Commission of Jurists, Nicholas Howen (2005a, 12), corporate complicity may refer to participation in human rights abuses committed by virtually anyone, that is, by "governments, armed opposition groups, other companies in the supply chain, joint venturers, sometimes even individuals." Because the most persistent form of wrongdoing deriving from the collaboration of two or more nonstate actors arguably happens within structural processes, this insight adds a further category to the earlier systematization, which I will call "structural complicity."

This leaves us with five basic but often interdependent categories of corporate complicity: *direct complicity* through active collaboration, *indirect complicity* through active or passive support, *beneficial complicity* through economic exploitation, *silent complicity* through nonopposition, and *structural complicity* through the active upholding and support of harmful economic structures. In the following paragraphs I will briefly examine these categories.

Direct Complicity   Direct complicity occurs when a corporation actively supports and collaborates with a principal perpetrator, that is, when a corporation directly assists, participates in, or supports a particular, well-defined case of human rights abuse. As pointed out earlier, it is not necessary that the corporation have an intention to do harm, but merely that it know or should know that its actions contribute to the wrongdoing. Deliberate collaboration based on a corporation's intent to violate human rights would likely exceed mere compliance and readily qualify as a kind of incitement or conspiracy (Wells and Elias 2005, 164).

Cases of direct corporate complicity do not cause major ambiguity. The operations of a corporation can be directly linked to a specific human rights violation, which clearly exposes the corporation to justified moral blame. For example, corporations' equipment might be directly used by the principal perpetrator to suppress human rights, as happened in 1997 with Enron in India. The police used Enron's corporate helicopters to survey demonstrations of activists, which were then, at least in some cases, violently suppressed (Human Rights Watch 1999a). There are countless similar cases in which corporations have reportedly made their premises available for interrogations, torture, and other harmful practices by security forces and local law enforcement. In 2001, for example, the International Labour Rights Fund filed a lawsuit under the Alien Tort Claims Act against Exxon Mobil charging the company with complicity in murder, torture, kidnapping, and sexual abuse by Indonesian soldiers in Aceh Province. Exxon Mobil was accused of providing barracks that were used by the military for torturing detainees and of lending heavy equipment like excavators that were used for digging mass graves. In March 2006 U.S. District Judge Louis Oberdorfer allowed this case to go forward (see Banerjee 2001; Renner 2006). Two years later, in August 2008, he concluded that there was sufficient evidence to let a jury decide whether Exxon

Mobil should be held liable in the case (Scarcella 2008). Although a trial date had not been set at the time of finalizing the manuscript for this book, the case of Exxon Mobil already is a major breakthrough in the debate on business and human rights. Especially in the extractive industries, which are commonly bound to particular locations, corporations often partner with repressive governments in order to gain access to valuable resources. Therefore, they often become complicit in the forceful relocation of whole communities or engage in so-called militarized commerce (Forcese 2000; 2001, 489), which means that they rely on state military forces, paramilitary forces, and private armies for the protection of their sites in regions that are unstable because of wars and conflicts. Such security forces are known for their "notorious human rights records" (Forcese 2000, 173). By accepting their support, corporations become an immediate part of the human rights violations committed by them. In some of these cases the concept of complicity might even fall short of capturing the full scope of responsibility of the involved corporation. Where corporations are effectively in control over these armed forces, that is, where they are in de facto command and thus knowingly tolerate or even encourage human rights abuses committed by their agents, they must be considered principal perpetrators rather than mere accomplices (Ratner 2001, 506).

The Human Rights Resource Centre website lists 21 categories of human rights abuses for which cases of corporate involvement can be found. Among them are crimes like genocide, killing, rape, slavery, and abduction. Furthermore, the list contains delicts like denial of freedom of association, movement, or expression. Large Internet and software companies have a reputation for being notorious in undercutting people's rights to access and distribute information. Because of the huge and tempting potential of the opening Chinese market, they have repeatedly put profit before principles and have actively assisted the Chinese government in the enforcement of its censorship policies. Some, like Google and Cisco, are actively facilitating the blocking of "politically sensitive" terms and sites in the Internet (see Thompson 2006). Others, like Yahoo, have even repeatedly been accused of actively collaborating with Chinese authorities in identifying and imprisoning dissidents through providing sensitive information drawn from their e-mail accounts.

Indirect Complicity   In cases of indirect complicity there is no direct link between particular corporate actions and a specific, well-defined case of human rights violation. The connection that links the corporation to the violation of human rights is more general. Indirect complicity may occur, for example, when a multinational corporation's activities generally help maintain an unjust regime's financial and commercial infrastructure (Wells and Elias 2005, 163). Hence the corporation does not directly participate in but rather facilitates human rights violations committed by the principal perpetrator. From this perspective, even the mere payment of taxes to an oppressive government can be problematic for a corporation, especially if these taxes are specifically directed at financing abusive security forces and the like (Howen 2005a, 14).

A persistent example of indirect complicity concerns the trade in so-called blood diamonds. Blood diamonds are mined in the conflict zones of, among other countries, Angola, Sierra Leone, and the Congo. The revenues generated through their trade are used to finance the wars over the diamond fields. The warring groups often gain control over the diamond fields through massive and brutal abuse of human rights. As a result, the diamond industry that trades in the conflict diamonds is accused of knowingly financing and thus indirectly supporting the wars and the human rights violations in these regions.

From a non-state-centric perspective, the maintenance of business relations with other corporations—contractors, suppliers, strategic partners—that engage in human rights abuse through forced labor, child labor, and other harmful practices also belongs to the category of indirect complicity. By maintaining such relationships, the corporation is not an immediate part of or directly involved in a particular case of human rights violation but provides general support to the primary perpetrator. Doing business with suppliers and producers that systematically tolerate human rights violations in their organizations and operations, as well as contracting and subcontracting with businesses with bad human rights records in the corporate value chain, renders multinational corporations complicit in the respective human rights violations.

Determining the scope of indirect complicity, especially in corporations' support of oppressive regimes, is not an easy task. Some have claimed that the mere presence of corporations in "rogue countries" constitutes a form of complicity. Accordingly, they argue that corporations should pull out of countries that are notorious for human rights violations. Others have argued quite differently. The presence of corporations in unjust regimes, they say, will promote economic development and contribute to the improvement of the situation. Both statements, however, seem too general to be of practical value. The former does not consider that corporations can and should indeed be a force of development and that pulling out often hurts the people more than the government. The latter ignores that economic growth does not always contribute positively to human development and hence that whether a corporation indeed serves as a force of development depends on additional factors and conditions.

The question whether a corporation should divest from countries with unjust regimes cannot be answered generally but only by carefully examining the specific situation. A corporation that reaches the conclusion that its operations contribute to and bolster a government's ability to carry out systematic human rights violations rather than building a counterforce to them might indeed have to withdraw. For example, in 1992 Levi Strauss decided that under "current circumstances" it was "not possible to do business in Myanmar without directly supporting the military government and its pervasive violations of human rights" (quoted in Avery 2000, 46). Levi Strauss was not alone. Macy's, Liz Claiborne, Eddie Bauer, and the oil giants Texaco and Amoco also ceased their operations in the country—in the case of Amoco even despite its announcement six months earlier that Burma was one of the company's most promising new locations for exploration (Spar 1998, 10). For Margaret Jungk (2000, 4) from the Danish Centre for Human Rights, there are three cases in which a corporation must refrain from operating in a particular area: when its presence conflicts with international sanctions against the country, when it undermines popular sovereignty, and when it legitimizes egregious human rights violators.

ABB's assessment of its business relations in war-torn Sudan in 2006 provides an example of a corporation that reached a different conclusion than Levi Strauss in 1992. ABB came under public attack, namely, from the Divest Sudan Campaign, for maintaining business projects and operations in Sudan and thereby supporting the Sudanese government in carrying out genocide against the non-Arab population in the Darfur region. In a well-reasoned response ABB, however, claimed that rather than contributing to the genocide, it was acting as a "force for progress in Sudan." Its involvement in the development of Sudan's infrastructure, it argued, benefited the people and helped realize their rights to education, health care, clean water, and other needs, rather than supporting the government's atrocities (ABB 2006). Public infrastructure, as seen earlier, is one of the critical practical dimensions of human development. However, as Craig Forcese argues, in oppressive regimes it often serves oppressive purposes. Forcese (1997, 22ff.) distinguishes four ways in which corporations may bolster rather than undermine the repressive capacity of an unjust regime. First, the firm may produce products that increase the regime's repressive capacity. Second, a company can be a source of revenue that increases a regime's repressive capacity. Third, the corporation may provide infrastructure such as roads, railways, and power stations that increases a regime's repressive capacity. Fourth, the firm may provide international credibility to an otherwise discredited regime.

It cannot be the aim of this analysis to determine whether ABB's contributions indeed benefited the rights of the population rather than the oppressive capacity of the genocidal regime in Khartoum. Nevertheless, the example shows that arguments in both directions are possible. Decisions must derive from good and credible reasons based on firm principles rather than from opportunism and must be validated in open public discourse. Even though evidence of genocide is generally an indicator of a regime that corporations need to avoid (Jungk 2000, 8f.), ABB's decision-making process seems to meet these requirements:

> In Sudan, our representatives have met government officials, NGOs, diplomats, other companies and representatives of international agencies to discuss the situation. No one in Sudan has advised us to withdraw, as proposed by certain concerned foreign investors; on the contrary, the people we have spoken to in Sudan have unanimously recommended that ABB remains there to help develop the country's economic and social infrastructure. To withdraw, they say, would undermine such efforts. As our discussions have progressed, ABB launched the idea of holding a broader meeting of interested parties in Sudan to discuss relevant issues. There has been considerable interest in this, and the meeting in Khartoum—organized by the UNDP—is now scheduled for May. Outside the country, ABB has been consulting with Amnesty International Business Group, an international human rights expert, Professor Alan Miller, as well as representatives of other organizations such as the UN Global Compact and the Business Leaders Initiative on Human Rights. Amnesty's position has been clear. It makes no recommendation on staying or withdrawing, but advises that once a company is in a country it should proceed with caution and engage in stakeholder dialogue. This is what we are doing. (ABB 2006)

Issues of indirect complicity must be analyzed on a case-by-case basis. Therefore, it is of critical importance that the corporation be open and transparent regarding its operations in problem areas and engage in clarifying dialogues with involved parties and independent observers. The fact that ABB eventually did pull out of Sudan in 2007 might be taken as a sign that it indeed took its ongoing stakeholder consultations seriously. Two special cases of indirect complicity are of particular relevance: beneficial complicity and silent complicity.

Beneficial Complicity   Beneficial complicity occurs when a corporation knowingly accepts a direct economic benefit connected to ongoing human rights violations and the continued partnership with the principal perpetrator (Ramasastry 2002, 150). The corporation does not need to be directly or indirectly involved in a particular wrongdoing in order to become complicit in human rights abuses; it is sufficient that it knowingly benefits from human rights abuses committed by a third party (Clapham and Jerbi 2001, 346).

Beneficial complicity can be direct or indirect. It counts as direct complicity if the benefits to the corporation arise from its direct involvement in human rights violations. An example of direct beneficial complicity is the case mentioned earlier in which corporations seek the protection of security forces that commit systematic human rights violations. Another example is the knowing acceptance of economic benefits deriving from the use of forced labor by suppliers or joint venturers. Indirect beneficial complicity, on the other hand, means that the corporation does not have a direct connection to a particular human rights violation but benefits from the opportunities or environment created by them (ICHRP 2002, 131). Craig Forcese (1997, 21f.) distinguishes three kinds of indirect beneficial complicity with unjust governments. First, governments may commit human rights violations in order to produce infrastructure designed for use by companies. Second, governments may commit human rights violations in order to provide companies with resources. Third, governments may accommodate commercial interests by resorting to repression to forestall labor unrest.

The case of indirect beneficial complicity illustrates the difference between moral and legal complicity. Although it is rather unlikely that a legal case can be established against a corporation for merely benefiting from human rights violations without any kind of direct involvement, there is a clear basis for moral blame (United Nations 2008a, 20f.). Benefiting from human rights violations means enhancing one's own position at the cost of other human beings' fundamental autonomy. A morality that tolerates such behavior cannot be based on inherent equality of human dignity and necessarily conflicts with the principle of equal moral concern and respect. Such a morality is inherently and inevitably unjust. Benefiting from human rights violations can never be morally justified. It denotes an indirect instrumentalization of the rights of human beings for the purpose of making profits. Therefore, it expresses both deep disregard for the dignity of the human beings whose rights are being violated and moral support for the principal perpetrators who are committing those violations.

Silent Complicity   There is growing agreement among scholars in human rights studies that corporations' silent acceptance of human rights violations committed by abusive governments is a form of indirect complicity. This "silent complicity" does not require a corporation's explicit connection to the human rights violations in the form of collaboration or interaction with the primary perpetrator, nor do the violations need to benefit the corporation in any way.

Margaret Jungk has opposed this far-reaching interpretation of corporate complicity. She argues that a company operating in a country with an oppressive government but without a direct or indirect relationship to the committed human rights violations does not have a responsibility to take action, because responsibility cannot be established on the mere grounds of location (Jungk 2001, 10). What Jungk seems to ignore, however, is that the mere absence of involvement or benefit for the corporation does not necessarily mean that it is morally entirely unconnected to certain human rights violations. On the contrary, the corporation might well be connected to them insofar as they occur within its general "sphere of influence." This means that a corporation turns into a silent accomplice in cases in which it effectively has the capabilities to stop, prevent, or reduce human rights violations but instead chooses to remain inactive. A corporation that has the power effectively to alter the course of (potential) human rights violations can hardly be considered a mere bystander. Thus silent complicity in general arises from the failure of a powerful actor to exercise influence. The combination of presence and authority constitutes assistance in the form of endorsement or moral support (Clapham and Jerbi 2001, 344; Howen 2005a, 15). Hence silence and inaction in the face of human rights violations committed by others are not a legitimate stance, especially for corporations acting in quasi-governmental positions. Turning away from human rights violations connotes toleration or even tacit approval rather than mere neutrality. Therefore, it plays a significant role in legitimizing the perpetrator's conduct (Ramasastry 2002, 104, 144).

Structural Complicity   Human rights violations do not occur only as a result of direct harmful actions by clearly identifiable perpetrators. On the contrary, the vast majority of them are the result of structural effects (Galtung 1994). Hunger, poverty, and disease in the developing world are not natural phenomena but the consequence of a highly unjust global institutional order that is "shaped by the better-off and imposed on the worse-off" in this world (Pogge 2002a, 199). Thus structural injustice derives from the regular activity and interaction of a variety of different agents. It indicates that some of the normal and generally accepted background conditions of our activities are morally unacceptable (Young 2004, 378). This is what makes structural complicity hard to grasp, and perhaps it is the reason that it is commonly overlooked in discussions of complicity. Nevertheless, if there is such a thing as structural injustice, then all participants in such structures are complicit, at least to some degree. The unjust global institutional order, after all, is not unalterable but could be shaped differently. Responsibility, in the first instance, is with all those who take part in such structures—from the consumer who buys cheap T-shirts at Western retail stores to the multinational corporation and its contractors and even to the exploited workers themselves. However, the main obligation arguably falls on those who have the political power fundamentally to transform such structures, and most attempts to do so have failed precisely because they have conflicted with the particular interests of such powerful actors.

By protecting the status quo, these economic and political powers—rich countries, international organizations, and multinational corporations—are knowingly engaging in the maintenance of a system that creates, sustains, and perpetuates poverty and desperation of millions of people scattered across the globe. Insofar as they take part in and lend their support to this system instead of pressing for its alteration, they are complicit in the structural violation of human rights on a massive scale. They are, as Pogge (2002a, 199) rightly notes, "causally deeply involved" in the misery of millions of people.

Corporations that facilitate the political systems of abusive governments by indirectly financing their unjust regimes and benefiting from or tolerating their human rights abuses are usually readily condemned for their complicity. Yet at the same time we tend to be very comfortable with watching corporations not only facilitate, benefit from, and silently accept a global economic system that keeps causing harm in unprecedented ways, but even control its rules and mechanisms to a large extent. If we accept the moral duty of corporations to avoid inflicting harm on others, as well as not to contribute to or benefit from unjust deprivations, we must not ignore the structural effects of unleashed global competitive markets. The corporate profits generated in global markets and the wealth they create for the rich parts of this world are structurally linked to poverty and starvation in the South. If multinational corporations do not want to be considered morally complicit in such human rights violations, they must start to address this problem seriously and thus publicly.

Preventing Injustice: The Duty to Protect Human Rights

There are no exclusively negative rights in a nonideal world. All rights, even the classical liberty rights, are connected to corresponding positive duties. As a result, the multinational corporation as an agent of justice bears not only an obligation to avoid deprivation caused by the direct or indirect violation of human rights but similarly a positive duty to protect human beings from deprivation caused by others. Although negative duties, at least in the case of direct abuse, derive from a causal link between a corporation's actions and a violation of human rights, the positive duty to protect is tied more closely to a corporation's capabilities.

Because the capability of a corporation to protect human beings from human rights violations is dependent on its proximity to the potential perpetrator, it is closely related to the concept of complicity in general and of silent complicity in particular. Evidently, the capability of a corporation to influence a potential perpetrator is based on the degree of the perpetrator's dependence on the corporation. Formulated from the perspective of the corporation, this means that its capabilities to protect increase with the degree of authority it factually enjoys over the potential perpetrator. Two contexts stand out as especially relevant in this regard: the relation of the corporation to its subsidiaries, contractors and subcontractors, and strategic partners and the relation of the corporation to its host governments.

Duties to Protect Along the Corporate Value Chain

Control breeds responsibility. A multinational corporation that maintains and controls subsidiaries overseas is accountable for their conduct and bears responsibility for potential human rights violations committed in their operations. Direct subsidiaries operate for and often in the name of the multinational corporation. Therefore, their misconduct can be attributed to the multinational itself. Even though there is no clear-cut legal obligation in this situation, the distribution of control on the one side and dependency on the other makes a clear moral case for the multinational's responsibility for its subsidiaries' human rights conduct. Because there is no real third-party perpetrator in this case, the duty of the multinational corporation regarding its direct subsidiaries is a duty to take adequate and specific organizational measures to avoid human rights violations within its multinational structure rather than a genuine duty to protect. Nevertheless, even this direct negative duty demands specific positive measures of the corporation.

However, the image of the multinational corporation as a vertically fully integrated organization is changing dramatically. Today multinationals are reducing the number of direct subsidiaries and increasingly organize their value chains as networks. Labor-intensive processes get outsourced to contractors and subcontractors overseas, while the multinational corporation itself focuses on the knowledge-based tasks and processes with a high added value. Especially in the apparel industry such contractors and subcontractors have been notorious for the maintenance of sweatshops and the systematic abuse of workers' rights. Multinational corporations that knowingly maintain and benefit from such business relations must, as argued earlier, be regarded as indirectly complicit in the respective human rights violations. Therefore, their dominant position within their supply chains is connected to undeniable moral obligations.

There is no doubt that multinational corporations have a moral obligation to avoid business relations with contractors or subcontractors that operate on the basis of systematic human rights violations. However, the responsibility of multinational corporations for their existing business relationships arguably entails more than a negative obligation simply to cut all ties to the offending supplier. As in the child labor example, the sudden termination of such relations would hardly lead to an actual improvement of workers' situations. Rather, it would jeopardize the livelihood of their families and force them to seek other opportunities to work, possibly under even worse conditions. Hence, rather than abandoning the problem, the corporation bears an obligation to improve the situation and thus to protect the rights of the exploited workers. The termination of existing business relations can only serve as a last resort if all other attempts to correct the contractor's conduct fail. Hence multinationals have a moral obligation to initiate corrective measures within their supply chains regardless of whether the human rights violations are committed by a direct subsidiary or by an "independent" contractor. In both cases the conduct of the abusive entity reflects on the performance of the company itself.

To deny any such corrective obligations on the basis of the argument that contractors are nominally independent and thus not a part of the corporation's organizational structure implies an overly narrow notion of control as ownership. It overlooks that contractors and subcontractors locked in multinational corporations' value chains are often heavily dependent on those multinationals. For example, the apparel market in the United States, like many other industries, is controlled by only a handful of gigantic retailers (Danaher and Mark 2003, 106). These retailers effectively set the conditions and decide what is and what is not possible in improving the rights of the workers in the factories of their suppliers all over the world. As long as the multinational corporation remains in de facto control over its contractors and subcontractors, that is, as long as they operate under its de facto authority, the multinational bears a large part of the responsibility for their human rights conduct. Hence the outsourcing of business processes certainly does not imply also the outsourcing of all moral responsibility. Asking multinationals to exercise their influence over their contractors to advance human rights is not an illusory or naïve request; after all, they have hardly ever hesitated to use their influence to demand cheaper prices for the production of their goods.

Levi Strauss and Company was one of the first multinational corporations explicitly to extend the scope of its human rights responsibilities to include its contractors and subcontractors. In correspondence with the earlier insight that an existing engagement in problematic business relations leads to a primary duty to protect rather than to pull out, Levi Strauss requires failing contractors to implement corrective action plans first and terminates the business relationship only if all else fails. The employment standards required by the Levi Strauss code of conduct for contractors include norms regarding child labor, forced labor, disciplinary practices, working hours, wages and benefits, freedom of association, discrimination, and health and safety. A similar code was released by Gap. This company reports on its website that its 90 vendor compliance officers conducted approximately 4,316 compliance inspections in 2,053 garment factories in 2006. Additionally, Gap has taken active steps to work with suppliers in order to help them understand and implement the code adequately. The impact of such measures, if carried out both seriously and carefully, is arguably more desirable than the termination of business relations.

Many corporations have realized that their responsibility for human rights does not stop at the doors of their own premises but systematically extends up and down their value chain. This moral responsibility grows in importance the more multinationals are operating as networks rather than as integrated wholes. Contractors and subcontractors often effectively operate in legal vacuums; in most cases they do not face any legal sanctions in their home countries, while their formal independence from the multinational company shields them from prosecution also in the multinational's home country. Therefore, it is essential that multinational corporations themselves start to make use of their capabilities and exercise positive influence over them.

Although there is increasing acceptance of such responsibilities of multinational corporations for the working conditions in their supply chains, the subject of complicity and consequent positive obligations within strategic partnerships has yet to be addressed adequately. As seen in part II of this book, such horizontal networks are a major determining force in the global economy, and their importance is likely to increase. Accordingly, it is of utmost importance that corporations start to take responsibility also for such strategic business relations. This insight refers to the same underlying argument as that concerning supply chains: corporations that maintain strategic relations with partners that lack respect for human rights turn into accomplices by either broadly contributing to, benefiting from, or silently accepting the partners' human rights violations. Hence corporations must choose their strategic partners with the same caution that is required for suppliers, and they must set the bar in human rights standards for their partners at least as high as they do for themselves. In case partners do not meet these standards, corrective measures must be deployed. If these measures fail, the relationship must be terminated. It is quite evident that the more important strategic networks become for corporations to be competitive in the global economy, the greater is the collective leverage of the network participants on potential laggards, for example, by introducing human-rights-based exclusion criteria and enforcement mechanisms. The potential impact of such networks on the global human rights situation is tremendous.

Duties to Protect Against Abusive Authorities

The state's obligation to protect human rights is normally interpreted as an obligation to adopt legislation in this regard. Evidently, corporations do not have this option. Nevertheless, even though multinational corporations lack this formal authority, their influence over what legislation and rules are being adopted by states and international institutions has grown steadily in the neo-liberal era. This suggests not only a general obligation for multinational corporations to promote and support existing attempts to further and improve national and international human rights legislation but also a specific one to exercise influence over unjust and oppressive governments, according to their capabilities. Situations in which governments deliberately disregard and abuse human rights create one of the contexts in which large multinationals are pushed into the role of primary agents of justice. Therefore, they face an obligation to protect human rights against abuse by governments. This obligation is in sharp contrast with the conventional view that assumes relevance only for the reverse case, that is, for governments having protective duties against "failed" corporations.

The obligation of powerful multinationals to protect human rights against violations committed by unjust governments derives from the concept of silent complicity described earlier. It implies a moral obligation for multinational corporations to use their economic and political clout, that is, their de facto authority, to speak out and pressure unjust governments and public (as well as private) authorities to respect and promote the rights of human beings. This includes the obligation to engage in a dialogue with authorities on their failed human rights policies, as well as to address specific cases of human rights violations publicly (Avery 2000, 44). The greater the importance of a multinational corporation for a country's position in the global economic game, the larger are its leverage and its bargaining power to demand adequate policies and enforcement for the protection of people's rights.

So far, however, corporate influence has had quite the reverse effect on governments' human rights policies. Multinational corporations have predominantly used their quasi-governmental influence to have restrictions and standards for the protection of people's rights loosened and removed rather than improved. For example, the sweatshop problem mentioned earlier is induced to a large extent by governments' unwillingness to adopt strict regulations because of the risk of pricing themselves out of the market (Danaher and

Mark 2003, 72). This competitive pressure on these governments comes, as seen earlier, directly from multinational corporations' threat to shift their production elsewhere.

When Ken Saro-Wiwa was executed by the Nigerian government, Shell stated that it would be "dangerous and wrong" for Shell to "intervene and use its perceived 'influence' to have the judgment overturned." "A commercial organization like Shell," it claimed further, "cannot and must never interfere with the legal processes of any sovereign state."[1] Shell's conviction was that what was needed was "quiet diplomacy" from all parties.[2] In 1996 a Shell manager reportedly stated:

> I am afraid I cannot comment on the issue of the Ogoni 9, the tribunal and the hanging. This country has certain rules and regulations on how trials can take place. Those are the rules of Nigeria. Nigeria makes its rules and it is not for private companies like us to comment on such processes in the country.[3]

The position expressed by Shell is evident: the business of business is business, not politics. However, Shell was thoroughly mistaken about its allegedly purely private nature. Corporate power, as we have seen, is always and inevitably public power. As such, it leads to similarly public responsibilities. The very fact that Shell effectively operated in a position that would have allowed it to speak out and to exercise influence over the government placed it in an inherently public role, irrespective of whether it actually made use of this possibility. The perception that commenting on the issue is publicly relevant, while remaining silent is not, is inherently flawed. The corporation is not an apolitical institution; Shell's silence was as much publicly relevant as explicit opposition would have been. Silence is not neutral but a sign of moral support, while speaking out would have put opposing pressure on the government. Hence once we uncover the private-public dichotomy that underlies Shell's position as an ideological construct, the duty of the corporation publicly to oppose and confront authorities that abuse human rights becomes very evident. For an institution operating in a quasi-governmental role, staying out of politics in such matters is not an option.

Shell's argument about Nigeria's sovereignty regarding its own laws is similarly irrelevant in connection with human rights violations. As the most essential universal moral rights, that is, as genuinely cosmopolitan claims, human rights transcend national sovereignty. Human rights are cosmopolitan rights, which means that no country can simply legislate them away as it pleases. Multinational corporations as quasi-governmental institutions at the global level have an obligation to speak out in defense of human rights. This does not constitute interference in domestic politics but is a wholly legitimate role for corporations; it must be part of their agenda (G. Chandler 1999, 43).

Restoring Justice: The Duty to Proactively Realize Human Rights

A large part of this book has focused on developing the analytical-ethical basis on which to normatively justify remedial duties of justice for multinational corporations. Although such positive obligations are intuitively comprehensible in cases where corporations have directly and actively contributed to bringing unjust situations about, they are less evident for situations in which no actor can be held directly responsible for causing a specific injustice. In the first part of this book I showed that the attribution of such imperfect obligations of justice must be based on the criterion of capability. In the second part I provided the foundation for holding multinational corporations directly responsible as primary agents of justice. In the following paragraphs I will finally engage in the concretization and systematization of such capability-based, remedial human rights obligations of multinational corporations.

Much of the current debate on business and human rights has been connected to the notion of the corporation's "sphere of influence." The first principle of the UN Global Compact, for example, states that "businesses should support and respect the protection of international human rights within their sphere of influence." Similarly, the UN Norms also refer to human rights obligations of corporations "within their respective spheres of activity and influence." The notion of the sphere of influence is specific to the business and human rights debate. That is, it is not adapted or imported from existing legal discussions on other subjects. Accordingly, it is still largely underexplored and subject to different and often conflicting interpretations. The capability focus can provide a fruitful alternative to conventional interpretations that usually start from a causality-based notion of influence. Such causality-based interpretations often lead to concentric-circle models of the sphere of influence in which the concentric circles represent stakeholder groups according to their proximity to the corporation. Proximity is interpreted as the intensity with which they are affected by the corporation's activities, which is often perceived as congruent with geographic distance. In these models employees and workers predominantly form the inner circle of responsibility, followed by the surrounding community and the countries in which multinational corporations operate.

I have already pointed out the flaws of such concentric-circle models of moral responsibility. They neither are compatible with a cosmopolitan understanding of justice nor adequately reflect the interconnectedness of our global society today. The proximity of multinational corporations to the violation of the human rights of the poor and vulnerable is often not geographic but structural. The popular claim that multinationals should act like good corporate citizens in the countries in which they operate (e.g., Hsieh 2004, 643) illustrates this misperception. It is at its core anticosmopolitan and turns a blind eye both on the transnational source of global problems and the inherently transnational capabilities of multinational corporations to address these problems at their source. Hsieh (2004, 650) suggests that corporations that "benefit directly from the burdensome conditions under which they operate" bear a duty of assistance. However, tying this principle to the physical presence of corporations in a particular country largely ignores that multinational corporations may benefit from burdensome conditions in other countries without actually operating in them. Pharmaceutical companies, for example, are investing tremendous amounts of money and time in lobbying for restrictive global intellectual property rules in order not to have to compete against more affordable generic drugs. Instead of securing the right to health of the people in developing countries, these restrictions rather aim at securing the margins of large multinational corporations. Thus thinking in concentric circles systematically fails to capture both the genuinely transnational responsibilities of multinational corporations and those positive responsibilities that arise beyond existing causal relations. Hence they lack an adequate answer precisely in those cases where we face genuinely global problems connected to highly imperfect obligations of justice.

Instead of defining the sphere of influence as the sphere of actual influence based on existing operations and their causal effects on people, we must focus on the sphere of potential influence based on the corporation's capabilities to make positive contributions to human development. This focus on capability rather than causality will not only considerably broaden the range of corporations' remedial responsibilities but also enlarge the scope of corporations addressed (Kline 2003, 2) and align it more consistently with their quasi-governmental role, that is, their position as primary agents of justice at the global level. Margolis and Walsh claim that instead of taking the (negative) effects of actual corporate conduct as a starting point for reflection, "we need to begin with the idea that organizations can play an effective role in ameliorating social misery" (Margolis and Walsh 2003, 283). From this perspective, they argue, we need to focus on questions about what firms are actually doing in response to social misery and what effects corporate actions have in this regard. Lee Tavis gets to the point without mincing words:

> When one person or group is in critical need, another individual or group in proximity to the situation must act to alleviate the need if they can. This is particularly true when other sources of assistance are not available in time to avoid a crisis. On this principle, a multinational manager who is in a position to aid the poor who cannot help themselves, incurs that responsibility. With the multinational direct and indirect links to the poor, managers would apply corporate resources where their firms could uniquely contribute to the relief of poverty, even though their firms were not involved in the cause. (Tavis 1982b, 132)

Multinational corporations' remedial duties of justice aim at the practical realization of human development. Human development, as a reminder, is rights-based processes aimed at expanding the real freedoms that people enjoy (Sen 2000, 3). The practical realization of human development, as shown earlier, takes place in the four dimensions of positivization of rights, internal capacity building, external arrangements consisting of public policies and local infrastructure, and enabling global superstructures. These four dimensions essentially span the relevant space or context for corporations' sphere of influence in their remedial human rights obligations. Thus the relevant capabilities that lead to remedial obligations of justice are the ones that may contribute to the enhancement of people's freedoms in one or several of those four practical dimensions of human empowerment. Accordingly, the process of assessing multinational corporations' remedial obligations of justice starts with the identification of those human rights to whose realization the corporation is believed to be able to make a significant contribution—the right to health for a pharmaceutical company, for example, or the right to water for the beverage industry. Once these rights are identified, the obligations can be specified in relation to the corporation's specific and unique capabilities to contribute to their realization within the four practical dimensions of human development.

Taking an abstract view of the capabilities of multinational corporations in general and matching them with the four practical dimensions of human development open up three broad areas or categories of remedial obligations in the corporation's sphere of influence. First, remedial obligations unfold at the corporate policy level and derive from corporation-specific capabilities. They follow from the purpose of the corporation and the social problems it is built to address. Thus corporations have an obligation to engage in finding innovative solutions to persistent human rights problems by making use of their economic core capabilities. I will refer to this category as the category of *business obligations*. Second, remedial duties of multinational corporations unfold at the social and public policy levels both nationally and globally. This second category of obligations essentially includes multinationals' engagement in public policy processes and in the provision of public goods and services, as well as in the maintenance of local infrastructure. Therefore, it largely is derived from industry-specific capabilities. However, especially in the area of corporate engagement in the maintenance of public infrastructure, it may heavily intersect also with the corporation-specific first category. This second category predominantly consists of *collaborative obligations* of multinationals. The third category of remedial obligations unfolds at the global economic policy level, which largely covers the dimension of global superstructures in the practical model of human development. At this level corporations have a quasi-governmental obligation to engage in the creation of an enabling global economic system through adequate regulatory measures. This category spans the corporation-specific as well as the industry-specific level and refers to the global economy at large, that is, to the *regulatory obligations* of multinational corporations in general.

In sum, the three categories of remedial obligations unfold at the corporate policy level (business obligations), the public policy level (collaborative obligations), and the global economic policy level (regulatory obligations). While the corporate and public policy levels refer to specific obligations in the multinationals' particular area of competence, the regulatory obligations at the global economic policy level derive from the general quasi-governmental capacity of multinationals, which may be largely independent of their particular area of competence.

Remedial Duties at the Corporate Policy Level: Business Obligations

In a 1996 article on multinational corporations' impact on human rights, William H. Meyer (1996, 368ff.) states that foreign direct investment is per se "positively associated with political rights and civil liberties as well as with economic and social rights in the third world." Meyer assumes that "to the extent that multinationals promote (economic) development, they must also enhance human rights." Thus Meyer essentially argues that multinational corporations' remedial duties toward poverty and other social grievances in the Third World can be met by simply investing in those countries; the rest will take care of itself. Therefore, he commits the fallacy of uncritically equating economic with societal development (see Meyer 1996, 376) and restates the trickle-down argument in the language of human rights. Even after the "disenchantment" of neoliberal globalization, Meyer's belief in the wondrous remedial powers of FDI still enjoys considerable popularity among scholars and practitioners. FDI is regarded as a catalyst of economic growth, a vehicle of technology and knowledge transfer, a creator of jobs, and a generator of tax income for poor countries. Some even claim that it promotes democracy and ultimately leads to the democratization of unjust regimes. My earlier elaborations, however, have shown that such general statements obscure, rather than adequately reflect, the real impact of multinationals on human rights.

FDI can indeed be instrumental in the fostering of human rights, but its impact on human rights depends on its quality rather than on its quantity. A positive effect of FDI on economic growth in developing countries is not guaranteed. In many cases the repatriation of profits, as well as the payment of royalties and licensing fees, has even turned the allegedly stimulating effect of FDI on economic growth into a net outflow of capital (Lippman 1985, 251). Furthermore, not all FDI yields equal spillovers in technology transfer (Stiglitz 2002b, 278). Similarly, jobs connected to exploitative and humiliating workplaces or to sweatshops and abusive child labor might generate economic growth, but they are inherently at odds with a rights-based interpretation of development. Not even the quantitative effects of FDI on job creation are as clear-cut as proponents like to make them seem. Oligopolistic behavior, domination of the local industrial sector, and the tendency of multinationals to buy from their own sources instead of local suppliers are just as likely to lead to a reduction of local employment by replacing or driving out domestic businesses. In order to be of real benefit to developing countries in the creation of jobs, multinationals must make a deliberate effort to support domestic private-sector development and encourage local firms, small-scale family enterprises, microbusinesses, and the informal sector to produce their inputs (J. Nelson 2002, 219ff.; Streeten 2004, 78).

The payment of taxes in oppressive regimes, to name another example, might also support rather than counteract human rights violations. Additionally, multinational corporations have stood out for their capabilities to avoid taxes rather than for their enthusiasm in contributing to the development of social infrastructures in poor countries. In many cases, as argued earlier, multinationals have not only largely avoided paying taxes but have actually even received substantial subsidies—corporate welfare—in order to build their facilities. In such cases they have diverted existing tax funds into their own pockets. The struggle for economic growth through attracting FDI often forces governments to cut back their spending for social policies and actually to lower their human rights standards (Ordentlicher and Gelatt 1993, 100f.; OECD 1996, 2000).

Hence the positive general contributions normally associated with multinationals operating in developing countries—jobs, taxes, and investment—are only beneficial to the realization of human rights if they are connected to a conscious and deliberate effort by the corporation to serve as a force of human development.[4] Furthermore, despite the dominant focus of the conventional economic development debate on such general contributions, the specific contributions to human development we can and should expect from multinationals must go much further.

Business Solutions for the Bottom of the Pyramid: C. K. Prahalad The most fundamental purpose of the economy is to prevent deprivation and social grievances by ensuring people's access to vital goods and services (Ulrich 2008, 192). Therefore, it fulfills an inherently public function. By delegating an ever-larger share of this function to "private" corporations, we automatically increase their public responsibility for the achievement of this goal. Hence the perception of the purpose and mission of a business as a purely private affair is flawed. It is public insofar as it should make a legitimate and meaningful contribution to the improvement of societal problems.

The more the economy transcends the national context and reaches truly global dimensions, the more globally we must interpret its fundamental purpose. The more globally we look at its purpose, however, the more drastically it appears to be unmet for a vast number of people. Consequently, the dominant position of multinational corporations in the global economy is naturally connected to their greater global responsibility to ensure people's access to the goods and services that are pivotal for a human life in dignity and instrumental in building capacities, improving capabilities, and achieving superior human functionings. From the perspective of rights-based justice, multinational corporations' specific positive contributions to human development depend, first, on their ability to interpret persistent societal problems in the developing world in terms of human rights instead of the rather simplistic categories of economic growth, and second, on how well their business model is able to serve the realization of those rights. Hence they depend on corporations' willingness to address human rights much more proactively and directly by reinterpreting the aim and purpose of their business in terms of rights and to come up with "positive responses to the issues arising from the condition of the poor in the Third World" (Tavis 1982a, 5).

Thus serious engagement of multinationals in the realization of human rights means not merely to donate a part of their revenues to good causes but to proactively address societal problems with their core competences and capabilities. Corporations are not merely asked to provide resources on a charitable and purely voluntary basis, as, for example, Dunfee and Hess (2000) demand in their concept of "direct corporate humanitarian investment." Rather, we expect them to innovate and leverage their core competences in their particular sectors in order to improve the access of the poor to essential goods and services such as medicines, clean water and sanitation, food, energy, technology, and education and to look for and deliver solutions beyond their wealthy customer base (Davies and Nelson 2003, 2). For some corporations and industries, such as the food and pharmaceutical industries, the connection between business purpose, core competences, and their possible contribution to the realization of rights is quite obvious. For others, more effort may be needed to unearth the relevant connections. Either way, corporations might find it helpful to assess their potential contributions in close interaction with other institutions, such as NGOs, international organizations, or government agencies. Once corporations start to engage in serious reflection on and discussion of their role and purpose in terms of rights, the potential to devise novel and innovative solutions for the practical empowerment of people is tremendous even for companies or industries that we do not primarily connect to the core of human development. Affordable skin-care products, for example, can vastly improve the lives of young Indian women working outdoors in the burning sun (see Hammond and Prahalad 2004, 36). Those who are unable to protect themselves against damaging sunlight have a much higher risk of skin cancer than those who can afford to do so (Chen, Evans, and Cash 1999, 293). Making products such as sunscreen available to the poor does not mean to sell them a luxury they do not need. It is a direct contribution to health equity and to economic justice. If we understand human development as a process of enhancing people's choices, then the availability of products and services that improve our quality of life is a crucial part of it. Human development is not simply about the quantity of goods and services produced, which is reflected in the aggregate measure of gross domestic product, but is crucially about their quality in addressing existing needs and deprivations (Galbraith 2001, 115).

The superior and often unique capabilities of multinational corporations, combined with their commanding position in the global production structure, suggest a general moral obligation to engage in the development of goods and services that have the potential to increase the living standard of the poor in the developing world. In other words, producing and distributing goods with an exclusive focus on the lucrative markets in the West or the privileged high-income classes in developing countries while leaving the problems of the poor up to other institutions must increasingly be considered an illegitimate stance for large multinationals.

Controlling the global production structure, as argued earlier, effectively means determining what is being produced and for whom. Hence the more control multinational corporations exert over what is being produced globally, the more they are directly responsible for ensuring distributive justice by securing poor people's access to the products and services that help secure a life in dignity. Thus their business decisions turn into a genuine matter of (global) justice.

University of Michigan economist C. K. Prahalad argues that big corporations should solve big problems. Therefore, they must start using the wealth and talents within their institutions to address the most pressing concern of all: the alleviation of global poverty (Prahalad and Hammond 2002, 57). Prahalad's work on business strategies that focus on the bottom of the economic pyramid has provided pathbreaking insights into the operationalization of this moral obligation. Prahalad shows that if addressing the needs of the poor is approached in new and innovative ways, it can even be economically interesting for multinational corporations. After all, only 100 million people worldwide earn more than $20,000 a year, while more than 4 billion earn less than $2,000; 1 billion of them live off less than $1 a day. Evidently, this is a market of colossal volume and tremendous economic potential. However, its profoundly different structure from high-income markets in the West requires some fundamental rethinking of common business logic: at the bottom of the economic pyramid, profits are not generated through large margins but through vast volumes of highly distributed small-scale operations with very low margins (Prahalad and Hammond 2002, 51ff; Prahalad and Hart 2002, 3f.). Hence addressing the needs of the poor requires corporations to reinvent common business models and to redesign products, technology, distribution channels, and logistics.

A few pioneer companies have risen to the challenge and have started to develop business models and strategies to better serve the Third World's poor. For example, they sell and distribute single-serving-sized products such as shampoo or detergent for only a few cents per unit. The idea behind smaller-unit packages evidently is to enable the poor to buy products they could not afford if they had to buy them in bulk. In India 60 percent of the value of the shampoo market and 95 percent of all shampoo units sold are now single-serving packages (Hammond and Prahalad 2004, 35). A similar concept has been applied to the financial sector by offering so-called microcredits or microinsurance to poor households. Furthermore, the model can be used to improve poor people's access to technology; cell phones, computers, and the Internet, for example, can be made available on a pay-per-use basis or by distributing low-amount prepaid cards. Shared-access models targeting the aggregate buying power of whole communities instead of individuals have also proved to be successful strategies for pioneer companies (Prahalad and Hammond 2002, 49ff.). However, groundbreaking innovations are necessary not only in pricing and distribution strategies but also in adequate product features. For example, in water-scarce regions hygiene products such as shampoo must be usable without large amounts of water. Where clothes are being washed in rivers, detergent must be designed to reduce its impact on the environment.

It is often the large multinationals with global reach that have the technological, managerial, and financial resources and capabilities necessary to create innovations that are effectively able to address poor people's needs adequately (Prahalad and Hart 2002, 14). Their commanding position in this regard even implies a corresponding moral obligation to do so. In opposition to this insight, Joseph Schumpeter claimed that the formation of large corporations actually slows down and destroys the innovation process in the economy (Berghoff 2004, 105). However, the question is whether a lack of ability or a lack of will to innovate leads to this process. Adolf Berle (1967, 209f.) had no doubt that the technical ability of big economic organizations, combined with their capacity to accumulate vast amounts of capital, provides them with the ability to introduce the innovations that bring society forward. For him, a lack of innovation rather points to a problem with the motives that lead large corporations to innovate. This corresponds to the earlier insight that the strategic use of political power by large corporations has partly replaced their need to innovate in order to be and stay competitive.

There is no doubt that enhancing poor people's access to the goods and services we take for granted in our lives can have a tremendous impact on their well-being and contribute a great deal to the realization of their human rights. However, it seems similarly evident that commercial products and services can always be only part of a more holistic solution. Thus Prahalad's approach has clearly defined limits and, if taken to the extreme, might even be counterproductive.

The Limitations of Prahalad's Paradigm   The mission of Prahalad's approach is to empower the poor by lifting them from the level of passive receivers of charity to the level of active consumers. In order to achieve this mission, Prahalad claims, corporations "need only act in their own self-interest, for there are enormous business benefits to be gained by entering developing markets" (Prahalad and Hammond 2002, 48). Prahalad and Hammond (2002, 57) suggest that the solution to poverty, disease, and related social and societal grievances in the developing world lies in a paradigm change from addressing them as social problems to addressing them as economic opportunities. However, precisely by attaching this element of absoluteness to their approach, they are undermining its main strengths. It seems that we must protect this innovative concept against the mischief of its creators.

Prahalad's concept can be an important part of the solution of the problems in the developing world, but it cannot solve all the problems, and certainly not on its own. We must think of it as embedded within the larger context of a holistic conception of moral obligation as it is presented in this book. Turning the concept into a paradigm, however, means disembedding it from this context and rendering it absolute. In other words, business strategies that address the needs of the world's poor are no longer seen as a mere contribution to an adequate solution but as its very essence. The market is turned into the panacea for coping with the problems of the poor (Prahalad 2002, 7).

Shifting the paradigm from problems to opportunities means looking for possible solutions to societal problems exclusively within the narrow scope of agents' self-interest and abandoning the idea of formulating truly moral obligations for them. It is symptomatic that S. L. Hart (2005: 3ff.) later reformulated this paradigm change as one "from obligation to opportunity." Hence we ultimately free corporations from all moral responsibilities that do not at the same time yield a positive impact on their bottom line. As a result, any social issue that does not provide a potential for making a profit, any humanitarian challenge that does not offer an economic opportunity, and any societal problem that in its complexity overstrains the scope of market-based remedies would have to be considered strictly beyond a corporation's concern. Thus within the paradigm of economic opportunity it is precisely these most persistent and urgent issues that will systematically remain unaddressed. Furthermore, even for the problems that are within the reach of a corporation's self-interest, the absence of any moral commitment renders it questionable whether a corporation will stick to its engagement in times when the prospective profit potential cannot be realized or if better opportunities come along. It also exempts corporations from reflecting on the problems that might potentially come with such an approach: what are the environmental and social implications of "exporting" a model of Western consumerism to the developing world, for example, and how can such worrisome tendencies be mitigated without having to give up on the approach altogether? Hence stating social grievances as opportunities instead of problems turns a blind eye on the truly moral obligations of corporations that are based on their superior and unique capabilities to make a positive contribution beyond the reach of the market mechanism.

Some might argue that if the private sector actually did address all the issues containing a business potential, the remaining ones not connected to any economic opportunities would fall into the domain and responsibility of public institutions. This, however, not only would confirm Friedman's dictum that the business of business is nothing else than business, but also would take us back to the questions that made this book necessary in the first place: what if those public institutions are too weak or unwilling to fulfill their duty? What if the societal problem at stake simply lies beyond the reach of state institutions? What if it is too complex to be solved by any one institution alone? An argument based on such traditional role allocations systematically overlooks the shifting patterns of influence and authority in the global political economy and fails to translate them into an adequate account of moral obligation. The changing nature of authority must be the starting point of any realistic evaluation of the potential for change in the global political economy (Strange 2002b, 226).

Take the example of large pharmaceutical corporations. Their dominant focus on opportunities rather than on problems has contributed little to solving the massive public health problems in developing countries so far. Out of 1,393 newly developed drugs approved between 1975 and 1999, only 13 specifically addressed tropical diseases (DNDWG 2001, 11). Of these 13, 5 were by-products of veterinary research and 2 had been commissioned by the military (Pogge 2006, 5). It seems difficult to argue that these companies have no moral obligation to engage much more in developing adequate treatments for tropical diseases, regardless of whether there is an immediate positive effect on their bottom line. Their command over relevant resources and knowledge, paired with their governing position in the global health structure, makes them indispensable in tackling health issues in the developing world. This clearly indicates a moral obligation actively to engage in the search for solutions beyond mere cost-benefit calculations.

The same goes for the large food and agribusiness companies that, as shown earlier, control today's global food system to a large extent. As the former UN special rapporteur on the right to food, Jean Ziegler (2005, 30), noted, instead of contributing to the equal realization of the right to food for everyone, as stipulated in Article 25 of the Universal Declaration of Human Rights, these corporations organize actual scarcities in order to exploit them according to the laws of profit maximization. Although this might well increase efficiency in the provision of such goods, it also drives up prices and excludes the poor from consumption (United Nations 2006b, 17). Similarly, current biotechnology that could make a significant contribution to the fight against hunger and starvation is predominantly driven by purely commercial imperatives and pays hardly any attention to the food security needs of the poorest (United Nations 2003, 11). The result, as Ziegler (2005, 100f.) continues, is that more than 10 million children under the age of five die every year from malnutrition and related diseases. This equals one child every seven seconds. Hunger is the main cause of human deaths on this planet; 36 million out of 62 million deaths per year are caused by hunger and related diseases. The sad fact, however, is that these people do not die because of an objective lack of goods but because of an artificially created one (Ziegler 2005, 31). Many of these deaths would be preventable if all agents who could make valuable contributions lived up to their moral obligation to do so.

As evident as it seems that such companies have a genuine moral obligation to focus much more on the development of adequate solutions for the poor, it is also evident that they do not have unlimited capacity to operate on a nonprofit basis. After all, corporations are profit-oriented organizations; their viability as social institutions is based on making a profit. This dilemma shows precisely the limits of purely market-based solutions to social and societal problems. In fact, it shows that in many regards the extension of the market mechanism over more and more aspects of social life is part of the problem rather than of the solution. Many of today's large social problems, such as poverty, hunger, and even famines, are inherently structural. therefore, any sustainable solution for their prevention or remedy must address and change the mechanisms of these structures themselves (O'Neill 1986, 9).

If global economic structures are in large part responsible for the persistence of poverty and desperation in the Third World, then Prahalad's (2002, 7) suggestion to shed our commitment to the public sector as fast as possible and instead to rely entirely on the market mechanism for the provision of solutions seems ill advised. His claim that wealth creation is more important than distributive justice clearly shows that his thinking is confined to the narrow limits of the empirical conditions that are currently in place. Subjecting these conditions themselves to ethical reflection, however, reveals that the very dichotomy between wealth creation and social justice is flawed. From a rights-based perspective, it is not about choosing between the two but about rendering the process of wealth creation itself an inherently just affair. Therefore, adequate solutions depend on whether we are able to strengthen our commitment to the public sector, where effective public policies and governance are not yet in place. Remedial obligations of justice are above all a call for structural change. Article 2 of the 1986 UN Declaration on the Right to Development, for example, states that all human beings, individually and collectively, have a responsibility for development and thus to "promote and protect an appropriate political, social and economic order" for achieving it. Similarly, Article 28 of the Universal Declaration on Human Rights states that "everyone is entitled to a social and international order in which the rights and freedoms set forth in this Declaration can be fully realized." The elaborations throughout this book show that we are far from meeting this demand. As quasi-governmental institutions, multinational corporations have an important role to play in the promotion, facilitation, and creation of such an order. This leads us to the second category of multinational corporations' remedial duties of justice, the category of collaborative obligations.

Remedial Duties at the Social Policy Level: Collaborative Obligations

The mere pursuit of business opportunities and the exclusive focus on private profits are inadequate guiding ideals for quasi-governmental institutions and will not solve the world's most pressing problems. As inspiring and important as Prahalad's proposal is, on its own, that is, without being backed by true moral competence and motivation of corporations, as well as by an adequate public policy framework, it will inevitably fall short. Integrating the world's poor into the marketplace as active consumers and enabling them to enjoy the choices that a functioning market is indeed able to offer would be a large step toward a more equitable world. However, this ideal does not hinge merely on the availability of products. Before the poorest of the poor have a chance to become active consumers, they must have access to a basic social infrastructure and to the most basic public goods and social services. The invention of effective drugs for tropical diseases, for example, will have little impact in the developing world without basic health infrastructure and services that make sure that they reach the patient and are adequately applied and integrated into a holistic treatment of the patient's illness.

Many developing countries, however, lack basic infrastructure or a clear and effective framework for providing public goods and social services. Some states might simply be too weak to provide such essential services. Others might be unwilling to do so. Even in the industrialized world the provision of social services and public goods has been cut back continuously in order to cope with the rising pressures of economic globalization. In either case it is the poorest part of the population that pays the price if these widening gaps are not filled by other institutions or if governments are not effectively pressured or enabled to reinstall the abandoned social infrastructure.

There are three concrete ways in which multinational corporations must step in and assume the role of the primary agent of justice in such situations. Corresponding to their capabilities, they have a moral obligation to actively engage in the building of infrastructure, the creation of effective social and public policies, and the provision of public goods and social services. In the first case, these obligations derive from multinational corporations' controlling position in specific public sectors based on former privatizations. In the second case, multinationals not only take over a specific public sector but replace governments altogether in certain geographic areas. Therefore, they must assume some of the most basic responsibilities currently associated with governments. The third case refers to multinational corporations' quasi-governmental role at the global level. As a consequence of their commanding position within global structures, they must assume public and political responsibility for the creation of a global social framework and the provision of global public goods and services. Let us look at each of these three cases in more detail.

Public Responsibility in Privatized Public Sectors: Fulfilling the Promise of Equal Access   The waves of privatizations in the 1980s and 1990s have shifted control over many genuinely public domains to private companies. Therefore, they have reduced the state's control over public infrastructure and the provision of public goods and social services.

Such active engagement of corporations in public sectors leads to immediate positive human rights obligations induced by the concept of justice. The privatization of state functions largely undermined the state's capacity to regulate and ensure human rights in these areas (Alston 2005, 27). As a consequence, the obligation to ensure the positive impact of such services on people's rights has shifted to the relevant companies. The assumption that the privatization of public domains denotes a transfer only of a hidden profit potential to a private corporation but not of the public responsibility associated with the provision of these services is fundamentally misguided. To the extent that corporations engage in the provision of public infrastructure, goods, and services, they must accept the public responsibility to ensure equal and non-discriminatory basic access for everyone. From the standpoint of justice, increased efficiency in providing public services cannot be an end in itself but is desirable only if it leads to an improvement of equitable access. Fulfilling governmental functions means accepting governmental responsibilities; private profits and efficiency are inadequate guides for the provision of public services.

Public Responsibility at the Local Level: Replacing Governments   There is no doubt that mobilizing resources, technologies, and capabilities of the private sector can have a substantial and positive impact on the improvement of infrastructure and the provision of public goods and services. Because markets help further the equal realization of rights only if they are embedded in adequate regulatory frameworks and flanked by an effective social and public infrastructure, corporations that are doing business in countries that lack such mechanisms have a direct responsibility to contribute to their improvement. Analogous to the obligations at the corporate policy level discussed in the previous section, a special obligation at this level arises for corporations that are directly concerned with business solutions in public and infrastructure sectors such as the water, sanitation, housing, information and communication technology, health services, education, transportation, and energy sectors. These corporations, too, have a direct obligation to leverage their capabilities and core competences to find innovative ways and adequate solutions for the provision of the respective services in the poverty-stricken areas in the developing world.

Existing attempts to integrate the private sector into the provision of public services and the operation of public and social infrastructure are predominantly based on public-private partnerships. Although these partnerships can indeed be an adequate and effective platform for corporations to meet their developmental responsibilities, it is of utmost importance to clarify their moral nature. Most important, they must not be misunderstood as or confused with ill-conceived privatization strategies formulated by the policy advisors of the Washington Consensus. In other words, it is not the provision of the service that must be shifted from the public into the private domain, as they would argue, but the "private" corporation that is partly integrated into the public sector. Thus the public sector is not being privatized but stays inherently public despite corporate involvement. As a consequence, it is the private corporation that must take on a public role connected to corresponding public responsibilities.

Hence the first and foremost concern of such partnerships and thus the reason for involving the private sector in the provision of public goods and services must be the improvement of people's access and coverage, especially in notoriously underserved areas, rather than the mere increase of their efficiency. The guiding principle for the provision of public services is social justice, not private profits; this holds for any institution involved. Accordingly, the division of labor within the partnerships must not be such that the profitable tasks are outsourced to the corporation while both the risks and the moral responsibilities remain the state's concern. On the contrary, involving the corporation as an agent of justice must lead to the transfer of an equal share of the public responsibility for ensuring equal access.

The share of a corporation's general public responsibility increases along with the transfer of authority from the government to the corporation. Multinationals, especially in the extractive industries, maintain extensive operations in developing countries. Therefore, their influence can go far beyond the exercise of certain specific powers beyond the reach of national governments; governments that are weak often allow such corporations effectively to take over specific areas or regions (Jungk 2001, 10). In such cases multinationals factually replace governments; they engage in building up the land, and they build health and transportation infrastructure, security facilities, and utilities, and provide other services and goods of public character. By doing so, they naturally create a demand also from the local population, which is often in desperate need of such services (Marsden 2000, 13). Hence when governments step back, whether because they do not have the capacity to meet their responsibilities adequately or simply because they do not have a desire to do so, multinationals often remain the only authority with superior capabilities and powers in the relevant areas. In such situations corporations must step into the government's role and take on some of the government's central functions and responsibilities for the protection of human rights and the furthering of human development (Jungk 2001, 10; Matten, Crane, and Chapple 2003, 116; Reinisch 2005, 78).

When corporations factually replace governments, their duties potentially reach far beyond their immediate specific area of expertise. Instead, they include a variety of very broad and general governmental tasks. In the practical dimensions of human development and empowerment, such tasks aim at the creation of enabling local environments favorable to furthering people's individual capacities and their transformation into effective capabilities. Corporate responsibilities here may include the provision of adequate infrastructure and of resources and utilities, including food and adequate access to water, as well as the provision of public goods and basic social services such as health care and education. Education in this context must be understood in a broad sense; it includes raising awareness of very practical issues such as gender inequality or health and human rights education. All these issues have a tremendous impact on the persistence and distribution of poverty in the developing world. Both corporations' proximity to and influence on people and communities can tremendously increase the effectiveness with which such messages reach people.

Unfortunately, as, for example, the interim report of the UN special representative on business and human rights (United Nations 2006a) showed, corporations have hardly lived up to this obligation so far. On the contrary, it is precisely in countries with weak governance that most corporate human rights abuses occur. Sadly, the corporate mind-set still seems to be programmed to exploit rather than remedy existing opportunities for human rights violations.

Public Responsibility at the Global Level: Public Policy Dialogue and Provision of Global Public Goods   Many of today's human rights problems, such as poverty and its consequences in ill health, malnutrition, and lack of access to water, housing, and energy, are, as argued earlier, structural problems. Thus most human rights violations are not a direct result of specific actions by specific agents but rather a result of the systemic interaction of a variety of different actors. These structures increasingly transcend national borders and move the sources of human rights problems beyond the reach of any one government. As a consequence, adequate public policy responses to such problems and the provision of public goods and services aimed at enhancing the well-being of human beings must increasingly shift to the global level (Reinicke 1998; Reinicke and Deng 2000; Kaul et al. 2003a). The global sphere in which such public policies must be located, however, is characterized by a lack of centralized governing and rule-making structures and by dispersed authority. This must inevitably render the design and the realization of public policy solutions, as well as the provision of global public goods and services, an inherently collaborative affair.

For example, public health depends on many variables that lie beyond the reach of communal and even national governments. Illness and disease do not stop at national borders and are often connected to poverty, whose sources similarly lie beyond the reach of national governments. In short, public health—recall severe acute respiratory syndrome (SARS) or the ongoing global scare about bird flu—is a genuinely global problem, and the effective cooperation of agents and agencies with relevant powers and knowledge is needed to influence and determine what adequate solutions are to look like. It is in this context that in her address to the fifty-fifth World Health Assembly, former World Health Organization (WHO) director general Gro Harlem Brundtland stated:

In a world filled with complex health problems, WHO cannot solve them alone. Governments cannot solve them alone. Nongovernmental organizations, the private sector and foundations cannot solve them alone. Only through new partnerships can we make a difference. And the evidence shows we are. Whether we like it or not, we are dependent on the partners, the resources and the energy necessary for at least a 30-fold scale up in effort—to bridge the gap and achieve health for all. (Brundtland 2002)

Although Brundtland refers to a number of different institutions as partners in such new collaborative efforts, the novelty in her plea is the explicit inclusion of the private sector—multinational corporations in particular—as a partner of WHO in global health policy making. Brundtland's plea, however, does not seem unreasonable. In fact, Kent Buse and Amalia Waxman (2001, 748) claim that partnerships between WHO and the commercial sector have become inevitable. Multinational corporations, as we saw in detail earlier, are effectively controlling the power structures in the global political economy. Furthermore, with the logics of the market increasingly penetrating and determining a growing part of the public sphere, multinational corporations have tremendously increased their influence also over genuinely social issues and are effectively exercising a large amount of control over those structures on which the well-being of human beings heavily depends. This holds also in regard to public health. Not only do the big multinationals in the pharmaceutical sector, for example, control the production structure of new drugs and treatments, but the spread of the global market has accelerated also the privatization of medical services and health knowledge (Chen, Evans, and Cash 1999, 292); the finance structure for such services and policies, as well as the structures connected to food, agriculture, and water, which play a similarly central role in the well-being and health of human beings, is also largely under corporate control. As a result, effective global public policy making and the provision of global public goods and services become increasingly dependent on the involvement and the contributions of multinational corporations.

Therefore, the call for stronger involvement of the private sector has become louder not only in WHO but also in many other UN agencies (J. Nelson 2002; Witte and Reinicke 2005). This has resulted in a growing number of public policy networks (see the section "Multinational Corporations as Public Policy Makers in the Global Political Arena" in chapter 7) and similar partnerships and alliances between UN agencies and the private sector at the global level.[5] The motivation of such collaborative approaches is to develop solutions that lie beyond the capacities of any one agency acting alone. The coordination of different actors with different experiences, backgrounds, and capabilities can open new perspectives on specific problems and lead to valuable synergies for their practical solution (Leisinger 2005, 590).

The current constellation of the global public sphere allows for all-embracing policy solutions only if all the multiple institutions that exercise authority over certain relevant domains are involved in a constructive dialogue. Policy processes that exclude some of these actors, on the other hand, will hardly lead to effective solutions (Kaul, Grunberg, and Stern 1999a, xxx). In fact, the current underprovision of global public goods, as Kaul, Grunberg, and Stern (1999b, 451) argue, is to a large extent caused by a "participation gap" that derives, they claim, "from the fact that we live in a multiactor world but international cooperation is still primarily intergovernmental." This participation gap is accompanied by an "operational gap" (Reinicke and Deng 2000, xiii, 2), which means that policy makers and public institutions increasingly lack the information, knowledge, and tools necessary to respond to the complexity of global policy issues. Because multinational corporations are covering more and more key positions in these areas, they have a direct obligation to support and to proactively engage in global public policy dialogues aiming at the design of effective public policy solutions.

In the section "Institutions and Collective Responsibility" in chapter 4 I argued that organized groups can have moral obligations based on the establishment of a formal decision-making method or process. However, in her seminal contribution to the topic, Virginia Held (1991) showed that random collections of loosely connected individuals (or institutions) can also be held responsible for neglecting to act if the actions called for in a given situation are obvious to any reasonable person. Moreover, there are certain special situations in which such random collections of people can at least be held responsible for not forming themselves into organized groups that would then be able to make decisions regarding which actions to take. This is the case for situations in which it is obvious to any reasonable person that action rather than inaction is needed but in which it is unclear what exactly the appropriate actions would be. This is precisely the situation we face for many pressing global problems today. Although it is obvious that action is needed, it is unclear who must do what. This reiterates multinational corporations' obligations to join and be an active part in the communicative processes that aim at the facilitation of the much-needed multiactor solutions to such problems. If we formulate these obligations from a negative perspective, this means that they must not obstruct or hinder public policies and the provision of public goods and services by refusing cooperation in cases where their support is required for making these policies work.

However, involvement alone does not guarantee success. There is a crucial difference between multinational corporations getting involved solely on the basis of a strategic intent to increase their power and political influence as an extension of their business and those corporations that use their involvement as a platform to put their powerful position up for discussion in light of potential claims and demands that may be raised within an inclusive policy dialogue. Only the latter, dialogue-oriented attitude can lead to successful public policies, while the former, interest-based attitude will inevitably lead to the failure of the enterprise. Hence the difficulty in providing effective global governance today is to increase the involvement of nonstate actors while at the same time avoiding the dangers of special-interest politics (Edwards and Zadek 2003, 200).

The moral obligation of multinational corporations concerning the facilitation of effective global public policies and the provision of global public goods and services is first and foremost a discursive one. This makes immediate sense, given that such positive obligations are always imperfect. Their allocation and distribution are determined by the default criterion of capability and the cutoff criterion of reasonableness (which includes the criterion of causality). Both, however, can be specified only within public discourse. Thus public policy dialogues not only serve for negotiating the design of adequate policy solutions but, before this, for evaluating what potential contributions we can reasonably ask of different actors for the realization of these solutions, as well as how their different capabilities ought to be coordinated in order to achieve outcomes most effectively.

Which actors will be charged with what specific obligations depends both on the broad policy problem addressed and on the specific solution proposed. Therefore, the involvement of multinational corporations is likely to occur because of two different categories of capabilities: first, capabilities that are characteristic of multinationals per se and valuable in a broad range of global public policy solutions, and second, specialized capabilities connected to a multinational corporation's particular business or industry. The latter are company or industry specific; the former include first and foremost multinational corporations' general global perspective (Kaul et al. 2003b, 30), as well as their unprecedented ability to act on a global scale (Marsden 2000, 11; 2005, 362) because of their specific management, organizational, and technical skills (Fiszbein and Lowden 1999, 20). There is simply no other institution—no international organization and certainly no national government—that could match this unique ability of multinational corporations. Multinational corporations are the first truly cosmopolitan institutions in an increasingly cosmopolitan world. Therefore, they naturally have unique capabilities for the advancement and realization of cosmopolitan justice. In addition to those already mentioned, these capabilities may include their versatility and adaptability, their speed and flexibility, their entrepreneurial mentality, and their knowledge about transferring capital, people, and technology, as well as how to work and communicate cross-culturally (Hesburgh 1982, 99).

Because of these general capabilities, the inclusion of multinationals in public policy processes may not only open up faster and more flexible ways to react to global problems but also help achieve a novel dimension of truly global reach for effective solutions. In 2001, for example, the Joint United Nations Programme on HIV/AIDS (UNAIDS) launched a partnership with the beverage giant Coca-Cola in order to make use of the company's unmatched global network of bottling partners and distributors for the support of local AIDS programs. This enabled it to reach some of the most remote villages in sub-Saharan Africa, which had been beyond its reach. A further element of the partnership was the use of the company's marketing skills for raising public awareness about AIDS by distributing educational material and testing kits and developing information campaigns (Jackson and Nelson 2004, 206).

Such partnerships must not be interpreted as a mere add-on to the normal business processes of a corporation but are themselves an integral part of how the corporation conducts its business. They provide a specific platform for multinational corporations to meet their moral responsibilities as social and public institutions (Ulrich and Wettstein 2005, 50f.). Accordingly, such partnerships are far more than mere charity programs; they are the foundation on which the legitimate public role and purpose of the corporation is being debated and ultimately defined. In other words, interaction with public agencies builds the foundation of doing business legitimately in the global sphere. From this perspective, the logical next step in the process is to move beyond the project focus that still characterizes most existing approaches and aim at their institutionalization within permanent structures on which a stable global public order and a global social framework can be built and in which the global market can effectively be (re)embedded.

Some Objections and Misunderstandings   Asking multinational corporations to replace governments or to get involved in global policy-making processes is controversial from both society's and the corporation's point of view. From the corporate standpoint, some might argue that their involvement in such partnerships distracts them from doing what they do best. After all, society built organizations, and thus corporations, for fulfilling specific, well-defined functions. Distracting them from doing so by broadening the range of their responsibilities, they argue, inevitably results in more harm than good. Peter Drucker (1994, 101), for example, argued that charging organizations with tasks that are "beyond their specialized competence, their specialized values, their specialized functions" is damaging to organizations. They are "special purpose organs" and are each good at only one task. After all, it is their very specialization that gives them the capacity to perform.

Drucker's warnings are to be taken seriously; but so is the context in which they must be interpreted. The corporation was not invented to fulfill its assigned purpose within a societal vacuum. Therefore, the demand for social responsibility both in the contribution of the corporation to society and in the way it pursues this contribution is built into the corporate task. Drucker was not blind to this fact; he was far from interpreting the purpose of business in a narrow Friedmanian sense. Drucker even criticized business ethics for being too narrowly focused on wrongdoings. Instead, he emphasised the question of positive contributions as the central problem of responsibility in the postcapitalist society (Drucker 1994, 99).

However, a global market that is detached from its social and political context can hardly make a positive contribution to society at large. It is able to contribute to human equality and well-being only within an adequate social and political framework. The same holds logically for those actors that are perceived to make their contribution in and through the market. Hence if corporations have an obligation to make a positive contribution to human well-being, they automatically bear an obligation also to engage in the promotion and, according to their capabilities, in the facilitation of such a framework. A corporation that refuses cooperation in this endeavor evidently cannot be seriously interested in fulfilling its obligation to make a positive contribution to human and societal development at the individual level. Hence denying this public and political responsibility of the corporation logically results in denying its obligation to make a positive contribution to society and human development in general.

Furthermore, let us not forget that Drucker (1994, 102) argued that charging corporations with tasks beyond their competence is detrimental to fulfilling their purpose. This insight does not go against the argument made in this book; after all, it is precisely my claim that the corporations' unique and superior capabilities, that is, their competences, lead to such moral obligations. Nevertheless, Drucker seriously doubted that social organizations have any competence in politics or are at all concerned with political power. This assumption is questionable, if not inadequate. Some of the very core competences of large multinationals today are inherently political (Boddewyn and Brewer 1994; M. T. Jones 2000); competitive advantages are not achieved solely through better products and services anymore but to a large extent are based on lobbying, influencing, and even manipulating political processes. Political power has become one of the core concerns of large multinationals. Hence the demand that this power be accompanied with corresponding moral obligations should be rather uncontroversial and is, at least in principle, confirmed by Drucker's (1994, 101) own critical position toward the increasing social power of corporations. Power, as he argues, must always be balanced by responsibility. Without responsibility it inevitably degenerates into nonperformance.

I am not denying that the involvement of multinationals in public policy dialogues and political processes is, at its core, problematic. As I showed earlier in this book, corporations might (mis)interpret it as an instrument to consolidate their quasi-governmental power rather than to put it up for discussion. However, it is important to remember the distinction between constitution and expression of political power. It is not that their active involvement in facilitating public policies or in the provision of public goods turns private corporations into public or political actors; they operate as politically relevant actors irrespective of whether they are an active part of any formal political processes. As quasi-governmental institutions, their actions and activities have public and political implications and relevance no matter what. In other words, multinational corporations' engagement in policy-making processes is not constitutive for their political power; rather, it is a specific expression of it. Hence involving them in public policy deliberations more formally does not mean an expansion of their power into new territory but can serve as an instrument to hold them accountable for their political clout, irrespective of such involvements, in order to direct it toward publicly more desirable goals and to institutionalize checks and balances on it. The unmanaged involvement of nonstate actors in policy-making processes, on the other hand, may lead to chaos and manipulation and the special-interest politics that largely characterizes today's international negotiations and many of the industrial democracies at the national level (Edwards and Zadek 2003, 208).

Those who reject the involvement of business in the provision of public goods or public policy dialogues based on a broader societal perspective, on the other hand, often point to the danger of blurring the boundaries between the public and the private spheres. Hence their concern is not that such cross-sectoral partnerships might reduce corporations' business performance but that they might facilitate and encourage the economization of the public sphere and thus the instrumentalization of the public sector for corporate profits. More specifically, they have warned that commercial actors could use such partnerships to gain access to political and market intelligence information in order to increase their political influence, as well as to gain a competitive edge in the market. Furthermore, some corporations might use their influence to set the global public agenda in their own interest and to "capture and/or sideline" intergovernmental public agencies (Richter 2004, 47). Others might simply aim at enhancing their reputation through creating a false sense of legitimacy by collaborating with a well-respected public agency. This last critique has featured prominently regarding some rather questionable member companies in the UN Global Compact that were said to use their membership merely to "blue-wash" their tarnished corporate image.[6] Some observers even raised concerns that such partnerships with the UN could lead to the privatization and the commercialization of the UN system itself (Bruno and Karliner 2000).

Some of these fears are perfectly justified and must be addressed with due concern, but the general assumption of a clear-cut separation between the private and the public spheres that normally underlies these objections is, as I showed earlier, problematic. It leads to the incorrect perception of the corporation as a purely economic institution with no other responsibility than to generate private profits, and it ultimately underpins the outdated realist and neorealist assumption that only states are of political relevance in the international sphere. The private and the public, as shown earlier, are by no means two separate and mutually exclusive domains. There is no such thing as an exclusively private sphere, because the question about its proper boundaries, that is, the question of what in a society should or should not be considered private, is itself an inherently public one. The definition of the private sphere is thus to be determined publicly. Hence the public does not exclude or, as commonly assumed, restrict the private but constitutes it. Thus business is to be considered private only insofar as these private actions and activities are publicly legitimized.

The corporation has always been a public institution serving a genuinely public purpose. Therefore, its contribution to finding adequate solutions for pressing societal problems is neither new nor unique. If we understand business itself as an inherently public institution, its engagement in facilitating the provision of public goods and policies because of its unique and superior competences seems a matter of course rather than a gimmick. It is a corporation's contribution to building the foundation on which the legitimate pursuance of "private" business becomes possible.

Evidently, this insight does not eliminate the practical danger of instrumentalization of the public sector for private interests, nor does it mean that any such imperialistic interpretation of private-public collaboration deserves support. Rather, it reconfirms the inherent ineptitude of the neoclassical business model in shaping public policy and clarifies the alternative underlying rationale required for the involvement of corporations in the design and realization of global public policy solutions. Understood as a moral obligation, the condition for corporate involvement is its genuine moral commitment and not its self-interest. The widespread and popular assumption, held also and especially in public agencies, that reaching out for the support of the private sector must necessarily be tied to creating some sort of a business case for their involvement is misguided. Win-win constellations, as Judith Richter (2004, 45) concludes with respect to WHO's partnership guidelines, are inadequate conditions for business involvement. The benefits of any private-public interaction must not be measured by the standard of mutual or shared benefits but by how well it serves the public.

Richter's argument is correct. If the reason for such partnerships is indeed the complexity of today's global challenges that allegedly overstrains the capacity of any single (public) actor, then the win-win criterion is neither a necessary nor a sufficient condition for the involvement of corporations. It is not necessary because if effective public policy making is impossible without the enabling support of corporations, then their moral obligation to provide this support derives from just that circumstance, combined with the corporation's inherently public role (Ulrich and Wettstein 2005, 49). Furthermore, the condition can never be sufficient simply because not all solutions to societal problems to which corporations can potentially make a positive contribution contain a profit potential for the private sector at the same time. After all, establishing and maintaining such partnerships is never cost free but demands considerable amounts of time and effort for making contracts, determining respective responsibilities and working procedures, improving systems of coordination, and other necessary tasks (Fiszbein and Lowden 1999, 15). To assume otherwise would mean to commit the same normative error that Prahalad committed in his approach and ultimately to collapse back into the rather naïve and metaphysical belief in a market that provides a one-size-fits-all solution for the entirety of societal problems. Hence the win-win paradigm is unlikely to provide an answer precisely to the most pressing societal issues because it is exactly these most persistent societal problems that will not yield any commercial opportunities (Ulrich and Wettstein 2005, 49).

Corporations that understand their engagement in public policy processes as moral obligations in a truly Kantian sense are aware of the fact that not their own but the public interest must be the guiding ideal and motivation that drives their commitment. From this perspective, they understand such collaborative partnerships not as an opportunity to extend their commercial interest into the public and political realm but, on the contrary, as a platform for meeting the moral obligations that necessarily come with their powerful position in the global sphere. This might appear as a detail, but it is absolutely crucial for the lasting success of such partnerships and public policy networks. A UNICEF official, for example, speculated "whether high-profile partnerships with pharmaceutical companies had delayed rather than improved poorer people's access to [. . .] essential medicines" (quoted in Richter 2004, 62). Such scenarios are indeed possible if the underlying rationale for the corporations' engagement is their own business interest and the vague assumption that pursuing their own agenda within such partnerships will automatically benefit the public interest at the same time. Such partnerships are not, as commonly assumed (see, e.g., Leisinger 2005, 580), about finding win-win situations that create synergies between different actors that all pursue their own interests and thereby magically improve the public good. Rather, it is about their willingness to commit to and work toward one overarching goal and thus to subordinate their particular interests to it. Once the different institutions are a part of the network, they must, as the World Bank's Jean-François Rischard (2002, 174) stated, "think and act as a global citizen, not as a staunch defender of narrow interest."

Thus where corporations are involved in public policy processes, adequate safeguards of the public interest must be in place. Because corporations are, after all, profit-oriented institutions, conflicts of interest may occasionally occur even for truly "enlightened" corporate actors. However, this is precisely why such public-spirited corporations will not understand such safeguards as a restriction or constraint on their freedom to act, but rather as a moral and institutional support for them to be able effectively to meet their obligation.

Stating a moral obligation for multinational corporations to engage in social policy making and the provision of global public goods inevitably leads to a somewhat paradoxical situation. Ultimately, as Ann Zammit (2004) argues perceptively, this means making the main protagonists of the neoliberal system the privileged actors to solve the problems resulting from it. Multinational corporations are expected to deliver solutions for social and societal problems that they are exacerbating at the very same time by upholding the neoliberal global economic system. Hence this second category of multinational corporations' remedial obligations of justice inevitably implies a third category that aims at the elimination of this contradiction. The third and most important category of remedial obligations aims at the transformation of the global economic system with the intent to make it work in favor of, rather than against, human development.

Remedial Duties at the Global Economic Policy Level: Regulatory Obligations

The creation of an adequate framework of social policies flanking the global market is a necessary but not a sufficient response to the unsatisfactory human rights situation on this planet. As long as the global economic system itself works against such policies, they will always be limited to fighting and remedying symptoms. Hence the single most important condition for realizing human rights on a large scale is the creation of an enabling global economic environment, that is, the taming of the destructive systemic forces of the global economic system and their transformation into positive mechanisms of human development.

Margaret Jungk (2001, 3) claimed that multinational corporations cannot be held responsible for systemic or structural shortcomings of the global economy. Asking individual businesses to solve collective problems that belong to the global market as a whole, she argues, is not only unreasonable but would effectively mean asking them to commit commercial suicide. This argument crucially misses the point. First, because multinational corporations control large parts of the power structures in the global political economy, it seems far from unreasonable to hold them responsible for the facilitation of structural change in the global economic system. Second, having them address such problems at the systemic level might in fact be the only way effectively to enable them to meet their individual moral responsibilities without committing commercial suicide. Let me elaborate on these two points in more detail.

Adjusting the Rules of the Game: The Obligation to Enable Effective Regulation   Charging multinational corporations with moral obligations concerning the remediation of the harmful effects of the global economic system is not unreasonable, as Margaret Jungk incorrectly argues, but the only reasonable strategy for creating lasting and sustainable solutions for the persistent human rights problems in the developing world. National governments that are caught in the golden straitjacket find it increasingly difficult to make autonomous regulatory decisions. At the same time, international institutions also are increasingly controlled by corporate interests. The result is the neoliberal paradox described earlier; multinational corporations themselves become the central institutions on whose willingness the transformation of the global economic system ultimately depends. After all, as I argued at length earlier, the capacity for structural change is the key determinant of corporations' new political power. Because multinational corporations are factually in charge of the global economic system, the likelihood of achieving any changes without their active support and advocacy is marginal.

The moral obligations deriving from multinational corporations' structural complicity (see the section "Avoiding Indirect Human Rights Violations: Corporate Complicity" earlier in this chapter) in maintaining and supporting a harmful global economic system are not merely negative ones to abstain from contributing to the structural violation of human rights. Because multinationals are operating in key political positions to alter this harmful system effectively, they have a moral obligation to protect people from its detrimental effects and to proactively engage in its transformation at both national and global levels.

At the national level, multinational corporations must use their power to enable governments to establish and maintain sound social and environmental regulation of the market instead of pressuring them continuously to loosen and ultimately abandon their existing frameworks. Instead of using their political clout to advance the continuous deregulation and liberalization of national markets, with potentially detrimental effects especially for the rights of the weaker and underprivileged parts of the population, multinational corporations should actively advocate rules and regulations that help secure those rights. Instead of lobbying against laws and regulations that are meant to protect human rights, they should throw their political weight behind initiating and enforcing such attempts. Furthermore, multinational corporations must refrain from using the coercive force of the exit threat to drive down social and environmental standards and to divert tax revenues into their own pockets. On the contrary, they should use the political power connected to the exit threat responsibly in those cases in which it can help pressure governments to abandon harmful policies and practices. Multinational corporations should use their political power to promote and facilitate the development of better and higher standards in the countries in which they choose to operate, as well as to pressure their own governments to adopt policies that are beneficial to poor countries (Garten 2002, 126).

At the global level, multinational corporations must take responsibility for the organization of the global economic system. As perhaps the most powerful actors in the global political economy, multinational corporations largely determine—whether by direct control or indirect influence on the relevant decision-making bodies—the way in which global economic structures are organized, what results they produce, and whom they do or do not benefit. Therefore, they bear an inherent moral obligation to organize these structures according to the principles of justice outlined earlier. Hence instead of shaping the rules of the global marketplace in their own favor by exerting influence over the relevant rule-making bodies, multinational corporations, as primary agents of justice, must use their power in the public interest and lend their support to and facilitate the creation of solutions that aim at making the global market work in the interest of those whose rights have remained unrealized. In certain cases, such as the WTO, this obligation may well include putting active pressure on an agency to find new solutions and change rules and regulations that are detrimental to human development—for example, the ones currently protecting intellectual property rights. Although nation-states have largely given up this possibility and have effectively subordinated themselves to the authority of the WTO, concerted action of multinational corporations could easily eliminate all harmful WTO regulations.

The WTO is arguably the most significant formal rule-making body in the global political economy and has traditionally promoted corporate rather than human interests in its rules and rulings. Accordingly, it has largely failed to take human rights into consideration in its rule-making process, despite the fact that most of its currently 153 member states have ratified or signed the UN Human Rights Covenants and other regional or bilateral treaties aimed at the protection of human rights (Wells and Elias 2005, 171). The WTO has adopted the dominant corporate perception that human rights are a hindrance or obstruction to, rather than a goal of, the global market. It has turned into an instrument to protect corporate rather than human rights.

To argue that such agreements are legitimate because of consensus and voluntary acceptance even by developing nations falls short of the criteria of justice elaborated in part I of this book. Such a contractarian argument turns a blind eye on the fact that developing nations seldom have a real choice to opt out of such unbeneficial rule systems, because this would effectively eliminate their access to the global market. Furthermore, because they lacked in-depth background knowledge about many of those rules (Pogge 2001a, 12), their bargaining position at the time of acceptance was generally weak. Many rules currently in place for governing the global economy are not only unjust in their outcomes but were negotiated and enacted under similarly illegitimate terms.

The regulatory obligations of multinationals not only refer to the formal rules and regulations that define the contours and build the frame of the global market but include the standardization of the principles on the basis of which those corporations compete. All the individual obligations of corporations described earlier, that is, obligations to abstain from human rights violations, to protect others from having their rights violated, and to remedy existing violations, must ultimately be backed by standards that effectively regulate global competition at both the industry level and the level of the economy at large. Without effective standards, meeting extensive human rights obligations may be an unreasonably heavy burden for any individual company competing in the global market. If the mechanism of competition itself is not subjected to sound human rights principles, all other attempts and approaches will ultimately collapse under the systemic pressure of global competition.

Even those critics who claim that charging individual corporations with human rights obligations means commercial suicide can hardly deny that once such obligations are built into the rules of competition itself and apply to all competitors equally, the danger of responsible corporations being driven out of the market will largely be averted. Regulation is thus to be understood not as a restriction on corporate freedom but as its enhancement: it is the precondition for corporations to choose to act responsibly.

However, those institutions that could take on a formal mandate to enact rules and legislation for the marketplace will be wary of acting against the interests of large multinationals on which they factually depend. Hence as long as multinational corporations are not pressing for such regulations themselves or, as is currently the case, even heavily oppose them, the hope for profound transformation in the global political economy will remain an illusion. There is no doubt in my mind that the largest impact of corporate action on the respect, protection, and realization of human rights will derive from how they put their power to use in the global political arena. David Vogel (2005, 171) is entirely right in claiming that the most critical dimension of corporate social responsibility today may be the corporation's impact on public policy. Hence a consistent conclusion from multinational corporations' de facto role as primary agents of justice is that they themselves must take responsibility for subjecting global competition to uniform human rights standards.

Leveling the Playing Field: A Case for Voluntary or for Mandatory Approaches?   The creation of and compliance with uniform human rights standards for global competition should not be perceived as an additional burden for multinational corporations. On the contrary, such standards must be interpreted as an instrument to disburden corporations from potential negative economic effects connected to meeting their individual moral obligations in an unregulated marketplace. In other words, if all companies adhered to the same standards, no single corporation would be put at an economic disadvantage for being responsible. Thus such collective action would effectively force a race to the top without negatively affecting companies' competitiveness in the marketplace (Spar 1998, 10). Such standards would be in the (enlightened) self-interest of all those corporations whose interest in the protection of human rights is indeed genuine and not just a marketing instrument (Ulrich 2002a, 145).

Thus multinational corporations with a genuine interest in the protection and promotion of human rights would welcome such approaches and standards on the basis of the experienced structural impossibility for any one of them truly to live up to the full range of their individual human rights obligations under current market conditions. In other words, truly enlightened companies support human rights regulation of global competition on the basis of their own interest in leveling the playing field, that is, their motivation to subject all corporations in the market to the same standards and principles. Leveling the playing field means nothing else than eliminating the (perceived) competitive disadvantage connected to the fulfillment of human rights obligations while competing in the global market. It aims at enhancing the reasonableness criterion, that is, the question of what corporations can reasonably be held responsible for under market conditions.

During the last few years we have witnessed the emergence of an increasing number of such standards at all levels, with the UN Global Compact being the most prominent and successful example among them. None of these standards, however, are endowed with regulatory force. They are entirely voluntary and lack comprehensive enforcement mechanisms even for the corporations that have signed them. Without tightening these conditions, however, it is unlikely that the existing standards will really be able to do the job. It is unlikely that companies will take such standards seriously when competitive disadvantage is the price they have to pay for doing so (Avery 2000, 44).

This suggests that only regulatory and thus mandatory and binding approaches will be able to breach the structural or "organized irresponsibility" (Beck 1988, 96ff.) of the global competitive system. "Structural irresponsibility" means that the current global neoliberal order requires a certain degree of irresponsibility from corporations in order for them to be able to stay competitive. As long as socially irresponsible behavior and the disregard of human rights are rewarded with an immediate economic benefit in the form of a competitive advantage, there will always be corporations ready and willing to exploit such opportunities. Thus the market suffers from an inherent free-rider problem in the extension of human rights obligations to multinational corporations (Muchlinski 2001, 35). Such moral free-riding of unscrupulous corporations undermines the attempts of those corporations that truly want to live up to their obligations because it forces them similarly to adopt certain irresponsible practices in order to stay competitive. This is just one manifestation of Virginia Haufler's (2001, 121) observation that self-regulation generally works poorly when the political system works against it and works best when there is some legal recourse.

Thus voluntary approaches will likely fall short in getting the destructive effects of the global competitive system under control. As long as such standards cannot be enforced for all corporations, there will likely be moral free-riders exploiting the opportunity to get an edge over their more responsible competitors. Kenneth Roth (2005), executive director of Human Rights Watch, argues that voluntary initiatives that are based predominantly on public pressure naturally focus heavily on large and prominent companies. If these companies are in competition with less visible companies, however, the competitive playing field is distorted. Less prominent firms might simply not see any reason (i.e., public pressure) to commit to the same standards as their more exposed peers. In some cases they might even gain a competitive advantage by deliberately pursuing socially irresponsible practices. Hence Roth concludes that only enforceable standards, can effectively avoid such double standards.

The willingness of corporations to commit voluntarily to human rights standards at the cost of real or perceived competitive disadvantages is still rather low. The number of member companies of the UN Global Compact is a reflection of this insight. The most successful of the current voluntary standards, the Global Compact has grown to an impressive number of 4,300 companies in 120 nations today, but relative to more than 70,000 transnational corporations and millions of local companies of all sizes worldwide, this number hardly indicates a major turnaround in corporate mentality. The impact of self-regulatory instruments in general is contested. For Noreena Hertz (2004, 206), civil and market-based forms of regulation are unlikely to have a significant impact on corporate behavior as a whole. Too many different standards, codes, and other self-regulatory instruments render public monitoring overall ineffective. Regulatory approaches, on the other hand, help solve these problems by delegating the monitoring task to the directly affected people themselves. For example, they empower exploited workers by establishing claimable rights, promoting their unionization, and building a countervailing force against abusive contractors (Danaher and Mark 2003, 101).

"If self-regulation and market forces were the best means to ensure respect for human rights," the International Council on Human Rights Policy (ICHRP 2002, 7) argues, one would expect that the number of human rights violations by companies would have diminished over the years. However, what we observe today is precisely the opposite. John Kenneth Galbraith (1952, 155) provides a comprehensive explanation of this connection. His argument is that self-regulation in an environment with no checks and balances is an illusion. It is the growth of countervailing power that strengthens the capacity of the economy for self-regulation. Precisely this countervailing power, however, is lacking today. Such insights make a clear case for subjecting global competition to mandatory human rights standards, which inevitably implies an indirect moral obligation of multinationals to support and facilitate approaches that aim at doing so. However, multinational corporations have been rather insensible to this concern so far. When, after a four-year preparation period, the UN Sub-commission on the Promotion and Protection of Human Rights released the UN Norms in 2003, only a handful even among the Global Compact member companies expressed their support for the venture, while the vast majority rejected it across the board.

The UN Norms were an attempt to translate existing international human rights law into the corporate context and to make it mandatory for all corporations. By applying to all companies equally, the UN Norms would have effectively been the first nonvoluntary human rights standard for corporations. The UN Norms would have carried the moral weight of a formal and authoritative process sanctioned by the UN (Amnesty International, 2004), but they were not meant to reach the status of a treaty and thus would not have achieved legal standing. This does not exclude the possibility, however, that they could have served as a basis for drafting what David Weissbrodt (2005, 288) calls "a human rights treaty on corporate social responsibility" later on.

Even though the UN Norms would not have been legally binding, compliance with them was meant to be subject to monitoring. Furthermore, the UN Norms called for compensation in case of their violation. However, the sub-commission's draft of the UN Norms did not gain the approval of the UN Commission on Human Rights, which was a precondition for their submission to the UN's Economic and Social Council and finally to the General Assembly for adoption (Weissbrodt 2005, 290).

The two biggest and most influential international business associations, the International Chamber of Commerce (ICC) and the International Organization of Employers (IOE), voiced harsh criticism of the UN Norms (ICC and IOE 2004, 1ff.). In their joint statement upon the release of the Norms, they condemned them as "an extreme case of privatization of human rights" that was based on a "legal error" because, in their opinion, only states can directly be held responsible under international human rights law. As a consequence, they claimed, human rights obligations can apply to corporations only on a strictly voluntary basis. Therefore, the IOE and ICC feared that the UN Norms might undermine the progress achieved by the UN Global Compact and even saw them as a threat to the institution of human rights per se. My earlier elaborations on the nature of human rights as moral rights, as well as on the status of the multinational corporation as a quasi-governmental institution, build a strong argumentative basis for the refutation of this critique as both morally too narrow and politically and legally outdated. I will not repeat these arguments at this point.

What seems even more surprising than the resistance by the IOE and the ICC, however, is that, as mentioned earlier, even most of the Global Compact member companies opposed the UN Norms vehemently. Considering that all these companies asserted their voluntary commitment to their human rights responsibilities when they signed the Global Compact, it seems hard to comprehend why they would oppose political attempts to hold their competitors accountable to such standards as well. A corporation that has committed to its human rights obligations on a voluntary basis has literally nothing to lose by rendering the respective standards mandatory unless it misinterprets voluntariness as opportunism, that is, as the possibility to opt out of its obligations whenever this might yield an economic advantage. For any truly committed, that is, nonopportunistic, corporation, however, such norms would be highly beneficial, because they effectively establish a level playing field.

Against this background, expressed and demonstrated support for mandatory human rights standards can be taken as the measure of proof for corporations' serious and genuine commitment to their human rights obligations. Rather than giving up their own responsible practices in order not to suffer competitive disadvantages, they are raising the bar for corporate responsibility in the competitive marketplace and fostering a mandate for the same standards for their less responsible peers (Wettstein and Waddock 2005, 312).

To be sure, this does not eliminate the simultaneous need for voluntary initiatives. On the contrary, voluntary and regulatory approaches are inherently complementary: while voluntary initiatives help develop mandatory standards, such standards provide the basis on which further voluntary initiatives are likely to flourish (Wettstein and Waddock 2005, 317). Regulatory approaches can never fully replace the need for the voluntary adoption of responsibility of corporations because they necessarily lag behind the development of moral insights. A complete replacement of voluntary approaches by mandated regulation would not even be desirable, because an economy in which we delegate all moral responsibility to the institutional market frame would lead us to a moderate Friedmanian stance that confirms the amoral nature of the corporation and dismisses the need for corporate integrity as long as corporations stay within the rules of the game. Thus we would confirm the stance that the corporation has no other responsibility than to run a financially successful business. Georg Kell, Global Compact executive head, and John Ruggie, the UN special representative on business and human rights, also point to this complementary relation between voluntary and mandatory approaches. Voluntary approaches, they claim, are not a substitute for government regulation and can at best fill a temporary void where governments are unable or unwilling to meet their responsibility (Kell and Ruggie 2004, 20). Hence opting for mandatory approaches is not a statement against complementary voluntary initiatives; we do not have to decide for one or the other. Rather, we need to decide what should be the right mix between the two (Howen 2005b, 321; Wettstein and Waddock 2005).

Chapter 10

A Look into the Future

Restoring Democracy in the Global Age

OSMOPOLITAN JUSTICE cannot be realized within a framework of political and institutional statism. The failure of the current statist interpretation of international human rights law is a prime example of this insight. If we are to take moral cosmopolitanism seriously, it must be followed by a sound institutional cosmopolitanism.

Institutional cosmopolitanism, as opposed to institutional statism, demands institutional pluralism. Hence instead of narrowly confining our focus to state action and thus to a decreasing number of solutions suitable for a globalizing world, we must shift our attention to all those institutions that can make valuable contributions to the realization of people's rights. In this book I have outlined the moral obligations of multinational corporations in this endeavor.

However, the very fact that multinational corporations are advancing to the position of key players in the realization of global justice illustrates a problem that is—at least at the current stage—endemic to the globalization process and concurrent attempts to realize global justice. If global justice is best interpreted as cosmopolitan justice and cosmopolitan justice implies institutional cosmopolitanism, and further, if institutional cosmopolitanism means focusing on a plurality of powerful global actors, then we are evidently confronted with the problem of democratic legitimation. Shifting moral responsibility to global institutions like multinational corporations is, as seen earlier, not only a necessary response to their increasing power but can also be a source for its consolidation. This, however, creates an evident dilemma between the moral justification of those global institutions' obligations deriving from their de facto powerful roles in the global political arena and the democratic political legitimation of these powerful roles.[1]

The quest for cosmopolitan justice is inevitably and inseparably tied to the call for the establishment of a global democratic order. Furthermore, the connection between global democracy and global justice is not merely causal but inherent. That is, democracy itself is to be considered an inherent part of global justice rather than an additional societal ideal connected to it. Self-government in the form of democratic rule is a crucial part of human self-determination and development. The realization of human beings' equality of private autonomy, as notably Habermas (2002, 202) argues, is tied to the appropriate use of their political autonomy as citizens. Whether there is a specific human right to democracy (see, e.g., Gould 2004, 184) is open to debate, but it seems that at the very least a consequent interpretation of our most basic human rights (including most notably the general political human rights) must necessarily require a democratic organization of society. The reverse relation also holds: the claim for democracy is at the same time a claim for the realization of our basic human rights, because "human rights institutionalize the communicative conditions for a reasonable political will-formation" (Habermas 2002, 201). Furthermore, freedom and equality of citizens are constitutional elements of any political order that deserves to be called democratic, and this holds as much for the global level as for local and national ones. Thus we can either have global justice and global democracy or none at all.

A Necessity for the Present

The call for global democracy is a logical consequence of the call for local and national democracy. Democratic decision making at the national and local levels, as seen earlier, is increasingly compromised and undermined by transnational economic processes and institutions. The idea that the citizens of any given community are able autonomously to determine their destiny, as Daniele Archibugi (1998, 205) rightly argues, becomes increasingly illusory in an inherently interdependent world. Only a global political order can bring those forces under control and create new space for local self-determination. Thus arguing against such a global order means sacrificing local democracy. Arguing in favor of a global order but against global democracy means falling back into premodern authoritarianism. Only the claim for a democratic, cosmopolitan world order is effectively able to secure human freedom in the global age. Hence the current stage of globalization effectively establishes a moral imperative for global democracy (Höffe 2002a, 11).

In the short run this insight implies an immediate demand for a massive democratic reform of existing governing institutions at the global level. This evidently affects the United Nations (see, e.g., Archibugi 1995; Höffe 2002c, 325ff.) and the Bretton Woods institutions; however, it similarly applies also to today's private governments such as large NGOs or, essentially, multinational corporations. The current global (dis)order is controlled by institutions that are characterized by exclusion rather than inclusion, by inadequate modes of representation and participation, and thus by a general lack of responsiveness. Responsiveness as a political concept refers to the readiness and willingness of an institution or representative to listen to others, as well as to respond to questions, challenges, impulses, or critiques raised by them (Müller 1999, 54). Thus it refers to the process of political legitimation.

Most international and supranational institutions do not represent people but governments. Individuals have no real role in international politics except as citizens of a state (Archibugi 1995, 128). Governments, however, represent national rather than global interests, which makes it hard if not impossible to find truly global solutions for inherently global problems (Archibugi 1998, 213). Thus the decisions reached in such institutions resemble international relations among states; they do not eliminate but reproduce the shortcomings and failures of the international, statist system. The move in the direction of truly cosmopolitan democracy must thus start with remedying the shortcomings of existing global, regional, and local institutions.

This takes us back to the problem of political legitimation of multinational corporations. Evidently, when we talk about democracy at the global level, the increasingly prominent role of multinational corporations on the global political stage must be addressed. Their powerful position in the global political economy, their quasi-governmental role, as I have described it earlier, has direct and obvious implications for the democratic constitution of our society. Only the previously described belief, still widely shared but nonetheless inadequate, in the apolitical nature of the corporation, as Charles Derber (1998, 119) notes, could seriously make us "believe that it is possible to have great concentrations of power and wealth in the 'private' sphere while still practicing true democracy in the public." This does not mean that any involvement of multinational corporations in global public policy processes must be condemned across the board. Precisely to the extent that multinational corporations can indeed make a genuine and positive contribution to the realization of human rights, they are also making an actual contribution to global democracy. The realization of human rights is an indispensable prerequisite for any democratic order. However, to the extent that this increasingly prominent position effectively allows multinational corporations to abuse their political power and to exert undue influence on public policy processes, they must be subjected to democratic checks and balances. This latter claim is not a remote suggestion thought out in the academic ivory tower but a logical consequence of multinational corporations' very real quasi-governmental role.

Establishing democratic checks and balances for multinational corporations ultimately means reembedding them in a system of democratically supported rules and regulations and subordinating them to the primacy of politics at the global level. As explained in the introductory thoughts to this book, a state in which private corporations factually operate beyond the authority of democratic institutions must strictly be thought of as a state in transition. What a conception of cosmopolitan democracy as the end goal of this transition could look like will be discussed shortly. For now, however, let us look at a more immediate claim for directly democratizing the multinational corporation itself by enhancing and institutionalizing responsiveness in its basic structure.

On the one hand, democratizing the multinational corporation means encouraging employees to execute their role as responsible citizens not only outside but also within and through the structures of the corporation. First of all, this means opening up organizational room that allows for and encourages autonomous ethical judgments of employees within daily business processes and operations. However, it also calls for greater employee representation in corporate decision-making processes. Such democratization of the workplace not only increases public legitimacy of corporate decisions but is inherently valuable because it increases the autonomy of employees and workers. Norman Bowie (1999, 82ff., 102f.) is a strong defender of workplace democratization along Kantian lines. A moral firm, he argues, would have to look like a representative democracy; everyone involved in the organization would have a voice in the rules and policies that govern the organization.

However, full democratization of the corporation must reach beyond mere employment relations into the broader society. The demography, as well as the representation of different worldviews and mentalities, in large organizations often resembles that of society quite accurately (Leisinger 2004, 184) and might thus be able to approximate the public interest, at least to some extent. It was John Stuart Mill (1991) who, on the basis of his general conviction that democracy is feasible only within reasonably small groups, suggested a model of representative deliberation for democratic societies that rests precisely on the idea of replacing deliberation among all citizens with deliberation within a representative group that reflects their demography and their points of view. However, even with greater employee representation, corporate decisions might still suffer from distortions caused by employee loyalty and identification and from the general underrepresentation of minorities, as well as from the fact that employees might be able to represent certain groups of people in general, but not in regard to their specific exposure to the corporation's actions and decisions. Thus the extension of the principle of representation and inclusion into the wider public is indispensable.

The possibilities regarding how to achieve greater societal representation in corporate decisions are manifold. It cannot be the aim of this concluding chapter to provide an in-depth inquiry into them. However, it seems evident that a holistic approach includes at least two dimensions. First, it requires the corporation's readiness and openness to enter into an ongoing constructive dialogue not only with all people who are directly affected by corporate policies and decisions but also with all others who want to express concerns and potential argumentative claims regarding corporate policies, decisions, and actions (Ulrich 2008, 423). This aspect represents the core of the concept of responsiveness; it requires an impact of the public on corporate decisions that is not merely accidental and transitory but regularized, unavoidable, ongoing, and significant (see Kuper 2004, 79).

This implies, second, the institutionalization of public representation within the internal governance and policy-making structures of the corporation through representative assemblies at the board level or other adequate and suitable measures. Although such models exist already in very broad terms, notably in Germany, there is an evident need for further research and investigation of how such attempts can be extended and improved in both scope and effectiveness.

A Vision for the Future

To be sure, in the long run the claim for cosmopolitan democracy exceeds the mere reform of existing—and in some cases inadequate—institutions and calls for the creation of new structures, laws, and institutions that are better suited to respond to the specific demands of cosmopolitan justice. What I am suggesting here is not the creation of a centralized global state. The danger of suppressing rather than enhancing democracy in a global state is, as Kant noted, too acute. A system of overlapping local, regional, and global mechanisms of self-determination seems more realistic and more appealing. In accordance with this insight, Archibugi (2003, 8) characterizes a truly cosmopolitan democracy as one that does not merely reproduce the organization of the state on a world scale. On the contrary, he associates it with a revision of the powers and functions of states that will "deprive them of the oligarchic power they now enjoy." First and foremost, however, cosmopolitan democracy aspires to enable individuals to be heard in global affairs and thus to structure institutions accordingly. Thus cosmopolitan democracy not only implies the creation of new global institutions that allow for the participation of global civil society in global political decision making (Archibugi 1998, 218), but similarly aims at reestablishing local and regional self-determination by reconfiguring it in the light of the new global context.

Nadia Urbinati (2003, 67) rejected cosmopolitan democracy "as a project of centralization and unification of power" rather than one based on decentralization and cooperation. Although her worries about the antidemocratic risks of global democracy are well justified in general, they do not apply to an adequate interpretation of cosmopolitan democracy. Quite contrary to her view, cosmopolitan democracy can be regarded as a project to restore and improve rather than to suppress the possibility of decentralization and localization under conditions of globalization. David Held (1995a, 113) proposes a model of decision making that refers to city and local levels those issues and policy questions that primarily affect the people living there, that is, those issues that refer to the conditions of their own association. At the national level we should decide issues and problems that stretch to, but no further than, the national frontiers. Those issues and policy questions that require transborder collaboration to be effectively resolved belong to the regional level. Hence regional decision making is legitimized only for those cases in which self-determination cannot be guaranteed by national governance alone. Similarly, for those cases in which neither local, national, nor regional governance leads to satisfying solutions, the democratic decision-making center must shift to the global level. Hence Held concludes:

> Decision-making centers beyond national borders are properly located when lower levels of decision–making cannot manage and discharge satisfactorily

transnational and international policy questions. [. . .] Democracy, thus, can only be adequately entrenched if a division of powers and competences is recognized across different levels of political interaction and interconnectedness. Such an order must embrace diverse and distinct domains of authority, linked both vertically and horizontally, if it is to be a creator and servant of democratic practice, wherever it is located. (D. Held 1995a, 113)

Cosmopolitan democracy does not imply a centralized global state. However, its consequent interpretation might well lead us toward a holistic conception of a democratic, federalist world republic, as proposed notably by Otfried Höffe (2002c). Such a world republic would not replace but merely complement nation-states (Höffe 2002a, 14, 21; 2002c, 14) and thus would essentially be subsidiary. Hence it would, as outlined by Held, propose global regulatory solutions precisely for those issues and problems that cannot be dealt with satisfactorily at the local, national, and regional levels. Therefore, it would not aim at global uniformity but would embrace difference as a constitutive element. Its universalistic stance is in fact the basis on which well-understood difference, whether cultural, national, or individual, becomes possible under conditions of globalization. This principle of subsidiarity evidently holds only vis-à-vis those states that are themselves well ordered, that is, constituted on democratic principles and in accordance with the universal requirements of cosmopolitan justice.

In correspondence with the notion and principles of justice put forth in this book, I hold that cosmopolitan democracy must be envisioned as deliberative democracy. Although the central institutional elements of a world republic would likely be some sort of cosmopolitan parliament, as well as a cosmopolitan legal order, the most important prerequisite for its deliberative interpretation is a functioning global public sphere that allows for a plurality of communicative forms and arenas for the use of public reason and democratic will formation. In other words, deliberative democracy aims at facilitating and institutionalizing free and inclusive public reasoning among equal citizens by providing favorable conditions for participation, association, and expression (J. Cohen 1996, 99). A world parliament would have to be sufficiently well connected to regions, nations, and localities (D. Held 1995a, 111) and perhaps consist of a house of citizens' representatives and a house of states' representatives (Höffe 2002a, 24). A constitutive cosmopolitan law, on the other hand, aims at the establishment of a well-ordered global coexistence not merely among nation-states (which is essentially a matter of international law) but among all human beings as genuine world citizens (Höffe 2002a, 21). A global public sphere must be thought of as an interlocking net of multiple forms of associations, networks, and organizations that together create what Seyla Benhabib (1996, 73ff.) calls "an anonymous 'public conversation'" that is not detached from but "flow[s] through" (Habermas 1996b, 28) the formal (and informal) institutional bodies of the republic. In other words, we must think of it as a "medium of loosely associated, multiple foci of opinion formation and dissemination" that are connected in "free and spontaneous processes of communication" (Benhabib 1996, 74). It is from these "noncoercive and nonfinal processes of opinion formation" that not only political legitimacy but also the "discursive rationalization" (Habermas 1996b, 28) of political decision making ultimately derive. The emergence and development of a shared, "global sense of justice" (Höffe 2002c, 341ff.) among free and equal world citizens, finally, is possible only within and through such inclusive communicative processes. Without the emergence of a global sense of justice, however, the practical realization of global justice will remain a distant dream. Thus any institutional realization of global democracy must be "centered around a procedure of free, public deliberation" within an unrestricted public sphere (Benhabib 1996, 85).

In regard specifically to multinational corporations, a cosmopolitan system of laws and regulations would establish global incorporation combined with global taxation of large multinationals. As cosmopolitan institutions that pursue and make profits within a global system, multinational corporations should be taxed for the maintenance of an effective global social system surrounding the global market. The distribution of such a global tax fund would be based on need rather than on the amount of profit generated in a particular country. Therefore, it would first of all benefit those countries and people who are affected by but not a part of the global economy. Hence it would end the illegitimate contemporary favoritism of compatriots at the expense of all other groups that contribute to global corporate profits, whether in an active manner or passively by being the losers in the global economy. Additionally, such constitutive regulations at the global level would effectively eliminate multinational corporations' capability to evade taxes and regulations. The conceptualization of a stringent and comprehensive global incorporation and taxation system is one of the foremost tasks on the way to a more equitable global economy.

On a more general level, cosmopolitan law picks up the Kantian idea of world citizens' rights, which complements national constitutions with the intent to secure equal freedom for all. Some might call this idea utopian, misguided, or downright wrong, and they are well entitled to do so. However, with increasing integration of our global society, this Kantian proposal is becoming a pressing necessity 200 years after it was initially formulated. It is the precondition for toleration and peaceful coexistence in the 21st century (D. Held 1995b, 228). It seems difficult to argue in favor of global justice but against its institutionalization through some form of global citizens' rights. At the very least it is up to opponents to demonstrate the plausibility of their argument against such a cosmopolitan law. As Nadia Urbinati correctly stated, "Post-Kant, the burden of proof is on those who want to argue against cosmopolitan civil rights" (Urbinati 2003, 67). This book should have made clear why.

Notes

Chapter 1

1. In this book I will use the term *liberal* in the traditional political philosophical sense rather than in reference to the cluster of political positions that are denoted as liberal (i.e., "leftist") in the Anglo-American discussion of current affairs. Neoliberalism, as used in this book, denotes a form of market liberalism that emerged in the early 1970s and found its most influential practical manifestation in the Reagan/Thatcher free-market doctrines. Underlying neoliberalism is a mind-set of libertarianism, which emphasizes personal liberty and the unrestricted pursuit of self-interest. For an in-depth analysis of the underlying premises and of the history of neoliberalism see David Harvey's short but concise book *A Brief History of Neoliberalism* (2007).

2. The difference between a thorough philosophical utilitarianism and such normative doctrines with utilitarian content can be made clear by following Thomas Scanlon's elaborations: "The term 'utilitarianism' is generally used to refer to a family of specific normative doctrines—doctrines which might be held on the basis of a number of different philosophical theses about the nature of morality. In this sense of the term one might, for example, be a utilitarian on intuitionist or on contractualist grounds. But what I will call 'philosophical utilitarianism' is a particular philosophical thesis that the only fundamental moral facts are facts about individual well-being" (Scanlon 1982, 108). Neoliberal doctrines, as we will see, unfold their utilitarian implications predominantly on contractarian—and thus Rawlsian—grounds.

Chapter 2

1. For Hume himself, the circumstances of justice essentially arise under conditions of scarcity of property and possessions. See Hume (1997, 13ff.; sec. 3, pt. 1), as well as Hume (1992, 484ff.; bk. 3, sec. 2).

2. It is in this aspect that Kant's attempt to derive an absolute justification from an understanding of pure reason as a transcendental human characteristic must necessarily fail. Kant's account of absolute, transcendental reason is problematic because it does not entirely succeed in overcoming traditionalistic conceptions of morals. In

fact, he merely replaces their adherence to traditional authorities with the authority of absolute reason. Thus he transforms the question of what we are reasonably able to want to do (and thus should do) into a question of what we objectively must do (Ulrich 2008, 54), based on our transcendental and thus absolute rational nature (Williams 1997, 94).

3. The importance of this distinction, especially from the perspective of a rights-based conception of justice, was pointed out very eloquently by John Stuart Mill (2001, 46): "The justice of giving equal protection to the rights of all is maintained by those who support the most outrageous inequality in the rights themselves. Even in slave countries it is theoretically admitted that the rights of the slave, such as they are, ought to be as sacred as those of the master, and that a tribunal which fails to enforce them with equal strictness is wanting in justice; while, at the same time, institutions which leave to the slave scarcely any rights to enforce are not deemed unjust because they are not deemed inexpedient." Hence an impartial application of norms is possible even under the condition of the most outrageous injustices against human beings. Only an impartial justification of the norms themselves can prevent such unjust outcomes.

4. Society's obligation to protect people's rights, according to Mill, can be justified only on the basis of utility (and not of these rights themselves). Therefore, he inevitably collapses back into an instrumental understanding of justice. He ultimately sacrifices the standpoint of justice to the criterion of the highest common good and undermines not only the principle of equal moral concern and respect but his whole theory of justice. Thus his theory of justice is self-contradictory, at least insofar as an instrumental understanding of justice contradicts his elaborations on the ethical standing of moral rights.

5. Shue's candidates for basic rights are the classical liberty rights, political rights, and some rights to subsistence. Patricia Werhane (1985, 16ff.), on the other hand, includes the right to equal consideration, the rights to security and subsistence (on the basis of Shue), and the right to life and not to be tortured, as well as the right to freedom, in the category of basic rights.

6. Donnelly's notion of universality is based on the de facto international consensus that has established human rights as "almost universally accepted" rights. Donnelly thus runs the risk of confusing acceptance with legitimacy, which may confront his theory with the problem of ethical relativism. Despite this flaw, Donnelly's theory of human rights is arguably one of the richest in the contemporary landscape of human rights literature. For an elaborate critique of Donnelly's approach, see Freeman (1994).

7. Evidently, the existence and resolution of rights conflicts presupposes some kind of distributive rule. One possibility to deal with rights conflicts, however, is their reinterpretation in terms of obligations. Thus rights conflicts arise when obligations deriving from one right are incommensurate with obligations generated by another right (Waldron 1993, 214). The distributive criterion for their resolution, as I will argue later, then is the "reasonableness" of these obligations (see the section "Gradation and Cutoff Criteria: Power and Reasonableness" in chapter 3).

8. The notion of cosmopolitanism was coined by Immanuel Kant. However, Kant's "cosmopolitan right" (*ius cosmopoliticum*) referred to the universal law of a possible union of all nations (Kant 1996, 121).

9. Rights in general are often associated with Western Enlightenment thought. If we insist on the very term *a right*, this association is most certainly correct. However, the basic underlying idea or concept of rights is not at all of uniquely Western heritage but can be found in many different moral traditions. To claim human rights as a unique legacy of the West reflects a piece of Western arrogance rather than one of Western imperialism, as is often claimed. For further elaboration on the culturally diverse roots of human rights, see Sen (1997; 2000, 232ff.).

10. For further elaboration of the distinction between universality of scope and universality of justification, see Pogge (1989, 212ff.) or Caney (2005, 25ff.).

11. In fact, Habermas aimed at showing that the moral principle is not only contained in the presuppositions of rational discourse but actually derives from them. This reduction of morality to the rational presuppositions of discourse, however, has rightly been criticized and rejected (e.g., Benhabib 1992, 23ff.; Maak 1999, 127ff.). The principle of equal moral respect and concern and thus the substantive equality of human beings must be regarded as inherently prior to the formal criteria of rational discourse. Hence the presuppositions contain strong ethical assumptions that precede the moral argument itself (Benhabib 1992, 29). Habermas's rational norms are thus to be interpreted as a reflexive reconstruction of preexisting relationships based on mutual recognition (Maak 1999, 128). Therefore, they provide an explication of the moral principle but not, however, its constitutive foundation.

12. For a specific and detailed account of communitarian rejection of the libertarian self, see Michael Sandel's (1982) critique of Rawls's theory of justice.

13. For an analysis of the substantive differences between statism and nationalism, see B. Barry (1999).

14. For overviews and further discussion of these and other arguments against cosmopolitanism, see, for example, C. Jones (1999), Caney (2001, 118ff.), Gosepath (2001), and Cabrera (2004).

15. Appiah (1996, 27) disagrees with this insight. In fact, he claims that if anything, it is the nation and not the state that is morally arbitrary, because all nations that are not coterminous with states today are, in his opinion, the legacy of older state arrangements. Even if this were true, however, it would not change the fact that statism does not have a theory about how boundaries should be drawn; it would simply refute the argument that nationalism does have one.

16. For an overview of the *Human Development Report*'s history and the concepts developed in it, as well as the idea of human development in general, see Mahbub ul Haq's *Reflections on Human Development* (1999).

17. For further elaboration of these categories, see Sen (1985b, 1993) or Fukada-Parr (2003).

18. For an extended defense of Sen's notion against this criticism, see Pettit (2001).

19. See the section "Human Rights as Principles of Minimal Justice" in this chapter on the definition of the term *basic*.

20. The notion of empowerment makes one important thing clear: development is not only a right but also a responsibility of its subjects. Kant rightly notes in the second book of *The Metaphysics of Morals* (1996, 154f.) that the "cultivation," that is, the development, of one's capacities is not only "an end" but also a duty. Understanding development as an empowerment process aims precisely at enabling human beings to discharge their own responsibility for development. Hence empowering human beings actively to take responsibility for their own development is quite different from fostering dependencies through passive and potentially limitless (predominantly financial) development aid.

21. Ulrich's framework does not contain such a global dimension. On the contrary, development is presented as a process that happens exclusively within the borders of a particular country. Accordingly, the external aspect of capabilities in his conception is given by national public policies and laws, as well as the "public infrastructure *of the state*" (Ulrich 2004a, 12; emphasis added, translation by the author). Such a conception might work for a contained national society in the Rawlsian sense. However, it fails to capture adequately our global reality and accordingly to realize the cosmopolitan ideal put forth in this book.

Chapter 3

1. For a critical examination of this "principle of alternate possibilities," see Frankfurt (1969, 1993) and Stump (1993).

2. This categorization of three kinds of moral action plus morally indifferent acts is slightly different from the one presented by James Fishkin (1982, 10ff.). Fishkin differentiates between a "zone of moral indifference" in which the individual can literally do as it pleases, a "zone of moral requirement" that is the zone of moral duties, and a "zone of supererogation" that contains those things we ought to do but that we are not blameworthy for failing to do. He thus distinguishes between indifferent acts, supererogatory acts, and required acts, whereas my categorization differentiates between morally owed acts, morally required acts, and supererogatory acts.

3. Grotius (1925, 330f.) speaks of "perfect promises" where they create a right for the second party to claim what is promised. He contrasts such perfect promises with moral obligations that give no right to the other party (such as, for example, the duty of having mercy and showing gratitude). Similarly, Grotius speaks of perfect rights if they are enforceable by legal process and of imperfect rights if they are not enforceable (Edmundson 2004, 20).

4. For in-depth elaborations on the public funding and support necessary to ensure the protection and enforcement of such rights, see Holmes and Sunstein's analysis in *The Cost of Rights* (1999), as well as Nickel (1987, 120ff.).

5. Parts of this section are adapted from my earlier article "Let's Talk Rights: Messages for the Just Corporation—Transforming the Economy Through the Language of

Rights," in *Journal of Business Ethics* 78/1 (2008): 247–263. With kind permission of Springer Science and Business Media.

6. Thomas Pogge (2001a, 14f.) identifies three general morally significant connections between us and the global poor: "First, their social starting positions and ours have emerged from a single historical process that was pervaded by massive grievous wrongs. The same historical injustices, including genocide, colonialism, and slavery, play a role in explaining both their poverty and our affluence. Second, they and we depend on a single natural resource base, from the benefits of which they are largely, and without compensation, excluded. [. . .] Third, they and we co-exist within a single global economic order that has a strong tendency to perpetuate and even to aggravate global economic inequality. Given these connections, our failure to make a serious effort toward poverty reduction may constitute [. . .] our active impoverishing, starving, and killing of millions of innocent people by economic means."

7. Fishkin's expression is (intentionally) contradictory. Heroism is commonly perceived as going beyond what one is morally obliged to do. We cannot be blamed for not being heroes, but we might be admired for heroic behavior. Heroism is thus more than merely doing one's duty; it is supererogatory, not obligatory (Fishkin 1982, 5). For Singer, the distinction between obligations and heroic acts is entirely meaningless. Heroism does not exist in utilitarianism. From a utilitarian perspective, every act that will result in more good than any alternative act is morally demanded and thus is not to be considered heroic. For further elaborations on heroism, see French (1992, 111ff.).

8. Kant stated for his virtue-based account of obligation, "How far should one expend one's resources in practicing beneficence? Surely not to the extent that he himself would finally come to need the beneficence of others" (Kant 1996, 202).

Chapter 6

1. See Grossman and Adams (1993) or Benson (2000) for in-depth elaborations on corporate charters, their history, and their relevance for our understanding of "private" business today.

Chapter 7

1. See http://www.eulobbytours.org/ for more information on corporate lobbying in the European Union.

Chapter 8

1. See Waddock (2004) for a systematic overview of the key terms used.

2. For a more detailed elaboration of the difference between legitimacy and acceptance, see Thielemann (2003), Thielemann and Ulrich (2003, 19ff.), and Ulrich (2008, 400).

3. See Ulrich (2001b) and Thielemann (2003, 2004a) on the concept of earned reputation.

4. This lack of a political-philosophical basis on which to reflect on the fundamental role and purpose of the corporation within society at large is a general characteristic and shortcoming of most stakeholder approaches.

Chapter 9

1. "Clear Thinking in Troubled Times," SPDC Press Statement, October 31, 1995, quoted in Human Rights Watch (1999b).

2. Statement by Mr. Brian Anderson, Managing Director, The Shell Petroleum Development Company of Nigeria Limited, SPDC Press Release, November 8, 1995, quoted in Human Rights Watch (1999b).

3. E. Imomoh, General Manager, Eastern Division, Shell Petroleum, on *Africa Express*, Channel 4 TV, UK, April 18, 1996, quoted in Avery (2000, 22).

4. For a general, balanced assessment of positive and negative aspects of FDI and multinationals in developing nations, see Lall and Streeten (1977). Also, see Smith, Bolyard, and Ippolito (1999) for a specific critique of Meyer's thesis, with particular emphasis on his underlying empirical data.

5. Such public-private interactions at the global public policy level can have very different shapes and implications. However, they are usually all referred to as public-private partnerships. This generalization has led to widespread and justified criticism (e.g., Martens 2003; Zammit 2003, 51ff.; Richter 2004), mostly because it trivializes the far-reaching implications of the term *partnership* for the division of risk, responsibility, or rights and duties between the partners.

6. "Blue-washing" derives from the term *green-washing*, which was initially used to mock corporate lip service paid to environmental protection. The term is an allusion to the official UN color. For an in-depth analysis of criticism of the UN Global Compact, see Waddock and Wettstein (2006).

Chapter 10

1. For further elaboration on this distinction, see Kuper (2004, 68ff.).

References

ABB. 2006. Reply of ABB to "Divest Sudan" Campaign. Human Rights Resource Centre, April 20. http://www.reports-and-materials.org/ABB-Sudan-reply-20-Apr-2006.doc.

Addo, Michael K. 1999. The Corporation as a Victim of Human Rights Violations. In *Human Rights Standards and the Responsibility of Transnational Corporations*, ed. Michael K. Addo, 187–196. The Hague; London; Boston: Kluwer Law International.

Albrow, Martin. 1997. *The Global Age: State and Society Beyond Modernity*. Stanford, CA: Stanford University Press.

Alston, Philip. 2005. The "Not-a-Cat" Syndrome: Can the International Human Rights Regime Accommodate Non-state Actors? In *Non-state Actors and Human Rights*, ed. Philip Alston, 3–36. Oxford; New York: Oxford University Press.

Alston, Philip, and Mary Robinson. 2005. The Challenges of Ensuring the Mutuality of Human Rights and Development Endeavours. In *Human Rights and Development: Towards Mutual Reinforcement*, ed. Philip Alston and Mary Robinson, 1–19. Oxford; New York: Oxford University Press.

Amnesty International. 2004. *The UN Human Rights Norms for Business: Toward Legal Accountability*. London: Amnesty International Publications. http://web.amnesty.org/aidoc/aidoc_pdf.nsf/Index/IOR420022004ENGLISH/$File/IOR4200204.pdf.

Anderson, Sarah, and John Cavanagh. 2000. *Top 200: The Rise of Corporate Global Power*. Washington, DC: Institute for Policy Studies.

Angell, Marcia. 2004. *The Truth About the Drug Companies: How They Deceive Us and What to Do About It*. New York: Random House.

Annese, Lucius. 1978. *The Purpose of Authority? A Recent Emphasis in American Political Thought in the United States and in American Churches*. Andover, MA: Charisma Press.

Apel, Karl-Otto. 1996. Limits of Discourse Ethics? An Attempt at a Provisional Assessment. In *Karl-Otto Apel: Selected Essays*. Vol. 2, *Ethics and the Theory of*

Rationality, ed. Eduardo Mendieta, 192–218. Atlantic Highlands, NJ: Humanities Press.

Appiah, Kwame A. 1996. Cosmopolitan Patriots. In *For Love of Country: Debating the Limits of Patriotism*, ed. Martha C. Nussbaum and Joshua Cohen, 21–29. Boston: Beacon Press.

Archibugi, Daniele. 1995. From the United Nations to Cosmopolitan Democracy. In *Cosmopolitan Democracy: An Agenda for a New World Order*, ed. Daniele Archibugi and David Held, 121–162. Cambridge, UK: Polity Press.

Archibugi, Daniele. 1998. Principles of Cosmopolitan Democracy. In *Re-imagining Political Community: Studies in Cosmopolitan Democracy*, ed. Daniele Archibugi, David Held, and Martin Köhler, 198–228. Cambridge, UK: Polity Press.

Archibugi, Daniele. 2003. Cosmopolitical Democracy. In *Debating Cosmopolitics*, ed. Daniele Archibugi, 1–15. London; New York: Verso.

Arendt, Hannah. 1969. *On Violence*. New York: Harcourt, Brace & World.

Arendt, Hannah. 1998. *The Human Condition*. Chicago; London: University of Chicago Press.

Aristotle. 1980. *The Nicomachean Ethics*. Transl. David Ross. Oxford; New York: Oxford University Press.

Avery, Christopher L. 2000. *Business and Human Rights in a Time of Change*. London: Amnesty International UK.

Bagdikian, Ben H. 2004. *The New Media Monopoly*. Boston: Beacon Press.

Bakan, Joel. 2004. *The Corporation: The Pathological Pursuit of Profit and Power*. New York: Free Press.

Banerjee, Neela. 2001. Lawsuit Says Exxon Aided Rights Abuses. *New York Times*, June 21.

Barnet, Richard J., and Ronald E. Müller. 1974. *Global Reach: The Power of the Multinational Corporations*. New York: Simon and Schuster.

Barry, Brian. 1989. *Theories of Justice*. Berkeley; Los Angeles: University of California Press.

Barry, Brian. 1995. *Justice as Impartiality*. Oxford: Clarendon Press.

Barry, Brian. 1999. Statism and Nationalism: A Cosmopolitan Critique. In *Nomos XLI: Global Justice*, ed. Ian Shapiro and Lea Brilmayer, 12–66. New York; London: New York University Press.

Barry, Christian. 2005. Applying the Contribution Principle. In *Global Responsibilities: Who Must Deliver on Human Rights?* ed. Andrew Kuper, 135–152. New York; London: Routledge.

Barstow, David. 2004. Security Companies: Shadow Soldiers in Iraq. *New York Times*, April 19.

Bartlett, Christopher A., and Sumantra Ghoshal. 1991. *Managing Across Borders: The Transnational Solution*. Boston: Harvard Business School Press.

Bauman, Zygmunt. 1998. *Globalization: The Human Consequences*. New York: Columbia University Press.

Bay, Christian. 1982. Self-Respect as a Human Right: Thoughts on the Dialectics of Wants and Needs in the Struggle for Human Community. *Human Rights Quarterly* 4/1: 53–75.

Beck, Ulrich. 1988. *Gegengifte: Die organisierte Unverantwortlichkeit.* Frankfurt a. M.: Suhrkamp.

Beck, Ulrich. 2000. *What Is Globalization?* Malden, MA: Polity Press.

Beck, Ulrich. 2003. Toward a New Critical Theory with a Cosmopolitan Intent. *Constellations* 10/4: 453–468.

Beck, Ulrich. 2006. *The Cosmopolitan Vision.* Cambridge, UK: Polity Press.

Beitz, Charles R. 1999a. *Political Theory and International Relations.* Princeton, NJ: Princeton University Press.

Beitz, Charles R. 1999b. Social and Cosmopolitan Liberalism. *International Affairs* 75/3: 515–529.

Benhabib, Seyla. 1992. *Situating the Self: Gender, Community, and Postmodernism in Contemporary Ethics.* New York: Routledge.

Benhabib, Seyla. 1996. Toward a Deliberative Model of Democratic Legitimacy. In *Democracy and Difference: Contesting the Boundaries of the Political,* ed. Seyla Benhabib, 67–94. Princeton, NJ: Princeton University Press.

Benner, Thorsten, and Wolfgang H. Reinicke. 1999. Politik im globalen Netz: Globale Politiknetzwerke und die Herausforderung offener Systeme. *Internationale Politik* 8: 25–32.

Benner, Thorsten, Wolfgang H. Reinicke, and Jan M. Witte. 2004. Multisectoral Networks in Global Governance: Towards a Pluralistic System of Accountability. *Government and Opposition* 39/2: 191–204.

Benner, Thorsten, Charlotte Streck, and Jan M. Witte. 2003. The Road from Johannesburg: What Future for Partnerships in Global Environmental Governance? In *Progress or Peril? Networks and Partnerships in Global Environmental Governance: The Post-Johannesburg Agenda,* ed. Jan M. Witte, Charlotte Streck, and Thorsten Benner, 59–84. Berlin; Washington, DC: Global Public Policy Institute.

Benson, Robert W. 2000. *Challenging Corporate Rule: The Petition to Revoke Unocal's Charter as a Guide to Citizen Action.* Croton-on-Hudson, NY: Apex Press.

Bentham, Jeremy. 2002. *Rights, Representation, and Reform: Nonsense upon Stilts and Other Writings on the French Revolution. The Collected Works of Jeremy Bentham.* Ed. Philip Schofield, Catherine Pease-Watkin, and Cyprian Blamires. Oxford: Clarendon Press.

Berghoff, Hartmut. 2004. *Moderne Unternehmensgeschichte: Eine themen- und theorieorientierte Einführung.* Paderborn; Munich; Vienna; Zurich: Ferdinand Schöningh.

Berle, Adolf A. 1967. *Power.* New York: Harcourt, Brace & World.

Berle, Adolf A., and Gardiner C. Means. 1991. *The Modern Corporation and Private Property.* New Brunswick, NJ; London: Transaction Publishers.

Berlin, Isaiah. 1969. Two Concepts of Liberty. In *Four Essays on Liberty,* ed. Isaiah Berlin, 118–172. Oxford; New York: Oxford University Press.

Bianchi, Stefania. 2005. Corporate Lobbyists in EU Face Closer Scrutiny. *Inter Press Service*, July 20.

Birnbaum, Jeffrey H. 2005. The Road to Riches Is Called K-Street: Lobbying Firms Hire More, Pay More, Charge More to Influence Government. *Washington Post*, June 22.

BLIHR. 2003. *Report 1: Building Understanding*. London; Amsterdam: Business Leaders Initiative on Human Rights.

Boddewyn, Jean J., and Thomas L. Brewer. 1994. International-Business Political Behavior: New Theoretical Directions. *Academy of Management Review* 19/1: 119–143.

Bodin, Jean. 1962. *The Six Bookes of a Commonweale*. Ed. Kenneth D. McRae. Cambridge, MA: Harvard University Press.

Bowie, Norman. 1999. *Business Ethics: A Kantian Perspective*. Malden, MA: Blackwell Publishers.

Bowman, Scott R. 1996. *The Modern Corporation and American Political Thought: Law, Power, and Ideology*. University Park: Pennsylvania State University Press.

Boxill, Bernard. 1987. Global Equality of Opportunity and National Integrity. *Social Philosophy and Policy* 5/1: 143–168.

Brinkman, Richard L., and June E. Brinkman. 2002. Corporate Power and the Globalization Process. *International Journal of Social Economics* 29/9: 730–752.

Brown, Chris. 1992. *International Relations Theory: New Normative Approaches*. New York: Columbia University Press.

Brundtland, Gro H. 2002. Address by Dr. Gro Harlem Brundtland, Director-General, to the Fifty-fifth World Health Assembly, May 13, World Health Organization, Geneva, Switzerland. http://www.who.int/directorgeneral/speeches/2002/english/20020513_addresstothe55WHA.html.

Bruno, Kenny, and Joshua Karliner. 2000. *Tangled Up in Blue: Corporate Partnerships at the United Nations*. San Francisco: TRAC–Transnational Resource and Action Center and Corp Watch.

Buchanan, Allen. 1990. Justice as Reciprocity Versus Subject-Centered Justice. *Philosophy and Public Affairs* 19/3: 227–253.

Buchanan, Allen. 1993. The Morality of Inclusion. In *Liberalism and the Economic Order*, ed. Ellen F. Paul, Fred D. Miller, and Jeffrey Paul, 233–257. Cambridge, UK: Cambridge University Press.

Buchanan, Allen E. 1989. Assessing the Communitarian Critique of Liberalism. *Ethics* 99/4: 852–882.

Buchanan, James M. 1985. *Liberty, Market, and State: Political Economy in the 1980s*. New York: New York University Press.

Buckley, Peter J., and Mark Casson. 1976. *The Future of the Multinational Enterprise*. London; Basingstoke, UK: Macmillan Press.

Bull, Hedley. 1966. The Grotian Conception of International Society. In *Diplomatic Investigations*, ed. Herbert Butterfield and Martin Wight, 51–73. London: George Allen & Unwin.

Burke, Edmund. 2003. *Reflections on the Revolution in France*. Ed. Frank M. Turner. New Haven, CT; London: Yale University Press.

Buse, Kent, and Amalia Waxman. 2001. Public-Private Health Partnerships: A Strategy for WHO. *Bulletin of the World Health Organization* 79/8: 748–754.

Business Week. 2000. Too Much Corporate Power? *Business Week*, September 11: 144–158.

Cabrera, Luis. 2004. *Political Theory of Global Justice: A Cosmopolitan Case for the World State*. London; New York: Routledge.

Caney, Simon. 2001. Cosmopolitan Justice and Equalizing Opportunities. *Metaphilosophy* 32/1–2: 113–134.

Caney, Simon. 2005. *Justice Beyond Borders: A Global Political Theory*. Oxford; New York: Oxford University Press.

Caporaso, James A., and Stephan Haggard. 1989. Power in the International Political Economy. In *Power in World Politics*, ed. Richard J. Stoll and Michael D. Ward, 99–120. Boulder, CO; London: Lynne Rienner Publishers.

Carroll, Archie B. 1979. A Three-Dimensional Conceptual Model of Corporate Performance. *Academy of Management Review* 4/4: 497–505.

Carroll, Archie B. 1998. The Four Faces of Corporate Citizenship. *Business and Society Review* 100/101: 1–7.

Carroll, Archie B., and Ann K. Buchholtz. 2003. *Business and Society: Ethics and Stakeholder Management*. Mason, OH: South-Western College Publishing.

Cavanagh, John, and Jerry Mander, eds. 2004. *Alternatives to Economic Globalization*. San Francisco: Berrett-Koehler.

Cerny, Philip G. 1990. *The Changing Architecture of Politics: Structure, Agency, and the Future of the State*. London: Sage Publications.

Cerny, Philip G. 1995. Globalization and the Changing Logic of Collective Action. *International Organization* 49/4: 595–625.

Chandler, Alfred D. 2002. *The Visible Hand: The Managerial Revolution in American Business*. Cambridge, MA; London: Harvard University Press.

Chandler, David. 2003. New Rights for Old? Cosmopolitan Citizenship and the Critique of State Sovereignty. *Political Studies* 51: 332–349.

Chandler, Geoffrey. 1999. Keynote Address: Crafting a Human Rights Agenda for Business. In *Human Rights Standards and the Responsibility of Transnational Corporations*, ed. Michael K. Addo, 39–45. The Hague; London; Boston: Kluwer Law International.

Chen, Lincoln C., Tim G. Evans, and Richard A. Cash. 1999. Health as a Global Public Good. In *Global Public Goods: International Cooperation in the 21st Century*, ed. Inge Kaul, Isabelle Grunberg, and Marc A. Stern, 284–304. New York; Oxford: Oxford University Press.

Chomsky, Noam. 1999. *Profit over People: Neoliberalism and Global Order*. New York; Toronto; London: Seven Stories Press.

Clapham, Andrew. 2004. State Responsibility, Corporate Responsibility, and Complicity in Human Rights Violations. In *Responsibility in World Business: Managing*

Harmful Side-Effects of Corporate Activity, ed. Lene Bomann-Larsen and Oddny Wiggen, 50–81. Tokyo; New York; Paris: United Nations University Press.

Clapham, Andrew, and Scott Jerbi. 2001. Categories of Corporate Complicity in Human Rights Abuses. *Hastings International and Comparative Law Review* 24: 339–350.

Cohen, Gerard A. 1988. Freedom, Justice, and Capitalism. In *History, Labor, and Freedom*, ed. Gerard A. Cohen, 286–304. Oxford: Clarendon Press.

Cohen, Gerard A. 1989. On the Currency of Egalitarian Justice. *Ethics* 99/4: 906–944.

Cohen, Gerard A. 1993. Equality of What? On Welfare, Goods, and Capabilities. In *The Quality of Life*, ed. Martha Nussbaum and Amartya Sen, 9–29. Oxford: Clarendon Press.

Cohen, Gerard A. 1997. Where the Action Is: On the Site of Distributive Justice. *Philosophy and Public Affairs* 26/1: 3–30.

Cohen, Joshua. 1996. Procedure and Substance in Deliberative Democracy. In *Democracy and Difference: Contesting the Boundaries of the Political*, ed. Seyla Benhabib, 95–119. Princeton, NJ: Princeton University Press.

Commission of the European Communities. 2006. Communication from the Commission to the European Parliament, the Council and the European Economic and Social Committee: Implementing the Partnership for Growth and Jobs; Making Europe a Pole of Excellence on Corporate Social Responsibility. Brussels, March 22. http://www.jussper.org/Resources/Corporate%20Activity/Resources/IMPLEMENTINGPARTNERSHIPJOBS.pdf.

Cooper, David E. 1991. Collective Responsibility. In *Collective Responsibility: Five Decades of Debate in Theoretical and Applied Ethics*, ed. Larry May and Stacey Hoffman, 35–46. Savage, MD: Rowman & Littlefield Publishers. Originally published in *Philosophy: The Journal of the Royal Institute of Philosophy* 43/65 (1968).

Corporate Europe Observatory. 2005. *Brussels the EU Quarter: Explore the Corporate Lobbying Paradise*. Amsterdam: Corporate Europe Observatory. http://www.corporateeurope.org/docs/lobbycracy/lobbyplanet.pdf.

Cortina, Adela. 1992. Ethik ohne Moral: Grenzen einer postkantischen Prinzipienethik? In *Zur Anwendung der Diskursethik in Politik, Recht und Wissenschaft*, ed. Karl-Otto Apel and Matthias Kettner, 278–295. Frankfurt a. M.: Suhrkamp.

Cox, Robert. 1985. Social Forces, States and World Orders: Beyond International Relations Theory. In *Neorealism and Its Critics*, ed. Robert O. Keohane, 204–254. New York: Columbia University Press.

Credit Suisse Group. 2004. *Sustainability 2004*. Zurich: Credit Suisse Group. http://www.creditsuisse.com/investors/doc/csg_sr_2004_en.pdf.

Crook, Clive 2005. The Good Company: A Survey of Corporate Social Responsibility. *Economist*, January 22.

Currie, David. 1999. The Global Corporation: Sharing the Regulatory Responsibility. *Business Strategy Review* 10/2: 19–24.

Cutler, A. Claire. 1999a. Locating "Authority" in the Global Political Economy. *International Studies Quarterly* 43/1: 59–81.

Cutler, A. Claire. 1999b. Private Authority in International Trade Relations: The Case of Maritime Transport. In *Private Authority and International Affairs*, ed. A. Claire Cutler, Virginia Haufler, and Tony Porter, 283–332. Albany: State University of New York Press.

Cutler, A. Claire. 2002. Private International Regimes and Interfirm Cooperation. In *The Emergence of Private Authority in Global Governance*, ed. Rodney B. Hall and Thomas J. Biersteker, 23–40. Cambridge, UK: Cambridge University Press.

Danaher, Kevin, and Jason Mark. 2003. *Insurrection: Citizen Challenges to Corporate Power*. New York; London: Routledge.

David, Wilfred L. 2004. *The Humanitarian Development Paradigm: Search for Global Justice*. Lanham, MD; Boulder, CO; New York; Toronto; Oxford: University Press of America.

Davies, Robert, and Jane Nelson. 2003. The Buck Stops Where? Managing the Boundaries of Business Engagement in Global Development Challenges. IBLF Policy Paper 2003, no. 2. London: International Business Leaders Forum.

De Greiff, Pablo, and Ciaran Cronin. 2002. Introduction: Normative Responses to Current Challenges of Global Governance. In *Global Justice and Transnational Politics: Essays on the Moral and Political Challenges of Globalization*, ed. Pablo De Greiff and Ciaran Cronin, 1–33. Cambridge, MA; London: MIT Press.

Derber, Charles. 1998. *Corporation Nation: How Corporations Are Taking Over Our Lives and What We Can Do About It*. New York: St. Martin's Griffin.

Derber, Charles. 2002. *People Before Profit: The New Globalization in an Age of Terror, Big Money, and Economic Crisis*. New York: St. Martin's Griffin.

Dicken, Peter. 1998. *Global Shift: Transforming the World Economy*. New York; London: Guilford Press.

Donaldson, Thomas. 1996. Values in Tension: Ethics away from Home. *Harvard Business Review* 74/5: 48–62.

Donnelly, Jack. 1985a. *The Concept of Human Rights*. New York: St. Martin's Press.

Donnelly, Jack. 1985b. Human Rights and Development: Complementary or Competing Concerns? In *Human Rights and Third World Development*, ed. George W. Shepherd Jr. and Ved P. Nanda, 27–55. Westport, CT; London: Greenwood Press.

Donnelly, Jack 2003. *Universal Rights in Theory and Practice*. Ithaca, NY; London: Cornell University Press.

Doremus, Paul N., William M. Keller, Louis W. Pauly, and Simon Reich. 1998. *The Myth of the Global Corporation*. Princeton, NJ: Princeton University Press.

Dornbusch, Rudiger. 2000. *Keys to Prosperity: Free Markets, Sound Money, and a Bit of Luck*. Cambridge, MA; London: MIT Press.

Drucker, Peter F. 1949. *The New Society: The Anatomy of the Industrial Order*. New York: Harper & Row.

Drucker, Peter F. 1989. *The New Realities: In Government and Politics, in Economics and Business, in Society and World View*. New York: Harper & Row.

Drucker, Peter F. 1993. *Concept of the Corporation*. New Brunswick, NJ; London: Transaction Publishers.

Drucker, Peter F. 1994. *The Post-capitalist Society*. New York: HarperBusiness.

Drucker, Peter F. 1997. The Global Economy and the Nation-State. *Foreign Affairs* 76/5: 159–171.

Drugs for Neglected Diseases Working Group (DNDWG). 2001. *Fatal Imbalance: The Crisis in Research and Development for Drugs for Tropical Diseases*. Geneva: Médecins sans Frontières and Drugs for Neglected Diseases Working Group. http://www.msf.org/source/access/2001/fatal/fatal.pdf.

Dunfee, Thomas W., and David Hess. 2000. The Legitimacy of Direct Corporate Humanitarian Investment. *Business Ethics Quarterly* 10/1: 95–109.

Dworkin, Ronald. 1977. *Taking Rights Seriously*. Cambridge, MA: Harvard University Press.

Dworkin, Ronald. 1984. Rights as Trumps. In *Theories of Rights*, ed. Jeremy Waldron, 153–167. Oxford; New York: Oxford University Press.

Dworkin, Ronald. 1985. Liberalism. In *A Matter of Principle*, 181–204. Cambridge, MA: Harvard University Press.

Dworkin, Ronald. 2000. *Sovereign Virtue: The Theory and Practice of Equality*. Cambridge, MA: Harvard University Press.

EarthRights International. 2008. Royal Dutch Shell to Go to Trial for Complicity in Torture and Murder of Nigerian Protesters. October 8. http://www.earthrights.org/content/view/578/41/.

Economist. 1999. Rupert Laid Bare. *Economist*, March 18.

Economist. 2005. Into Africa: Can South Africa Ride the Outsourcing and Offshoring Wave? *Economist*, August 27.

Edmundson, William A. 2004. *An Introduction to Rights*. Cambridge, UK; New York: Cambridge University Press.

Edwards, Michael, and Simon Zadek. 2003. Governing the Provision of Global Public Goods: The Role and Legitimacy of Nonstate Actors. In *Providing Global Public Goods: Managing Globalization*, ed. Inge Kaul, Pedro Conceição, Katell Le Goulven, and Ronald U. Mendoza, 200–224. New York; Oxford: Oxford University Press.

Elster, Jon. 1982. Sour Grapes—Utilitarianism and the Genesis of Wants. In *Utilitarianism and Beyond*, ed. Amartya Sen and Bernard Williams, 219–249. Cambridge, UK: Cambridge University Press.

Elster, Jon. 1983. *Sour Grapes: Studies in the Subversion of Rationality*. Cambridge, UK: Cambridge University Press.

Eucken, Walter. 1932. Staatliche Strukturwandlungen und die Krise des Kapitalismus. *Weltwirtschaftliches Archiv* 84: 297–331.

Feinberg, Joel. 1973. *Social Philosophy*. Englewood Cliffs, NJ: Prentice-Hall.

Feinberg, Joel. 1980. *Rights, Justice, and the Bounds of Liberty: Essays in Social Philosophy*. Princeton, NJ: Princeton University Press.

Feinberg, Joel. 1988. *Harmless Wrongdoing*. New York: Oxford University Press.

Feinberg, Joel. 1991. Collective Responsibility. In *Collective Responsibility: Five Decades of Debate in Theoretical and Applied Ethics*, ed. Larry May and Stacey Hoffman, 53–71. Savage, MD: Rowman & Littlefield Publishers. Originally published in Joel Feinberg, *Doing and Deserving: Essays in the Theory of Responsibility* (Princeton, NJ: Princeton University Press, 1970).

Fields, A. Belden. 2003. *Rethinking Human Rights for the New Millennium*. New York; Houndsmills, Basingstoke, Hampshire, UK: Palgrave Macmillan.

Fishkin, James S. 1982. *The Limits of Obligation*. New Haven, CT; London: Yale University Press.

Fiszbein, Ariel, and Pamela Lowden. 1999. *Working Together for a Change: Government, Civic, and Business Partnerships for Poverty Reduction in Latin America and the Caribbean*. Washington, DC: World Bank.

Fletcher, George P. 1993. *Loyalty: An Essay on the Morality of Relationships*. Oxford: Oxford University Press.

Forcese, Craig. 1997. *Putting Conscience into Commerce: Strategies for Making Human Rights Business as Usual*. Montreal: International Centre for Human Rights and Democratic Development.

Forcese, Craig. 2000. Deterring "Militarized Commerce": The Prospect of Liability for "Privatized" Human Rights Abuses. *Ottawa Law Review* 31: 171–211.

Forcese, Craig. 2001. ATCA's Achilles Heel: Corporate Complicity, International Law and the Alien Tort Claims Act. *Yale Journal of International Law* 26: 487–515.

Frankena, William K. 1973. *Ethics*. Englewood Cliffs, NJ: Prentice-Hall.

Frankfurt, Harry. 1969. Alternate Possibilities and Moral Responsibility. *Journal of Philosophy* 66/23: 829–839.

Frankfurt, Harry. 1993. What We Are Morally Responsible For. In *Perspectives on Moral Responsibility*, ed. John M. Fischer and Mark Ravizza, 286–295. Ithaca, NY; London: Cornell University Press.

Frankfurt, Harry. 1997. Equality and Respect. *Social Research* 64/1: 3–15.

Frankfurt, Harry. 2000. Gleichheit und Achtung. In *Gleichheit oder Gerechtigkeit: Texte der neuen Egalitarismuskritik*, ed. Angelika Krebs, 38–49. Frankfurt a. M.: Suhrkamp.

Fraser, Nancy. 1997. *Justice Interruptus: Critical Reflections on the "Postsocialist" Condition*. New York; London: Routledge.

Fraser, Nancy, and Axel Honneth. 2003. *Redistribution or Recognition? A Political-Philosophical Exchange*. London; New York: Verso.

Freeman, Michael. 1994. The Philosophical Foundations of Human Rights. *Human Rights Quarterly* 16/3: 491–514.

French, Peter A. 1984. *Collective and Corporate Responsibility*. New York: Columbia University Press.

French, Peter A. 1991. The Corporation as a Moral Person. In *Collective Responsibility: Five Decades of Debate in Theoretical and Applied Ethics*, ed. Larry May and Stacey Hoffman, 133–149. Savage, MD: Rowman & Littlefield Publishers. Originally published in *American Philosophical Quarterly* 16/3 (1979).

French, Peter A. 1992. *Responsibility Matters.* Lawrence: University Press of Kansas.

Frey, Bruno S. 1984. *International Political Economics.* New York: Basil Blackwell.

Friedman, Milton. 1962. *Capitalism and Freedom.* Chicago; London: University of Chicago Press.

Friedman, Milton. 1970. The Social Responsibility of Business Is to Increase Its Profits. *New York Times Magazine,* September 13.

Friedman, Richard B. 1990. On the Concept of Authority in Political Philosophy. In *Authority,* ed. Joseph Raz, 56–91. New York: New York University Press.

Friedman, Thomas L. 2000. *The Lexus and the Olive Tree.* New York: Anchor Books.

Fukada-Parr, Sakiko. 2003. The Human Development Paradigm: Operationalizing Sen's Ideas on Capabilities. *Feminist Economics* 9/2–3: 301–317.

Fukada-Parr, Sakiko, and Ruth Hill. 2002. The Network Age: Creating New Models of Technical Cooperation. In *Capacity for Development: New Solutions to Old Problems,* ed. Sakiko Fukada-Parr, Carlos Lopes, and Khalid Malik, 183–201. London; Sterling, VA: Earthscan Publications.

Fukuyama, Francis. 1992. *The End of History and the Last Man.* New York: Free Press.

Galbraith, John K. 1952. *American Capitalism: The Concept of Countervailing Power.* Boston: Houghton Mifflin.

Galbraith, John K. 1973. *Economics and the Public Purpose.* Boston: Houghton Mifflin.

Galbraith, John K. 1977. *The Age of Uncertainty.* Boston: Houghton Mifflin.

Galbraith, John K. 1996. *The Good Society: The Humane Agenda.* Boston; New York: Houghton Mifflin.

Galbraith, John K. 2001. The Proper Purpose of Economic Development. In *The Essential Galbraith,* ed. John K. Galbraith and Andrea D. Williams, 109–117. Boston; New York: Houghton Mifflin. Originally published in John K. Galbraith, *Economics, Peace, and Laughter* (Boston: Houghton Mifflin, 1971).

Galbraith, John K. 2004. *The Economics of Innocent Fraud: Truth for Our Time.* Boston; New York: Houghton Mifflin.

Galtung, Johan. 1994. *Human Rights in Another Key.* Cambridge, UK: Polity Press.

Garred, Jason. 2004. Offshore Finance, Onshore Compliance. GPF Major Policy Papers 30. http://www.globalpolicy.org/publications/majorpapers.htm.

Garrett, Geoffrey. 2000. Global Markets and National Politics. In *The Global Transformation Reader: An Introduction to the Globalization Debate,* ed. David Held and Anthony McGrew, 301–318. Cambridge, UK; Malden, MA: Polity Press.

Garten, Jeffrey E. 2002. *The Politics of Fortune: A New Agenda for Business Leaders.* Boston: Harvard Business School Press.

Gauthier, David. 1986. *Morals by Agreement.* Oxford: Clarendon Press.

Gay, William C. 1997. The Violence of Domination and the Power of Nonviolence. In *Philosophical Perspectives on Power and Domination: Theories and Practices,* ed. Laura D. Kaplan and Laurence F. Bove, 15–28. Amsterdam; Atlanta: Rodopi.

Geuss, Raymond. 2001. *History and Illusion in Politics*. Cambridge, UK: Cambridge University Press.

Gewirth, Alan. 1984. Are There Any Absolute Rights? In *Theories of Rights*, ed. Jeremy Waldron, 91–109. Oxford; New York: Oxford University Press. Originally published in *Philosophical Quarterly* 31 (1981).

Gewirth, Alan. 1996. *The Community of Rights*. Chicago; London: University of Chicago Press.

Giddens, Anthony. 2002. Introduction to *The Protestant Ethic and the Spirit of Capitalism*, by Max Weber, vii–xxiv. London; New York: Routledge.

Gilpin, Robert. 2000. *The Challenge of Global Capitalism: The World Economy in the 21st Century*. Princeton, NJ: Princeton University Press.

Gilpin, Robert. 2001. *Global Political Economy: Understanding the International Economic Order*. Princeton, NJ: Princeton University Press.

Glazer, Nathan. 1996. Limits of Loyalty. In *For Love of Country: Debating the Limits of Patriotism*, ed. Martha C. Nussbaum and Joshua Cohen, 61–65. Boston: Beacon Press.

Glendon, Mary A. 1991. *Rights Talk: The Impoverishment of Political Discourse*. New York: Free Press.

Global Policy Forum. N.d. Multilateral Agreement on Investments and Related Initiatives. http://www.globalpolicy.org/socecon/bwi-wto/maimia/index.htm.

Gloub, Stephen. 2005. Less Law and Reform, More Politics and Enforcement: A Civil Society Approach to Integrating Rights and Development. In *Human Rights and Development: Towards Mutual Reinforcement*, ed. Philip Alston and Mary Robinson, 297–324. Oxford; New York: Oxford University Press.

Goodin, Robert E. 1985. *Protecting the Vulnerable: A Reanalysis of Our Social Responsibilities*. Chicago; London: University of Chicago Press.

Goodpaster, Kenneth E. 1983. The Concept of Corporate Responsibility. *Journal of Business Ethics* 2/1: 1–22.

Goodpaster, Kenneth E. 1991. Business Ethics and Stakeholder Analysis. *Business Ethics Quarterly* 1/1: 52–71.

Gordimer, Nadine. 1989. *The Ultimate Safari*. London; New York: Granta.

Gosepath, Stefan. 2001. The Global Scope of Justice. *Metaphilosophy* 32/1–2: 135–159.

Gosepath, Stefan. 2003. Verteidigung egalitärer Gerechtigkeit. *Deutsche Zeitschrift für Philosophie* 51/2: 275–297.

Gosepath, Stefan. 2004. *Gleiche Gerechtigkeit: Grundlagen eines liberalen Egalitarismus*. Frankfurt a. M.: Suhrkamp.

Gould, Carol C. 2004. *Globalizing Democracy and Human Rights*. Cambridge, UK; New York: Cambridge University Press.

Graham, Edward M. 1996. *Global Corporations and National Governments*. Washington, DC: Institute for International Economics.

Gray, John. 1995. *Liberalism*. Minneapolis: University of Minnesota Press.

Gray, John. 1998. *False Dawn: The Delusions of Global Capitalism*. New York: New Press.

Green, Michael. 2005. Institutional Responsibility for Moral Problems. In *Global Responsibilities: Who Must Deliver on Human Rights?* ed. Andrew Kuper, 117–133. New York; London: Routledge.

Green, Reginald H. 1981. Basic Human Rights/Needs: Some Problems of Categorical Translation and Unification. *Review of the International Commission of Jurists* 27: 53–58.

Greenpeace. N.d. Ken Saro-Wiwa's Closing Statement to the Nigerian Military Appointed Tribunal. http://archive.greenpeace.org/comms/ken/state.html.

Grossman, Richard L., and Frank T. Adams. 1993. *Taking Care of Business: Citizenship and the Charter of Incorporation.* Cambridge, MA: Charter Ink.

Grotius, Hugo. 1925. *De jure belli ac pacis libri tres.* Vol. 2. Oxford: Clarendon Press.

Habermas, Jürgen. 1977. Hannah Arendt's Communications Concept of Power. *Social Research* 44/1: 3–24.

Habermas, Jürgen. 1978. *Knowledge and Human Interests.* London: Heinemann.

Habermas, Jürgen. 1987. *The Theory of Communicative Action.* Vol. 2, *The Critique of Functionalist Reason.* Cambridge, UK: Blackwell Publishers.

Habermas, Jürgen. 1991. *Erläuterungen zur Diskursethik.* Frankfurt a. M.: Suhrkamp.

Habermas, Jürgen. 1995. Reconciliation Through the Public Use of Reason: Remarks on John Rawls' Political Liberalism. *Journal of Philosophy* 92/3: 109–131.

Habermas, Jürgen. 1996a. *Between Facts and Norms: Contributions to a Discourse Theory of Law and Democracy.* Cambridge, MA: MIT Press.

Habermas, Jürgen. 1996b. Three Normative Models of Democracy. In *Democracy and Difference: Contesting the Boundaries of the Political,* ed. Seyla Benhabib, 21–30. Princeton, NJ: Princeton University Press.

Habermas, Jürgen. 1998. *The Inclusion of the Other: Studies in Political Theory.* Cambridge, MA: MIT Press.

Habermas, Jürgen. 2002. On Legitimation Through Human Rights. In *Global Justice and Transnational Politics: Essays on the Moral and Political Challenges of Globalization,* ed. Pablo De Greiff and Ciaran Cronin, 197–214. Cambridge, MA; London: MIT Press.

Hall, Rodney B., and Thomas J. Biersteker. 2002. The Emergence of Private Authority in the International System. In *The Emergence of Private Authority in Global Governance,* ed. Rodney B. Hall and Thomas J. Biersteker, 3–22. Cambridge, UK: Cambridge University Press.

Hammond, Allen L., and C. K. Prahalad. 2004. Selling to the Poor. *Foreign Policy* 142: 30–37.

Haq, Mahbub ul. 1999. *Reflections on Human Development.* Delhi; Calcutta; Chennai; Mumbai: Oxford University Press.

Harris, David. 1987. *Justifying State Welfare: The New Right Versus the Old Left.* Oxford: Blackwell.

Hart, H. L. A. 1984. Are There Any Natural Rights? In *Theories of Rights,* ed. Jeremy Waldron, 77–90. Oxford; New York: Oxford University Press. Originally published in *Philosophical Review* 64 (1955).

Hart, Stuart L. 2005. *Capitalism at the Crossroads: The Unlimited Business Opportunities in Solving the World's Most Difficult Problems.* Upper Saddle River, NJ: Wharton School Publishing.

Harvard Law School Human Rights Program. 1999. *Business and Human Rights: An Interdisciplinary Discussion Held at Harvard Law School in December 1997.* Cambridge, MA: Harvard Law School Human Rights Program.

Harvey, David. 2007. *A Brief History of Neoliberalism.* Oxford; New York: Oxford University Press.

Haufler, Virginia. 2001. *A Public Role for the Private Sector: Industry Self-Regulation in a Global Economy.* Washington, DC: Carnegie Endowment for International Peace.

Hayek, Friedrich A. 1976. *The Mirage of Social Justice.* Chicago: University of Chicago Press.

Held, David. 1995a. Democracy and the New International Order. In *Cosmopolitan Democracy: An Agenda for a New World Order,* ed. Daniele Archibugi and David Held, 96–120. Cambridge, UK: Polity Press.

Held, David. 1995b. *Democracy and the Global Order: From the Modern State to Cosmopolitan Governance.* Stanford, CA: Stanford University Press.

Held, David. 2000. Regulating Globalization? In *The Global Transformation Reader: An Introduction to the Globalization Debate,* ed. David Held and Anthony McGrew, 420–430. Cambridge, UK; Malden, MA: Polity Press.

Held, David. 2004. *Global Covenant: The Social Democratic Alternative to the Washington Consensus.* Cambridge, UK; Malden, MA: Polity Press.

Held, Virginia. 1991. Can a Random Collection of Individuals Be Morally Responsible? In *Collective Responsibility: Five Decades of Debate in Theoretical and Applied Ethics,* ed. Larry May and Stacey Hoffman, 89–100. Savage, MD: Rowman & Littlefield Publishers. Originally published in *Journal of Philosophy* 68/14 (1970).

Herman, Barbara. 2002. The Scope of Moral Requirement. *Philosophy and Public Affairs* 30/3: 227–256.

Hertz, Noreena. 2001. *The Silent Takeover: Global Capitalism and the Death of Democracy.* London: William Heinemann.

Hertz, Noreena. 2004. Corporations on the Front Line. *Corporate Governance* 12/2: 202–209.

Hesburgh, Theodore M. 1982. The Capability for Unique Contributions. In *Multinational Managers and Poverty in the Third World,* ed. Lee A. Tavis, 94–101. Notre Dame, IN; London: University of Notre Dame Press.

Hinsch, Wilfried. 2002. *Gerechtfertigte Ungleichheiten: Grundsätze sozialer Gerechtigkeit.* Berlin; New York: Walter De Gruyter.

Hirst, Paul, and Grahame Thompson. 1999. *Globalization in Question: The International Economy and the Possibilities of Governance.* Malden, MA: Polity Press.

Höffe, Otfried. 2002a. Globalität statt Globalismus: Über eine subsidiäre und föderale Weltrepublik. In *Für und wider die Idee einer Weltrepublik,* ed. Matthias Lutz-Bachmann and James Bohman, 8–31. Frankfurt a. M.: Suhrkamp.

Höffe, Otfried. 2002b. *Politische Gerechtigkeit: Grundlegung einer kritischen Philosophie von Recht und Staat.* Frankfurt a. M.: Suhrkamp.

Höffe, Otfried. 2002c. *Demokratie im Zeitalter der Globalisierung.* Munich: C. H. Beck.

Höffe, Otfried. 2003. *Aristotle.* Albany: State University of New York Press.

Höffe, Otfried. 2004a. *Wirtschaftsbürger, Staatsbürger, Weltbürger: Politische Ethik im Zeitalter der Globalisierung.* Munich: C. H. Beck.

Höffe, Otfried. 2004b. *Gerechtigkeit: Eine philosophische Einführung.* Munich: C. H. Beck.

Holmes, Stephen, and Cass R. Sunstein. 1999. *The Cost of Rights: Why Liberty Depends on Taxes.* New York: W. W. Norton & Company.

Hout, Thomas, Michael E. Porter, and Eileen Rudden. 1998. How Global Companies Win Out. In *On Competition,* ed. Michael E. Porter, 289–308. Boston: Harvard Business School Press.

Howen, Nicholas. 2005a. Responsibility and Complicity from the Perspective of International Human Rights Law. In *The 2005 Business and Human Rights Seminar Report: Exploring Responsibility and Complicity,* ed. Matt Shinn, 12–15. London: Business & Human Rights Seminar Ltd.

Howen, Nicholas. 2005b. "Voluntary or Mandatory: That Is (Not) the Question": A Comment. *Zeitschrift für Wirtschafts- und Unternehmensethik* 6/3: 321–323.

Hsieh, Nien-he. 2004. The Obligations of Transnational Corporations: Rawlsian Justice and Duty of Assistance. *Business Ethics Quarterly* 14/4: 643–661.

Hu, Yao-Su. 1992. Global or Stateless Corporations Are National Firms with International Operations. *California Management Review* 34/2: 107–126.

Human Rights Watch. 1999a. *The Enron Corporation: Corporate Complicity in Human Rights Violations.* New York; Washington, DC; London; Brussels: Human Rights Watch. http://www.hrw.org/reports/1999/enron/.

Human Rights Watch. 1999b. *The Price of Oil: Corporate Responsibility and Human Rights Violations in Nigeria's Oil Producing Communities.* New York; Washington, DC; London; Brussels: Human Rights Watch. http://www.hrw.org/reports/1999/nigeria/.

Hume, David. 1992. *Treatise of Human Nature.* Buffalo, NY: Prometheus Books.

Hume, David. 1997. *An Enquiry Concerning the Principles of Morals.* Ed. Tom L. Beauchamp. Oxford; New York: Oxford University Press.

ICHRP. 2002. *Beyond Voluntarism: Human Rights and the Developing International Legal Obligations of Companies.* Versoix, Switzerland: International Council on Human Rights Policy.

Illich, Ivan. 1978. *The Right to Useful Unemployment and Its Professional Enemies.* London: Boyars.

International Chamber of Commerce and International Organization of Employers (ICC and IOE). 2004. *Joint Views of the IOE and ICC on the Draft "Norms on the Responsibilities of Transnational Corporations and Other Business Enterprises with Regards to Human Rights."* Paris; Geneva: ICC and IOE.

http://www.reportsandmaterials.org/IOEICCviews-UN-norms-March-2004
.doc.

International Labour Office. 2005. *A Global Alliance Against Forced Labour: Global Report Under the Follow-up to the ILO Declaration on Fundamental Principles and Rights to Work 2005*. Geneva: International Labour Office.

Ismail, M. Asif. 2005. Prescription for Power: Drug Makers' Lobbying Army Ensures Their Legislative Dominance. Center for Public Integrity, April 28. http://projects.publicintegrity.org/lobby/report.aspx?aid=685.

Ismail, M. Asif. 2008. A Record Year for the Pharmaceutical Lobby in '07: Washington's Largest Lobby Racks Up Another Banner Year on Capitol Hill. Center for Public Integrity, June 24. http://projects.publicintegrity.org/rx/report.aspx?aid=985.

Jackson, Ira A., and Jane Nelson. 2004. *Profits with Principles: Seven Strategies for Delivering Value with Values*. New York; London; Toronto; Sydney; Auckland: Currency Doubleday.

Jacoby, Neil H. 1973. *Corporate Power and Social Responsibility*. New York; London: Macmillan Publishers/Collier Macmillan Publishers.

James, Susan. 2005. Realizing Rights as Enforceable Claims. In *Global Responsibilities: Who Must Deliver on Human Rights?* ed. Andrew Kuper, 79–93. New York; London: Routledge.

Jonas, Hans. 1984. *The Imperative of Responsibility: In Search of an Ethics for the Technological Age*. Chicago; London: University of Chicago Press.

Jones, Charles. 1999. Patriotism, Morality, and Global Justice. In *Nomos XLI: Global Justice*, ed. Ian Shapiro and Lea Brilmayer, 125–170. New York; London: New York University Press.

Jones, Charles. 2001. *Global Justice: Defending Cosmopolitanism*. Oxford; New York: Oxford University Press.

Jones, Geoffrey. 1996. *The Evolution of International Business: An Introduction*. London; New York: Routledge.

Jones, Geoffrey. 2003. Multinationals. In *Business History Around the World*, ed. Franco Amatori and Geoffrey Jones, 353–371. Cambridge, UK: Cambridge University Press.

Jones, Marc T. 2000. The Competitive Advantage of the Transnational Corporation as an Institutional Form: A Reassessment. *International Journal of Social Economics* 27/7–10: 943–958.

Jonker, Jan. 2005. CSR Wonderland: Navigating Between Movement, Community, and Organization. *Journal of Corporate Citizenship* 20: 19–22.

Jungk, Margaret. 2000. *Deciding Whether to Do Business in States with Bad Governments*. Copenhagen: Danish Centre for Human Rights.

Jungk, Margaret. 2001. *Defining the Scope of Business Responsibility for Human Rights Abroad*. Copenhagen: Danish Centre for Human Rights.

Kahler, Miles, and David A. Lake. 2003. Globalization and Changing Patterns of Political Authority. In *Governance in a Global Economy: Political Authority in*

Transition, ed. Miles Kahler and David A. Lake, 412–438. Princeton, NJ: Princeton University Press.

Kaiser, Helmut. 1992. *Die ethische Integration ökonomischer Rationalität: Grundelemente und Konkretion einer "modernen" Wirtschaftsethik.* Bern; Stuttgart; Vienna: Haupt.

Kant, Immanuel. 1996. *The Metaphysics of Morals.* Transl. Mary Gregor. Cambridge, UK; New York: Cambridge University Press.

Kant, Immanuel. 1997. *Groundwork of the Metaphysics of Morals.* Transl. Mary Gregor. Cambridge, UK; New York: Cambridge University Press.

Kant, Immanuel. 2001a. Answer to the Question: What Is Enlightenment? Transl. Thomas K. Abbott. In *Basic Writings of Kant,* ed. Allen W. Wood, 133–141. New York: Modern Library.

Kant, Immanuel. 2001b. To Eternal Peace. Transl. Carl J. Friedrich. In *Basic Writings of Kant,* ed. Allen W. Wood, 433–475. New York: Modern Library.

Kaplan, Morton A. 1976. *Justice, Human Nature, and Political Obligation.* New York; London: Free Press.

Kaul, Inge, Pedro Conceição, Katell Le Goulven, and Ronald U. Mendoza. 2003a. Why Do Global Public Goods Matter Today? In *Providing Global Public Goods: Managing Globalization,* ed. Inge Kaul, Pedro Conceição, Katell Le Goulven, and Ronald U. Mendoza, 2–20. New York; Oxford: Oxford University Press.

Kaul, Inge, Pedro Conceição, Katell Le Goulven, and Ronald U. Mendoza. 2003b. How to Improve the Provision of Global Public Goods. In *Providing Global Public Goods: Managing Globalization,* ed. Inge Kaul, Pedro Conceição, Katell Le Goulven, and Ronald U. Mendoza, 21–58. New York; Oxford: Oxford University Press.

Kaul, Inge, Isabelle Grunberg, and Marc A. Stern. 1999a. Introduction to *Global Public Goods: International Cooperation in the 21st Century,* ed. Inge Kaul, Isabelle Grunberg, and Marc A. Stern, xix–xxxviii. New York; Oxford: Oxford University Press.

Kaul, Inge, Isabelle Grunberg, and Marc A. Stern. 1999b. Conclusion: Global Public Goods; Concepts, Policies and Strategies. In *Global Public Goods: International Cooperation in the 21st Century,* ed. Inge Kaul, Isabelle Grunberg, and Marc A. Stern, 450–507. New York; Oxford: Oxford University Press.

Kell, Georg, and John G. Ruggie. 2004. Voluntary and Regulatory Approaches Needed in Establishing Business Case for Human Rights. *Financial Times,* April 14.

Keohane, Robert O. 2000a. Sovereignty in International Society. In *The Global Transformation Reader: An Introduction to the Globalization Debate,* ed. David Held and Anthony McGrew, 109–123. Cambridge, UK; Malden, MA: Polity Press.

Keohane, Robert O. 2000b. Foreword to *Strange Power: Shaping the Parameters of International Relations and International Political Economy,* ed. Thomas C. Lawton, James N. Rosenau, and Amy C. Verdun, ix–xvi. Aldershot, UK; Burlington, VT; Singapore; Sidney: Ashgate.

Kersting, Wolfgang 1996. Weltfriedensordnung und globale Verteilungsgerechtigkeit. In *Zum ewigen Frieden*, ed. Reinhard Merkel and Roland Wittman, 172–212. Frankfurt a. M.: Suhrkamp.

Kersting, Wolfgang. 2000. *Theorien der sozialen Gerechtigkeit*. Stuttgart; Weimar: Verlag J. B. Metzler.

Khan, L. Ali. 1996. *The Extinction of Nation-States: A World Without Borders*. The Hague; Boston: Kluwer Law International.

Klein, Naomi. 1999. *No Logo: Taking Aim at the Brand Bullies*. New York: Picador.

Kline, John M. 2003. Political Activities by Transnational Corporations: Bright Lines Versus Grey Boundaries. *Transnational Corporations* 12/1: 1–25.

Knott, Alex. 2005. Industry of Influence Nets More Than $10 Billion: Shadowy Lobbyists Ignore Rules and Exploit Connections. Center for Public Integrity, April 7. http://projects.publicintegrity.org/lobby/report.aspx?aid=675.

Kobrin, Stephen J. 1997. The Architecture of Globalization: State Sovereignty in a Networked Global Economy. In *Governments, Globalization, and International Business*, ed. John Dunning, 146–171. Oxford: Oxford University Press.

Kobrin, Stephen J. 1998. Neo-medievalism and the Post-modern World Economy. *Journal of International Affairs* 51/2: 361–386.

Kobrin, Stephen J. 2002. Economic Governance in an Electronically Networked Global Economy. In *The Emergence of Private Authority in Global Governance*, ed. Rodney B. Hall and Thomas J. Biersteker, 43–75. Cambridge, UK: Cambridge University Press.

Kohlberg, Lawrence. 1981. *Essays on Moral Development*. Vol. 1, *The Philosophy of Moral Development*. San Francisco: Harper & Row.

Korsgaard, Christine M. 1996. The Authority of Reflection. In *The Sources of Normativity*, ed. Christine M. Korsgaard, 90–130. Cambridge, UK: Cambridge University Press.

Korsgaard, Christine M. 1997. Introduction to *Groundwork of the Metaphysics of Morals*, by Immanuel Kant, vii–xxx. Cambridge, UK; New York: Cambridge University Press.

Korten, David C. 1995. *When Corporations Rule the World*. West Hartford, CT; San Francisco: Kumarian Press and Berrett-Koehler Publishers.

Krasner, Stephen D. 2000. Compromising Westphalia. In *The Global Transformation Reader: An Introduction to the Globalization Debate*, ed. David Held and Anthony McGrew, 124–135. Cambridge, UK; Malden, MA: Polity Press.

Krebs, Angelika. 2000. Einleitung: Die neue Egalitarismuskritik im Überblick. In *Gleichheit oder Gerechtigkeit: Texte der neuen Egalitarismuskritik*, ed. Angelika Krebs, 7–37. Frankfurt a. M.: Suhrkamp.

Krebs, Angelika. 2003. Warum Gerechtigkeit nicht als Gleichheit zu begreifen ist. *Deutsche Zeitschrift für Philosophie* 51/2: 235–253.

Kuper, Andrew. 2004. *Democracy Beyond Borders: Justice and Representation in Global Institutions*. Oxford; New York: Oxford University Press.

Lall, Sanjaya, and Paul Streeten. 1977. *Foreign Investment, Transnationals and Developing Countries*. Boulder, CO: Westview Press.

Lawton, Thomas C., James N. Rosenau, and Amy C. Verdun. 2000. Introduction: Looking Beyond the Confines. In *Strange Power: Shaping the Parameters of International Relations and International Political Economy*, ed. Thomas C. Lawton, James N. Rosenau, and Amy C. Verdun, 3–18. Aldershot, UK; Burlington, VT; Singapore; Sidney: Ashgate.

Lazich, Robert S., ed. 2008. *Market Share Reporter 2008: An Annual Compilation of Reported Market Share Data on Companies, Products, and Services*. Vols. 1 and 2. Detroit: Thomson Gale.

Lehman, Karen, and Al Krebs. 1996. Control of the World's Food Supply. In *The Case Against the Global Economy: And for a Turn Toward the Local*, ed. Jerry Mander and Edward Goldsmith, 122–130. San Francisco: Sierra Club Books.

Leisinger, Klaus M. 2004. Zur Umsetzung unternehmensethischer Ambitionen in der Praxis. In *Ethik im Management: Ethik und Erfolg verbünden sich*, ed. Hans Ruh and Klaus M. Leisinger, 151–202. Zurich: Orell Füssli Verlag.

Leisinger, Klaus M. 2005. The Corporate Social Responsibility of the Pharmaceutical Industry: Idealism Without Illusion and Realism Without Resignation. *Business Ethics Quarterly* 15/4: 577–594.

Lewis, H. D. 1991. Collective Responsibility. In *Collective Responsibility: Five Decades of Debate in Theoretical and Applied Ethics*, ed. Larry May and Stacey Hoffman, 17–33. Savage, MD: Rowman & Littlefield Publishers. Originally published in *Philosophy: The Journal of the Royal Institute of Philosophy* 24/83 (1948).

Lincoln, Bruce. 1994. *Authority: Construction and Corrosion*. Chicago; London: University of Chicago Press.

Lippman, Matthew. 1985. Multinational Corporations and Human Rights. In *Human Rights and Third World Development*, ed. George W. Shepherd Jr. and Ved P. Nanda, 249–272. Westport, CT; London: Greenwood Press.

Lipschutz, Ronnie D., and Cathleen Fogel. 2002. "Regulation for the Rest of Us?" Global Civil Society and the Privatization of Transnational Regulation. In *The Emergence of Private Authority in Global Governance*, ed. Rodney B. Hall and Thomas J. Biersteker, 115–140. Cambridge, UK: Cambridge University Press.

Logsdon, Jeanne M., and Donna J. Wood. 2002. Business Citizenship: From Domestic to Global Level of Analysis. *Business Ethics Quarterly* 12/2: 155–187.

Lucas, J. R. 1997. Against Equality. In *Equality: Selected Readings*, ed. Louis P. Pojman and Robert Westmoreland, 104–112. Oxford; New York: Oxford University Press. Originally published in *Philosophy* 40 (1965).

Lukes, Steven. 1990. Perspectives on Authority. In *Authority*, ed. Joseph Raz, 203–217. New York: New York University Press.

Lunau, York, and Florian Wettstein. 2004. *Die soziale Verantwortung der Wirtschaft: Was Bürger von Unternehmen erwarten*. Bern; Stuttgart; Vienna: Haupt.

Maak, Thomas. 1999. *Die Wirtschaft der Bürgergesellschaft*. Bern; Stuttgart; Vienna: Haupt.

MacDonald, Margaret. 1984. Natural Rights. In *Theories of Rights*, ed. Jeremy Waldron, 21–40. Oxford; New York: Oxford University Press. Originally published in *Proceedings of the Aristotelian Society, 1947–48*.

MacIntyre, Alasdair. 1981. *After Virtue: A Study in Moral Theory.* Notre Dame, IN: University of Notre Dame Press.

Mackie, John L. 1984. Can There Be a Right-Based Moral Theory? In *Theories of Rights,* ed. Jeremy Waldron, 168–181. Oxford; New York: Oxford University Press. Originally published in Peter A. French, Howard K. Wettstein, and Theodore E. Uehling, eds., *Studies in Ethical Theory* (Minneapolis: University of Minnesota Press, 1978).

Malanczuk, Peter. 2002. Globalisierung und die zukünftige Rolle souveräner Staaten. In *Weltstaat oder Staatenwelt? Für und wider die Idee einer Weltrepublik,* ed. Matthias Lutz-Bachmann and James Bohman, 171–200. Frankfurt a. M.: Suhrkamp.

Mann, Michael. 2000. Has Globalization Ended the Rise and Rise of the Nation-State? In *The Global Transformation Reader: An Introduction to the Globalization Debate,* ed. David Held and Anthony McGrew, 136–147. Cambridge, UK; Malden, MA: Polity Press.

Margalit, Avishai. 1996. *The Decent Society.* Cambridge, MA; London: Harvard University Press.

Margalit, Avishai. 1997. Decent Equality and Freedom: A Postscript. *Social Research* 64/1: 147–160.

Margolis, Joshua D., and James P. Walsh. 2001. *People and Profits? The Search for a Link Between a Company's Social and Financial Performance.* Mahwah, NJ: Lawrence Erlbaum Associates.

Margolis, Joshua D., and James P. Walsh. 2003. Misery Loves Companies: Rethinking Social Initiatives by Business. *Administrative Science Quarterly* 48/2: 268–305.

Marsden, Chris. 2000. The New Corporate Citizenship of Big Business: Part of the Solution to Sustainability? *Business and Society Review* 105/1: 9–25.

Marsden, Chris. 2005. In Defence of Corporate Responsibility. *Zeitschrift für Wirtschafts- und Unternehmensethik* 6/3: 359–373.

Marsden, Chris, and Jörg Andriof. 1998. Towards an Understanding of Corporate Citizenship and How to Influence It. *Citizenship Studies* 2/2: 329–352.

Martens, Jens. 2003. *The Future of Multilateralism After Monterrey and Johannesburg.* Berlin: Friedrich Ebert Stiftung.

Martin, Hans-Peter, and Harald Schumann. 1997. *The Global Trap: Globalization and the Assault on Prosperity and Democracy.* London; New York: Zed Books.

Masci, Alessandra, and Salil Tripathi. 2005. Business and Human Rights: The Value of the UN Norms. *Sustainable Development International* 13: 23–26.

Mathews, Jessica T. 1997. Power Shift. *Foreign Affairs* 76/1: 50–66.

Matten, Dirk, Andrew Crane, and Wendy Chapple. 2003. Behind the Mask: Revealing the True Face of Corporate Citizenship. *Journal of Business Ethics* 45/1–2: 109–120.

Mellema, Gregory F. 1997. *Collective Responsibility.* Amsterdam; Atlanta: Rodopi.

Merriam, Charles E. 1934. *Political Power: Its Composition and Incidence.* New York; London: Whittlesey House.

Meyer, William H. 1996. Human Rights and MNCs: Theory Versus Quantitative Analysis. *Human Rights Quarterly* 18/2: 368–397.

Micklethwait, John, and Adrian Wooldridge. 2003. *The Company: A Short History of a Revolutionary Idea*. New York: Modern Library.

Mill, John S. 1991. *Considerations on Representative Government*. Amherst, NY: Prometheus Books.

Mill, John S. 2001. *Utilitarianism*. Indianapolis; Cambridge, MA: Hackett Publishing Company.

Mill, John S. 2005. *Autobiography*. Boston: Adamant Media Corporation.

Miller, David. 1988. The Ethical Significance of Nationality. *Ethics* 98/4: 647–662.

Miller, David. 1995. *On Nationality*. Oxford; New York: Oxford University Press.

Miller, David. 1998. The Limits of Cosmopolitan Justice. In *International Society: Diverse Ethical Perspectives*, ed. David R. Mapel and Terry Nardin, 164–181. Princeton, NJ: Princeton University Press.

Miller, David. 1999. *Principles of Social Justice*. Cambridge, MA; London: Harvard University Press.

Miller, David 2005. Distributing Responsibilities. In *Global Responsibilities: Who Must Deliver on Human Rights?* ed. Andrew Kuper, 95–115. New York; London: Routledge.

Miller, Peter. 1987. *Domination and Power*. London; New York: Routledge & Kegan Paul.

Miller, Richard. 1998. Cosmopolitan Respect and Patriotic Concern. *Philosophy and Public Affairs* 27/3: 202–224.

Morriss, Peter T. 1987. *Power: A Philosophical Analysis*. New York: St. Martin's Press.

Muchlinski, Peter. 2001. Human Rights and Multinationals: Is There a Problem? *International Affairs* 77/1: 31–47.

Müller, Jörg P. 1999. *Der politische Mensch—menschliche Politik: Demokratie und Menschenrechte im staatlichen und global Kontext*. Basel; Geneva; Munich: Helbling & Lichtenhahn and C. H. Beck.

Mytelka, Lynn. 2000. Knowledge and Structural Power in the International Political Economy. In *Strange Power: Shaping the Parameters of International Relations and International Political Economy*, ed. Thomas C. Lawton, James N. Rosenau, and Amy C. Verdun, 39–56. Aldershot, UK; Burlington, VT; Singapore; Sidney: Ashgate.

Mytelka, Lynn, and Michel Delapierre. 1999. Strategic Partnerships, Knowledge-Based Networked Oligopolies, and the State. In *Private Authority and International Affairs*, ed. A. Claire Cutler, Virginia Haufler, and Tony Porter, 129–149. Albany: State University of New York Press.

Nagel, Thomas. 1973. Rawls on Justice. *Philosophical Review* 83: 220–234.

Nagel, Thomas. 1979. *Mortal Questions*. Cambridge, UK: Cambridge University Press.

Nagel, Thomas. 1991. *Equality and Partiality*. New York; Oxford: Oxford University Press.

Nelson, Jane. 2002. *Building Partnerships: Cooperation Between the United Nations System and the Private Sector*. New York: United Nations.

Nelson, Jane. 2004. The Public Role of the Private Enterprise: Risks, Opportunities, and New Models of Engagement. Working Paper of the Corporate Social Responsibility Initiative. Cambridge, MA: John F. Kennedy School of Government.

Nelson, William. 1974. Special Rights, General Rights, and Social Justice. *Philosophy and Public Affairs* 3/4: 410–430.

Nickel, James W. 1987. *Making Sense of Human Rights: Philosophical Reflections on the Universal Declaration of Human Rights.* Berkeley; Los Angeles; London: University of California Press.

Nozick, Robert. 1974. *Anarchy, State, and Utopia.* New York: Harper & Row.

Nussbaum, Martha C. 1990. Aristotelian Social Democracy. In *Liberalism and the Good*, ed. R. Bruce Douglass, 203–252. New York: Routledge.

Nussbaum, Martha C. 1996a. Patriotism and Cosmopolitanism. In *For Love of Country: Debating the Limits of Patriotism*, ed. Martha C. Nussbaum and Joshua Cohen, 1–17. Boston: Beacon Press.

Nussbaum, Martha C. 1996b. Reply. In *For Love of Country: Debating the Limits of Patriotism*, ed. Martha C. Nussbaum and Joshua Cohen, 131–144. Boston: Beacon Press.

Nussbaum, Martha C. 2000. *Women and Human Development: The Capabilities Approach.* Cambridge, UK: Cambridge University Press.

Nussbaum, Martha C. 2001. Adaptive Preferences and Women's Options. *Economics and Philosophy* 17/1: 67–88.

Nussbaum, Martha C. 2002. Capabilities and Human Rights. In *Global Justice and Transnational Politics: Essays on the Moral and Political Challenges of Globalization*, ed. Pablo De Greiff and Ciaran Cronin, 117–149. Cambridge, MA; London: MIT Press.

Nussbaum, Martha C. 2003. Capabilities as Fundamental Entitlements: Sen and Social Justice. *Feminist Economics* 9/2–3: 33–59.

Nussbaum, Martha C. 2006. *Frontiers of Justice: Disability, Nationality, Species Membership.* Cambridge, MA; London: Belknap Press of Harvard University Press.

Nussbaum, Martha C., and Jonathan Glover, eds. 1995. *Women, Culture, and Development: A Study of Human Capabilities.* Oxford: Clarendon Press.

Nye, Joseph S. 1990. *Bound to Lead: The Changing Nature of American Power.* New York: Basic Books.

Nye, Joseph S. 2004. *Soft Power: The Means to Success in World Politics.* New York: Public Affairs.

OECD. 1996. *Trade, Employment and Labour Standards: A Study of Core Workers' Rights and International Trade.* Paris: OECD Publishing.

OECD. 2000. *International Trade and Core Labour Standards.* Paris: OECD Publishing.

Ohmae, Kenichi. 1995a. *The End of the Nation State, The Rise of Regional Economics; How New Engines of Prosperity Are Reshaping Global Markets.* New York: Free Press.

Ohmae, Kenichi. 1995b. Putting Global Logic First. In *The Evolving Global Economy: Making Sense of the New World Order*, ed. Kenichi Ohmae, 129–137. Boston: Harvard Business Review.

Okin, Susan. 2003. Poverty, Well-Being, and Gender: What Counts, Who's Heard? *Philosophy and Public Affairs* 31/3: 280–316.

O'Neill, Onora. 1986. *Faces of Hunger: An Essay on Poverty, Justice and Development*. London: Allen & Unwin.

O'Neill, Onora. 1991. Transnational Justice. In *Political Theory Today*, ed. David Held, 276–304. Stanford, CA: Stanford University Press.

O'Neill, Onora. 1993. Justice, Gender, and International Boundaries. In *The Quality of Life*, ed. Martha Nussbaum and Amartya Sen, 303–323. Oxford: Clarendon Press.

O'Neill, Onora. 1996. *Towards Justice and Virtue: A Constructive Account of Practical Reasoning*. Cambridge, UK; New York: Cambridge University Press.

O'Neill, Onora. 2000. *Bounds of Justice*. Cambridge, UK: Cambridge University Press.

O'Neill, Onora. 2001. Agents of Justice. *Metaphilosophy* 32/1–2: 180–195.

O'Neill, Onora. 2004. Global Justice: Whose Obligations? In *The Ethics of Assistance: Morality and the Distant Needy*, ed. Deen K. Chatterjee, 242–259. Cambridge, UK; New York: Cambridge University Press.

Ordentlicher, Diane F., and Timothy A. Gelatt. 1993. Public Law, Private Actors: The Impact of Human Rights on Business Investors in China. *Northwestern Journal of International Law and Business* 14/1: 96–102.

Orlitzky, Marc, Frank L. Schmidt, and Sara L. Rynes. 2003. Corporate Social and Financial Performance: A Meta-analysis. *Organization Studies* 24/3: 403–441.

Paine, Lynn S. 2000. Does Ethics Pay? *Business Ethics Quarterly* 10/1: 319–330.

Paine, Thomas. 1985. *The Rights of Man*. New York: Penguin Books.

Palazzo, Guido, and Andreas G. Scherer. 2006. Corporate Legitimacy as Deliberation: A Communicative Framework. *Journal of Business Ethics* 66/1: 71–88.

Palazzo, Guido, and Andreas G. Scherer. 2008. The Future of Global Corporate Citizenship: Toward a New Theory of the Firm as a Political Actor. In *Handbook of Research on Global Corporate Citizenship*, ed. Andreas G. Scherer and Guido Palazzo, 577–590. Cheltenham, UK; Northampton, MA: Edward Elgar.

Passerin d'Entrèves, Maurizio. 1994. *The Political Philosophy of Hannah Arendt*. London; New York: Routledge.

Pava, Moses, and Joshua Krausz. 1996. The Association Between Corporate Social-Responsibility and Financial Performance: The Paradox of Social Cost. *Journal of Business Ethics* 15/3: 321–357.

Pettit, Philip. 2001. Capability and Freedom: A Defence of Sen. *Economics and Philosophy* 17/1: 1–20.

Pieper, Annemarie. 2003. *Einführung in die Ethik*. Tübingen; Basel: A. Francke Verlag.

Pierer, Heinrich von. 2003. Zwischen Profit und Moral? In *Zwischen Profit und Moral: Für eine menschliche Wirtschaft*, ed. Heinrich von Pierer, Karl Homann, and Gertrude Lübbe-Wolff, 7–34. Munich; Vienna: Carl Hanser Verlag.

Plato. 1992. *Republic*. Transl. G. M. A. Grube. Indianapolis; Cambridge, MA: Hackett Publishing Company.

Pogge, Thomas W. 1989. *Realizing Rawls*. Ithaca, NY: Cornell University Press.

Pogge, Thomas W. 1992. Cosmopolitanism and Sovereignty. *Ethics* 103/1: 48–75.

Pogge, Thomas W. 1998. Menschenrechte als moralische Ansprüche an globale Institutionen. In *Philosophie der Menschenrechte*, ed. Stefan Gosepath and Georg Lohmann, 378–400. Frankfurt a. M.: Suhrkamp.

Pogge, Thomas W. 2001a. Priorities of Global Justice. *Metaphilosophy* 32/1–2: 6–24.

Pogge, Thomas W. 2001b. Introduction. *Metaphilosophy* 32/1–2: 1–5.

Pogge, Thomas W. 2002a. *World Poverty and Human Rights*. Cambridge, UK; Malden, MA: Polity Press.

Pogge, Thomas W. 2002b. Cosmopolitanism: A Defence. *Critical Review of International Social and Political Philosophy* 5/3: 86–91.

Pogge, Thomas W. 2003. The Influence of the Global Order on the Prospects for Genuine Democracy in Developing Countries. In *Debating Cosmopolitics*, ed. Daniele Archibugi, 117–140. London; New York: Verso.

Pogge, Thomas W. 2004. "Assisting" the Global Poor. In *The Ethics of Assistance: Morality and the Distant Needy*, ed. Deen K. Chatterjee, 260–288. Cambridge, UK; New York: Cambridge University Press.

Pogge, Thomas W. 2006. Incentives for Pharmaceutical Research: Must They Exclude the Global Poor from Advanced Medicines? Paper presented at the conference "Equality and the New Global Order," John F. Kennedy School of Government at Harvard University, Cambridge, MA, May 11–13.

Polanyi, Karl. 2001. *The Great Transformation: The Political and Economic Origins of Our Time*. Boston: Beacon Press.

Porter, Michael E. 1998a. Introduction to *On Competition*, by Michael E. Porter, 1–17. Boston: Harvard Business School Press.

Porter, Michael E. 1998b. The Competitive Advantage of Nations. In *On Competition*, by Michael E. Porter, 155–196. Boston: Harvard Business School Press.

Porter, Michael E., and Victor E. Millar. 1998. How Information Gives You Competitive Advantage. In *On Competition*, by Michael E. Porter, 75–98. Boston: Harvard Business School Press.

Prahalad, C. K. 2002. Strategies for the Bottom of the Economic Pyramid: India as a Source for Innovation. *Reflections* 3/4: 6–17.

Prahalad, C. K., and Allen L. Hammond. 2002. Serving the World's Poor, Profitably. *Harvard Business Review* 80/9: 48–57.

Prahalad, C. K., and Stuart L. Hart. 2002. The Fortune at the Bottom of the Pyramid. *Strategy and Business* 26: 2–14.

Presbey, Gail M. 1997. Hannah Arendt on Power. In *Philosophical Perspectives on Power and Domination: Theories and Practices*, ed. Laura D. Kaplan and Laurence F. Bove, 29–40. Amsterdam; Atlanta: Rodopi.

Public Citizen. 2003. *The Other Drug War 2003: Drug Companies Deploy an Army of 675 Lobbyists to Protect Profits*. Washington, DC: Public Citizen. www.citizen.org/documents/Other_Drug_War2003.pdf.

Ramasastry, Anita. 2002. Corporate Complicity: From Nuremberg to Rangoon; An Examination of Forced Labor Cases and Their Impact on the Liability of Multinational Corporations. *Berkeley Journal of International Law* 20/1: 91–159.

Ratner, Steven R. 2001. Corporations and Human Rights: A Theory of Legal Responsibility. *Yale Law Journal* 111/3: 443–545.

Rawls, John. 1971. *A Theory of Justice*. Cambridge, MA: Belknap Press of Harvard University Press.

Rawls, John. 1996. *Political Liberalism*. New York: Columbia University Press.

Rawls, John. 1999a. *The Law of Peoples*. Cambridge, MA; London: Harvard University Press.

Rawls, John. 1999b. The Law of Peoples. In *John Rawls: Collected Papers*, ed. Samuel Freeman, 529–564. Cambridge, MA; London: Harvard University Press.

Raz, Joseph. 1984. Right-Based Moralities. In *Theories of Rights*, ed. Jeremy Waldron, 182–200. Oxford; New York: Oxford University Press.

Raz, Joseph. 1986. *The Morality of Freedom*. Oxford: Oxford University Press.

Raz, Joseph. 1990a. Introduction to *Authority*, ed. Joseph Raz, 1–19. New York: New York University Press.

Raz, Joseph. 1990b. Authority and Justification. In *Authority*, ed. Joseph Raz, 115–141. New York: New York University Press.

Raz, Joseph. 2000. Strenger und rhetorischer Egalitarismus. In *Gleichheit oder Gerechtigkeit: Texte der neuen Egalitarismuskritik*, ed. Angelika Krebs, 50–80. Frankfurt a. M.: Suhrkamp.

Reich, Charles A. 1995. *Opposing the System*. New York: Crown Publishers.

Reich, Robert B. 1995. Who Is Them? In *The Evolving Global Economy: Making Sense of the New World Order*, ed. Kenichi Ohmae, 161–181. Boston: Harvard Business Review.

Reich, Robert B. 2001. Corporate Power in Overdrive. *New York Times*, March 18.

Reich, Robert B. 2002. *The Future of Success: Working and Living in the New Economy*. New York: Vintage Books.

Reinicke, Wolfgang H. 1998. *Global Public Policy: Governing Without Government?* Washington, DC: Brookings Institution Press.

Reinicke, Wolfgang H., and Francis Deng. 2000. *Critical Choices: The United Nations, Networks, and the Future of Global Governance*. Ottawa, ON: International Development Research Centre.

Reinisch, August. 2005. The Changing International Legal Framework for Dealing with Non-state Actors. In *Non-state Actors and Human Rights*, ed. Philip Alston, 37–89. Oxford; New York: Oxford University Press.

Renner, M. 2006. Exxon Mobil in Aceh. Global Policy Forum, April 17. http://www.globalpolicy.org/opinion/2006/0417exxonaceh.htm.

Richards, David A. J. 1982. International Distributive Justice. In *Nomos XXIV: Ethics, Economics, and the Law*, ed. Roland Penncock and John Chapman, 275–299. New York: New York University Press.

Richter, Judith 2004. *Public-Private Partnerships and International Health Policy-Making: How Can Public Interests Be Safeguarded?* Helsinki: Ministry for Foreign Affairs of Finland.

Rinderle, Peter. 2006. John Stuart Mills liberale Theorie der Gerechtigkeit. In *John Stuart Mill: Der vergessene politische Ökonom und Philosoph*, ed. Peter Ulrich and Michael S. Assländer, 79–123. Bern; Stuttgart; Vienna: Haupt.

Rischard, Jean-François. 2002. *High Noon: Twenty Global Problems, Twenty Years to Solve Them.* New York: Basic Books.

Robinson, Mary. 2005. What Rights Can Add to Good Development Practice. In *Human Rights and Development: Towards Mutual Reinforcement*, ed. Philip Alston and Mary Robinson, 25–41. Oxford; New York: Oxford University Press.

Rodrik, Dani. 2002. Feasible Globalizations. Faculty Research Working Paper Series RWP02-029. Cambridge, MA: John F. Kennedy School of Government at Harvard University.

Rondinelli, Dennis A. 2002. Transnational Corporations: International Citizens or New Sovereigns? *Business and Society Review* 107/4: 391–413.

Rondinelli, Dennis A. 2003. Transnational Corporations: International Citizens or New Sovereigns? *Business Strategy Review* 14/4: 13–21.

Rosenau, James N. 2000. Governance in a Globalizing World. In *The Global Transformation Reader: An Introduction to the Globalization Debate*, ed. David Held and Anthony McGrew, 181–190. Cambridge, UK; Malden, MA: Polity Press.

Ross, W. D. 1930. *The Right and the Good.* Oxford: Clarendon Press.

Roth, Kenneth. 2005. Rules on Corporate Ethics Could Help, Not Hinder, Multinationals. *Financial Times*, June 21.

Rousseau, Jean-Jacques. 1968. *The Social Contract.* London; New York: Penguin Books.

Rousseau, Jean-Jacques. 1984. *A Discourse on Inequality.* London; New York: Penguin Books.

Ruggie, John G. 1993. Territoriality and Beyond: Problematizing Modernity in International Relations. *International Organization* 47/1: 139–174.

Ruggie, John G. 2003. Taking Embedded Liberalism Global: The Corporate Connection. In *Taming Globalization: Frontiers of Governance*, ed. David Held and Mathias Koenig-Archibugi, 93–129. Cambridge, UK; Malden, MA: Polity Press.

Ruigrok, Winfried, and Rob van Tulder. 1995. The Persistent Myth of the "Global" Corporation. *Holland Management Review* 146/46: 17–25.

Sampson, Anthony. 1995. *Company Man: The Rise and Fall of Corporate Life.* London: HarperCollins.

Sandel, Michael J. 1982. *Liberalism and the Limits of Justice.* Cambridge, UK; New York: Cambridge University Press.

Sassen, Saskia. 1996. *Losing Control? Sovereignty in an Age of Globalization.* New York: Columbia University Press.

Sassen, Saskia. 2002. The State and Globalization. In *The Emergence of Private Authority in Global Governance*, ed. Rodney B. Hall and Thomas J. Biersteker, 91–114. Cambridge, UK: Cambridge University Press.

Satz, Debra. 1999. Equality of What Among Whom? Thoughts on Cosmopolitanism, Statism, and Nationalism. In *Nomos XLI: Global Justice*, ed. Ian Shapiro and Lea Brilmayer, 67–85. New York; London: New York University Press.

Scanlon, Thomas M. 1982. Contractualism and Utilitarianism. In *Utilitarianism and Beyond*, ed. Amartya ·Sen and Bernard Williams, 103–128. Cambridge, UK: Cambridge University Press.

Scanlon, Thomas M. 1984. Rights, Goals, and Fairness. In *Theories of Rights*, ed. Jeremy Waldron, 137–152. Oxford; New York: Oxford University Press. Originally published in *Erkenntnis* 2/1 (1977).

Scanlon, Thomas M. 1998. *What We Owe to Each Other*. Cambridge, MA; London: Belknap Press of Harvard University Press.

Scarcella, Mike. 2008. Judge Rejects Summary Judgment in Human Rights Lawsuit Against Exxon. *Legal Times*, August 28.

Scheffler, Samuel. 1999. The Conflict Between Justice and Responsibility. In *Nomos XLI: Global Justice*, ed. Ian Shapiro and Lea Brilmayer, 86–106. New York; London: New York University Press.

Scherer, Andreas G. 2003. *Multinationale Unternehmen und Globalisierung: Zur Neuorientierung der Theorie der Multinationalen Unternehmung*. Heidelberg: Physica-Verlag.

Scherer, Andreas G., and Guido Palazzo. 2007. Toward a Political Conception of Corporate Responsibility: Business and Society Seen from a Habermasian Perspective. *Academy of Management Review* 32/4: 1096–1120.

Scherer, Andreas G., Guido Palazzo, and Dorothee Baumann. 2006. Global Rules and Private Actors: Toward a New Role of the Transnational Corporation in Global Governance. *Business Ethics Quarterly* 16/4: 505–532.

Schumpeter, Joseph A. 1976. *Capitalism, Socialism, and Democracy*. London: George Allen & Unwin.

Schwartz, Herman M. 2000. *States Versus Markets: The Emergence of a Global Economy*. New York: St. Martin's Press.

Sen, Amartya. 1973. *On Economic Inequality*. Oxford: Clarendon Press.

Sen, Amartya. 1979. Welfarism and Utilitarianism. *Journal of Philosophy* 76/8: 463–489.

Sen, Amartya. 1980. Equality of What? In *Tanner Lectures on Human Values*. Vol. 1, ed. Sterling M. McMurrin, 197–220. Cambridge, UK: Cambridge University Press.

Sen, Amartya. 1982. Rights and Agency. *Philosophy and Public Affairs* 11/1: 3–39.

Sen, Amartya. 1985a. *Commodities and Capabilities*. Amsterdam; New York; Oxford: North-Holland.

Sen, Amartya. 1985b. Well-Being, Agency, and Freedom: The Dewey Lectures, 1984. *Journal of Philosophy* 82/4: 169–221.

Sen, Amartya. 1985c. Rights and Capabilities. In *Morality and Objectivity: A Tribute to J. L. Mackie*, ed. Ted Honderich, 130–148. London: Routledge & Kegan Paul.

Sen, Amartya. 1985d. Rights as Goals. In *Equality and Discrimination: Essays in Freedom and Justice*, ed. Stephen Guest and Alan Milne, 11–25. Stuttgart: Franz Steiner.

Sen, Amartya. 1990. Justice: Means Versus Freedoms. *Philosophy and Public Affairs* 19/2: 111–121.

Sen, Amartya. 1992. *Inequality Reexamined*. Cambridge, MA: Harvard University Press.

Sen, Amartya. 1993. Capability and Well-Being. In *The Quality of Life*, ed. Martha Nussbaum and Amartya Sen, 30–53. Oxford: Clarendon Press.

Sen, Amartya. 1997. Human Rights and Asian Values. *New Republic*, July 14–21: 33–40.

Sen, Amartya. 2000. *Development as Freedom*. New York: Anchor Books.

Sen, Amartya. 2004a. Elements of a Theory of Human Rights. *Philosophy and Public Affairs* 32/4: 315–356.

Sen, Amartya. 2004b. Capabilities, Lists, and Public Reason: Continuing the Conversation. *Feminist Economics* 10/3: 77–80.

Sennett, Richard. 1980. *Authority*. New York: Alfred A. Knopf.

Shapiro, Ian, and Lea Brilmayer. 1999. Introduction to *Nomos XLI: Global Justice*, ed. Ian Shapiro and Lea Brilmayer, 1–11. New York; London: New York University Press.

Shepherd, George W., Jr., and Ved P. Nanda. 1985. Introduction: Human Rights and Third World Development—Do They Mix? In *Human Rights and Third World Development*, ed. George W. Shepherd Jr. and Ved P. Nanda, 3–10. Westport, CT; London: Greenwood Press.

Shklar, Judith N. 1986. Injustice, Injury, and Inequality: An Introduction. In *Justice and Equality Here and Now*, ed. Frank S. Lucash, 13–33. Ithaca, NY; London: Cornell University Press.

Shklar, Judith N. 1990. *The Faces of Injustice*. New Haven, CT; London: Yale University Press.

Shue, Henry. 1980. *Basic Rights: Subsistence, Affluence, and U.S. Foreign Policy*. Princeton, NJ: Princeton University Press.

Shue, Henry. 1983. The Burdens of Justice. *Journal of Philosophy* 80/10: 600–608.

Shue, Henry. 1988. Mediating Duties. *Ethics* 98/4: 687–704.

Singer, Peter. 1972. Famine, Affluence, and Morality. *Philosophy and Public Affairs* 1/3: 229–243.

Singer, Peter W. 2004. Outsourcing the War. *Salon.com*, April 16.

Slaughter, Anne-Marie. 2004. *A New World Order*. Princeton, NJ: Princeton University Press.

Slivinski, Stephen. 2007. The Corporate Welfare State: How the Federal Government Subsidizes U.S. Businesses. Cato Institute, Policy Analysis no. 592, May 14. http://www.cato.org/pub_display.php?pub_id=8230.

Smith, Adam. 1985. *An Inquiry into the Nature and Causes of the Wealth of Nations*. New York: Modern Library.

Smith, Adam. 2002. *The Theory of Moral Sentiments*. Ed. Knud Haakonssen. Cambridge, UK: Cambridge University Press.

Smith, Anthony D. 1986. *The Ethnic Origins of Nations*. Oxford: Blackwell.

Smith, Jackie, Melissa Bolyard, and Anna Ippolito. 1999. Human Rights and the Global Economy: A Response to Meyer. *Human Rights Quarterly* 21/1: 207–219.

Sontag, Susan. 2003. *Regarding the Pain of Others*. New York: Picador.

Spar, Debora L. 1998. The Spotlight and the Bottom Line: How Multinationals Export Human Rights. *Foreign Affairs* 77/2: 7–12.

Spar, Debora L. 1999. The Public Face of Cyberspace. In *Global Public Goods: International Cooperation in the 21st Century*, ed. Inge Kaul, Isabelle Grunberg, and Marc A. Stern, 344–362. New York; Oxford: Oxford University Press.

Srivastava, Amit. 2006. Coca-Cola and Water—An Unsustainable Relationship. India Resource Center, March 8. http://www.indiaresource.org/campaigns/coke/2006/cokewwf.html.

Steinhardt, Barry, and Jay Stanley. 2005. Protecting the Future of the Free Internet. In *News Incorporated: Corporate Media Ownership and Its Threat to Democracy*, ed. Elliot D. Cohen, 237–254. Amherst, NY: Prometheus Books.

Steinhardt, Ralph G. 2005. Corporate Responsibility and the International Law of Human Rights. In *Non-state Actors and Human Rights*, ed. Philip Alston, 177–226. Oxford; New York: Oxford University Press.

Stiglitz, Joseph E. 2001. Foreword to *The Great Transformation: The Political and Economic Origins of Our Time*, by Karl Polanyi, vii–xvii. Boston: Beacon Press.

Stiglitz, Joseph E. 2002a. *Globalization and Its Discontents*. New York; London: W. W. Norton & Company.

Stiglitz, Joseph E. 2002b. Knowledge of Technology and the Technology of Knowledge: New Strategies for Development. In *Capacity for Development: New Solutions to Old Problems*, ed. Sakiko Fukada-Parr, Carlos Lopes, and Khalid Malik, 271–280. London; Sterling, VA: Earthscan Publications.

Stiglitz, Joseph E. 2003. *The Roaring Nineties: A New History of the World's Most Prosperous Decade*. New York: W. W. Norton & Company.

Stopford, John M., and Susan Strange. 1991. *Rival States, Rival Firms: Competition for World Market Shares*. Cambridge, UK; New York: Cambridge University Press.

Story, Jonathan. 2000. Setting the Parameters: A Strange World System. In *Strange Power: Shaping the Parameters of International Relations and International Political Economy*, ed. Thomas C. Lawton, James N. Rosenau, and Amy C. Verdun, 19–38. Aldershot, UK; Burlington, VT; Singapore; Sidney: Ashgate.

Strange, Susan. 1988. *States and Markets*. London: Pinter Publishers.

Strange, Susan. 1994. Wake Up, Krasner! The World *Has* Changed. *Review of International Political Economy* 1/2: 209–219.

Strange, Susan. 1996. *The Retreat of the State: The Diffusion of Power in the World Economy*. Cambridge, UK: Cambridge University Press.

Strange, Susan. 1998. *Mad Money: When Markets Outgrow Governments*. Ann Arbor: University of Michigan Press.

Strange, Susan. 2000. The Declining Authority of States. In *The Global Transformation Reader: An Introduction to the Globalization Debate*, ed. David Held and Anthony McGrew, 148–155. Cambridge, UK; Malden, MA: Polity Press.

Strange, Susan. 2002a. What Is Economic Power and Who Has It? In *Authority and Markets: Susan Strange's Writings on International Political Economy*, ed. Roger Tooze and Christopher May, 197–208. Houndsmills, Basingstoke, Hampshire, UK; New York: Palgrave Macmillan.

Strange, Susan. 2002b. Territory, State, Authority and Economy: A New Realist Ontology of Global Political Economy. In *Authority and Markets: Susan Strange's Writings on International Political Economy*, ed. Roger Tooze and Christopher May, 225–238. Houndsmills, Basingstoke, Hampshire, UK; New York: Palgrave Macmillan.

Streck, Charlotte. 2002. Global Public Policy Networks as Coalitions for Change. In *Global Environmental Governance: Options and Opportunities*, ed. Daniel C. Esty and Maria Ivanova, 121–140. New Haven, CT: Yale School of Forestry and Environmental Studies.

Streeten, Paul. 1979. A Basic Needs Approach to Economic Development. In *Directions in Economic Development*, ed. Kenneth P. Jameson and Charles K. Wilber, 73–129. Notre Dame, IN: University of Notre Dame Press.

Streeten, Paul. 2004. Human Rights—A Business Affair? In *Human Rights and the Private Sector: International Symposium Report*, ed. Lucy Amis, Klaus M. Leisinger, and Karin Schmitt, 71–78. Basel; London: Novartis Foundation for Sustainable Development and the Prince of Wales International Business Leaders Forum (IBLF).

Stump, Eleonore. 1993. Intellect, Will, and the Principle of Alternate Possibilities. In *Perspectives on Moral Responsibility*, ed. John M. Fischer and Mark Ravizza, 237–262. Ithaca, NY; London: Cornell University Press.

SustainAbility and WWF. 2005. *Influencing Power: Reviewing the Conduct and Content of Corporate Lobbying*. London; Godalming, UK: SustainAbility Ltd. and WWF UK.

Sutherland, Peter. 1999. Global Interdependence, the Corporation and the Changing World. *Business Strategy Review* 10/3: 47–55.

Tamir, Yael. 1993. *Liberal Nationalism*. Princeton, NJ: Princeton University Press.

Tavis, Lee A. 1982a. Introduction to *Multinational Managers and Poverty in the Third World*, ed. Lee A. Tavis, 1–6. Notre Dame, IN; London: University of Notre Dame Press.

Tavis, Lee A. 1982b. Developmental Responsibility. In *Multinational Managers and Poverty in the Third World*, ed. Lee A. Tavis, 127–139. Notre Dame, IN; London: University of Notre Dame Press.

Taylor, Charles. 1985. *Philosophy and the Human Sciences*. Philosophical Papers, Vol. 2. Cambridge, UK: Cambridge University Press.

Thielemann, Ulrich. 1996. *Das Prinzip Markt: Kritik der ökonomischen Tauschlogik*. Bern; Stuttgart; Vienna: Haupt.

Thielemann, Ulrich. 2003. Moral als Ausweg aus der Vertrauenskrise? In *Wege aus der Vertrauenskrise: 18 Lösungsansätze für eine neue Wirtschaftskultur,* ed. Robert Jakob and Jörg Naumann, 305–329. Frankfurt a. M.: Redline Wirtschaft.

Thielemann, Ulrich. 2004a. Akzeptanz oder Legitimität? Die Idee verdienter Reputation. CCRS Occasional Paper Series 05/04. Zurich: Center for Corporate Responsibility and Sustainability.

Thielemann, Ulrich. 2004b. *Freiheit unter den Bedingungen des Marktes: Oder doch gegenüber der Marktlogik? Vom verfehlten Umgang mit Sachzwängen.* Berichte des Instituts für Wirtschaftsethik der Universität St. Gallen 101. St. Gallen: Institut für Wirtschaftsethik.

Thielemann, Ulrich, and Peter Ulrich. 2003. *Brennpunkt Bankenethik: Der Finanzplatz Schweiz in wirtschaftsethischer Perspektive.* Bern; Stuttgart; Vienna: Haupt.

Thompson, Clive. 2006. Google's China Problem (and China's Google Problem). *New York Times,* April 23.

Thomson, Janice E., and Stephen D. Krasner. 1989. Global Transactions and the Consolidation of Sovereignty. In *Global Changes and Theoretical Challenges: Approaches to World Politics for the 1990s,* ed. Ernst-Otto Cziempel and James N. Rosenau, 195–219. Lexington, MA; Toronto: Lexington Books.

Thurow, Lester. 2003. *Fortune Favors the Bold: What We Must Do to Build a New and Lasting Global Prosperity.* New York: HarperBusiness.

Touraine, Alain. 2001. *Beyond Neoliberalism.* Malden, MA: Polity Press.

Tugendhat, Ernst. 1992. *Philosophische Aufsätze.* Frankfurt a. M.: Suhrkamp.

Tugendhat, Ernst. 1993. *Vorlesungen über Ethik.* Frankfurt a. M.: Suhrkamp.

Ulrich, Peter. 1977. *Die Grossunternehmung als quasi-öffentliche Institution: Eine politische Theorie der Unternehmung.* Stuttgart: C. E. Poeschel Verlag.

Ulrich, Peter. 1986. *Transformation der ökonomischen Vernunft: Fortschrittsperspektiven der modernen Industriegesellschaft.* Bern; Stuttgart: Haupt.

Ulrich, Peter. 1998. *Integrative Economic Ethics—Towards a Conception of Socioeconomic Rationality.* Berichte des Instituts für Wirtschaftsethik der Universität St. Gallen 82. St. Gallen: Institut für Wirtschaftsethik.

Ulrich, Peter. 2001a. *Integrative Wirtschaftsethik: Grundlagen einer lebensdienlichen Ökonomie.* Bern; Stuttgart; Vienna: Haupt.

Ulrich, Peter. 2001b. Integritätsmanagement und "verdiente" Reputation. *ioManagement* 1/2: 42–47.

Ulrich, Peter. 2002a. *Der entzauberte Markt: Eine wirtschaftsethische Orientierung.* Freiburg; Basel; Vienna: Herder.

Ulrich, Peter. 2002b. Ethics and Economics. In *Ethics in the Economy: Handbook of Business Ethics,* ed. Laszlo Zsolnai, 9–37. Bern: Peter Lang.

Ulrich, Peter. 2004a. Was ist "gute" sozioökonomische Entwicklung? Eine wirtschaftsethische Perspektive. *Zeitschrift für Wirtschafts- und Unternehmensethik* 5/1: 8–22.

Ulrich, Peter. 2004b. *Unternehmensethik—integrativ gedacht: Was ethische Orientierung in einem "zivilisierten" Wirtschaftsleben bedeutet.* Berichte des Instituts für Wirtschaftsethik 102. St. Gallen: Institut für Wirtschaftsethik.

Ulrich, Peter. 2008. *Integrative Economic Ethics: Foundations of a Civilized Market Economy.* Cambridge, UK: Cambridge University Press.

Ulrich, Peter, and Florian Wettstein. 2005. Öffentlich-private Partnerschaften—ein tragfähiges Konzept entwicklungspolitischer Mitverantwortung der Privatwirtschaft? In *Schweizerisches Jahrbuch für Entwicklungspolitik 24/2: Öffentlich-private Partnerschaften und internationale Entwicklungszusammenarbeit,* 45–58. Geneva: Institut universitaire d'études du développement.

UNCTAD. 1992. *World Investment Report 1992: Transnational Corporations as Engines of Growth.* New York; Geneva: United Nations.

UNCTAD. 1998. *World Investment Report 1998: Trends and Determinants.* New York; Geneva: United Nations.

UNCTAD. 1999. *World Investment Report 1999: Foreign Direct Investment and the Challenge of Development.* New York; Geneva: United Nations.

UNCTAD. 2003. *World Investment Report 2003: FDI Policies for Development; National and International Perspectives.* New York; Geneva: United Nations.

UNCTAD. 2004. *World Investment Report 2004: The Shift Towards Services.* New York; Geneva: United Nations.

UNCTAD. 2008. *World Investment Report 2008: Transnational Corporations and the Infrastructure Challenge.* New York; Geneva: United Nations.

Underhill, Geoffrey, R. D. 1997. Private Markets and Public Responsibility in a Global System: Conflict and Co-operation in Transnational Banking and Securities Regulation. In *The New World Order in International Finance,* ed. Geoffrey R. D. Underhill, 17–49. New York: St. Martin's Press.

Underhill, Geoffrey R. D. 2000. Global Money and the Decline of State Power. In *Strange Power: Shaping the Parameters of International Relations and International Political Economy,* ed. Thomas C. Lawton, James N. Rosenau, and Amy C. Verdun, 115–135. Aldershot, UK; Burlington, VT; Singapore; Sidney: Ashgate.

UNDP. 1999. *Human Development Report 1999: Globalization with a Human Face.* New York; Oxford: Oxford University Press.

UNDP. 2000. *Human Development Report 2000: Human Rights and Human Development.* New York; Oxford: Oxford University Press.

UNDP. 2002. *Human Development Report 2002: Deepening Democracy in a Fragmented World.* New York; Oxford: Oxford University Press.

UNDP. 2004. *Water Governance for Poverty Reduction: Key Issues and the UNDP Response to Millennium Development Goals.* New York: United Nations Development Programme.

UNESCO. 2003. *Water for People, Water for Life—UN World Water Development Report.* Paris: UNESCO Publishing.

United Nations. 2003. *The Right to Food: Note by the Secretary General.* General Assembly, Fifty-eighth Session, A/58/330. http://daccessdds.un.org/doc/UNDOC/GEN/N03/484/16/PDF/N0348416.pdf?OpenElement.

United Nations. 2006a. *Promotion and Protection of Human Rights: Interim Report of the Special Representative of the Secretary-General on the Issue of Human Rights and Transnational Corporations and Other Business Enterprises.* Commission on Human Rights, Sixty-second Session, E/CN.4/2006/97. http://daccessdds.un .org/doc/UNDOC/GEN/G06/110/27/PDF/G0611027.pdf?OpenElement.

United Nations. 2006b. *Economic, Social, and Cultural Rights: The Right to Food; Report of the Special Rapporteur on the Right to Food, Jean Ziegler.* Commission on Human Rights, Sixty-second Session, E/CN.4/2006/44. http://daccessdds .un.org/doc/UNDOC/GEN/G06/118/82/PDF/G0611882.pdf?OpenElement.

United Nations. 2008a. *Protect, Respect and Remedy: A Framework for Business and Human Rights.* Report of the Special Representative of the Secretary-General on the Issue of Human Rights and Transnational Corporations and Other Business Enterprises, John Ruggie. Human Rights Council. Eighth Session, A/HRC/8/5. http://daccessdds.un.org/doc/UNDOC/GEN/G08/128/61/PDF/ G0812861.pdf?OpenElement.

United Nations. 2008b. *Clarifying the Concepts of "Sphere of Influence" and "Complicity.* Report of the Special Representative of the Secretary-General on the Issue of Human Rights and Transnational Corporations and Other Business Enterprises, John Ruggie. Human Rights Council, Eighth Session, A/HRC/8/16. http://www.reports-and-materials.org/Ruggie-companion-report-15-May -2008.pdf.

Urbinati, Nadia. 2003. Can Cosmopolitan Democracy Be Democratic? In *Debating Cosmopolitics*, ed. Daniele Archibugi, 67–85. London; New York: Verso.

Van Parijs, Philippe. 1995. *Real Freedom for All: What (If Anything) Can Justify Capitalism?* Oxford: Clarendon Press.

Velasquez, Manuel G. 1991. Why Corporations Are Not Morally Responsible for Anything They Do. In *Collective Responsibility: Five Decades of Debate in Theoretical and Applied Ethics*, ed. Larry May and Stacey Hoffman, 111–131. Savage, MD: Rowman & Littlefield Publishers. Originally published in *Business and Professional Ethics Journal* 2/3 (1983).

Vernon, Raymond. 1971. *Sovereignty at Bay: The Multinational Spread of U.S. Enterprises.* New York; London: Basic Books.

Vernon, Raymond. 1993. Sovereignty at Bay: Twenty Years After. In *Multinationals in the Global Political Economy*, ed. Lorraine Eden and Evan H. Potter, 19–24. New York: St. Martin's Press.

Vernon, Raymond. 1998. *In the Hurricane's Eye: The Troubled Prospects of Multinational Enterprises.* Cambridge, MA; London: Harvard University Press.

Vlastos, Gregory. 1984. Justice and Equality. In *Theories of Rights*, ed. Jeremy Waldron, 41–76. Oxford; New York: Oxford University Press. Originally published in *Social Justice*, ed. R. B. Brandt (Englewood Cliffs, NJ: Prentice-Hall, 1962).

Vogel, David. 2005. *The Market for Virtue: The Potential and Limits of Corporate Social Responsibility.* Washington, DC: Brookings Institution Press.

Waddock, Sandra. 2002. *Leading Corporate Citizens: Vision, Values, Value Added.* New York: McGraw-Hill.

Waddock, Sandra. 2004. Parallel Universes: Companies, Academics, and the Progress of Corporate Citizenship. *Business and Society Review* 109/1: 5–42.

Waddock, Sandra. 2007. Corporate Citizenship: The Dark-Side Paradoxes of Success. In *The Debate over Corporate Social Responsibility*, ed. Steven May, George Cheney, and Juliet Roper, 74–86. New York; Oxford: Oxford University Press.

Waddock, Sandra, and Samuel Graves. 1997. The Corporate Social Performance-Financial Performance Link. *Strategic Management Journal* 18/4: 303–319.

Waddock, Sandra, and Florian Wettstein. 2005. The Shifting Agenda of Corporate Citizenship. *Forum TTN* 14: 40–52.

Waddock, Sandra, and Florian Wettstein. 2006. The UN Global Compact in a Context of Voluntary Responsibility Assurance. In *Unternehmensethik im Spannungsfeld der Kulturen und Religionen*, ed. Johannes Wallacher, Michael Reder, and Tobias Karcher, 146–161. Stuttgart: Kohlhammer.

Waldron, Jeremy. 1993. *Liberal Rights: Collected Papers, 1981–1991*. Cambridge, UK; New York: Cambridge University Press.

Walzer, Michael. 1983. *Spheres of Justice: A Defense of Pluralism and Equality*. New York: Basic Books.

Weber, Max. 1958a. Religious Rejections of the World and Their Directions. In *From Max Weber: Essays in Sociology*, ed. H. H. Gerth and C. Wright Mills, 323–359. New York: Oxford University Press.

Weber, Max. 1958b. Class, Status, Party. In *From Max Weber: Essays in Sociology*, ed. H. H. Gerth and C. Wright Mills, 180–195. New York: Oxford University Press.

Weber, Max. 1958c. Structures of Power. In *From Max Weber: Essays in Sociology*, ed. H. H. Gerth and C. Wright Mills, 159–179. New York: Oxford University Press.

Weber, Max. 1962. *Basic Concepts in Sociology*. New York: Philosophical Library.

Weber, Max. 1968. *Economy and Society: An Outline of Interpretive Sociology*. New York: Bedminster Press.

Weber, Max. 2002. *The Protestant Ethic and the Spirit of Capitalism*. London; New York: Routledge.

Weissbrodt, David. 2005. Corporate Human Rights Responsibilities. *Zeitschrift für Wirtschafts- und Unternehmensethik* 6/3: 279–297.

Wells, Celia, and Juanita Elias. 2005. Catching the Conscience of the King: Corporate Players on the International Stage. In *Non-state Actors and Human Rights*, ed. Philip Alston, 141–175. Oxford; New York: Oxford University Press.

Werhane, Patricia H. 1985. *Persons, Rights, and Corporations*. Englewood Cliffs, NJ: Prentice-Hall.

Westen, Peter. 1990. *Speaking of Equality: An Analysis of the Rhetorical Force of Equality in Moral and Legal Discourse*. Princeton, NJ: Princeton University Press.

Wettstein, Florian. 2005. From Causality to Capability: Towards a New Understanding of the Multinational Corporation's Enlarged Global Responsibilities. *Journal of Corporate Citizenship* 19: 105–117.

Wettstein, Florian. 2008. Let's Talk Rights: Messages for the Just Corporation; Transforming the Economy Through the Language of Rights. *Journal of Business Ethics* 78/1: 247–263.

Wettstein, Florian, and Sandra Waddock. 2005. Voluntary or Mandatory: That Is (Not) the Question; Linking Corporate Citizenship to Human Rights Obligations for Business. *Zeitschrift für Wirtschafts- und Unternehmensethik* 6/3: 304–320.

Wildt, Andreas. 1998. Menschenrechte und moralische Rechte. In *Philosophie der Menschenrechte*, ed. Stefan Gosepath and Georg Lohmann, 124–145. Frankfurt a. M.: Suhrkamp.

Wilkins, Mira. 1997. The Conceptual Domain of International Business. In *International Business: An Emerging Vision*, ed. Brian Toyne and Douglas Nigh, 27–110. Columbia: University of South Carolina Press.

Wilkins, Mira. 1998a. The Free-Standing Company Revisited. In *The Free-Standing Company in the World Economy, 1830–1996*, ed. Mira Wilkins and Harm Schröter, 3–64. Oxford; New York: Oxford University Press.

Wilkins, Mira. 1998b. Multinational Enterprise and Economic Change. *Australian Economic History Review* 38/2: 103–134.

Williams, Bernard A. O. 1997. The Idea of Equality. In *Equality: Selected Readings*, ed. Louis P. Pojman and Robert Westmoreland, 91–101. New York; Oxford: Oxford University Press. Originally published in *The Idea of Equality*, ed. Peter Laslett and W. G. Runciman (Oxford: Basil Blackwell, 1962).

Williamson, Oliver E. 1986. *Economic Organization: Firms, Markets and Policy Control*. New York; London; Toronto; Sydney; Tokyo; Singapore: Harvester Wheatsheaf.

Willke, Helmut. 2001. *Atopia: Studien zur atopischen Gesellschaft*. Frankfurt a. M.: Suhrkamp.

Witte, Jan M., and Wolfgang Reinicke. 2005. *Business Unusual: Facilitating United Nations Reform Through Partnerships*. New York: United Nations.

Wood, Donna, and Raymond Jones. 1995. Stakeholder Mismatching: A Theoretical Problem in Empirical Research on Corporate Social Performance. *International Journal of Organizational Analysis* 3/3: 229–267.

World Bank. 2008. *Global Monitoring Report 2008: MDGs and the Environment: Agenda for Inclusive and Sustainable Development*. Washington, DC: The International Bank for Reconstruction and Development/The World Bank. http://siteresources.worldbank.org/INTGLOMONREP2008/Resources/4737994-1207342962709/8944_Web_PDF.pdf.

Young, Iris. 2003. From Guilt to Solidarity: Sweatshops and Political Responsibility. *Dissent* 50/2: 39–44.

Young, Iris M. 2004. Responsibility and Global Labor Justice. *Journal of Political Philosophy* 12/4: 365–388.

Young, Iris M. 2008. Responsibility and Global Justice: A Social Connection Model. In *Handbook of Research on Global Corporate Citizenship*, ed. Andreas G. Scherer and Guido Palazzo, 137–165. Cheltenham, UK; Northampton, MA: Edward Elgar.

Zammit, Ann. 2003. *Development at Risk: Rethinking UN-Business Partnerships*. Geneva: South Centre and UNRISD.

Zammit, Ann. 2004. Die Vereinten Nationen und die Wirtschaft: Von der Polarisierung zur Partnerschaft. In *Unternehmen in der Weltpolitik: Politiknetzwerke, Unternehmensregeln und die Zukunft des Multilateralismus*, ed. Tanja Brühl, Heidi Feldt, and Brigitte Hamm, 44–72. Bonn: Verlag J. H. W. Dietz.

Ziegler, Jean. 2005. *Das Imperium der Schande: Der Kampf gegen Armut und Unterdrückung.* Munich: C. Bertelsmann.

Zimmermann, Michael J. 1996. *The Concept of Moral Obligation.* Cambridge, UK; New York: Cambridge University Press.

Zürn, Michael. 2008. The Politicization of Economization? On the Current Relationship Between Politics and Economics. In *Handbook of Research on Global Corporate Citizenship*, ed. Andreas G. Scherer and Guido Palazzo, 293–311. Cheltenham, UK; Northampton, MA: Edward Elgar.

Index